# Foulois and the U.S. Army Air Corps  1931-1935

The United States Air Force General Histories

# Foulois and the U.S. Army Air Corps

## 1931-1935

By

# John F. Shiner

GOVERNMENT REPRINTS PRESS
Washington, D.C.

© Ross & Perry, Inc. 2002 on new material. All rights reserved.

No claim to U.S. government work contained throughout this book.

Protected under the Berne Convention.

Printed in The United States of America
Ross & Perry, Inc. Publishers
216 G St., N.E.
Washington, D.C. 20002
Telephone (202) 675-8300
Facsimile (202) 675-8400
info@RossPerry.com

SAN 253-8555

Government Reprints Press Edition 2002

Government Reprints Press is an Imprint of Ross & Perry, Inc.

Library of Congress Control Number: 2002106454
http://www.GPOreprints.com

ISBN 1-932080-37-6

Book Cover designed by Sapna. sapna@rossperry.com

☉ The paper used in this publication meets the requirements for permanence established by the American National Standard for Information Sciences "Permanence of Paper for Printed Library Materials" (ANSI Z39.48-1984).

All rights reserved. No copyrighted part of this publication may be reproduced, stored in a retrieval system, or transmitted, in any form or by any means, electronic, photocopying, recording, or otherwise, without the prior written permission of the publisher.

# Foreword

Few nations in modern times have been prepared for war. Even the aggressors who have initiated conflicts have not been fully ready, for they could never be certain how their victims would react or what the clash of arms would bring. Nor, since the industrial revolution of the 19th century accelerated the pace of technological change, could a nation predict the impact of new weapons on battle and decide upon new tactics and strategies necessary for victory.

For most of its history, the United States did not trouble itself deeply with problems of preparing for war. With wide oceans separating it from the major powers of the world, and with a tradition isolating it from the balance of power system which governed international relations, this country could afford a military policy predicated on mobilizing after hostilities had begun. Its small peacetime military and naval establishment was designed for border security, for patrol of distant seas and a vast continental interior, for exploration, and after the dawn of the 20th century, for a cadre and training base which would absorb the manpower and materiel of the nation for wartime armed forces.

Beginning late in the 19th century, however, technology began to render such a policy increasingly dangerous. The introduction of steel and steam in ship construction and improvements in naval weaponry pushed the nation into overhauling and expanding the peacetime Navy. While the oceans would still provide a barrier and afford an interval for mobilization, defeat at sea would transform the barrier into a highway for invasion. To surrender the command of the sea was perceived by the early 20th century to offer an enemy the opportunity to defeat the United States.

Similarly, air power shrank the world and promised as much danger as opportunity to the country in defending itself. Proponents of air power realized that command of the air by an enemy could lay the nation open to bombardment and perhaps defeat. To prevent such a catastrophe required extensive preparation and much practice, thus prompting the expenditure of considerable resources in peacetime. And yet the nation, in the aftermath of World War I—the "war to end all wars"—saw little need for much spending on the implements of war. And in the 1930s, with the onset of the worst depression in American history, economic theory called for reduced government expenditure. For the pioneers of the American air forces, these were difficult years in a struggle as part of the army to forge the air weapons they believed so strongly would decide future warfare.

In this thoroughly researched and lucidly written volume, Lt. Col. John F. Shiner describes the Air Corps' effort to prepare the nation for war; to gain money, aircraft, and, even more important, independence; and to achieve a capability to wage aerial war. The focus of the work is Maj. Gen. Benjamin Foulois and his tenure as Chief of the Air Corps between 1931 and 1935. But the implications of Shiner's findings go beyond either the personalities or the issues. They encompass the whole character of developing United States military policy and its ascendancy to leadership in aviation during World War II. At the beginning of Foulois' stewardship, the Air Corps lacked both a "specific mission" and a "clearly defined doctrine." It possessed neither the aircraft not the organization for an independent role in conflict. War Department leaders were convinced that future war would be decided in ground fighting and that the most logical and effective mission for air power was in support of the land forces. On its part, the Navy was determined to develop its own air arm and to prevent army aviation from gaining any mission that overlapped into the naval environment.

From these battles merged the foundations of the large air fleets that helped to bring victory in World War II. Shiner shows that Army leaders were neither as backward nor as resistant to aviation as had been previously thought. Out of Foulois' term as Chief of the Air Corps came a fully articulated doctrine of long-range bombardment, its acceptance as part of official Army doctrine, the beginning of the program for the procurement of the B-17, and the missions for Army aviation of air and coastal defense. Even more important, pressed by Foulois' badgering, the Army established GHQ Air Force, a major step toward autonomy which allowed the Air Corps to unify its strike forces, to concentrate them under a single air commander, and to train and develop the striking forces which could command the air and attack and enemy's heartland.

This is also a human story. Benjamin Foulois made many mistakes, not the least of which was his unqualified assurance to President Roosevelt in 1934 that the Air Corps could fly the domestic mails, an episode that Shiner brings to life in dramatic terms. Foulois clashed repeatedly with the War Department. He believed passionately in the burgeoning importance of the Army air arm and its need for freedom from Army control. He liked nothing better than being in the cockpit, in the operations post, or in the airplane repair shop. (Thirty years later, in his eighties, Foulois told a young pilot that writing memoirs "cut into his flying time.") While clearly more at home among his airmen than in front of a congressional committee, Benjamin Foulois relentlessly pressured and bargained with the War Department, emerging as one of the most significant founders of air power.

Colonel Shiner has illuminated a critical period in aviation history. His is the story of the complicated relationships between equipment, doctrine, and organization—relationships which invariably raise the issue of the proper roles and missions of air power. It is a story as timely today as it was forty years ago, when aviation was just emerging as a major force in modern war.

*Richard H. Kohn*
*Chief, Office of Air Force History*

# The Author

Lieutenant Colonel John F. Shiner is a career Air Force officer. He holds a B. S. in Education from Capital University (1964), an M. A. in History from the University of Maryland (1966), and a Ph. D. in Military History from the Ohio State University (1975). He was commissioned through the Air Force ROTC program in 1964 and entered active duty in 1966. A command pilot with over 3,100 flying hours, Shiner has served as a KC-135 tanker aircraft commander with SAC and as a C-123 tactical airlift instructor pilot and flight examiner in the Republic of Vietnam.

He joined the faculty of the Department of History, U. S. Air Force Academy, in 1972. In 1979, Professor Shiner assumed duties as Director of Military History, and in 1981 he became the Acting Department Head. Shiner is presently assigned to the Directorate of Plans, Headquarters US Air Force. His articles on military aviation history and defense policy have appeared in *Aerospace Historian*, *Military Affairs*, and *Modern Warfare and Society*.

# Preface

For the Army Air Corps the first half of the 1930s was a time of great transition. While few issues relevant to military aviation were conclusively settled between 1931 and 1935, it was an era of rapid change in air doctrine, mission, organization, and equipment. Doctrinally, the age produced more clearly defined employment concepts. Likewise, it bred a fervent belief among Air Corps officers that independent strategic bombing operations could achieve decisive results in warfare, and that air power alone could prevent a hostile invasion of the United States. Organizationally, it was a time of centralization. The War Department allowed the air arm's striking elements, previously divided among the various ground commanders, to be concentrated under a senior Air Corps commander in one General Headquarters Air Force (GHQ Air Force). The era also created a clear and immediate mission for the air arm—the air defense of the United States and its overseas possessions. In addition, it was an age of rapid technological advancement in aeronautics, spawning aircraft such as the B-17 that could turn the potential of air power into reality.

Benjamin D. Foulois directed the Army air arm during this time of tremendous transition. An aviation pioneer who had flown with the Wright brothers, Foulois had been involved in military aviation since its inception. Short in stature, an ex-enlisted man with only a high school education, and possessing no exceptional gifts as a public speaker, he lacked the charisma of a Billy Mitchell. Yet he believed just as firmly as Mitchell in the importance of military aviation and fought equally as hard to remove it from the ground-minded control of the Army General Staff. Foulois made mistakes in judgment during his tenure as Chief of the Air Corps, but they were usually based on deep convictions about military aviation and what it could and should do. The officers and men of the Air Corps respected him, and he, for his part, did a credible job of representing their interests.

None of the previous works on the history of the Air Force cover this age of transition in detail. Nor have authors heretofore attempted to assess Foulois' impact upon military aviation development. The present volume seeks to fill both of these voids. It will trace topically the various changes between 1931 and 1935 and Foulois' part therein. It will also attempt to shed some light on why this four-year period produced widespread and important alterations that set the tenor for America's Army air effort in World War II.

General Foulois played the role of a leading advocate for change. Using his official position, he agitated tirelessly for improvements in organization, force structure, and employment doctrine during his first two and one-half years as Chief of the Air Corps. By applying persistent pressure on the General Staff, he encouraged that conservative body to rethink its position on a number of aviation-related subjects. The chapters that follow examine this War Department-Air Corps interplay and relate how it usually resulted in a period of negotiation that would culminate in the General Staff altering its official position in the direction of that advanced by Foulois and his aviation associates. In this manner, the Air Corps was able to make appreciable gains during the first half of the 1930s. The only issues the General Staff adamantly refused to negotiate were those of increased autonomy or independence for the Air Corps and continued expansion of the air arm at the expense of the rest of the Army.

This volume is intended as neither a detailed history of the Air Corps nor a biography of Maj. Gen. Benjamin D. Foulois. Instead, it is a study of the time and the man during an important period in the U.S. Air Force's past—a period of change and progress.

No work of this scope could be written without the assistance of many people. One such individual is my mentor and good friend, Prof. Allan R. Millett of The Ohio State University. As my Ph.D. adviser, he spent many hours and an untold quantity of blue ink offering valuable suggestions as I prepared a substantial portion of this study for my dissertation committee. His encouragement and that of Lt. Col. David MacIsaac, formerly the Deputy for Military History at the U.S. Air Force Academy, were extremely important. Colonel MacIsaac read the entire manuscript and offered very useful advice. I also must thank Brig. Gen. Alfred F. Hurley, USAF, Ret., who served so effectively as the Chairman of the Academy's Department of History until his retirement in 1980. General Hurley was responsible for first interesting me in the Air Corps during the Foulois years. A caring boss, he gave me his unflagging support.

I received considerable research assistance from Maj. Gen. John W. Huston, USAF, and his staff in the Office of Air Force History. General Huston, Mr. Eugene P. Sagstetter, Mr. Herman S. Wolk, and Mrs. Barbara C. Fleming in the Air Force History Office provided excellent editorial advice as well. Mr. Lawrence J. Paszek, Senior Editor, and Vanessa D. Allen selected the photography and designed the layout for the volume. These photographs were selected from collections at the Defense Audiovisual Agency, the Library of Congress, and the National Archives. Likewise, James N. Eastman, Jr., Chief of the Historical Research Branch, and the people at the Albert F. Simpson Historical Research Center, Maxwell Air Force Base, Alabama, helped me locate important document collections.

The staff at the National Archives was equally helpful. Dr. Timothy K. Nenninger of the Navy and Old Army Branch deserves special praise. He spent countless hours in the Archives locating pertinent boxes of documents. His advice and willingness to help went well beyond the call of duty. Dr. Dean C. Allard and his people in the Naval History Division, Department of the Navy, also provided valuable assistance; Dr. Allard steered me directly to the relevant collections and made me feel right at home.

A number of other institutions and individuals also assisted my research efforts. Mr. Duane J. Reed, in the Special Collections Branch at the U.S. Air Force Academy Library, was very helpful. So too were the staffs of the Manuscript Division, Library of Congress; the Nimitz Library at the U.S. Naval Academy; and the Franklin D. Roosevelt Library, Hyde Park, New York. Miss Janice E. McKenney and others in the U.S. Army Center of Military History went out of their way to locate obscure manuals and other materials for me.

I owe a special thank you to one other individual—my wife, Beverly. She typed and retyped the chapters of this volume many times, offering free editorial advice—often unsolicited—as she went. Her loving support and ability at the keyboard to turn my scribbling into something more intelligible were very important. To her, to my children Steve and Laurie, and to my mother, Helene, I dedicate this book.

# United States Air Force
# Historical Advisory Committee

(As of December 1, 1983)

Lt. Gen. Charles G. Cleveland, USAF
*Commander,* Air University, ATC

Mr. DeWitt S. Copp
The National Volunteer Agency

Dr. Philip A. Crowl
Annapolis, Maryland

Dr. Warren W. Hassler, Jr.
Pennsylvania State University

Brig, Gen. Harris B. Hull,
USAF, Retired
National Aeronautics and Space Administration

Dr. Alfred F. Hurley
Brig. Gen. USAF, Retired
North Texas State University

Mr. David E. Place,
*The General Counsel,* USAF

Gen. Bryce Poe II,
USAF, Retired

Lt. Gen. Winfield W. Scott, Jr.
*Superintendent,* USAF Academy

Dr. David A. Shannon *(Chairman)*
University of Virginia

# Contents

|  | Page |
|---|---|
| Foreword | iii |
| Preface | vii |
| I. Foulois and the Air Arm, 1908–1931 | 1 |
| II. Doctrine, Mission, and Employment Concepts, 1931–1933 | 43 |
| III. Organization: Toward a GHQ Air Force, 1932–1933 | 76 |
| IV. Funds, Aircraft, and Personnel, 1931–1933 | 101 |
| V. The Air Mail Fiasco | 125 |
| VI. Procurement Troubles, 1933–1935 | 150 |
| VII. The Chief in Trouble, 1934–1935 | 171 |
| VIII. Organization, 1934–1935: The GHQ Air Force | 193 |
| IX. Doctrine, Mission, and Employment Concepts, 1934–1935 | 212 |
| X. Funds, Aircraft, Personnel, and Bases, 1934–1935 | 236 |
| XI. An Age of Transition | 256 |
| Notes | 266 |
| Glossary | 309 |
| Bibliographic Note | 313 |
| Index | 321 |

# ILLUSTRATIONS AND PHOTOGRAPHS

|  | Page |
|---|---|
| Benjamin D. Foulois | xvii |
| Lt. Foulois, Ft. Sam Houston, Texas, 1910; the Army's first aeroplane, type Wright B | 4 |
| Ft. Sam Houston, Texas; Orville and Wilbur Wright with Foulois at Ft. Myer, Virginia | 5 |
| Scenes from Mexican expedition | 7 |
| Capt. Foulois, 1914; Brig. Gen Foulois with Gen. Pershing, 1918 | 10 |
| Map of the United States showing air activities of the Air Service, 1918 | 13 |
| Sec. of War, Newton D. Baker and Chief of Air Service, Maj. Gen. Charles T. Menoher, Bolling Field, May 1920 | 14 |
| Sinking of the German battleship, *Ostfriesland* | 20 |
| Generals Patrick and Mitchell, Selfridge Field, Michigan, 1922 | 22 |
| Wreckage of the *Shenandoah* | 26 |
| President Coolidge, Sec. Weeks, and Generals Patrick and Mitchell meet the "World Fliers," 1924; witnesses in the Billy Mitchell courtmartial: Lts. Leigh Wade, Orvil A. Anderson, Hiram W. Sheridan, Maj. Sumpter Smith, and Lt. Eugene Eubanks | 28 |
| Lt. Col. Foulois, commander of Mitchel Field, Long Island; Maj. Horace M. Hickam | 30 |
| Map sketch of routes designed for Air Corps bombardment units, May 1931 exercises | 36 |
| Fairfield Air Depot, Wright Field, Ohio; B-2 Condors over Staten Island, May 1931 exercises | 37 |

Curtis A-3s; B-2 Condors over Ocean City, New Jersey; staff and group commanders of the 1st Provisional Pursuit Wing for the May 1931 exercises .................................. 38

Howard S. Smith, Lt. Col. H. H. Arnold, Orville Wright, Maj. Carl A. Spaatz, Brig. Gen. Foulois, Maj. A. L. Sneed, and Brig. Gen. H. C. Pratt; Hiram Bingham presents the Mackay Trophy to Foulois, Ass't. Sec. of War for Air, F. Trubee Davison looks on ........................................ 39

Organization Chart, Office, Chief of the Air Corps, July, 1931 .. 41

Air Corps Tactical School, Maxwell Field, Alabama ............ 44

B-9 monoplane; B-10 ..................................... 49

Maj. Gen. Patrick with Adm. Moffett ....................... 53

Adm. William V. Pratt ..................................... 55

Bombing of *Mt. Shasta* off Virginia Capes .................... 57

Brig. Gen. Foulois, Ass't. Sec. of War for Air F. Trubee Davison, Maj. Gen. Fechet, and Brig. Gen. Pratt ................... 60

Rear Adm. Ernest J. King .................................. 71

Congressman John J. McSwain .............................. 79

Gen. Douglas MacArthur ................................... 80

President Roosevelt with 2d Lt. William B. Bogen, SSgt. Roy D. Dodd, Sgt. Thomas J. Rogers, and Maj. Gen. Foulois ...... 82

Maj. Gen. Hugh A. Drum ................................... 91

Sec. of War Patrick J. Hurley .............................. 105

Ft. Defiance, Arizona, southern Navajo agency headquarters for the relief of snowbound Indians ......................... 113

Will Rogers with Sec. of War Patrick J. Hurley .............. 134

Foulois explains air routes in Air Corps' operation of air mail in 1934; radio station at Las Vegas ......................... 142

Aircraft used in air mail operations in 1934: Boeing P-12, Thomas Morse 0-19, and Curtiss B-2 Condor ...... 143

P-26 ...... 168

Brig. Gen. George S. Simonds; Brig. Gen. Charles E. Kilbourne; Maj. Gen. John W. Gulick ...... 177

Sec. of War Newton D. Baker ...... 194

Clark Howell ...... 200

Organization of the GHQ Air Force ...... 205

Ass't. Sec. of War Harry H. Woodring and Gen. Malin Craig .. 208

Lt. Col. "Hap" Arnold and the Alaskan Flight of Martin B-10s 218

Sec. of War George H. Dern and Maj. Gen. Foulois greet Col. Arnold upon his return from the Alaskan Flight, Bolling Field ...... 219

Boeing XB-15 ...... 232

Douglas XB-19 ...... 233

Douglas B-18A ...... 235

Brig. Gen. Frank M. Andrews ...... 246

Maj. Gen. Oscar Westover ...... 253

Organization Chart, Office of the Chief of the Air Corps ...... 261

B-17 bomber developed in late 1930s; first B-17 to land at Langley Field, Virginia, greeted by Maj. Gen. Andrews ...... 264

Benjamin D. Foulois.

# CHAPTER I

# FOULOIS AND THE AIR ARM, 1908-1931

Benjamin Delahauf Foulois, a man destined to leave his mark on American military aviation, was born in the quaint country village of Washington, Connecticut, on December 9, 1879. Son of Henry and Sarah Augusta Foulois, "Benny" completed eleven years of schooling and at the age of sixteen went to work in his father's prosperous business as an apprentice plumber and steamfitter. Two years later, news of the sinking of the battleship *Maine* and the possibility of war with Spain filled the newspapers. Yearning for excitement, young Foulois ran off to New York City to join the military. He first tried the Navy but was rejected because he lacked seafaring experience and was small in stature. Benny subsequently visited the Army recruiting station and enlisted in the 1st U.S. Volunteer Engineers.[1]

Foulois' early military experiences took him to both Puerto Rico and the Philippines. He served with the Engineers in Puerto Rico during the Spanish-American War and was mustered out of the service as a sergeant in January 1899. Savoring his first taste of military life, he immediately sought an appointment to West Point. This effort was unsuccessful due to what Foulois later called a "lack of theoretical school training."[2] He thereupon enlisted as a private in Company G, 19th Infantry, of the Regular Army, which was soon assigned to duty in the Philippines. The Connecticut youth experienced rapid advancement between 1899 and 1901, rising to become first sergeant of Company G. His coolness in combat and leadership must have been the major factors in his superiors' decision to commission him a second lieutenant in February 1901. Foulois recalled later that "I didn't win my commission on the basis of the answers on the [commissioning] test. Whatever value they attached to my two years of field service with troops must have outweighed my ignorance."[3]

1

## FOULOIS AND THE U.S. ARMY AIR CORPS

After a second tour of duty in the Philippines, Foulois in 1905 entered the Army's professional education program—his avenue to eventual involvement in aeronautics. He did not compile a very impressive record as a student in the Infantry and Cavalry School at Fort Leavenworth, Kansas, due to trouble with his eyes. When informed by the post surgeon he would have to either stop studying or wear glasses, Foulois made his decision: "I stopped studying—and as a result, graduated (1906) about two or three numbers from the bottom of my class." His lack of academic excellence did not, however, keep him from being assigned to the Army Signal School upon graduation. This new course had barely gotten under way when trouble erupted in Cuba. Foulois was ordered to rejoin his regiment, which was to become a portion of the Army of Cuban Pacification. After several months of fighting insurgents and mapping the countryside, he returned to the signal school in August 1907. By this time the Signal Corps, which had charge of all military balloon activity, had created an aeronautical division. Foulois' school thesis, "The Tactical and Strategical Value of Dirigible Balloons and Aerodynamical Flying Machines," and the general interest he showed toward military aviation while at the school, caused him to be detailed to the Signal Corps upon graduation in July 1908. The Army at once ordered him to Washington, D.C., for aviation duty.[4]

For the next year and a half, Lieutenant Foulois was intimately connected with the U.S. Army's first real flying experiences.[5] Assigned to the Office of the Chief Signal Officer, he became a member of the Aeronautical Board for the 1908-09 airship and airplane trials. The Army had just purchased its first dirigible and was about to evaluate for the first time a heavier-than-air flying machine. Foulois flew on the Army dirigible in 1908 but was not very impressed with the machine's military capabilities. He did not take part in the test trial of the Wright brothers' airplane at Fort Myer, Virginia, which ended in disaster on September 17, 1908. Lieutenant Thomas E. Selfridge was killed and Orville Wright badly injured when the propeller broke and the aircraft crashed. However, after the Wright brothers rebuilt the plane, Foulois became directly involved in the July 1909 continuation of the evaluation. He not only laid out the trial course between Fort Myer and Alexandria, Virginia, but also flew as the navigator-observer during the final test flight.[6] Foulois explained: "I would like to think that I was chosen on the basis of intellectual and technical ability, but I found out later that it was my short stature, light weight, and map-reading experience that had tipped the decision in my favor."[7]

Based on the July 1909 tests, the Army purchased the Wright aircraft and contracted with the inventors to establish a temporary flying school at College Park, Maryland. There Foulois received his first instruction in piloting a plane. Because he had made disparaging remarks concerning the worth of dirigibles which were contrary to the official War Department view, or so he believed, the recent Signal Corps School graduate was not among the first two Army officers selected for the training. His superiors allowed him to join the College Park program in October 1909, but soon after, the original two trainees, Lieutenants Frank P. Lahm and Frederic E. Humphreys, badly damaged the airplane. Since the Wright brothers had technically fulfilled the terms of their contract when these two men soloed, the training program ended before Foulois could be given an opportunity to take the aircraft up alone. The Wrights repaired the aircraft and departed.[8]

Both Lahm and Humphreys, who had been serving on detached duty for aviation training, were ordered back to their regular billets, leaving Foulois and the Wright aircraft to constitute the Army's entire heavier-than-air flying force.[9] In December the War Department ordered the little-experienced aviator to take the plane to Fort Sam Houston in San Antonio, Texas. Foulois delighted in recounting the directive given him by Brig. Gen. James Allen, Chief Signal Officer, who told him: "Your orders are simple, Lieutenant. You are to evaluate the airplane. Just take plenty of spare parts—and teach yourself to fly." The lieutenant did just that.[10]

As the Army's one-man air force, the young flyer learned a great deal and achieved a number of U.S. military aviation firsts during 1910-11. Foulois and his small crew of nine enlisted men arrived at Fort Sam Houston with the crated aircraft in early February 1910. After reassembling the plane and erecting the catapult that helped the plane take off, the lieutenant made his initial solo flight on March 2. He went aloft four times that day, establishing three personal firsts—his first solo takeoff, first solo landing, and first crackup. During the succeeding months the Army's only officer assigned to flying duty completed numerous flights, gaining valuable aviation experience. He corresponded frequently with the Wright brothers on questions of pilot technique. He also modified the airplane they had designed and built, substituting wheels for the original skids. This enabled him to take off without using the catapult. He also installed the first aircraft seatbelt, after nearly being thrown out of the plane while approaching the field for landing. Foulois showed the airplane's practical application to military operations by carrying out aerial mapping, photography, and observation of troops. When trouble erupted along the Mexican border, he set a cross-country distance record of 106 miles on March 3, 1911, while on a reconnaissance flight in support of American ground troops. That same year he designed the first military air-to-ground wireless communications system and demonstrated its practicality.[11]

# FOULOIS AND THE U.S. ARMY AIR CORPS

Lt. Foulois at the controls, Ft. Sam Houston, Texas, 1910.

The Army's first aeroplane, type Wright B, accepted at Ft. Myer, Va., 1909.

# FOULOIS AND THE AIR ARM, 1908-1931

Ft. Sam Houston, Texas.

Orville and Wilbur Wright with Foulois, at Ft. Myer, Va.

The Army was not impressed with its one-aircraft, one-pilot air arm. The plane was quite fragile and usually had to spend about three weeks in the repair shop after each week of flying. Crackups were not infrequent. The War Department furnished Foulois only $150 to keep his aircraft going during the remainder of fiscal year 1910, and the aviator had to spend more than $300 of his own money to subsidize the operation. Likewise, he "begged, borrowed, and stole material from the Quartermaster Department" to carry out continual airplane repairs.[12] In 1910-11 Foulois sought to awaken a reluctant Army to the "value" of the airplane through such actions as flying "over the tents occupied by sleeping officers of the division headquarters staff at about ten feet" and executing "a power dive over the headquarters latrine." However, these activities did not seem to noticeably improve the outlook of ground officers toward military aviation.[13]

Irrespective of Foulois' antics, the War Department by 1911 had taken slightly more notice of miltiary aviation. The Army assigned additional officers to flying duty and purchased a few new planes. The fiscal year 1911 War Department budget for the first time included a specific appropriation for aviation—a sum of $125,000. Nevertheless, the Army's increased interest in the airplane was quite limited. In 1914, just prior to the outbreak of World War I, the United States stood fourteenth in total funds allocated for military aviation—well below such world powers as Greece and Bulgaria. Not until July 1914 did Congress pass a law to provide permanent personnel for Army aviation, establishing a small Aviation Section of the Signal Corps containing 60 officers and 260 enlisted men.[14]

The Army removed Foulois from aviation activities in 1912 and did not reassign him to flying duty until early 1914. Since he had spent in excess of four years on detached service with the Signal Corps, he was required by federal law to perform troop duty with his own branch, the Infantry.[15] Foulois spent little time in the infantry assignment before working his way back into a flying job. By January 1914 he secured for himself the position of troubleshooter for the commandant of the new aviation school at San Diego. Accidents had been all too frequent prior to the little aviator's arrival. Foulois, never afraid to get his hands dirty, promptly organized and personally instructed a course for the flying students in engine overhaul and repair. With the young flyers more knowledgeable about aircraft powerplants, the school's casualty rate dropped to near zero.[16]

In 1914-15 Foulois personally organized the Army's first tactical air unit (the 1st Aero Squadron) at San Diego, and in 1916 took this small force into Mexico as part of the punitive expedition. The War Department gave him the order to establish the squadron in 1914. However, according

# FOULOIS AND THE AIR ARM, 1908–1931

Scenes from Mexican expedition. Above: Lt. Herbert A. Dargue in a JN-2; right: Capt. Foulois (seated) and Lt. Joseph E. Carberry return to camp via a Mexican cart, after the crash on May 15, 1916; below: JN-2s refuel at Casas Grandes.

to Foulois, "I had no instructions and received no information of any definite plan as to what we should organize or how we should organize, so we proceeded to organize by ourselves."[17] Assigned to Brig. Gen. John J. Pershing's command in 1916, the unit's pilots and eight training aircraft struggled to carry out their reconnaissance and liaison duties, but the task of operating at relatively high altitudes (above 10,000 feet) over the mountainous terrain of northern Mexico proved too demanding for the squadron's underpowered planes. By the end of the sixth week all the aircraft were either worn out, in need of major repair, or wrecked in crashes. The 1st Aero Squadron's accomplishments in Mexico had been extremely meager. Foulois and the other flyers had gained some valuable experience but their military usefulness, aside from the liaison role, "could be summed up in one successful scouting mission: they had once found a lost and thirsty cavalry column."[18]

The dearth of suitable American flying equipment during the Mexican punitive expedition indicated how far the United States lagged behind Europe in military aviation. With World War I nearly two years old, the Army had but one tactical squadron in 1916 and it was equipped with underpowered training planes. From the War Department's purchase of its first airplane in 1909 until the United States' entry into the World War in April 1917, the Army had acquired a total of 224 aircraft. Few of these were still in commission in 1917, and none were combat models by European standards. When America declared war, the Army possessed just 55 planes (all trainers) located at two flying fields. Pershing declared that 51 of these were obsolete and 4 obsolescent.[19]

After the punitive expedition and a brief tour of duty as aeronautical officer for the Army's Southern Department, in March 1917 Foulois moved to the Aviation Section, Office of the Chief Signal Officer, in Washington. He soon began drafting a program for the wartime expansion of the air arm. Several weeks work yielded plans for an air organization sufficient to meet the needs of an army of three million men. His proposal contained estimates for the required appropriations and a draft of the legislation needed to support the program. The plan carried a price tag of $640 million and was approved by Congress on July 24, 1917.[20] Looking back over his military career four decades later, Foulois would consider formulating and winning congressional approval for the 1917 legislative proposal his most significant contribution to military aviation, for it laid the foundation for America's World War I and postwar aviation organization and development.[21]

The pioneer flyer had his first direct clash with the General Staff over the issue of the $640 million expansion program. As a result, he adopted a style or method of action that he would resort to in succeeding years when differing with War Department policy or decisions. After submitting the program to the General Staff and having it returned disapproved, Foulois went before the House Military Affairs Committee and testified in behalf of the plan:

> I found that if the issues were serious enough there were always means of getting the ear of Congress. Air Service officers would be called upon to testify before Congressional committees of inquiry and they were free to give honest appraisals of the situation without danger of War Department reprisals. ... If the issue were especially important and there was no chance of obtaining a hearing from the War Department there were always ways of taking the matter before Congress and still remain within the limitations of military command.[22]

This approach was extremely successful for Foulois in 1917 and in later years allowed him to express his disapproval of General Staff control of aviation without bringing on War Department retribution. However, his attempts to undercut the General Staff in testimony before Congress would eventually backfire in 1934.

As a temporary brigadier general, in November 1917 Foulois traveled to France to assume the duties of Chief of the Air Service, American Expeditionary Force (AEF). According to the aviator's memoirs, General Pershing had personally requested him for the job and wanted him to end the chaos within the Air Service in France.[23] However, the arrival of Foulois and his staff did not bring order. Instead, it merely produced more friction and confusion. The air officers already in France were for the most part Regulars. They resented having Foulois' cortege, which included quite a few recently commissioned civilians, imposed on them. Brig. Gen. Billy Mitchell, Air Service commander for the Zone of Advance, was highly displeased with Foulois' staff and referred to them as "carpetbaggers."[24] Pershing, AEF commander in chief, summed up his new air staff by calling them "a lot of good men running around in circles." In May 1918 he reorganized the AEF Air Service and brought in as its new chief, Brig. Gen. Mason M. Patrick, a ground officer.[25] Foulois was appointed Chief of the Air Service, First Army, but soon requested that he be made Patrick's assistant and that Mitchell be given the First Army job. This was approved by Patrick and the change took place on August 1, 1918.[26]

Even though Foulois recommended Mitchell for the post of Chief of the Air Service, First Army, the two men harbored an intense and lasting dislike for one another. Senior to Foulois prior to the war, Mitchell bitterly resented Foulois' elevation to Chief of the Air Service, AEF, and complained directly to Pershing about Foulois' alleged inefficiency. For his part, Foulois considered Mitchell one of his biggest headaches, being both insubordinate and ill-informed on questions of logistics. Still Foulois was clear-sighted enough to recognize Mitchell's leadership abilities and honest enough to recommend him for the prestigious job of leading the combat air efforts as Chief of the Air Service, First Army.[27]

Foulois and Mitchell had life styles and personalities which were so different that there is little chance that they would have been friends even had they not clashed over issues of command in France. Mitchell was flamboyant, relatively wealthy, and a flashy dresser. Foulois, the ex-enlisted man, came from more humble origins. He preferred a pair of overalls to a neatly tailored uniform and felt at home amidst the dirt and grime of the aircraft repair shop. While Mitchell moved in the higher circles of society, Foulois enjoyed a good drinking party and a game of poker with his fellow officers. Foulois was not a particularly articulate

Capt. Foulois (left photo), 1914, became Brig. Gen. in 1918; shown with Gen. Pershing (right) at Issoudun, France.

public speaker nor did he seem to relish the public role. He possessed a wealth of practical knowledge on aviation, while the more publicity-oriented Mitchell was a parvenu. Their differences in style easily carried over into the methods each adopted in the postwar struggle to free military aviation from ground officer control. Mitchell directed much of his effort toward public opinion. Foulois, believing that officers should keep the struggle within established channels, tried to exert pressure in testimony before Congress and other official investigative bodies.[28]

U.S. Army aviation entered World War I quite late and was employed almost exclusively in a tactical ground support role. Senior American flying officers wanted to eventually undertake a strategic bombardment campaign against Germany, but they never got the chance. American air units did not go into combat until April 1918. In September the Air Service, American Expeditionary Force, directed its first large operation, involving 1,481 aircraft in support of the ground advance on the St. Mihiel salient. However, only 609 of the planes were from U.S. squadrons. Throughout the war the AEF continued to use its air units for reconnaissance, artillery spotting, close air support, interdiction of enemy lines of communications in the immediate vicinity of the trenches, and to deny the Germans use of the air space along the front.[29] Even had Pershing and his staff been advocates of strategic bombing, the state of aviation technology would have severely limited the effectiveness of such an undertaking. Aircraft range and load-carrying capability were quite limited in 1918.

With the close of the war in Europe and the swift demobilization of American forces, the issue of aviation's place in the U.S. postwar defense structure immediately arose. Pershing had removed American air units in France from Signal Corps control in June 1917, establishing the Air Service, AEF, with its own chief. President Woodrow Wilson followed suit for the entire Army air arm in May 1918, using the provisions of the recently passed Overman Act that allowed him to reorganize the wartime functions of government agencies.[30] There was no question of returning Army aviation to the Signal Corps at the end of the war. Still, the size of the postwar Air Service and its degree of freedom from General Staff control were vital issues both for the flyers and the Army's ground leadership.

The air arm's wartime expansion had been proportionately greater than that of the rest of the Army. If the Air Service were to remain relatively large in the postwar period, it might have to be at the expense of the rest of the Army, a situation dictated by the popular desire to return to the normal small peacetime expenditures for defense. Air officers, realizing the economics of the situation, feared that the General Staff would seek to reduce the Air Service to its prewar size to free more funds for the Army's traditional combat branches. Consequently, many Army flyers began to champion the formation of a separate service as the sole means of preserving what they believed to be an important element in the nation's defense structure. The rapid demobilization of the wartime air organization (a drop in officer strength from twenty thousand to little more than two hundred in 1919) intensified the fears of the Army aviators.[31]

The dispute over Air Service independence that ensued between the flyers and the War Department in 1919-20 did not so much involve a doctrinal conflict over the decisiveness of air power as it did the issues of adequate funding, development, and leadership for military aviation. Air Service officers did not claim that air power alone could win wars or replace the "queen of battles," the Infantry. But many of them insisted aviation represented an important offensive striking arm which must be properly developed. Aviation advocates were displeased with the War Department's view that military aviation was only an auxiliary to be used to directly aid the infantry.[32]

In 1919 the Army completed a series of studies on aviation's place within the national defense structure. In April, General Pershing appointed a board of officers to consider the lessons of the war. That group's report on aviation stressed the auxiliary nature of the Army's air arm. In May, Secretary of War Newton D. Baker ordered Assistant Secretary Benedict Crowell to head a new board to make a more thorough investigation of military aviation. Reporting in July, the Crowell Board recommended concentrating all of the government's air activities in a single national air service, coequal with the War, Navy, and Commerce Departments. Both Secretary Baker and the General Staff were upset with this conclusion. The War Department did not want to lose control of its useful auxiliary force. Baker, while wanting the air arm to grow, was totally opposed to the idea of separation. He therefore buried the Crowell report and authorized the Chief of Air Service, Maj. Gen. Charles T. Menoher, to organize a new investigative group. Menoher, a nonflyer, produced a study more to the War Department's liking. Completed in October, the report opposed the creation of an independent department of air and maintained that a separate air force would violate the principle of unity of command and that air action could not in itself be decisive against ground forces.[33]

The War Department was under considerable congressional pressure during 1919-20, for no less than eight separate bills were introduced seeking to create a Department of Aeronautics. As expected, ranking officers of the Army and Navy testified against all such legislative proposals. They regarded military flyers as upstarts, and could see no reason for granting independence to what they considered a valuable auxiliary combat arm. Not unexpectedly, the Army's aviators staunchly supported the legislation.[34]

Foulois, who did not return to the United States until mid-1919, im-

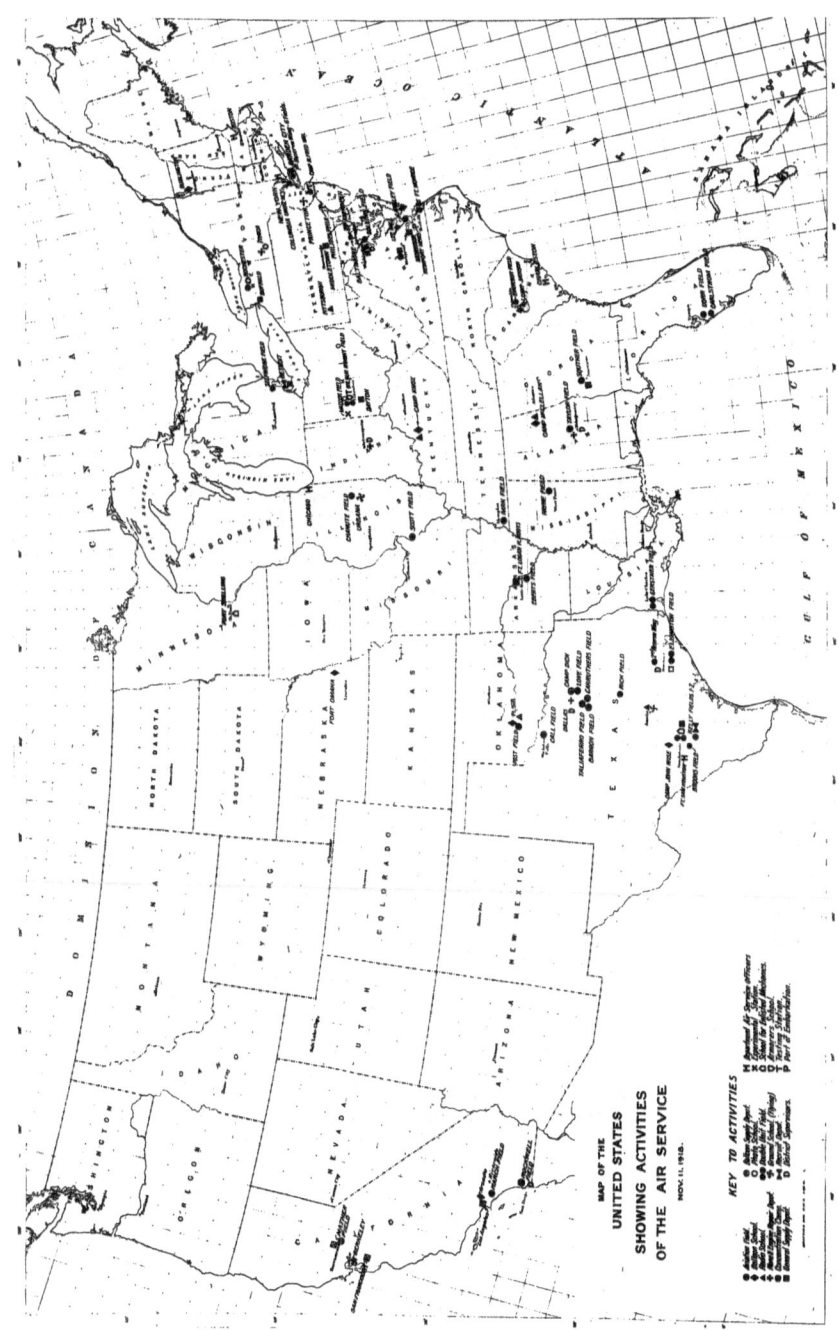

## FOULOIS AND THE U.S. ARMY AIR CORPS

Sec. of War, Newton D. Baker and Chief of Air Service, Maj. Gen. Charles T. Menoher, watch air tournament at Bolling Field, May 1920.

mediately became one of the leading advocates of a separate Department of Aeronautics. He and General Patrick had remained behind in France and worked on the aviation terms of the Treaty of Versailles. Returning home in July to head the Liquidation Division in the Office of the Chief of the Air Service, Foulois appeared frequently before congressional committees considering various bills relating to the future of the Air Service.[35]

The aviation pioneer, now a major, [36] campaigned for independence on the basis of the War Department's inability to adequately provide for and direct the Army's air arm, rather than on the issue of whether there existed a separate mission that only aviation could carry out. What he sought was a single government agency that would have charge of both civil and military aviation.[37] Like other flyers, Foulois was quite upset by the General Staff's postwar aviation policy, introduced as House Bill S.2715 on August 4, 1919. While the legislative proposal provided for an Air Service strength of 1,923 officers and 21,753 enlisted men, none were to be assigned permanently. All would be detailed from the Army's other branches and arms and would return whence they came after a period of time.

In the ensuing hearings before the House Military Affairs Committee, Foulois vigorously protested against the detail system. He charged that such an arrangement would result in

> creating a service without permanency and with constantly shifting personnel who would hardly be in the Air Service long enough to learn the names of all the different tools and instruments (to say nothing of their efficient use) until they, by law, would have to give up their work and try something else.[38]

He also claimed that such a system would result in a "high state of inefficiency with maximum expenditures of public funds and maximum waste of equipment." Foulois criticized the failure of the bill to specify that flying officers should hold the command positions in the Air Service. He pointed out that if the bill became law, due to the relatively low rank of Air Service personnel, 191 out of 193 vacancies in the ranks of major through colonel would have to be filled with nonflying officers from the Army at large. Foulois, other Air Service officers, and their supporters so convinced the committee that the bill should not become law that it was not reported out of committee.[39]

During the last quarter of 1919, Foulois testified on three occasions before congressional committees. Each time he defiantly attacked the General Staff as an organization ill-suited to administer, control, and provide for the growth of military aviation. On October 7, 1919, he told the House Committee on Military Affairs:

> The General Staff of the Army is the policy making body of the Army and, either through lack of vision, lack of practical knowledge, or deliberate intention to subordinate the Air Service needs to the needs of the other combat

arms, it has utterly failed to appreciate the full military value of this new military weapon and, in my opinion, has utterly failed to accord it its just place in our military family.[40]

He went on to damn the General Staff's prewar lack of concern for aviation that had resulted in the gross weakness of the Army's air arm at the onset of hostilities in 1917. Speaking of the present circumstances of the Air Service and the American aviation industry, he asserted:

I frankly state that in my opinion the War Department through its policy-making body, the General Staff of the Army, is primarily responsible for the present unsatisfactory, disorganized, and most critical situation which now exists in all aviation matters throughout the United States.[41]

He repeated his criticism of the War Department a week later before the Senate Military Affairs Committee, again emphasizing the General Staff's inept handling of the air arm. He attacked that body for its inability to understand the full value of military aviation and for seeking to use it almost exclusively in what he considered the "defensive" roles of observation and artillery spotting. He decried the lack of aviation development at the hands of the General Staff and angrily asserted that

based on a practical experience in Army aviation, ever since its birth in 1908, I can frankly state that in my opinion, the War Department has earned no right or title to claim further control over aviation or the aviation industry of the United States.[42]

Foulois believed that the offensive capabilities of military aviation could never be developed under General Staff control. He again argued this point in December 1919 before the House Committee on Military Affairs, pointing out that the Army had not as yet recognized the great value of aviation in operations beyond the areas occupied by ground troops. He called for turning "defensive" observation aircraft over to the Army and operating the rest as a national air force under a separate department. He explained he had great respect for the General Staff's expertise in ground operations; however, he was "not a believer in anyone trying to run something unless they know something about it themselves." Therefore, the War Department should definitely not be charged with running America's offensive air arm.[43] Years later, when he was serving as Chief of the Air Corps, Foulois still maintained this 1919 view of the inappropriateness of General Staff control.

While the future chief was the most aggressive Air Service spokesman for independence in 1919-20, Billy Mitchell, Hap Arnold,* and others also participated in the crusade. Mitchell agreed with his former commander that the American military air arm could not properly develop under the disinterested hand of the General Staff. However, he based the bulk of his argument for independence on the existence of a separate air mission. He

---

*Maj. Henry H. Arnold.

testified before the House Military Affairs Committee that military aviation's principal function was to obtain a decision over the enemy's aviation—essentially an air problem which provided the rationale for a distinct air arm mission.[44]

Foulois believed that in any future war the opposing air fleets would battle for control of the air, but he did not play upon this mission as justification for a separate service. Nor did he seek to diminish the prevailing paramount position held by the Infantry in Army doctrinal thinking. What he was after was the reorganization of America's defense structure, so that military aviation might grow to realize its offensive potential, becoming second in importance only to the "queen of battles."[45]

Most Air Service officers now favored separation from the War Department. As might be expected, General Menoher, the nonflying Chief of the Air Service, was an exception: He vehemently opposed separation. Lt. Col. Oscar Westover was one of a handful of aviators who agreed with Menoher. Westover believed it was all a question of submitting to proper authority, in this case the War Department. He asserted that officers advocating independence were being insubordinate.*[46]

Irrespective of the campaign conducted by Foulois, Mitchell, and other Air Service officers and the efforts of aviation supporters in Congress, the Army Reorganization Act passed on June 4, 1920, gave the air arm neither independence nor autonomy. The act did formally recognize the Air Service as a combat arm and raised its authorized personnel strength to 1,516 officers and 16,000 enlisted men. It provided for a Chief of the Air Service with the rank of major general and a brigadier general assistant. The law specified that no more than ten percent of Air Service officers could be nonflyers, and that all flying units would have aviators for commanders.[47]

The advocates of air arm independence saw the act as a crushing defeat—and it was. By leaving the General Staff-Air Service relationship unchanged, it left the destiny of military aviation in the hands of those who viewed it only as a force that might help the advance of the infantry. The General Staff's subsequent tactical reorganization of Army aviation showed what the Army's senior officers prized most from military aviation. Of twenty-seven squadrons called for in the War Department plan, fifteen were to be observation and four surveillance. The Air Service's striking power would be confined to four bombardment and four pursuit squadrons. Further, the General Staff insisted that all of the squadrons operate as integral parts of the Army's divisions and corps. The War Department gave command and control of each of the Air Service's tactical

---

*Stressing loyalty above all else, Westover would serve as Foulois' Assistant Chief of Air Corps from January 1932 to December 1935, and would give full support to his anti-General Staff chief.

squadrons to the commander of the corps area in which the squadron was based.[48] One could not expect those who advocated a strong air arm to be pleased with the resultant decentralized and offensively impotent aviation organization fostered by the General Staff.

Not unexpectedly, the cleavage between the aviators and the Army ground officers controlling the General Staff deepened during the first half of the 1920s. The flying officers felt stymied in their campaign to win a voice in the nation's military aviation destiny. Between 1920 and 1925, many aviation bills were introduced, innumerable investigations and hearings were held and reports rendered, but virtually no important legislation resulted. To make matters worse, Congress, after passing the 1920 Army Reorganization Act, failed to provide the funds to build and keep the Army at the authorized force level of 280,000 enlisted men and slightly over 17,000 officers. By 1922 the economy-minded lawmakers had lowered enlisted strength to 137,000, and in 1927 cut it to 118,750. By 1926 the government had pared officer strength to nearly 12,000. The Air Service suffered accordingly. By March 1923, the Army air arm contained only 880 officers and 8,399 enlisted men, including 91 aviation cadets—well below the 1,516 officers and 16,000 enlisted men (including 2,100 flying cadets) authorized by the 1920 act. General Patrick, appointed Chief of the Air Service in 1921, compounded the Air Service officer shortage by refusing to fill vacancies through the transfer of senior ground officers to the flying arm. More important than the manpower shortage was the dearth of acceptable flying equipment. Of 1,970 aircraft of all types in the Army inventory in 1923, 1,531 were obsolescent models built during the war. Since very few new aircraft were being purchased, aviation officers feared that in the next three years normal attrition would reduce the total number of planes on hand to below 300.[49]

These conditions stimulated those who believed in the value of military aviation, both within and outside the Army, to intensify their campaign to win independence—or at least a measure of autonomy—for the air arm. With Foulois serving a four-year tour as air attache in Berlin between 1920-24, Brig. Gen. Billy Mitchell, Assistant Chief of the Air Service, easily became the leading crusader. Beginning with theoretical air raids on U.S. cities and the ship bombing tests in 1921, he kept himself and the issue of air power before the American people for almost five years. Mitchell was an excellent propagandist. When his provisional brigade of one hundred aircraft sank the old German battleship *Ostfriesland*, his claims that the airplane had made the battleship obsolete received wide press coverage, much to the chagrin of the Navy. In 1924 Mitchell wrote a series of controversial magazine articles proclaiming the importance of air power to the defense of the United States. He also was a frequent witness before congressional committees and other investigative bodies looking into the condition and organization of military aviation. By writing, testifying, and lecturing on the importance of air power, Mitchell apparently believed he could win the support of public opinion, which in turn might force the War Department to change its aviation policy. Although making claims hardly justified by the performance of existing aircraft, he did arouse widespread public interest in military aviation.[50]

By 1925 Mitchell had articulated the doctrine of strategic bombardment and used it to substantiate his claim that a separate air mission existed. Others abroad and in the United States may have previously advocated this method of warfare, but he was the first American to popularize it. Mitchell's approach was to explain to the public what another nation could do to the United States by launching air attacks on its industrial, transportation, and commercial centers. He emphasized that this type of warfare would force a nation to make peace, regardless of the disposition of that country's land and naval forces. To be victorious would no longer entail "the tedious and expensive processes of wearing down the enemy's land forces by continuous attacks." By explaining that only an air force could stop another air force and thus prevent the horrors of strategic air attack, Mitchell identified the existence of a mission—air defense—that required an independent air arm. Only a separate air force controlling its own training, doctrine, and resources could turn back a strategic air attack on a nation's vital centers. Deeming naval vessels extremely vulnerable to air attack, Mitchell claimed that the mission of coast defense against both aircraft and surface ships clearly belonged to the air arm.[51]

In order to placate the American abhorrence of total war and its concomitant destruction of "innocent" civilians, Mitchell publicly played up the defensive nature of independent air operations. He merely hinted that the United States might also undertake strategic bombardment of enemy vital centers. In dealing with his fellow Air Service officers, he was more candid. In 1923 he created an unofficial manual on bombardment listing as acceptable military targets the enemy's industry, transportation system, and food and water supplies. However, it asserted that purely civilian targets would be hit only in reprisal.[52]

Mitchell and other Army flyers held that the airplane, being able to bypass ground and sea forces and go directly to important targets, represented an entirely new kind of warfare, a view not shared by the ground officers who dominated the Army. The 1926 edition of Training Regulations (TR) 440-15 aptly summed up the General Staff's attitude: "The organization and training of all air units is based on the fundamental doctrine that their mission is to aid the ground forces to gain decisive success." Though continuing to view military aviation as an auxiliary arm, by 1926 the General Staff had begun to appreciate the airplane's offensive

# FOULOIS AND THE U.S. ARMY AIR CORPS

Sinking of the old German battleship, *Ostfriesland*.

uses. According to TR 440-15:

> The mission of the Air Service is to assist the ground forces to gain strategical and tactical successes by destroying enemy aviation, attacking enemy ground forces and other enemy objectives on land and sea, and in conjunction with other agencies to protect ground forces from hostile aerial observation and attack. In addition it furnishes aerial observation for information and for artillery fire, and also provides messenger service and transportation for special personnel.[53]

Mitchell increasingly antagonized senior officers of the War and Navy departments with his claims that an independent air mission dictated the separation of aviation from the two existing services. His persistent assertion that air power had replaced sea power as the nation's first line of defense and his public criticism of the Army and Navy for their failure to develop military aviation increased the disdain which ground and sea officers held for the Army's aviation crusaders. Army and Navy leaders believed the airplane was incapable of conducting decisive independent air operations. Likewise, they could see no reason for creating a separate air defense force; given the state of aviation technology, no overseas nation could launch air attacks on the United States. Moreover, both services prized their respective air arms as important auxiliaries and were by no means willing to give them up without an intense struggle. Mitchell's ceaseless carping led to his removal as Assistant Chief of the Air Service and his eventual court-martial in 1925 and resignation in 1926.[54]

Nearly all of Mitchell's fellow Air Service officers agreed with his concepts of air power and his aim to create a strong, independent air force, but many disagreed with his tactics. They appreciated the military potential of strategic bombing and considered the creation of a counter-air force vital to the future security of the United States. Further, they believed, as he did, that military aviation could only achieve defensive and offensive potential if guided in its development by those interested in it. Yet many Army flyers disliked Mitchell's exaggerated claims for air power.[55] Foulois, no friend of Mitchell's, probably summed up the feelings of many Army aviators when he wrote: "I have no quarrel about Mitchell's championing the need for airpower before the American public. It was his methods and his lack of judgment about what he said that I deplored."[56]

In the unreceptive political environment during the first half of the 1920s, the campaign by the Army flyers for military reorganization produced few positive results. Presidents Warren G. Harding and Calvin Coolidge opposed independence as did the powerful Naval and Military Affairs Committees of Congress. Consequently, the War and Navy Departments had powerful allies in their quest to preserve the status quo. The crusade led by Mitchell nonetheless engendered a public awareness of military aviation, and his arguments for a separate air arm helped his

## FOULOIS AND U.S. ARMY AIR CORPS

Generals Patrick (left) and Mitchell converse at the 1922 Detroit air races, Selfridge Field, Mich.

fellow flyers think more coherently about air power.[57]

General Patrick, Chief of the Air Service/Air Corps, 1921-1927, favored air arm autonomy within the War Department rather than outright independence; he was quite active in the air arm's behalf in the early 1920s. Following a course of action far different from that of his volatile assistant, Patrick worked for change exclusively within established channels. In mid-1922 he complained to the War Department that the Air Service had been virtually demobilized and could no longer discharge even its peacetime duties. On December 18, 1922, the General Staff directed him to study the Air Service situation and submit recommendations. Patrick's response of February 1923 underscored the air arm's inadequate size and faulty organization. The report criticized the permanent assignment of air elements to individual ground units and called for a change in that policy. Patrick suggested the Air Service be divided into two components. One would consist of observation squadrons and balloon companies serving as integral parts of the ground units. The other would comprise an enlarged air force of pursuit, attack, and bombardment squadrons, which would operate independently of the ground forces, under the command of the General Headquarters (GHQ) commander. Patrick realized the War Department was not willing to give its air arm autonomy, but he probably thought that gaining General Staff acceptance of the principle of air force concentration would be a step in the proper direction. Furthermore, he was convinced of the military value of such a tactical reorganization.[58]

On March 17, 1923, Secretary of War John W. Weeks convened a board of General Staff officers under the chairmanship of Maj. Gen. William Lassiter to consider Patrick's recommendations. After studying the Chief of the Air Service's report, in late March the board issued its findings which essentially concurred with Patrick's views. The board deplored the poor condition of the Army air arm and called for a ten-year program to build up Air Service personnel and aircraft strength. It recommended that the air arm have a minimum peacetime establishment of 4,000 officers, 25,000 enlisted men, 2,500 aviation cadets and 2,500 aircraft. In general the board endorsed Patrick's plans for tactical reorganization with but one major change: it favored assigning of some attack and pursuit aviation directly to each field army. More important, the members accepted Patrick's proposal that most combat aircraft be concentrated as an air force:

> An Air Force of bombardment and pursuit aviation and airships should be directly under General Headquarters for assignment to special and strategical missions, the accomplishment of which may be either in connection with the operation of ground troops or entirely independent of them. This force should be organized into large units, insuring great mobility and independence of action.[59]

The War Department adopted the Lassiter Board report as its aviation policy. Unfortunately, the tactical reorganization was not carried out because the department did not secure the legislation to put the ten-year program into effect. Secretary Weeks approved the report and sent it to the Joint Board for coordination with the Navy. The sea service agreed in principle with the program but was somewhat concerned over the possible impact of the Army's aviation buildup on naval aircraft procurement. While the Lassiter report was still before the Joint Board, Secretary Weeks proposed to the Secretary of the Navy that the two services agree on what proportion of military aviation appropriations their two air arms should receive. The Navy Department wanted no part of such a plan, for it would give the War Department a voice in determining how much the sea service would receive for its air activities. The War Department submitted a second proposal specifying a two-thirds/one-third split of aviation funds, with the Army getting the lion's share. In response the Navy refused to consider further either the fund split proposal or the Lassiter report. The Lassiter program therefore languished awaiting further War Department action that never came.[60]

In the meantime the House of Representatives undertook its own investigation of military aeronautics. On March 24, 1924, the Speaker appointed a nine-man select committee drawn from the Military and Naval Affairs Committees and chaired by Representative Florian Lampert of Wisconsin. This Select Committee of Inquiry into the Operations of the United States Air Services (better known as the Lampert Committee) began hearings in October and took testimony until March 1925.[61]

Patrick and Mitchell, both disgusted with War Department inaction on the Lassiter report, ably presented Air Service views before this committee.[62] Mitchell's testimony, as might be expected, was the more sensational. He blamed the General Staff for the Army air arm's weakened condition, attacked the Navy as a waste of tax dollars, and called for a separate Department of Aeronautics coequal with the War and Navy Departments.[63] Patrick, reflecting the attitude of many Air Service officers now willing to accept autonomy in lieu of the much-sought-after but illusive independence, campaigned before the committee for removal of the air arm from General Staff control. He explained that he had recently recommended that the General Staff draft and forward legislation "for the reorganization of the Air Service as an air corps apart from the War Department, but under the Secretary of War." This, he said would afford the air arm financial and doctrinal autonomy. Patrick also asserted that great confusion presently reigned over whether the Army or Navy had responsibility for coast defense. He claimed that this mission should be given to an autonomous air corps thus ending the duplication and confusion.[64]

The Lampert Committee's report—not released until December 1925, and therefore superseded by events—supported both Patrick's and Mitchell's views. As a short-term solution to the problems of Army and Navy aviation, it recommended that the War and Navy Departments be required to spend $10 million a year on aircraft procurement; that the two air arms be given their own separate, all-inclusive budgets; and that the Army and Navy be required to give adequate representation on their respective General Staff and General Board to members of their air services "who will firmly support the full and complete use of Army and Navy aviation for the defense of the country." As a permanent solution the committee wanted established "a single department of national defense, headed by a civilian secretary, specially charged with the coordination of the defenses of the country." This last proposal implied air arm equality with the land and sea forces in the new organization. However, the report did not state that the single department would contain three coequal subdivisions.[65]

## FOULOIS AND THE AIR ARM, 1908-1931

By autumn 1925, President Coolidge determined that another investigation of military aviation was warranted. The economy-minded chief executive was just as much opposed to a separate air arm as were the War and Navy Departments, and conditions prevailing in September indicated that it was time to act. The Lampert Committee, quite friendly to the aviation advocates during its hearings, would probably recommend some kind of costly reorganization.[66] Further, on September 5, Mitchell, upset over the recent crash of the dirigible *Shenandoah,* charged that such accidents were "the direct results of incompetency, criminal negligence and almost treasonable administration of the national defense by the War and Navy Departments." These charges resulted in Mitchell's court-martial, but Coolidge feared they might also prompt a public outcry for a sweeping aviation investigation.[67] Likewise, the President did not want to allow Mitchell to make his court-martial the focal point of attention. So on September 12, Coolidge ordered the formation of the President's Aircraft Board and secured the consent of his life-long friend Dwight W. Morrow to head the new investigation. He directed Morrow and his committee of distinguished civilians to have their report ready by the end of November, presumably to take the sting out of the court-martial action.[68]

Where the Lampert Committee had been sympathetic to the views of the Army aviators, the Morrow Board seemed to encourage witnesses who opposed any measure of independence for the Air Service. The board gave the officers from the Army air arm a chance to speak their piece for greater autonomy or separation but in the end endorsed the General Staff's view of military aviation. Dwight Morrow's group submitted its report on December 3, two weeks before the announcement of the Mitchell court-martial verdict and prior to the publication of the Lampert Committee's report.[69] No doubt President Coolidge and the War Department were well pleased with the timing as well as the findings.

The report called for some increased recognition of the air arm but in general vindicated the status quo. Concerning the issue of separating the Air Service from the rest of the Army, the board held that air power had not as yet "demonstrated its value for independent operations." It also asserted that the United States was in no danger of hostile air attack, thus undermining much of the rationale for independence by denying the need for a separate air defense force. The board did recommend upgrading the Air Service's status by designating it the Air Corps and giving it two additional brigadier generals and special representation on the General Staff. The report also called for the creation of an additional Assistant Secretary of War (for air) and for further study of the need for an Army aviation expansion program.[70]

The Air Service was amply represented in the Morrow Board hearings. Mitchell, Patrick, Foulois, and others presented their cases for vary-

25

# FOULOIS AND THE AIR ARM, 1908-1931

Wreckage of the *Shenandoah*.

## FOULOIS AND THE U.S. ARMY AIR CORPS

Above: President Coolidge (third from left), Sec. Weeks, and Gens. Patrick and Mitchell (in background) meet the "World Fliers" in 1924; below: witnesses for Billy Mitchell in the famous courtmartial pass time before testifying: (l. to r.) Lts. Leigh Wade, Orvil A. Anderson, Hiram W. Sheridan, Maj. Sumpter Smith, and Lt. Eugene Eubanks.

ing degrees of air arm independence. Mitchell renewed his demand for a Department of National Defense containing three service departments. He charged that Army and Navy nonflying officers were "psychologically unfit" to properly employ military aviation and blamed the General Staff for the "deplorable" condition of the Air Service. He stressed that the air arm was the only organization capable of keeping an enemy's aircraft and ships away from the United States. Further, it was the only one of the military forces that could "smash an enemy's centers of power, manufactures, and means of transportation on land so that he can be conquered." Such a force, according to Mitchell, was no mere auxiliary. Instead, it was a main force in America's defense structure and should be given its proper place.[71]

Foulois, now a lieutenant colonel and commander of Mitchel Field, Long Island, New York, supported General Patrick's plea for autonomous status for the Air Service, much like the relationship between the Marine Corps and the Navy Department. Both men testified that the ultimate solution to the military aviation problem required the creation of a separate air organization within a single department of defense, but that the time was not yet ripe for such a change. For the present, they favored the immediate establishment of an autonomous air corps directly under the Secretary of War. Foulois resorted to the same arguments he had used in 1919 to justify the proposed reorganization—the inability of the General Staff to adequately develop and properly employ military aviation:

> Based on my knowledge of the past 17 years of effort for proper recognition of the air branch of the Army, I am fully convinced that aviation will never reach its proper place in the scheme of national defense so long as it remains in the control of the War Department General Staff.[72]

While the aviation pioneer now sought something less than complete independence for the air arm, he and most other Air Service officers believed that ending General Staff control would bring basically the same benefits to military aviation. It would let the fliers themselves chart the air arm's material and doctrinal development. Then, too, the goal of autonomy might be more easily achieved than complete independence. The essential thing for the Air Service officers was to wrest control of military aviation from the nonflyers. Maj. Horace M. Hickam summed up the aviators' feelings before the Morrow board: "I am confident that no general thinks he can command the Navy, or no admiral thinks he can operate an army, but some of them think they can operate an air force."[73]

While Air Service officers found the Morrow Board report wanting, the War Department was quite willing to accept its recommendations over those of the Lampert Committee. The Army adopted the board's program and used it during the first months of 1926 to counter the wave of congressional resolutions and bills calling for the creation of a unified depart-

# FOULOIS AND THE U.S. ARMY AIR CORPS

Left: Foulois, as a lieutenant colonel and commander of Mitchel Field, Long Island, N.Y.

Below: Maj. Horace M. Hickam, with an SE-5 in the background.

ment of defense or some form of air autonomy which had been introduced in the aftermath of Billy Mitchell's court-martial and the publication of the Lampert report. The bitter congressional debate over Air Service legislation ended with passage of the Air Corps Act of July 2, 1926—a law based primarily on the Morrow Board report.[74]

The 1926 act left Army aviation under General Staff control, but it also increased the air organization's military strength and its prestige and influence within the War Department. The law changed the name of the Air Service to the Air Corps; gave it representation in each General Staff division; and authorized a five-year expansion program of the Air Corps to a strength of 1,650 officers, 15,000 enlisted men (including up to 2,500 flying cadets), and 1,800 serviceable airplanes. Further, it provided for a major general as Chief of the Air Corps with three brigadier general assistants. The major general, at least two of the brigadier generals, and ninety percent of the officers in each grade below brigadier general had to be flyers. The act also authorized an additional Assistant Secretary of War "to aid the Secretary of War in fostering military aeronautics."[75]

The law conferred no added measure of autonomy on the Air Corps, but it did offer significant gains to the Army aviators. With Billy Mitchell gone and with the appointment of an assistant secretary for aviation who could act as a special pleader, the Air Corps grew more tractable during the next half decade. Air officers had not abandoned their goal of autonomy or independence, but they were more concerned for the present with carrying out the expansion authorized by the act.

The Air Corps readied plans specifying what would be purchased, constructed, or organized during each of the five annual increments. At its completion, the Air Corps program provided for one air wing each on the east and west coasts, one in the southern United States, one each in Panama and Hawaii, one air group on the northern United States border, and another in the Philippines. It also provided for schools and depots to support this expanded fighting organization. The War Department approved the Air Corps plan, and it became the official five-year expansion program.[76]

It soon became apparent that, although Congress had authorized the five-year program, neither it nor President Coolidge was eager to spend sufficient funds to bring the Air Corps to the specified strength in aircraft and personnel. This situation was bound to exacerbate the temporarily relaxed tensions between the air arm and the rest of the Army. Coolidge, taking full advantage of the permissive nature of the 1926 legislation, delayed the start of the program until fiscal year 1928. During the next five years the executive branch neither requested nor did the Congress appropriate enough funds for the Air Corps to assemble eighteen hundred serviceable airplanes or to build military installations to support them.[77]

While never achieving the number of airplanes authorized by the Air Corps Act during the life of the five-year program, the Air Corps did enlarge its aircraft inventory. In 1926 the Air Corps, together with the aviation units of the National Guard, possessed something less than 900 planes. By 1931 that number had climbed to approximately 1,650, no small feat considering that military aircraft were usually worn out and had to be replaced after five years' service.[78]

Nevertheless, the 1931 total was somewhat deceiving, for it included the more than twelve percent of the fleet undergoing depot overhaul. Assistant Secretary of War for Air F. Trubee Davison argued in 1930 and 1931 that such aircraft should not be counted as "serviceable" under the provisions of the 1926 Air Corps Act. The Attorney General agreed, and as a result the War Department no longer counted the planes in depot as part of the 1,800 "serviceable" authorized by Congress. Based on this decision, Davison asserted in his 1931 annual report that the Air Corps actually needed a total of 2,058 aircraft to meet Congress' goal of 1,800 "serviceable" planes. He also explained that the Army air arm really had only 1,476 "serviceable" aircraft on hand as of July 18,1931, 183 short of the 1,659 called for at the end of the fourth increment in the five-year plan.[79]

The personnel expansion under the Air Corps Act posed a more complicated problem than aircraft procurement. Congress authorized substantial enlargement of Air Corps officer and enlisted strength, but between 1926 and 1935 both the President and Congress opposed any change in the overall size of the Army. Consequently, Air Corps growth had to come at the expense of other Army elements. The War Department diligently carried out the transfer of enlisted men, at the cost of great resentment in the other combatant arms over losing manpower to the air arm. Between July 1927 and July 1931 the enlisted strength of the Air Corps rose from 9,079 to 13,190.[80]

Increasing the air arm's commissioned strength while keeping the Army's total number of officers at a constant 12,000 presented a thornier problem. The War Department needed only a limited number of new officers each year to fill the few vacancies which occurred, and by 1930 West Point was able to supply all of them. Virtually all of the Air Corps new officers had to be aviators, but not many military academy graduates were willing to accept flying training as their first active duty assignment. This set of circumstances left the Air Corps with only one source for additional officers—those who voluntarily transferred from the Army's other arms and branches.

While the Air Corps did increase its commissioned strength from 960 officers at the end of fiscal year 1927 to 1,266 on July 1, 1930, it experienced very limited growth in the following five years. On July 1, 1935, the air arm contained 1,385 officers, a figure well short of the 1,650 authorized by Congress. Not enough officers had volunteered and qualified as aviators to do much more than offset the Air Corps' high attrition rate caused by accidents. The leaders of the Army air arm wanted to cure the officer shortage by continuing to award Regular commissions to some of the hundreds of flying cadets who graduated annually from the Air Corps' pilot training program after 1930. But because of the 12,000 officer ceiling imposed on the Army and the necessity of commissioning all West Point graduates who desired to enter the Army, this was not possible.[81]

The War Department supported the five-year program, but administration and congressional niggardliness in funding the program eventually helped to renew distrust between the flyers and the ground officers. The transfer of enlisted men had cost the other combat arms dearly, resulting by 1930 in the deactivation of five battalions of infantry and almost a complete regiment of field artillery. By fiscal year 1931 the Air Corps was receiving over twenty percent of the funds appropriated for War Department military activities, nearly double the percentage it had received in 1926. Ground commanders thought this was excessive, but members of the air arm asserted it was not enough. Air Corps leaders pointed with dismay to the deep cuts made annually by the Secretary of War in their requests for funds, apparently not realizing that these reductions were largely due to the economy-mindedness of Presidents Coolidge and Hoover. The flyers knew that their aircraft procurement program was lagging badly and believed this showed a lack of War Department support for the five-year program.[82]

The General Staff, however, was guilty only of obeying the Executive's decisions on budget limitations, and of making no effort since the inception of the Air Corps expansion program to go over the President's head and request more funds from Congress. The War Department had the financial needs of the other combat arms and services to consider. Faced with declining federal revenues, in mid-1930 President Hoover intensified the growing Air Corps-War Department discord by ordering the Army not to spend $65 million of the $509 million appropriated by Congress for fiscal year 1931. The Air Corps vigorously protested its share of the reduction. Finally, the General Staff relented and restored $2 million of the cut, taking the funds from the other arms and services. This of course angered those who had to surrender the $2 million. They could see no reason for allowing the Air Corps what appeared to be unwarranted special privileges.[83]

Lt. Col. Benny Foulois was not in Washington at the time of the passage of the 1926 Air Corps Act and subsequent formulation of the five-year program, though he had tried to be on hand. In early 1925, news was circulating within the Air Service that Mitchell would not be renewed as Assistant Chief, Foulois, then a student at the Command and General Staff School, began a letter writing campaign to senior Army officers and politicians in an attempt to gain the post. Foulois' efforts failed, and Lt. Col. James E. Fechet was assigned to the Assistant Chief's position. In mid-1925 Foulois journeyed to New York to take command at Mitchel Field, where he remained until 1927.[84]

When it became clear in mid-1927 that Patrick would soon retire and Fechet would replace him as Chief of the Air Corps, Foulois again resorted to letter writing in an effort to secure the Assistant Chief's office. Governor John H. Trumbull of Connecticut wrote the Secretary of War in his constituent's behalf but received the noncommital reply that "your letter will be given every consideration" when it comes to the matter of appointing a new Assistant Chief of the Air Corps.[85] Near the end of 1927, General Patrick called Foulois to Washington and asked him if he would like the job when Fechet was elevated to chief. Foulois, delighted, said yes. He moved to Washington and on December 20, 1927, assumed the new position, which carried with it the temporary rank of brigadier general.[86]

Foulois spent the next three and one-half years preparing himself for the day when Fechet would retire and he might be selected to succeed him. As Fechet's principal assistant, he initially went to work as head of the Training and Operations Division, the most important of the nine subdivisions within the Office of the Chief of the Air Corps (OCAC). This gave Foulois a wide range of experience, for the Training and Operations Division was responsible for war plans preparation, War Department strategic estimates, legislative proposals, coordination of regulations governing tactical principles and organization, and recommendations to the Chief of the Air Corps on all policy matters and on issues relating to training and Army air operations. After serving eighteen months in this capacity Foulois arranged a one-year exchange of duties with Brig. Gen. William E. Gilmore, Chief of the Air Corps Materiel Division. This enabled him to become more familiar with the air arm's research and development and procurement activities, for which the division based at Dayton, Ohio, had responsibility. When back in Washington in July 1930, as Assistant Chief, Foulois took over direction of the Plans Division, which had been recently created to assume the planning and policy formation functions of the Training and Operations Division.[87]

In 1931 General Fechet selected his assistant to command the annual Air Corps maneuvers. This would be the fourth time in as many years that the Army air arm had pursued this undertaking, but the 1931 edition was by far the largest Army air exercise ever attempted by the United States. The OCAC had decided on forming a provisional air division of approximately 670 aircraft, using it to test the Air Corps' mobility and to determine the problems connected with handling such a large force. The tentative plan envisioned a series of aerial demonstrations over the major cities in the Great Lakes region and the eastern United States. Organizing and directing this force would be no easy matter. It would mean assembling most of the Army's U.S.-based planes in one area and shifting the entire force to various other locations as the maneuvers progressed. Foulois and his staff set to work at once planning what proved to be a tremendous logistics exercise.[88]

Foulois was an excellent choice to organize and command the maneuvers. A "doer" rather than a great thinker, he performed best when dealing with the real and the tangible. He was not afraid to make decisions or experiment. As he wrote the following year in a magazine article: "I am a firm believer, however, in the theory that the best way to learn how to do something is to do it."[89]

After nearly four months of preparation, portions of the huge air armada and the division staff moved on May 12 toward the initial concentration point at Wright Field near Dayton. This operation was a major undertaking in itself, for it involved transferring twenty-four of the twenty-five regular Army Air Corps bombardment, pursuit, attack, and observation squadrons from all across the United States, along with flights from nineteen National Guard units and eight provisional squadrons from the Air Corps Training Center at San Antonio. All units were to be in place in the Dayton area by the eighteenth. General Foulois and his staff left by air from Washington on May 12. The first flight of three single-seat aircraft led by Foulois himself, ran into bad weather near Cumberland, Maryland. An excellent pilot, the general pressed on through the weather, while his much younger fellow aviators headed back to Bolling Field and clear skies. A second flight of three did the same. Arriving safely at Wright Field, the good-humored Foulois had a big laugh at the expense of his Washington cohorts when they finally arrived much later in the day.[90]

The general's remarkably large provisional air organization took to the air as a unit during the last week and a half of May and carried out demonstrations over many cities in the Great Lakes region and along the Atlantic Coast. The operation generated tremendous public interest as millions of Americans got a chance to witness a massive, though not very militarily potent, aerial display. Antiwar groups in New York and a few other cities protested the maneuvers, but generally the public fully supported them. Both Chief of Staff Gen. Douglas MacArthur and President Herbert Hoover were delighted with the smoothness of the operation.[91]

Foulois, leading the operation from his own plane, could be justifiably proud. His force had flown nearly thirty-eight thousand hours,

Sketch of routes designed for Air Corps bombardment units flying from home stations to and from the May 1931 exercises.

# FOULOIS AND THE AIR ARM, 1908-1931

Right: the air armada was initially concentrated at Fairfield Air Depot, adjacent to Wright Field, Ohio, for the 1931 maneuvers; below: B-2 Condor bombers flying over Staten Island docks during the exercises, May 27, 1931.

# FOULOIS AND THE U.S. ARMY AIR CORPS

# FOULOIS AND THE AIR ARM, 1908-1931

Above: The exercises also drew some notable figures in aviation: (l. to r.) Howard S. Smith, Chairman of Aeronautical Committee, Dayton Chamber of Commerce, Lt. Col. H. H. Arnold, Orville Wright, Maj. Carl A. Spaatz, Brig. Gen. Foulois, Maj. A. L. Sneed, and Brig. Gen. H. C. Pratt; right: for organizing and executing the flawless maneuvers, Hiram Bingham presented the Mackay Trophy to Foulois on behalf of the National Aeronautics Association. Ass't. Sec. of War for Air, F. Trubee Davison looks on.

The grouping of these illustrations indicates the vast scope of the May 1931 exercises. On the adjacent page (top) is a formation of Curtiss A-3s taking part in the maneuvers; center: a flight of B-2 Condors over Ocean City, N.J.; bottom: staff and group commanders of the 1st Provisional Pursuit Wing formed for the event.

sometimes in close formation for up to four hours at a time with over six hundred aircraft in the sky at once, and not one serious accident had occurred. This was a remarkable safety record for its day. In recognition the National Aeronautic Association awarded Foulois the Mackay Trophy for 1931.[92]

The Assistant Chief of the Air Corps' credible performance as commander of the provisional air division probably had much to do with his selection to succeed General Fechet as chief. Shortly after the conclusion of the maneuvers, Fechet announced that he would retire in December. At the end of the first week in June news stories appeared in some of the leading eastern newspapers asserting that Foulois had already been selected to replace Fechet and lauding the Assistant Chief's fine record.[93] The War Department was somewhat disturbed, since President Hoover had apparently not as yet reached a final decision. Assistant Secretary of War for Air Davison wrote Foulois about the news stories, seeking their source. The general's response was not completely truthful: "During my entire period of service in the Army, I have consistently discouraged the efforts of political, or other outside influences, desiring to further my advancement in the Service."[94] Whether Foulois or some of his friends had sought in this instance to influence the Secretary of War's and President's attitudes by planting the news stories is open to speculation. Regardless, on July 13 The Adjutant General informed the Assistant Chief that the President had appointed him to succeed Fechet upon the present chief's retirement. The rank and file of the Air Corps seemed genuinely pleased with the Chief Executive's selection.[95]

Fechet applied for and was granted a three months' leave of absence, effective September 8. Hence, Foulois actually took over the duties of the chief at that time. On December 21 he formally assumed command and pinned on his second star.[96]

As Chief of the Air Corps the new major general could not exercise operational control over the Air Corps' tactical units. These organizations belonged to the corps area commanders, as did all combat units in the United States. The OCAC administered only those installations and organizations involved in aircraft procurement and maintenance or specialized training related to aviation—these being specifically exempted from corps area control by War Department directives. The Chief of the Air Corps and his subordinates supplied the aeronautical equipment to the tactical squadrons and performed their depot maintenance; determined how the tactical units would be organized and who would command them; wrote the Army regulations governing aircraft operations and unit and individual training; and decided how much of the Air Corps appropriations each air arm organization would spend and for what. Thus, while not having actual operational control over tactical air units, the chief did have a tre-

Organization Chart of the Office, Chief of the Air Corps, July 1931.

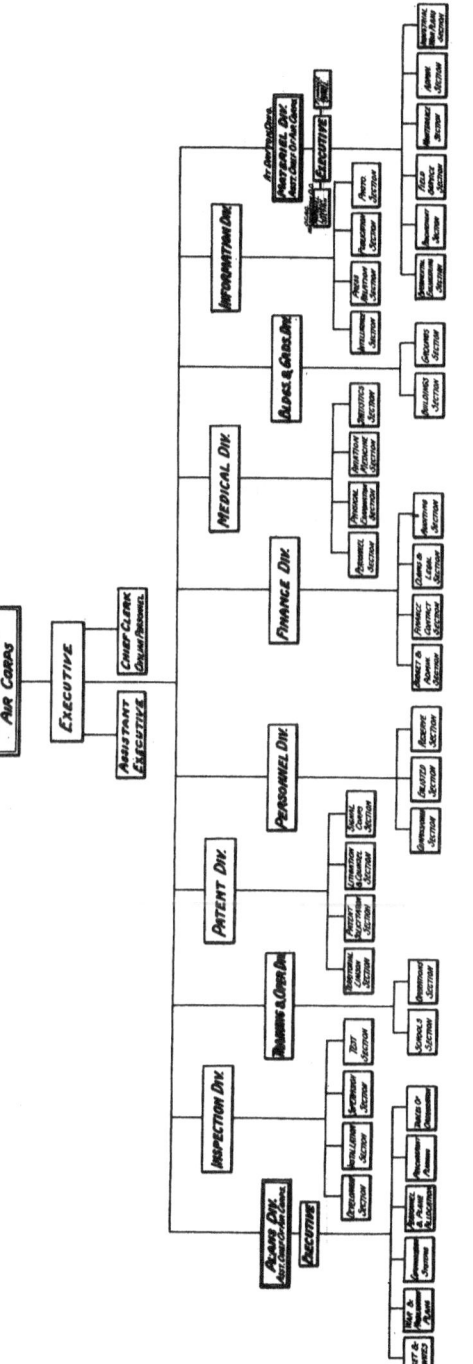

mendous voice in what these organizations did.[97] However, Foulois and most other Air Corps officers were not satisfied with this arrangement. Experiencing temporary operational control in the 1931 air maneuvers, the new chief worked almost from the start to centralize all Army flying units within the United States under Air Corps command.

Foulois had only a limited say in choosing his new Assistant Chief. He had initially proposed that the War Department jump over several senior Air Corps officers and select a younger man for the post. Assistant Secretary of War for Air Davison disagreed. General MacArthur joined in the discussion, and to break the stalemate suggested Lt. Col. Oscar Westover for the job. Eventually both men agreed and on January 13, 1932, Westover took office with the temporary rank of brigadier general.[98]

The military aviation pioneer who had opposed General Staff control of the air arm during most of his career was about to begin his first full year at the helm of the Air Corps. Beside him, ready to take over in his absence, was a man who in 1919 had been vocal in his support of War Department control. Together, and in apparent harmony, they would lead the Army air arm through one of its greatest periods of transition.

## CHAPTER II

## DOCTRINE, MISSION, AND EMPLOYMENT CONCEPTS, 1931-1933

When Benjamin Foulois became Chief of the Air Corps, air doctrine was in a state of confusion; despite years of thought, Air Corps officers had developed no comprehensive statement on the employment of air power. Certainly Mitchell's comments on the importance of attacking the enemy's vital centers and his belief that the airplane represented an entirely new method of warfare continued to win advocates within the Air Corps during the late 1920s. Still, circumstances prevented the doctrine of strategic bombardment from becoming paramount in the Army air arm by 1931. The Air Corps possessed no aircraft capable of traveling great distances with heavy bombloads. Further, American national policy discouraged offensive military strategy. Government leaders believed national defense should be just that—defense. President Hoover made this very clear on October 27, 1931, in his Navy Day statement: "Ours is a force of defense, not offense."[1]

General Staff thinking also acted as an inhibiting agent. The War Department had by 1926 acknowledged a multitude of tasks that military aviation could perform—some far removed from the battlefield. Yet the General Staff's central premise remained unchanged throughout the 1920s: air power was an auxiliary force to assist American ground forces in destroying the enemy land army.[2] This attitude was anathema to strategic bombing advocates, for it denied aviation's ability to independently influence the outcome of future wars. However, the General Staff controlled the formation of all official doctrine within the entire Army. With so many checks to the concept of strategic bombardment, air officers also continued to think and write about the two most obvious alternative missions—air defense of the homeland and battlefield support for the ground forces. Having arrived at no single concept of employment, Air Corps doctrine remained fluid.[3]

## FOULOIS AND THE U.S. ARMY AIR CORPS

The Air Corps Tactical School (ACTS) was the primary participant in air doctrine development during the 1920s and 1930s. Originally established in 1920 at Langley Field, Virginia, as the Air Service Field Officer's School, it was renamed the Air Service Tactical School in 1922. In 1931 the school, by then known as the Air Corps Tactical School, moved to newly constructed facilities at Maxwell Field, Alabama. The War Department originally organized the school as the air arm's counterpart to the principal service schools of the other branches, but by the mid-1920s ACTS had begun to reach beyond instruction in air tactics, organization, and administration to questions of doctrine.[4]

The school first challenged War Department employment concepts with its 1926 text for the course, "Employment of Combined Air Force." This volume asserted that the goal in war was not the destruction of the enemy's field forces, but to destroy his morale and will to resist. Any effective means, including the annihilation of his army, could be used to achieve this goal, but at the outset of hostilities the best method might be air attack on the enemy's interior. The text explained: "It is a means of imposing will with the least possible loss by heavily striking vital points rather than wearing down an enemy to exhaustion." If shattering the enemy's morale through attacks on the interior were not possible at the onset of hostilities, the air force should seek such objectives as the hostile air

Air Corps Tactical School, Maxwell Field, Ala.

force, ground troops, lines of communications, and industrial and transportation centers that would demolish the enemy's military strength. The concepts expressed in "Employment of Combined Air Force" did not, however, reflect a unified Air Corps Tactical School doctrinal viewpoint. Texts for other 1926 courses accepted the auxiliary role of aviation propagated by the General Staff.[5]

In 1928, seeking to establish a common air doctrine throughout the Army, the tactical school faculty wrote and forwarded for War Department consideration a paper entitled "The Doctrine of the Air Force." The paper's major premises showed the doctrinal confusion existing at the time. While stating that the Air Force may be able to break the will of the enemy alone, "The Doctrine of the Air Force" went on to say that actual or threatened occupation of enemy territory would be necessary to bring hostilities to a close. Further, it asserted that the air component "always supports the ground forces, no matter how decisive its [the Air Force's] operations may be, or how indirect the support."[6]

The Chief of the Air Corps, General Fechet, and his staff usually looked to the tactical school for leadership on doctrinal questions. However, in this instance they were appalled by the military conservatism expressed in the school's proposal. The OCAC officers believed the paper underplayed the independent decisiveness of air power. They rejected it, explaining:

> In considering the attached study the impression throughout is conveyed that the Air Force is subsidiary to the ground forces and is entirely an auxiliary for the purpose of assisting them in accomplishing their mission. As pointed out above, this is contrary to the prevailing ideas on the proper mission of an Air Force, as the application of air power has gained sufficiently in importance as a means of national defense to greatly influence, if not entirely remove, the necessity in some cases, particularly at the beginning of a campaign, of ground forces ever coming in contact.[7]

In succeeding years the views of the Air Corps Tactical School and the Office of the Chief of the Air Corps returned to harmony. By 1931 the tactical school was again the doctrinal innovator, fully supported by the OCAC. In the years following 1931 the ACTS gradually led the Air Corps to a fuller articulation of the strategic bombardment doctrine, the concept that the enemy could be defeated by strategic air operations alone.[8]

The tactical school texts in 1930 made no mention of the decisiveness of military aviation in warfare. They did, however, call bombardment the "basic arm of the Air Force" and urged its use against industrial and transportation centers and lines of communications.[9] But they also acknowledged the military importance of other targets. "The Air Force" course (the most important of the school's offerings) taught in 1930 that the enemy's air force was the primary objective in war, with attacks on strategic targets next in importance. The course text further mentioned coast defense and support of ground troops as meaningful missions. The book's statements on defense of the United States again indicated the doctrinal confusion that reigned at the time:

> The peacetime organization of our air force should be predicated upon the defense of our country against invasion by the most probable coalition of powers. The composition and strength of the Air Corps should be developed primarily for the purpose of successfully driving home our bombardment attacks against the invading forces.[10]

Thus, while mentioning the military significance of offensive strategic bombardment, the text called for air arm organization and development based on the more politically acceptable mission of coast defense.

Air Corps officers at the school and elsewhere also continued to think about ground support, the mission the General Staff deemed most essential.[11] By 1930 the air arm had clearly defined its employment concepts respecting its relationship to the ground forces, and it did not change its position during the next thirteen years. According to the 1930 text "The Air Force," the air arm could best help the ground forces by achieving air superiority, interdicting supplies, destroying production facilities, and striking troop concentrations. The book shunned the close air support role that the General Staff so prized: "Rarely will troops engaged in battle be suitable air force objectives." It explained that such targets were hard to hit, and since the outcome of ground combat was always determined by the timely employment of reserves, it would be far more beneficial to interdict them instead.[12]

Between 1931 and 1935 the Army aviators considered the Air Corps to have three major missions: strategic bombardment, coast defense, and ground army support. During these years the air arm more clearly defined the strategic bombardment doctrine, fully embraced the coast defense mission, and retained its 1930 attitudes toward field army support. General Foulois took no active part in doctrinal development during 1931-35. He vigorously sought Army and Navy acceptance of the Air Corps' primacy in coast defense, but otherwise deferred to the Air Corps Tactical School and his assistant, General Westover, who had been commandant of that school in the mid-1920s.[13] By 1935 the Air Corps had developed a body of doctrine based on one type of mission—strategic bombardment—while fully accepting and championing the air arm's paramount importance in another—coast defense.

In 1931, the instructors at the tactical school moved closer to open advocacy of the decisiveness of air power. The text for the course "Bombardment Aviation" maintained: "There will probably be certain vital objectives comparatively limited in number which, if destroyed, will contribute most to the success of the combined arms of the nation."[14] The text

CONCEPTS, 1931-1933

for "The Air Force" course agreed, pointing out that the decision to accept defeat in the Civil War and World War I "was largely based upon the condition and sufferings of the noncombatants at home." It asserted that the ability of an air force "to strike directly the rear of the enemy's army, or the heart of his country, may have a profound effect upon his will to wage war." Yet it hedged on the issue of air power's ability to independently win a war:

> Some men of vision prophesy a time when wars will be fought principally and decided absolutely by air forces. He is egotistical, to say the least, who will set a limit for future development of aviation in war or peace. But if the future course of war follows past development, the next war will begin about where the last ended, and the air force will be subordinate, although a most important auxiliary, to the ground forces. It is improbable that any nation today has sufficient airpower to overcome any other strong nation by that means alone.[15]

In 1932-33 the tactical school clung to its equivocal position on the decisiveness of independent air operations, but produced a conclusive statement on the significance of air superiority:

> It remains to be proved that an air force alone can break a nation's national resistance—its will to fight. Whatever our personal opinions may be, we must admit that. But while it also remains to be proved by future wars, we are firmly of the belief that there is no hope for victory for these land forces and sea forces, if their air force has been overcome, and the enemy has control of the air.[16]

Faculty members used this rationale to emphasize the importance of the air arm in the defense of the United States and its overseas possessions. They believed that if the Air Corps defeated an invader's air component, no land invasion could take place [17]—a supposition confirmed in Britain in 1940. But the doctrinal innovators at Maxwell Field also easily converted this defensive function into one requiring offensive strategic bombing operations. They claimed that the best way to destroy the enemy air force was to attack its airdromes, factories, depots, and supporting industries. The notes used to teach a unit on counterair operations quoted an unnamed European's comments: "To quickly get rid of a race of birds it is not sufficient to shoot down in flight all that we encounter. This method is the most inefficient imaginable. It will be far better to systematically destroy the nests and the eggs therein."[18]

The Air Corps made direct use of Giulio Douhet's theories on air power in 1933. Under the direction of General Westover, Capt. George C. Kenney and an ACTS civilian employee translated an article containing his major concepts that Douhet had written for a French magazine. The Italian general had maintained for years that military aviation would be the decisive element in future wars. He believed victory would go to the side whose aerial bombardment most rapidly destroyed its adversary's ma-

47

terial and moral resistance. He considered the army and navy as defensive elements which would prevent a surface invasion while the air force conducted its victory-winning air campaign. Most Air Corps officers were not well acquainted with Douhet's thoughts prior to the 1933 translation. Yet the new translation signaled no radical increase in his influence among Army aviators. They would conveniently quote Douhet from time to time if his words supported their own theories on air power, but the American doctrine of strategic bombardment continued to evolve on its own. However, General Foulois, who completely endorsed the ACTS's work on air doctrine and realized the educational and propaganda value of the translated article, saw that it was widely distributed within the Air Corps and the House Committee on Military Affairs.[19]

By the early 1930s, Billy Mitchell's ideas on the value of strategic air attack differed little from Douhet's. Like his Italian counterpart, Mitchell now believed land and sea operations would be largely superfluous to achieving victory. Mitchell contended the enemy's population centers and production facilities had to be attacked to bring about the rapid collapse of his will to resist. While Mitchell continued to correspond with Air Corps officers after his resignation from the service in 1926, he, like Douhet, had slight direct impact on the Army air arm's doctrinal development during the 1930s.[20]

By 1934, instructors at the Air Corps Tactical School no longer quibbled over the decisiveness of independent air operations in warfare. The "Bombardment" text for the 1933-34 school year boldly proclaimed: "Bombardment aviation, properly employed, can shatter a nation's will to resist; it can destroy the economical and industrial structures which make possible the very existence of modern civilization." However, aware of the dichotomy between this offensive doctrine and the defense mission of the Air Corps as set forth in national policy, the text cast bombardment aviation in defensive terms:

> It can make untenable the establishment or occupation of bases from which air operations could be conducted against the industrial and financial heart of our nation; it constitutes, if properly organized, controlled and employed, the very bulwark of our national defense.[21]

On the adjacent page, the B-9 (above) represented Boeing's new aerodynamic concept. The all-metal monoplane was designed specifically as a bomber, in contrast to earlier multi-purpose designs. Though not adopted by the Army, all of its new design features were incorporated into the B-10 (below), which went into service in 1933.

CONCEPTS, 1931-1933

Even so, the lectures to the class stressed the offensive strength of air power. The instructors made it clear that the goal in war was not to destroy the adversary's army but his will to resist, and this could best be carried out by bombing his industrial and transportation centers.[22]

Technological progress contributed to this growing doctrinal boldness. The Boeing B-9, introduced into the Air Corps inventory in 1931, represented a quantum leap forward in aircraft design and performance. A twin-engine, all-metal, low-wing monoplane with retractable landing gear, it could carry 2,000 pounds of bombs at a top speed of 186 miles-per-hour and had a service ceiling of 20,000 feet. Though not adopted as the Army's standard bomber, the B-9 was a tremendous technological improvement over existing wood and fabric biplanes, the best of which could not attain speeds above 135 miles-per-hour. The Martin B-10, which began Air Corps operations in 1933, incorporated all of the new design features of the B-9 and was capable of even better performance. It possessed a maximum speed of around 210 miles-per-hour and a ceiling of over 21,000 feet. Neither plane, however, had a combat range in excess of 600 miles. Nonetheless, the great aeronautical advances embodied in the B-9 and B-10 must have been heartening to airpower advocates.[23]

The Army General Staff at no time during the 1920s and 1930s gave encouragement to the growing Air Corps belief that military aviation, of itself, was capable of producing a decision in warfare. It continued to believe that the only route to victory lay in the destruction of the enemy's armed forces.[24] However, by the late 1920s the War Department more fully appreciated the military usefulness of air operations beyond the battlefield. A 1929 War Plans Division report, while affirming that the air arm was "an auxiliary of the basic arm, the Infantry," stated that

> the Air Corps possesses certain characteristics which enable it to conduct separate operations. In combat with enemy air forces, in long-distance reconnaissance, and in long-distance bombardment, it must frequently conduct its operations entirely apart from the other arms, although such operations are always dependent on general tactical or strategic considerations.[25]

The General Staff accepted the theory of independent air operations only insofar as they could be shown to affect the outcome on the battlefield. It was hostile to any thought of strategic bombing as an alternative method of gaining victory. Since it controlled the formation and dissemination of doctrine, the General Staff forced the Air Corps to moderate its official position on this subject. All manuals written by the air arm and the other branches had to win War Department approval to become official publications. This, of course, necessitated some watering down of the tactical school's theories before they could appear in Army publications.[26]

General Staff officers of the early 1930s were not unthinking reactionaries consciously seeking to stymie the full development of military aviation. It was true that as a group they had a strong conservative bent.

CONCEPTS, 1931-1933

It was also true that in their reaction to the claims of the Army aviators they were frequently motivated by institutional self-interest and were merely seeking to preserve the Army's already skimpy land warfare resources. But their attitude toward air power was more fundamentally based on two other considerations: they could see no evidence of the decisiveness of strategic bombing operations, and they valued military aviation for its ability to assist the ground forces in combat.[27] Strategic bombardment had never before been widely employed in warfare, and current American aircraft were neither technologically capable nor numerous enough to attempt an effective strategic bombing campaign. Moreover, the General Staff officers realized that any aircraft diverted to such militarily questionable operations would not be available to assist the ground forces. Given the slim financial resources annually available to the War Department in the 1930s, such a diversion might leave ground troops without adequate air support. General Staff officers refused to let this potentially dangerous situation come to pass. All of them knew that wars were won on the ground by infantrymen. They insisted that the Air Corps accept its responsibilities as an auxiliary and prepare to properly support the foot soldier.

Members of the General Staff were quite displeased with the seemingly disloyal comments of those Air Corps officers who publicly proclaimed aviation as a new mode of warfare, capable in itself of achieving victory. Maj. Gen. George Van Horn Moseley, a former Deputy Chief of Staff, complained bitterly in 1934 that "too many of the Air Corps officers have the idea in the event of war tomorrow that the Army is one problem, and they are going somewhere else and are going to do something more or less spectacular."[28] Brig. Gen. Charles E. Kilbourne, Chief of the War Plans Division and certainly no reactionary, probably expressed the general sentiment of the War Department when he wrote: "For many years the General Staff of the Army has suffered a feeling of disgust amounting at times to nausea over statements publicly made by General William Mitchell and those who followed his lead." He contended Mitchell and others had far overstated the abilities of military aviation in order to gain preferential treatment for the air arm.[29] A paper from Kilbourne's office in early 1934 explained that in their zeal to advance the interests of military aviation, Air Corps officers "adopted the tactics of attacking and belittling all other elements of our national defense forces, sea and land. This course of action led many officers to instinctively close their minds to perfectly legitimate and honest claims" presented by these same military aviators.[30]

Although the Air Corps and the General Staff officers differed as to the decisiveness of strategic air operations, by 1931 they generally agreed that Army rather than Navy aviation should be charged with the aerial coast defense of the United States. The sea service, however, did not agree. Prior to the advent of military aviation, the dividing line for coast defense responsibility had been clear—the Navy controlled all operations beyond the range of Army coastal batteries. This well-defined line became blurred as aircraft entered the picture. The Army and Navy had been discussing the issue at meetings of the Joint Board, off and on, since the close of World War I. The Joint Board, never a very useful agency for resolving deep-rooted differences between the two services, could not produce a clearly worded statement defining coast air defense responsibilities. Resorting to vague generalities in its "agreements" on the issue during the 1920s, the Joint Board simply papered over the question, allowing each service to interpret the wording as it saw fit.[31]

The crux of the disagreement centered around the Army's claim to exclusive control over land-based combat aircraft, and the Navy's assertion that all overwater aerial operations came under its jurisdiction.[32] The War Department appropriations act for fiscal year 1921 sought to clarify the matter:

> the Army Air Service shall control all aerial operations from land bases, and Naval Aviation shall have control of all aerial operations attached to the fleet, including shore stations whose maintenance is necessary for operations connected with the fleet, for construction and experimentation, and for the training of personnel.[33]

But this statement allowed the Navy numerous loopholes for justifying the operation of aircraft from land bases, and did not touch directly on the issue of aerial coast defense.

Between 1921 and 1926, Mitchell and Chief of the Air Service Patrick campaigned continuously for the Army air arm to have complete responsibility for coastal air defense. Patrick reemphasized the air arm's position to the War Department in February 1926 explaining that naval aviation traveled with the fleet and consequently could not be counted on to assist with coast defense. The War Department was mildly sympathetic toward the Air Service's view but did not press the issue in discussions with the Navy. Neither the General Staff nor the Navy believed there was much danger of air attack on the United States.[34]

The War Department was nevertheless quite concerned over the increasing buildup of naval land-based aviation taking place in the mid-1920s. The Joint Board took up the matter in 1926 and produced an imprecise agreement concerning which types of aircraft the Navy could operate from shore installations: "To avoid duplication in peacetime procurement, the Navy's land-based aircraft . . . will be limited to those primarily designed and ordinarily used for scouting and patrolling over the sea." Each service placed its own interpretation on the agreement. To the dismay of the General Staff and the Air Corps, the Navy continued to

# CONCEPTS, 1931–1933

Maj. Gen. Patrick with Adm. Moffett.

increase the number of combat aircraft at its land installations. In 1927 the War Department became particularly perturbed when the sea service began stationing torpedo planes ashore in Hawaii and Panama.[35]

In 1928, after the Army had argued that the issue should go to the President for resolution, the Navy agreed to join in a new Joint Board agreement. The resulting rather ambiguous paper authorized the Navy to base some strike aircraft ashore if the primary functions of these planes were scouting and patrol. It also recognized the Army's chief responsibility in resisting attacks on the coasts of the United States and its possessions.[36] However, the 1928 paper also contained vague statements from the 1926 agreement that did not clearly specify who would control aerial defense operations beyond the shoreline:

(a) The air component of the Army conducts air operations over the land and such air operations over the sea as are incident to the accomplishment of Army functions.

(b) The air component of the Navy conducts air operations over the sea and such operations over the land as are incident to the accomplishment of Navy functions.[37]

Hence, the issue of who was responsible for aerial coast defense continued unresolved into the 1930s.

In truth, the Navy favored reinstituting the old dividing line for coast defense responsibility—at or near the shoreline. Naval aviators were adamant about this by the mid-1920s, but they secured only lukewarm support from their blue-water superiors. Rear Adm. William A. Moffett, Chief of the Bureau of Aeronautics, vigorously fought the Air Corps encroachment on what he and his colleagues considered a naval air mission.

He likewise crusaded for the buildup of naval shore-based patrol and strike aircraft so the Navy could handle the aerial coast defense mission efficiently.[38] In 1926 he argued before Congress that offshore scouting and attacks on enemy forces at sea were "essentially naval operations" which comprised "the major elements of aerial defense required along the coasts." Shore-based naval aircraft were vital to this mission. Leaving no doubt as to where he would draw the dividing line, Moffett said "it is the Navy's duty to prevent the movement of enemy forces over the sea. The Army is concerned only when the enemy forces reach the immediate vicinity of the coasts."[39]

As Air Corps leaders pressed in the late 1920s for control of all coastal air defense functions out to the limit of the radius of action of existing land planes (approximately 250 miles), Navy resistance intensified. Expressing the War Department's view, Assistant Secretary of War for Air Davison had to agree with the Navy on one score: It was not the Air Corps' job to venture far out over the high seas in search of the enemy's navy. Yet he and his uniformed associates argued that Air Corps aircraft were responsible for interdicting air or surface invasion forces anytime those hostile forces were located within range of Army planes.[40] The Navy's position remained unchanged: Army air responsibility stopped at the water's edge or just beyond it. As one admiral asserted in 1929, "The aerial coast defense of our country is purely a naval function."[41]

After Patrick J. Hurley became Secretary of War and Douglas MacArthur took office as Chief of Staff in 1930, a definite shift occurred in the War Department's attitude toward the Air Corps' right to full responsibility for coastal air defense. No longer was the War Department willing to accept some fuzzily worded compromise statement. Instead, it wanted the Navy's unambiguous concurrence that the mission of aerial coast defense of the United States coasts and its overseas holdings belonged exclusively to the Air Corps. Encouraged by President Hoover, who wanted to avoid duplication in aircraft procurement, MacArthur eventually resorted to personal negotiations with the Chief of Naval Operations (CNO), Adm. William V. Pratt. The two men met and on January 7, 1931, arrived at what MacArthur believed was a final settlement of the issue.[42] A War Department press release recorded the unwritten understanding:

> The Naval Air Force will be based on the fleet and move with it as an element in solving the primary missions confronting the fleet. The Army Air Forces will be land based and employed as an essential element to the Army in the performance of its mission to defend the coasts both at home and in our overseas possessions, thus assuring the fleet absolute freedom of action without any responsibility for coast defense.[43]

The War Department had finally received the Navy's concurrence that the aerial coast defense mission belonged to the Air Corps. But as the *Army and Navy Journal* cautioned when announcing the MacArthur-Pratt

CONCEPTS, 1931-1933

agreement: "Nothing is said in the agreement, and at the Departments it is said that there is no specific understanding, as to the scope of the term 'aerial coast defenses'."[44]

Admiral Pratt was not a reluctant partner in the agreement. From the time of his appointment as CNO in September 1930, he had taken steps on his own to clear up the aerial coast defense controversy. Pratt was most concerned for the mobility and striking power of the fleet, for he believed that the fleet should meet and destroy a hostile invasion force far out to sea. Since carrier-based aircraft would play a crucial part in such an operation, he favored spending the Navy's meager aviation funds for planes that could go to sea.[45]

Barely two months after taking office, Pratt promulgated a new naval air operating policy giving force to his views and paving the way for agreement with MacArthur. According to the new policy: "All aircraft assigned to tactical units will be mobile in order to operate with the fleet. Mobility will be achieved by the use of carriers and [seaplane] tenders."

Adm. William V. Pratt.

Coastal patrol remained a secondary mission for naval aviation, but the Navy would not earmark resources for it during peacetime. Pratt's directive required that shore naval air stations supporting the fleet be renamed fleet air stations and be controlled by the fleet commander. The stations and their aircraft

> are not intended for and will not be allowed to be diverted from their fleet objectives, for any reasons of coast defense, except for the most urgent, when upon request of the Commandant of a particular Naval District the forces therein may be permitted to cooperate with other military forces.[46]

The Navy's patrol and strike aircraft based ashore were now part of the fleet. In time of crisis, they were to travel on carriers or tenders in support of the fleet's mission. As a consequence of his views, the Chief of Naval Operations readily joined with the Chief of Staff in the MacArthur-Pratt agreement. Admiral Moffett, his fellow aviators, and many other senior naval officers disliked the new aviation policy and the MacArthur-Pratt agreement. They wanted to avoid giving the Air Corps the chance to absorb the coast defense mission in its entirety. For the time being, however, there was little they could do.[47]

The Air Corps was delighted with the informal agreement between Pratt and MacArthur. At last the Army air arm had a clearly defined semiautonomous mission consistent with American national policy. While not deserting the concept of offensive strategic bombardment, the Air Corps fully accepted the coast defense mission in its own right. This was no facade behind which the air arm clandestinely prepared itself to fight World War II. Military aviators believed that air defense was an important mission, and worked to develop the plans, proper organization, and equipment to carry it out. Air leaders might have had strategic bombing operations in the back of their minds when they sought longer range aircraft and a unified striking force, but during the years Foulois was at the Air Corps' helm, they were primarily thinking about what the Army air arm needed to best carry out the mission of aerial coast defense.

Events in August 1931 called into question the Air Corps' ability to carry out its new mission even before it had begun to prepare itself for the task. With General Staff approval, the shipping board donated an old freighter, the *Mount Shasta*, to the Air Corps for use in bombing practice. The Office of the Chief of the Air Corps planned no publicity for the operation. The ship was to be towed into shallow water not far from Langley Field and anchored there as a static target for continuous use. However, the Virginia State Commission of Fisheries objected, so it was decided to move the *Mount Shasta* about fifty-five miles out to sea and use it for a one-time exercise. Apparently the commanding officer at Langley Field handled all the arrangements and did not keep the OCAC fully informed. Word of the impending exercise reached the newspapers,

CONCEPTS, 1931-1933

and they reacted as if it were going to be a reenactment of Billy Mitchell's exploits of the early 1920s. Generals Fechet and Foulois knew little about the proposed exercise until the press began to emphasize it. Although neither of them favored the wide publicity, they did nothing to halt the August operation.[48] They were both probably quite willing to reap whatever benefits might accrue to the Air Corps from the wide public interest.

At Langley Field a provisional squadron of nine bombers commanded by Maj. Herbert A. Dargue took off on August 11 and headed out to sea to locate and attack the old freighter. The planes carried only 300-pound bombs, which the optimistic Dargue believed would be ample to sink the ship. Much to the embarrassment of the Air Corps, the squadron ran into rainy weather en route, could not locate the *Mount Shasta*, and was forced to return to Langley Field. The bombers tried again on August 14. This time the squadron found the freighter but could not sink it with the lightweight bombs. The planes from Langley Field scored several direct hits setting the *Mount Shasta* on fire, but a Coast Guard cutter had to be called in to finish off the freighter.[49]

While the press was not overly critical of the Air Corps' effort, the Navy used it as an excuse for rather heavy heckling of the Army air arm. *The New York Times* explained that, while none of the bombers found the ship on August 11, this was due in part to the vessel being cut free from the towship earlier than planned. The paper also pointed out that a number of Army observation planes had successfully located her and that the Air Corps would have quickly sent the old freighter to the bottom, had the aircraft dropped 1,000-pound bombs instead of the small 300-pounders. The Navy used the August 11 failure to embarrass the Air

Bombing of *Mt. Shasta* off Virginia Capes.

Corps by publicly offering its services to guide the Army bombers to the *Mount Shasta* and, if necessary, sink the old hulk.[50] All this was ostensibly done in good fun, but a poem passed to the press by naval officers on August 13 revealed in its last verse something of the sea service's attitude toward Army air operations beyond the coast:

> Oh Navy take back your coast defense
> For we find that the sea is rough;
> We thought on one hand it would help us expand
> We find we are not so tough.
> The sea is your right, you hold it by might
> We would if we could but we can't.
> It seems that the sea is entirely Navy,
> Army planes should remain o'er the land,
> The land, the land.
> Army planes should remain o'er the land.[51]

The Air Corps was concerned over its poor showing in the exercise. Lt. Col. Hap Arnold probably expressed the fears of many of his fellow officers when he wrote: "I cannot help but feel that it will have a very detrimental effect on this newly assigned Coast Defense project." Arnold believed the Navy would likely capitalize on the *Mount Shasta* fiasco and attempt to convince Congress that the Air Corps could not locate or sink ships at sea.[52] Hanson W. Baldwin, *The New York Times'* military affairs editor and a U.S. Naval Academy graduate, must have intensified Air Corps fears with his August 30 editorial. Baldwin wrote that the bomb squadron's inability to locate the ship on its first try was

> illustrative of the inefficiency of land-based pilots over water. . . . The inability of the army aviation, however, to find a floating target not more than sixty miles away—a problem which is solved almost monthly by Navy fliers—is certainly a definite example of the value of specific training for a specific task.[53]

Baldwin implied that aerial operations against hostile ships should be left to the Navy. He also used the occasion to proclaim that aviation was incapable of acting as America's first line of defense.[54]

General Foulois, about to take over as Acting Chief of the Air Corps, was sorely distressed by the entire affair. He blamed the commander of Langley Field and subordinates in the OCAC for not giving the chief adequate advance notice of the exercise's changed scope. Presumably, this would have enabled Fechet or Foulois to keep the operation from becoming a publicity stunt. Foulois was so angry that he decided to quietly relieve a number of officers in the chief's office as soon as he was in a position to do so.[55]

Foulois and other Air Corps officers believed the *Mount Shasta* exercise pointed up the need for the Air Corps to conduct specialized overwater training, if it hoped to keep the coastal air defense mission exclusively its own. The OCAC had already contemplated setting up a special

CONCEPTS, 1931-1933

overwater navigation coast defense school in July 1931, but the events of August spurred Foulois and his subordinates to move more quickly on the issue. On October 9 the acting chief requested permission from the General Staff to establish a school to develop coast defense navigation and plotting equipment and tactics.[56]

The War Department response was somewhat confusing. Senior Army officers agreed that the Air Corps was neither trained nor equipped to carry out all-weather coast defense operations, but the General Staff did not believe the situation warranted creation of a permanent school. The War Department stressed in its November 21 reply to the Air Corps request that

> coast defense is a problem which appertains to the Army at large and invokes the utilization of all branches of the Army. The work of the Air Corps, therefore, along such lines, instead of being segregated in an exempted school, should be coordinated under the normal agencies in the line of command of the Army.[57]

However, the War Department memo directed the Air Corps to submit plans for putting overwater navigation training into effect throughout the Army air arm.[58] Apparently, the General Staff did not think the Air Corps should intercept ships at sea without coordinating such operations with coast artillery and mobile ground units. Likewise, it appeared that the General Staff did not understand the exclusively air-oriented technological and tactical problems needing to be solved to make air defense workable.

General MacArthur expressed surprise upon receiving Foulois' October 9 memo, for he presumed the Air Corps was already engaged in coast defense training. After Foulois met with the Chief of Staff and clarified the matter, MacArthur on February 18, 1932, approved Air Corps plans for a scaled-down version of the proposed school. In April the school opened at Bolling Field, Washington, D.C., and for the next two years carried out research and development on the problems of coastal air defense equipment, technique, and tactics. The Air Corps, however, did not establish an extensive formal coast defense training program for its tactical units and pilots. Only the 19th Bombardment Group at Rockwell Field, California, actively participated in a continuing program stressing instrument flying and overwater operations in 1932-33.[59]

In 1931, before the Bolling Field project had been authorized, the Office of the Chief of the Air Corps was already concerned over the question of how the Army air arm could best be used to carry out the coastal air defense mission. The air officers were dismayed by the absence of a definite War Department policy on the subject. Army Training Regulations 440-15, *Fundamental Principles for the Employment of the Air Service,* had not been updated since January 1926, and it gave no indica-

59

## FOULOIS AND THE U.S. ARMY AIR CORPS

Brig. Gen. Foulois, Ass't. Sec. of War for Air F. Trubee Davison, Maj. Gen. Fechet, and Brig. Gen. Pratt.

tion of how the Air Corps should be employed to stop an air attack on the United States.[60] General Fechet, before departing on terminal leave, convinced General MacArthur to sign a letter to the Director of the Bureau of the Budget stating that under the MacArthur-Pratt agreement the Army air arm had "the primary responsibility for all defensive air operations by the United States, except those required for furthering the operation of the high seas Fleet."[61] But aside from this recognition of Air Corps responsibility the General Staff did nothing to explain how it intended to use the air arm to fulfill its mission.

Foulois began carping at the General Staff for its lack of policy as soon as he took over as acting chief of the air arm. Responding to War Department notification that a Harbor Defense Board would soon be constituted to revise existing harbor defense projects, he pointed out in September that while the Air Corps had a portion of the Army's responsibility for coast defense, it had never been asked for its views. He opposed the practice of leaving the planning of defense operations to corps area commanders and requested that the Chief of the Air Corps be charged with preparing air defense plans. Foulois likewise asked that the Chief of Coast Artillery be permitted to carry out his own portion of coast defense planning. He and his Coast Artillery counterpart could then get together and coordinate their respective programs.[62]

The General Staff reply, coming two months later, showed that the War Department did not want the Air Corps to design its own program for air defense employment. The memo asserted firmly that the air arm's sole responsibility in coast defense was to support the mobile land army: "Neither the Chief of the Air Corps nor the Chief of Coast Artillery has any responsibility in planning for Coast Defense other than to collaborate when called upon with the proper planning agencies of the War Depart-

CONCEPTS, 1931-1933

ment in preparation of such a plan." It pointed out that "Corps Area Commanders in their capacity as Frontier Commanders" would prepare the necessary subordinate plans in cooperation with local Navy commanders. The General Staff memo did say, however, that the Harbor Defense Board would soon hold a meeting, and Foulois, as a member, could "present his recommendations with reference to the employment of aircraft in harbor defense."[63]

Apparently undismayed by this rebuff, Foulois kept up his struggle to force the War Department to develop a plan for aerial coast defense. He worked equally hard to assure an Air Corps voice in formulating that plan. In January 1932 he told the House Appropriations Committee that the War Department had no air policy, but he qualified this by saying he had been instructed to help develop one—perhaps referring to the latitude given him as a member of the Harbor Defense Board. Having spoken personally to MacArthur of the need for an air defense policy, Foulois probably felt reasonably certain the Chief of Staff favored the creation of one.[64]

In April 1932, Foulois won the Harbor Defense Board's endorsement of an Air Corps-sponsored statement of basic air defense principles. The paper affirmed that "Air Corps projects pertaining to the employment of Army aircraft in the defense of the coast will be based upon the assumption that no assistance can be expected from naval aviation." It then broke down the Air Corps' coast defense mission into three phases. During the first phase the air arm would operate reconnaissance and strike aircraft out to the limit of their combat radius to locate and attack the enemy invasion force. This air action was to be independent of local ground force control, with directions coming from Army General Headquarters. During the second phase of the engagement—when the enemy had come within range of shore guns—the Air Corps would spot for the coast artillery and make complementary attacks from the air. The air arm would continue to serve in this capacity until the invasion force had been driven off or the battle had reached its third phase. In this last canto the air arm would directly support the ground forces in their struggle to repel the invader from the beaches "in accordance with its use in general land operations."[65]

Foulois directed his subordinates in the OCAC to use the statement of principles in preparing a more comprehensive coastal air defense employment proposal. Three months later, the Chief of the Air Corps submitted his staff's labors to the Harbor Defense Board. Titled "Employment of the Army Air Forces in Defense of our Seacoast Frontiers," the proposal received the board's endorsement on July 7, 1932, and was sent on for General Staff approval.[66]

The proposal restated the three phases of combat air operations and provided for the division of United States coastal areas into six geographical zones. Each zone was to contain an air force composed of observation, pursuit, attack, and bombardment planes under a single zone air force commander. Each of these air forces would include a "Zone Air Patrol equipped with long-range aircraft located at suitable stations along the coast, and in such numbers that the sea approaches will be patrolled and observed seaward to the limit of their radius of action." Apart from the zone air patrol, the paper did not propose manning the various zone air forces permanently with tactical units. Concentration of available Air Corps units would depend in each case upon the particular threat and war plan involved. However, the proposal did call for establishing the six zones and preparing the necessary airfields and facilities within them so that all would be ready in time of emergency.[67]

The War Plans Division of the General Staff studied the July 7 proposal but refused to recommend its acceptance. Instead, over the next three months it developed an extremely vague alternate plan, which recommended that frontier defense sectors be formed, but with all forces located therein responsible to the sector ground commander. It said nothing about the use of the air arm in various phases of an attack on the United States. It did, however, call for the concentrated employment of all Air Corps tactical units—in the form of a General Headquarters Air Force (GHQ Air Force) under the direct control of the overall Army field commander—in one or more of the defense sectors on mobilization day, depending on the scope of the threat. In essence the War Plans Division proposal said nothing about how the Air Corps should actually be employed to carry out its air defense mission. When the Chief of the War Plans Division, Brig. Gen. Charles Kilbourne, circulated the proposal for the concurrence of the other General Staff divisions and the Air Corps, only the latter disapproved.[68]

The differences between the War Plans Division and the Air Corps on the coast defense issue heightened the tension between the General Staff and the air arm, and kindled a lasting ill will between Kilbourne and Foulois. While generally supporting the air arm and exhibiting more appreciation for the value of military aviation than most of his General Staff associates, Kilbourne deplored the absence of team spirit as well as the pushiness of airpower advocates. Foulois, by virtue of his position as the official spokesman for the airpower crowd, must have struck Kilbourne as one of the worst offenders. The Chief of the Air Corps, in turn, disliked General Staff resistance to what the members of the air arm believed were quite valid requests concerning policy and organization. Since the War Plans Division was largely responsible for such issues and Kilbourne was the division chief, Foulois probably perceived him as one of the prominent War Department hindrances to Air Corps development, which he was not. The numerous paper wars between the War Plans Division and the OCAC over issues of doctrine and employment no doubt sharpened the ill feelings between the two men.

Foulois critiqued the War Plans Division's alternate employment proposal on October 11 in a blunt ten-page memo to the Chief of the War Plans Division. The air chief, quite feisty when agitated, took Kilbourne to task for maintaining that the original Harbor Defense Board proposal had not sufficiently considered the possible presence of the Navy. Foulois averred that the War Department had previously advised his office that the Air Corps could not expect the Navy to assist in coastal air defense. Addressing the crux of the proposal circulated by Kilbourne, he found it too "ambiguous and indefinite" to provide a basis for air employment planning. He next attacked the War Plans Division chief for basing most of his proposal on the Joint Board agreement of 1926, which through its vague phrasing appeared to leave to the Navy responsibility for all offshore operations. He pointed out that the MacArthur-Pratt agreement had superseded the 1926 written agreement. The Chief of the Air Corps also highlighted a glaring inconsistency in Kilbourne's proposal. While calling for the ground commander's supervision of air units in each coastal defense sector, the War Plans Division paper noted that wartime air operations from these sectors would be under the control of GHQ Air Force, which was not subordinate to sector ground commanders.[69]

As part of his memo, Foulois redrafted the War Plans Division's proposal, reinserting virtually all the recommendations contained in the program submitted through the Harbor Defense Board, save one: The plan for six separate Air Force zones was dropped in favor of common Army defense sectors. But this revision made clear that "The Air Force in any emergency initially will operate under the direct control of GHQ" and that "the basic plan for the concentration and operation of the Air Force in coast defense will be provided by the War Department"—not by the local ground commanders.[70]

Foulois' redraft, like his July 7 offering, allowed for long-range air patrols in each coastal area. Kilbourne counterattacked on this issue almost immediately. He contended in an October 27 memo to the Chief of the Air Corps that this would entail a costly "chain defense" system. He quite correctly pointed out that it would be impossible to secure appropriations for the many aircraft and installations required in such a system. He also apprised Foulois that "no emergency requiring such an all around defense is visualized in war plans."[71] Foulois responded saying that centrally controlled long-range reconnaissance was vital to adequate air defense. He explained that such units operating under GHQ Air Force control would not constitute a linear defense system: "Due to the mobility of these units, with centralized control, they can be shifted to or concentrated in support of any threatened area at the proper time."[72]

After considerable give-and-take between the Office of the Chief of the Air Corps and the War Plans Division during November and early December and a personal talk between MacArthur and Foulois, the air chief eventually agreed to accept a second War Plans Division draft proposal, one which embodied some of the items in the Air Corps' July 7 plan. Foulois accepted the compromise because he must have realized that, by continuing to hold out for General Staff acceptance of the Air Corps' original proposal, he would only intensify the bitterness while producing few additional positive results. As it was, the air arm had at least gained some semblance of a coast defense employment strategy and had been able to influence its formation. Foulois was not completely pleased with the outcome, but under the circumstances he probably got all that was possible at the time.[73] Kilbourne also was willing to give on some issues, for he deemed it important to have a definite air defense policy. He understood that without one the Chief of the Air Corps would have nothing concrete on which to base his peacetime planning for procurement and distribution of units. Nor would the General Staff be able to adequately prepare war plans for the defense of the United States.[74]

MacArthur published the compromise employment doctrine on January 3, 1933, in a policy letter titled "Employment of Army Aviation in Coast Defense." While adopting the Air Corps' three phases of employment, the letter did not restrict control of the air arm during the first, or independent, phase to Army GHQ but authorized theater or frontier commanders to direct the air arm if circumstances warranted. MacArthur accepted the need for long-range reconnaissance "beyond the range of corps and army observation aviation." He said, "these aircraft are to be equipped with radio and that certain of them are to be equipped with navigation and plotting facilities and will be in constant communication with one or more shore stations." This pleased Foulois and the other Air Corps members. However, the policy letter made no mention of zone air forces and continuing zone air patrols. In line with the recent Army ground force reorganization creating the nucleus of four field armies in the continental United States each of the four army commanders was charged with the security of one of the nation's frontiers. The letter gave them the responsibility for planning the emergency use of all units—including air—that might be assigned to them under the particular war plan involved, but it reserved to the War Department formulation of plans involving the use of the conglomerate of Air Corps striking power, the GHQ Air Force. Possibly as a further sop to the air arm, the compromise air defense policy statement explained that cooperation with naval forces would be based on the 1926 Joint Board agreements "as modified by the Joint agreement between the Chief of Staff and the Chief

CONCEPTS, 1931-1933

of Naval Operations of 1931 making the Army solely responsible for coast defense including air operations in connection therewith."[75]

Members of the Air Corps could not have been much dissatisfied with the January 3 policy statement. It affirmed the air arm's right and responsibility to range far out to sea in search of the enemy fleet and approved air operations unrelated to ground troop activity when the enemy was not in contact with American ground forces. Further, it endorsed the need for long-range reconnaissance aircraft. It also afforded centralized planning for, and employment of, a consolidated Air Corps strike force and reaffirmed the Army air arm's claim to sole responsibility for aerial coast defense. Certainly the two War Department principals involved in formulating this program—Kilbourne and MacArthur— could not be considered foes of the Air Corps.

Even so, Foulois and his subordinates in the Office of the Chief of the Air Corps desired a more specific employment plan. They therefore drafted one and forwarded it for General Staff consideration on March 15, 1933. The plan listed what the Air Corps needed to execute its aerial coast defense mission and described how this force should be disposed. In many ways the plan restated the proposal of July 7, 1932. It designated six key coastal areas (New England, Chesapeake Bay, Florida, and the areas around Seattle, San Francisco, and San Diego) and called for permanently stationing one bombardment group and long-range coastal patrol units in each of them: "The disposition and operations of the Air Force and the disposition and movements of the ground forces will depend largely on the information furnished by these patrols." The plan called for a total of six air wings within the United States, consisting of three pursuit groups, six bombardment groups, three attack groups, three observation groups, and five coast defense patrol groups. Three additional composite wings were to be stationed overseas—one each in Panama, Hawaii, and the Philippines. In a May memo to the War Department, Foulois added Alaska to the list. One composite group and two long-range coast patrol units were to be assigned there.[76]

In the March plea to the General Staff, Foulois' staff accented the nation's need for a suitable air defense system:

The danger of concentrated air attacks upon nerve centers of communication, industry, and government, with the object of paralyzing the nation's power to resist and thus facilitating decisive action of ground forces, is a factor which makes it imperative that the nation's peacetime air strength be adequate to meet such an attack upon the outbreak of war.[77]

The Air Corps' proposal also stressed that no air defense system presently existed: "The coastal air defense of the United States has been relinquished by the Navy. Until it is physically undertaken by the War Department, there actually will be no coastal air defense in the United States."[78]

## FOULOIS AND THE U.S. ARMY AIR CORPS

The General Staff was unsympathetic to the OCAC plan. The War Department realistically assessed it as far too costly to implement and deemed it unrealistic in view of the dearth of air striking power possessed by America's potential enemies. Sustained carrier-borne strategic air power did not exist, and effective long-range air attacks on the United States from overseas land bases were technologically impossible in 1933. Moreover, the General Staff considered the Air Corps plan an unwarranted departure from MacArthur's January 3 letter. The War Department was even more disturbed when Foulois, contrary to regulations, sent a copy of the plan to Assistant Secretary of War Harry H. Woodring. Army officials feared this might be a prelude to a wider distribution of the unsanctioned proposal. According to the General Staff, here was real evidence of a lack of team spirit. General MacArthur directed his War Plans Division chief, Kilbourne, to try to iron out the differences on the employment issues existing between the OCAC and the War Department, but this proved to be an impossible task.[79]

Many officers of the Air Corps believed in the vital importance of their aerial coast defense mission, and had come to consider the Army air arm the nation's first line of defense. The aviators thought the Air Corps, without the aid of land and sea forces, could, if properly organized and equipped, repel an invasion force before it could land on American beaches. Bombers would smash the enemy's air might by sinking his carriers and then would destroy his transports. Should the enemy gain positions ashore in countries bordering the United States before the onset of hostilties, the Army air arm would destroy his airfields and lines of communications. This would make the forward advance of the enemy land army impossible. Foulois and his Army aviators believed the Air Corps must be both strong and properly disposed in peacetime to carry out this vital mission during a national emergency. In April 1933, the air chief and one of his key officers, Lt. Col. James E. Chaney, were given a chance to appear before the House Military Affairs Committee. They testified that air attacks on the United States were now possible, and asked for congressional support for the Army air arm's March 15 aerial coast defense program.[80]

In June, while Kilbourne was still working to settle differences with the OCAC, General MacArthur decided to allow the Air Corps to try its hand at writing specific air defense plans based upon the War Department's "color" war plans. The 1932 Four Army Plan reorganization of the ground forces caused reconsideration of the various plans for the defense of the United States. Besides, word had been circulated to Congress and the press—probably with the help of the Air Corps—that the Army had no plans for the air defense of the United States. On June 3 at the Chief of Staff's behest, the General Staff requested Foulois' recommenda-

CONCEPTS, 1931-1933

tions for employment of the GHQ Air Force if war plans RED (Britain), RED-ORANGE (Britain-Japan), or GREEN (Mexico) were activated. The memo from The Adjutant General directed the Chief of the Air Corps to use eighteen hundred serviceable aircraft (the number called for in the five-year expansion program) as a basis for planning. However, the Air Corps was authorized to suggest a larger force if the OCAC planners found eighteen hundred planes unequal to the task. The Air Corps proposal was to include the geographic disposition and plan for concentration and use of the air arm under each of the color plans. General Kilbourne counseled the air planners at the outset not to place in their proposal a bold demand for large numbers of aircraft that the War Department could not support in appropriations hearings.[81]

After some delay, the OCAC submitted its plan on July 13, 1933. Much to the annoyance of the General Staff, it did not provide what had been asked for. The "Air Plan for the Defense of the United States" began by denying the relevance of current Army defense plans to initial air defense activities:

> There is a phase in the defense of the United States in which air power plays a distinct part operating either alone or in conjunction with the Navy. And in either case the plan for the use of air power initially will bear little relation to the details of any of the existing colored war plans.[82]

It also asserted there was no need to tie the initial offshore operations to plans for ground force deployment. Foulois must have believed that persistence would eventually wear down General Staff resistance, for the plan enumerated seven critical areas needing air protection (adding the Great Lakes region to the six areas listed in the 1932 Harbor Defense Board proposal) and called for continuous air reconnaissance outward from these areas to a distance of 250 to 300 miles. It likewise required the deployment of portions of the GHQ Air Force to the most critical of these regions, just prior to the onset of hostilities. Once the main enemy threat had been determined, all available air power would be shifted to the affected region.

The plan touched on deployment under the three color plans, but complained that the Air Corps would be hopelessly outclassed if the United States were attacked at the same time on both its coasts by a British-Japanese coalition. In fact, claimed the OCAC, the Army air arm lacked adequate numbers of planes to deal with the RED threat alone, for Britain could mass superior air strength in Canada before beginning hostilities. All this was done to prove that the Air Corps needed more aircraft. The paper then arrived at the ideal number of planes needed to defend the seven critical areas in the continental United States as well as America's overseas possessions—4,459.[83] Foulois, who was absent from Washington on the day the plan reached the General Staff, was shocked by the furor it caused. He lamely explained to War Department superiors: "This is a tentative plan only and was prepared hastily because of the short time limit imposed by the original instructions."[84]

The plan had spawned an immediate and entirely negative General Staff reaction. Kilbourne wrote MacArthur on July 25 that "the report submitted is of no value either for war planning or for a logical determination of the strength at which the Air Corps should be maintained." He complained the plan just repeated earlier proposals submitted by the Chief of the Air Corps to justify requests for more aircraft at a time when the existing threat was quite low. Kilbourne was incensed over the air arm's claim to separate war planning privileges and was fearful that air officers were being "falsely indoctrinated" as to the abilities of the Air Corps to carry out the coast defense mission alone. He complained that this and other papers submitted by the Office of the Chief of the Air Corps had departed from War Department principles "to a degree which indicates a complete lack of desire to conform to instructions issued by proper authority."[85] General MacArthur disapproved the Air Corps plan. On August 11 he directed the formation of a special committee of the General Council, chaired by Deputy Chief of Staff Maj. Gen. Hugh A. Drum, to review and revise the OCAC proposal.[86]

From the General Staff's point of view there was obviously a great deal wrong with the July 13 Air Corps proposal. It bore no relation to any probable air threat to the United States, and the cost of the program was prohibitive. Most important, the plan represented a deep divergence of views between the War Department and its air arm:

> The General Staff held that strategic and tactical operations in pursuance of the Army plan as a whole, both in land campaign and coast defense, was the primary mission of the Air Force, while the Office of the Chief of the Air Corps held the opinion that there should be a special plan for the Air Corps defense of the United States and that organization and training for this purpose should take priority over all other considerations.[87]

The Drum Board soon set to work studying the question of Air Corps employment in coast defense. Besides Drum, its membership included Kilbourne, Foulois, Maj. Gen. John W. Gulick, Chief of Coast Artillery, and Maj. Gen. George S. Simonds, Commandant of the Army War College. The board first met as a group on September 15 and almost at once concluded that the General Staff memo directing the preparation of the July 13 Air Corps plan was somewhat vague and might have misled the Air Corps chief and his subordinates as to the study's purposes. The board decided to disregard the July 13 plan, and to develop its own program for the use of the air arm in coast defense.[88]

During the ensuing weeks of discussion, the other board members gave the Chief of the Air Corps ample opportunity to voice the air arm's

CONCEPTS, 1931-1933

views. Being outnumbered four to one by nonflying officers, perhaps Foulois was cowed. Maybe he believed that the conclusions reached by the board were the best possible under the circumstances. Regardless, he did not strike a controversial pose, but instead worked harmoniously with the other members. He gave the impression that Air Corps difficulties were due to a dearth of appropriations rather than to General Staff-Air Corps differences. General Simonds reported later: "In these conversations he appeared willing and anxious to cooperate with the General Staff in the formulation of policies and in carrying them out. He appeared to be in the belief that we were all working to a common end."[89] The ground generals, also apparently given to compromise, allowed the air chief to prepare a list of general principles upon which the board based its conclusions on Air Corps coast defense employment.[90]

Released in October, the Drum Board report made clear that the air arm was an integral part of the Army:

> The terminology, "air defense of the United States," frequently employed in writings, gives an erroneous and false view of the employment of air forces. Whether operating in close conjunction with the Army or the Navy, or at some distance therefrom, all of these agencies must operate in accordance with one general plan of national defense.[91]

Acknowledging that aviation had greatly increased the difficulties of overseas invasion, the report underscored the importance of long-range reconnaissance and air attack on enemy expeditions "by a properly constituted GHQ Air Force" before they reached the American shoreline. Nevertheless, it declared that the present state of aviation technology made a serious air attack on the vital areas of the United States impossible. The report adopted the seven vital coast defense areas as designated in the July 13 Air Corps plan, but it maintained that the air arm alone could not prevent the invasion of these areas, and that it would be unwise permanently to station air defense units in each of them.[92]

Concerning air employment under the color plans, the Drum Board examined only RED-ORANGE. The report explained this plan represented the worst circumstances the United States could expect to meet. Faced with war against a Japanese-British coalition, the RED-ORANGE plan called for defensive action against Japan while exerting full military pressure against Great Britain in the northwest Atlantic and Canada. The Drum Board determined it would be the GHQ Air Force's tasks to secure air superiority in the major theater of operations, support the advance of the ground forces into southeastern Canada, conduct any necessary joint actions with the fleet, and assist the ground forces in coast defense should the fleet be absent or unable to maintain control of the sea. To carry out these operations, the board judged that the Air Corps required 2,320 aircraft, 980 to be assigned to the consolidated striking force, the GHQ Air Force.[93]

## FOULOIS AND THE U.S. ARMY AIR CORPS

The board's report did not tamper with the three phases of coast defense approved in the Chief of Staff's January 3 letter, but it did provide a breakdown of how the air striking force would be used in land operations:

> Strategically, this will be used for long range reconnaissance, for interdicting enemy reconnaissance, for demolition of important installations, and for interdiction of enemy movement. Tactically, the GHQ Air Force will be used in support of the ground forces in preparation for battle by combat against enemy air forces engaged in missions of reconnaissance, demolition, and interdiction, during battle by actual participation, and after battle by exploitation of victory or minimizing enemy exploitation in event of defeat.[94]

Though still tying the air arm to tactical ground operations, the report acknowledged the importance of independent strategic air missions. In effect, its statement on employment in land operations struck a balance between what the airpower advocates and the ground commanders each prized most in military aviation. While the report did not endorse strategic bombardment per se, its statement on strategic employment was so broad it could not have displeased the air advocates. General MacArthur approved the Drum Board report on October 12, making it an official War Department policy statement.[95]

While the Air Corps and the War Department were forging an employment doctrine for the Army air arm in its coast defense mission, the Navy refused to fully acknowledge that the MacArthur-Pratt agreement had stripped it of all responsibility for coast defense. In fact, there were signs that the sea service had every intention of replacing the Air Corps as the primary vehicle for the air defense portion of that mission. In spite of Pratt's new naval air policy and his informal agreement with the Army Chief of Staff, the Navy Department continued to develop land-based aircraft, expand naval air stations, and deploy bombers ashore (calling them patrol aircraft). Purportedly these resources were for fleet support, but even the Navy's General Board argued within the sea service that the Navy should also have coastal air defense responsibility.[96]

The Air Corps was quite concerned over these developments. As it became clear in the fall of 1933 that Congress would soon authorize a new naval air expansion program, the Chief of the Air Corps as well as the Chief of the War Plans Division, became extremely worried. Until then, the Navy had only been authorized 1,000 serviceable aircraft while the Air Corps was allowed 1,800. Now it seemed the Navy would build up to 2,492. Both Foulois and Kilbourne reasoned that naval numerical superiority might reduce Army air arm appropriations and cause loss of a portion or all of the aerial coast defense mission to the sea service.[97]

These were not the only indications of Navy dissatisfaction with the

# CONCEPTS, 1931-1933

MacArthur-Pratt agreement. On February 21, 1933, MacArthur sent the Joint Board a draft of changes to the 1926 Joint Board agreement, designed to bring the instructions in the pamphlet, "Joint Action of the Army and the Navy," into accord with the 1931 agreement on aerial coast defense. The Navy members of the Joint Board informally disagreed with the draft but refused to request a conference to resolve the matter. This spurred the Chief of Staff to write Admiral Pratt on June 23. MacArthur stressed the importance of resolving the contradictions between the obsolete pamphlet on joint action and the instructions in his January 3 letter on the employment of the air arm in coast defense. He said the Army wanted to issue new regulations based on the 1931 agreement but they would contradict the pamphlet. Admiral Pratt replied the same day saying he was retiring at the end of June and the matter would have to be taken up with his successor.[98] This boded ill for the War Department's efforts to gain formal Navy acceptance of the MacArthur-Pratt Agreement.

Rear Adm. Ernest J. King arrives aboard USS *Lexington*, June 1936.

Moffett, his successor, Rear Adm. Ernest J. King, and their fellow flyers had continued to affirm within the Navy family that coast defense was a proper naval aviation mission. By 1933 they were winning a wider following. No one, save the departing Chief of Naval Operations, wished to further compromise the Navy's claim to this significant mission. Yet most senior naval officers were more concerned with two other aviation issues: (1) the need to continue building up the fleet's air resources; and (2) the persistent Air Corps assertions that MacArthur's January policy letter had given Army aviation responsibility for distant overwater aerial patrolling, a direct infringement on an established Navy mission.[99]

After Pratt's retirement, Ernest King, now Chief of the Bureau of Aeronautics, announced that neither the Secretary of the Navy nor the new Chief of Naval Operations, Vice Adm. William H. Standley, recognized the MacArthur-Pratt Agreement.[100] The Navy Department reopened Joint Board discussions on the issue of responsibility for aerial coast defense operations, but the Navy spokesman denied that this was solely an Air Corps mission. He insisted that the Navy had responsibility for "air operations in support of local naval defense forces operating for the protection of lines of sea communications and coastal zones against attacks by hostile submarines and surface raiders."[101] If this were true, the Navy would control antisubmarine and antiraider air activities along the U.S. coasts. The crux of the dispute was actually much simpler: the Navy wanted to control all overwater air operations, while the Air Corps claimed responsibility for coastal air defense operations out to three hundred miles off the coast.[102] The debate on coastal air defense, reopened in 1933, continued unabated for the next sixteen months.

Part of the debate in late 1933 focused on the types of aircraft the Navy and Air Corps would develop. The Army flyers opposed the sea service's increased purchase of shore-based amphibian patrol aircraft, while the Navy denied the Air Corps' right to buy amphibian planes of its own. Foulois had been considering using amphibians for long-range reconnaissance in connection with the air arm's coast defense mission ever since the spring of 1932. He and his staff desired a large aircraft with a 1,000-mile range, capable of landing and taking off from the ocean, and able to carry a 2,200-pound bombload so that it could also perform as a bomber.[103]

General Kilbourne and the War Plans Division initially supported the air arm's outlook on amphibian reconnaissance planes, considering them an essential element in the Air Corps' coast defense program. However, when General Foulois exerted heavy pressure to buy such airplanes in the last six months of 1933 with funds made available as part of the National Industry Recovery Act, Kilbourne turned cold to the idea. His opposition appears to have been based on both a desire to limit the range of Air

## CONCEPTS, 1931-1933

Corps overwater operations in order to reduce friction with the Navy and on technical considerations associated with the Air Corps' proposed method of employing the amphibians. Foulois had contended that these aircraft could best be used by deploying them approximately three hundred miles out to sea. The planes would land on the water and from time to time take off and fly laterally to patrol an assigned sector of the sea. With several of these aircraft watching adjacent sectors, the United States would have a complete air reconnaissance cordon far from its shore. Kilbourne objected, claiming amphibians capable of landing and taking off from the open sea as well as land would be far too costly to construct and to maintain for the benefit they would provide. He considered a reconnaissance cordon financially prohibitive. While endorsing smaller, lighter weight, long-range amphibians, since they would not normally land at sea and thus intrude on the Navy's preserve, neither he nor other members of the General Staff favored spending the limited National Industrial Recovery Act funds for a large amphibian.[104]

The War Department informed Foulois in November that amphibians would not be purchased at present, but that the idea of using bomb-carrying amphibian aircraft for long-range reconnaissance still had General Staff support. Brig. Gen. Robert E. Callan, Assistant Chief of Staff, G-4, while agreeing that the Air Corps needed such aircraft, voiced the opinion to MacArthur in January 1934 that the development of land-based, long-range bombers should be afforded priority.[105] The OCAC was soon to reach the same conclusion.

Kilbourne believed the Air Corps' coast defense mission demanded that the air arm be able to fly reconnaissance far from the shore. However, he did not agree that its mission justified the Air Corps' assertion that it had the responsibility for air operations up to three hundred miles from the coast. Deducing correctly that this claim had been a leading cause of the renewed Army-Navy controversy over coast defense responsibilities, the War Plans Division chief worked in the fall and winter, 1933-34, to bring about a restatement of the scope of the air arm's responsibility. Kilbourne presumed that patrolling the coastal shipping lanes was the Navy's job, and Air Corps combat operations should normally be confined to close-in waters "where the maximum damage to the enemy may be inflicted with the least damage to our own forces." In November he sent Deputy Chief of Staff Drum a series of suggestions on aerial coast defense policy, and proposed that the War Department use them in discussions with the Navy. The War Plans Division chief believed the suggestions would allay the Navy's fears of Air Corps encroachment, and thus lead to a new agreement on the division of responsibility for anti-invasion operations.[106]

Kilbourne's recommendations affirmed that the Army was responsible for coast defense and the Navy for control of the seas. If sufficient naval force was available to engage an enemy approaching the American coast, the Navy would have paramount interest, and the Army would assist as requested. In the absence of adequate naval force, paramount interest would rest with the Army, and the Navy would assist on request. Kilbourne's proposals also maintained that "the Army may omit seaward reconnaissance and depend entirely upon the naval forces for information" if elements of the fleet were present or the naval district commandant had the means to ensure the detection of enemy forces. Kilbourne explained: "The normal mission of the Army Air Corps is to conduct air operations in support of the ground forces in land campaigns including coast defense." However, "the use of Army aircraft acting under Army command, in the attack of enemy naval forces, is contemplated only in a threat to the coast and in the absence of sufficient naval forces to meet and defeat such threat."[107] Some, but not all, of these recommendations found their way into the coast defense agreement reached between the Army and the Navy a year later.

Kilbourne judged the Air Corps the chief culprit in stirring up the renewed Army-Navy dispute, but the Air Corps took a different view. Foulois and his subordinates believed the 1931 MacArthur-Pratt Agreement had established that the fleet could not be depended upon for assistance in coast defense. Hence, they simply disregarded the Navy in their defense planning. Further, they thought MacArthur's January 3, 1933, policy letter gave the air arm the authority to operate against the enemy fleet up to three hundred miles off the coast. It said that during the first phase of aerial coast defense operations Army aircraft would undertake "reconnaissance and offensive operations between the limit of range of the Air Force and the line of contact with ground forces." [108] While Kilbourne might have been correct when he alleged that the Chief of Staff had never accepted the Air Corps' idea of attempting to control sea lanes three hundred miles off the coast, MacArthur's January 3 letter certainly implied a degree of approval. The OCAC viewed actions by General Staff officers to restrict the air arm's range in coast defense operations as a clear demonstration of lack of support. By late fall 1933, Foulois and many other air officers believed the War Department was selling out the air arm's principal mission for the sake of Army-Navy harmony.[109]

A poem in the *Washington Sunday Star* reflected the growing conflict between the Air Corps and the War Department at the close of 1933 over how far from the coast the air arm should range in quest of enemy forces:

>Mother, may I fly out to sea?
>  Yes my darling daughter,
>But keep your eye on the land and me,
>  And hurry away from the water. [110]

## CONCEPTS, 1931-1933

Under Foulois' leadership, the Air Corps had made some significant gains between 1931 and 1933. Besides further clarifying its strategic bombardment doctrine, it had acquired a key defense mission as well as a body of general employment concepts for that mission. The War Department had admitted the military importance of the air arm in coast defense, and given a general endorsement to strategic air operations in support of land campaigns. Even so, at the end of 1933, many issues involving air doctrine, mission, and employment concepts remained unresolved.

# CHAPTER III

# ORGANIZATION: TOWARD A GHQ AIR FORCE, 1932-1933

During the 1920s Army flyers had been displeased with their place in the War Department organization, and this dissatisfaction continued unabated into the early 1930s. Air Corps leaders no longer carried on a public campaign like that of the Mitchell era, but they still sought an autonomous arrangement under the Secretary of War or independence within a Department of National Defense. When given the opportunity to do so in 1932 and 1933, Foulois and his OCAC subordinates expressed this position to congressional committees, but they rarely assumed an uncompromising stand favoring immediate defense reorganization. In the winter of 1933-34, however, the air chief and his staff secretly drafted a bill that would have given the air arm autonomy.[1]

In early 1932, Foulois received his first opportunity as Chief of the Air Corps to make his views known to the lawmakers. In December 1931, Representative William Williamson of South Dakota introduced a bill calling for the consolidation of the War and Navy Departments into a single department containing three subdivisions headed by assistant secretaries. In January, Representative Joseph W. Byrns of Tennessee sponsored similar legislation. Both proposals were presented as economy measures to reduce defense expenditures at a time of severe economic depression. The Hoover administration opposed the bills but met stiff resistance from House Democrats who were seeking partisan issues for the 1932 elections. The Democrat-controlled House assigned the measures to the Committee on Expenditures in the Executive Departments, where the bills might receive more sympathetic treatment. In subsequent hearings, the committee did not invite MacArthur or other General Staff officers to testify, thus making the Chief of the Air Corps the principal Army witness.[2]

## ORGANIZATION: 1932-1933

Foulois appeared on February 4 to discuss military aviation and the form reorganization should take. He had originally intended only to answer questions put to him by the congressmen, but disparaging remarks about the Air Corps made before the committee by Representative Charles H. Martin of Oregon—a retired Army general—prompted him to change his mind. Martin had strongly opposed air arm independence, warning that Army flyers were extravagant, undisciplined, unruly, and would cost the taxpayers a fortune if given their own organization. Aroused by these remarks, the air chief denounced them as untrue.[3]

Foulois did not support the bills under discussion. He explained that the proposed legislation was overly general and requested Congress to undertake an "exhaustive study" to "definitely fix the relative roles of the land, the air, and the sea forces." He wanted the national defense structure reorganized to afford the air arm equality with the Army and Navy, but only after Congress had given the matter sufficient study: "I believe in a year or two more, military aviation will have reached the stage in its development, that it will then be time to take the Air Forces and put them in their proper place in the scheme of our national defense." [4]

Foulois went on to propose his own reorganization. Rather than forming a Department of National Defense with one secretary and a single "super staff," he favored building on current arrangements. With creation of an independent air force, by combining the Army and Navy air arms, the military services could coordinate planning and resolve differences through a Defense Commission composed of the three service secretaries. Supplementing this would be a War Council consisting of the military commanders of the three services. He pointed out that this system would produce clearer decisions, since voting on issues could no longer end in a tie. The Air Corps Chief believed the existing Joint Board, expanded to give the Air Force equal representation, could carry on the functions of a Joint Staff. Foulois stressed throughout his testimony that a careful study by Congress should precede service reorganization. He wanted independence for the military air arm but not until the recommended investigation had been completed.[5]

It is questionable if Foulois' proposed defense structure would have furnished the air arm the freedom to conduct an independent strategic bombing campaign in wartime. In his "majority rules" decision-making structure, no doubt the Army and Navy representatives would have voted the Air Force down had they felt a need for tactical air support. Foulois himself had told the committee that the land forces were the most important element in warfare and should head a unified command arrangement for combat operations. To dramatize this point the Chief of the Air Corps said:

> I would not hesitate a minute if I was in charge of the air forces for instance,

in an invasion of the eastern coast of the United States, if the President places one of the Army nurses in charge of those land operations, I would assume it was my job to get under her command and do as she told me under the principles of "Unity of Command."[6]

The leaders of the War and Navy Departments were completely opposed to service unification and any other change that would remove aviation from their control. MacArthur, while not called as a witness, presented his views on the pending bills in a letter that Representative Charles H. Martin read to the committee:

> No other measure proposed in recent years seems to me to be fraught with such potential possibilities of disaster for the United States as is this one. The proven agencies which have successfully conducted this country through six wars in a period of 125 years are now under the apparent dictation of a measure of economy to be launched on an adventure, which, under certain conditions might involve the very life of the nation.[7]

MacArthur and the General Staff were quite concerned. The Chief of Staff allowed Foulois to speak freely before the committee, but directed the War Plans Division to prepare a paper showing that the pending bills would promote neither greater economy nor combat efficiency. A solid front of adamant opposition formed against the proposed legislation, consisting of the General Staff, the two service secretaries, and Navy leaders including Admiral Moffett, Chief of the Bureau of Aeronautics.[8]

Opposed by the Hoover administration and the armed services and having but moderate congressional support, neither of the pro-Air Corps bills was reported out of committee. However, advocates of service unification attached similar provisions to an economy bill which reached the floor of the House in April 1932. There the measure was defeated by a vote of 153 to 135. Proponents of air arm independence and/or military unification did not give up, but at no time during the next four years were they again able to get such a measure before the whole House.[9]

Congress was not generally sympathetic toward air independence during Foulois' years as Chief of the Air Corps. However, one influential figure on Capitol Hill, Representative John J. McSwain, consistently championed the Air Corps' cause throughout the first half of the 1930s. McSwain, a Democrat from South Carolina, took over the chairmanship of the House Military Affairs Committee in February 1932, and immediately announced his position on the relative importance of the Army air arm:

> I would place the highest emphasis upon the power of aviation, whether in the Regular Army or in the Reserves or National Guard. This powerful modern instrumentality for both transportation and combat must receive the greatest possible aid, consistent with reasonable economy, in our scheme of preparedness. On the contrary, I recognize that the cavalry is almost obsolete. . . . It is amusing to me that money is spent teaching young men to ride.[10]

McSwain was one of the ardent backers of the 1932 legislative proposals

ORGANIZATION: 1932-1933

Congressman
John J. McSwain.

for service unification and air arm equality. After Foulois had appeared before the Committee on Expenditures on February 4, McSwain wrote him a personal letter praising both the Chief of the Air Corps and his testimony:

> It is very gratifying to my feelings that an enlisted man has risen by force of merit to the rank of Major General and the headship of the most technical and I believe important branch of our national defense organization. The contrast between the dignity and force of your statement and the confusion and lack of dignity of the statement of a certain blue blood of the Army [MacArthur] is very striking.[11]

While McSwain's feelings for Foulois cooled considerably in succeeding years, his support for air power grew. Annually between 1933 and 1936, he sponsored legislation to give the Air Corps either complete independence or a greater measure of autonomy within the War Department.

In his 1932 annual report, General MacArthur set forth many of the General Staff's reasons for resisting Air Corps independence. The Chief of Staff explained that strong air units were essential to Army and Navy combat operations. Even if the air force were separate from the Army and Navy, the land and sea services would still need large contingents assigned to them, thus necessitating an immediate redivision. Further, an independent air arm would be costly, for it would have to create its own overhead agencies to replace the support presently supplied by the Army and Navy. As is evident in MacArthur's report, traditional military conservatism affected the General Staff's attitude toward change:

> Governmentally we have today, from the standpoint of national strategy and policy, the strongest possible organization for war. It seems almost incomprehensible that this organization which incidentally has been the envy of soldiers, sailors, and statesmen abroad, should be tampered with in its military elements in favor of a highly speculative experiment.[12]

MacArthur did not develop the point in 1932, but another vital element in the General Staff's rationale was its disbelief in the ability of aviation to independently influence the outcome of war.[13]

In December, Foulois requested that the War Department delegate to the Chief of the Air Corps and the Assistant Secretary of War for Air all procurement and budget functions pertaining to the Air Corps. This, in effect, would have given the Army air arm a measure of autonomy. Foulois asserted it would be just as economical and far more efficient for the Air Corps to administer all Army funds connected with aviation under a single appropriation. He considered this far better than continuing the present system where the Chief of Ordnance, Chief Signal Officer, and others requested and controlled the funds for aircraft weapons, radios, and other auxiliary equipment. The General Staff, however, turned a deaf ear to this request. It refused to relinquish any of its control over military aviation.[14]

Army Chief of Staff Gen. Douglas MacArthur.

ORGANIZATION: 1932-1933

When President Franklin D. Roosevelt took office in 1933, some people, Billy Mitchell among them, hoped the new Commander in Chief would quickly sponsor legislation providing the Air Corps greater independence. Mitchell campaigned heavily in Roosevelt's behalf, and a few individuals believed the ex-general would be rewarded with the post of Assistant Secretary for Air. After the election, Mitchell and Roosevelt met and discussed military aviation, but once in office, Roosevelt failed to appoint Mitchell to public office and disregarded the ex-Army flyer's advice on air independence. The new President's attitude toward military reorganization paralleled Hoover's. Both men refused to sanction any change which might increase defense costs.[15]

Roosevelt probably never really entertained any serious thoughts about creating a separate air force. In 1919, while serving as Assistant Secretary of the Navy, he had opposed "the creation of another and separate branch of national defense,"[16] and nothing occurred in the intervening years to change his mind. In 1933, the nation's tremendous economic problems and not military reorganization, were foremost on his mind.[17] When Roosevelt did concern himself with defense issues, his interest focused on his old love—the Navy. As Billy Mitchell said in 1935 after seeing the President's desk covered with naval mementos: "I wish I could have seen one airplane in that collection."[18] Those who believed FDR would intervene in the Army air arm's behalf were victims of their own wishful thinking.

The new President's first action respecting military aviation was one of omission rather than commission. He refused to fill the post of Assistant Secretary of War for Air. This move pleased the General Staff and the Army's other arms and branches, for they had never really approved of allowing the Air Corps a special representative to the Secretary of War. When F. Trubee Davison resigned in the fall of 1932 to run for Lieutenant Governor of New York, MacArthur advocated leaving the post vacant, using the twin excuses of economy and War Department consolidation. Hoover did not name a replacement during the remainder of his term, and Roosevelt failed to fill the position during his first months in office. In June 1933 the administration announced the permanent abandonment of the post.[19]

Over a year later, Secretary of War George H. Dern, a man who had rapidly become a staunch supporter of almost all General Staff views, spelled out the Roosevelt administration's position. Dern wrote in his annual report for fiscal year 1934 that the vacancy was not filled "because the Air Corps, like the other branches of the Army, now functions directly under the Chief of Staff, to the mutual benefit of the Air Corps and the Army as a whole."[20] The Secretary's confusing comment mixed up cause and effect. Nevertheless, it indicated acceptance by the administration of

## FOULOIS AND THE U.S. ARMY AIR CORPS

At his desk covered with naval mementos, President Roosevelt presents the Cheney Award for 1933 to (l. to r.) 2d Lt. William L. Bogen, SSgt. Roy D. Dodd, and Sgt. Thomas J. Rogers. Gen. Foulois looks on.

the War Department view. The Air Corps no longer had its special advocate.

MacArthur and his General Staff subordinates were well pleased with the turn of events. They saw the Office of the Assistant Secretary of War for Air as an instrument of division. MacArthur voiced this view to the Senate Committee on Appropriations in 1934:

> To all intents and purposes within the Army there was an independent fighting branch, the Air Corps, which had its own Assistant Secretary for Aviation, who had delegated to him, by the Secretary of War, the complete authority which, where the rest of the army at large [is concerned], is exercised by the General Staff.[21]

This was a grave distortion of truth, but it accurately reflected the General Staff's consternation over an avenue outside the chain of command, used for Air Corps procurement decision making and special pleading to the Secretary of War. On July 1, 1933, Air Corps procurement reverted to control of the remaining Assistant Secretary of War, Harry H. Woodring, and the General Staff assumed the other supervisory functions previously

## ORGANIZATION: 1932-1933

delegated to the Assistant Secretary for Air. The air arm was now in step organizationally with the other branches of the Army.[22]

Foulois and his fellow aviators were bitter over the decision to abolish the post of Assistant Secretary for Air. The administration's apparent acceptance of the General Staff position on the issue in the spring of 1933 might have deepened the resolve of Air Corps officers to work for freedom from War Department control. Believing this might be the case, Army officials tried to curb OCAC support for reorganization in the March-April 1933 congressional hearings on a new Department of National Defense bill. They acted too late.

Chairman McSwain of the House Military Affairs Committee introduced the new measure (House Bill 4318) on March 29. The bill provided for three military services within one executive department. Each service would be supervised by an assistant secretary, who, in turn, would report to a single Secretary of National Defense. Although the bill was assigned to the Committee on Expenditures in the Executive Departments, McSwain immediately opened hearings on the measure in his own committee and called General Foulois to testify on March 31.[23] The Chief of the Air Corps told the committee he favored combining Army and Navy tactical air units into a single service, but acknowledged that the sea and land forces would need their own observation and support aviation. He claimed the air arm had now replaced the Navy as the nation's first line of defense and thus deserved priority in defense spending. He again petitioned Congress to thoroughly review American defense policy. In Foulois' opinion, such a study would show the importance of military aviation, substantiate the Air Corps' right to independence, and justify greater air defense expenditures.[24]

The General Staff must have had a representative present at the hearings, for it was immediately aware of Foulois' comments. The War Department expressed its displeasure over having no advance warning of the air chief's appearance. Westover replied, explaining Foulois had only received the committee's call on the evening of March 30 and had telephoned MacArthur regarding the summons to appear. While keeping a careful eye on the hearings, the General Staff took action seemingly designed to avoid a repetition of the Air Corps Chief's open advocacy of independence. On April 10, General Drum, the Deputy Chief of Staff, instructed Kilbourne that any further evidence to be presented at the hearings by War Department personnel would be coordinated by the War Plans Division and that no presentation would be made without the Chief of Staff's approval.[25]

Kilbourne immediately requested copies of the testimony already given by Air Corps officers as well as copies of papers prepared for future use before the Military Affairs Committee. Foulois was gone from Wash-

83

ington at the time, so Westover spoke for the Air Corps in a meeting with Drum on April 13. Apparently Westover advised the Deputy Chief of Staff that the new restrictions on testimony were coercive and departed from the established policy of allowing Air Corps officers to express their professional views before Congress. Later in the day, Drum sent Westover a note saying his April 10 memo had been misunderstood. He had not intended to restrict what officers said before congressional committees. The prior approval of the Chief of Staff just concerned material being gathered by the War Plans Division to explain the War Department's official position on the bill. Whether this was true or not, the General Staff took no further action in 1933 to prevent Air Corps officers from voicing their own opinions. However, restrictions were unnecessary. The Military Affairs Committee called no additional Air Corps officers, and the McSwain bill, lacking any real congressional support, never reached the House floor.[26]

Save for sending thirty copies of the translation of Giulio Douhet's article on air power to McSwain in May, Foulois took no further direct action during the remainder of the year to advance Air Corps independence. There is evidence, however, that he did use his new friendship with Representative Ross A. Collins of Mississippi (another of the limited number of air arm independence advocates in Congress) to influence members of the legislative branch. Unknown to the War Department, Foulois had been feeding Collins information on the needs and the importance of the Army air arm. On April 15, 1933, Collins testified before McSwain's committee that the War Department had no air policy and that he favored consolidating Army and Navy aviation into a separate service. Whether the Congressman's views were due to Foulois' influence or to Collins' enduring disdain for the Army General Staff is impossible to determine. Perhaps the Chief of the Air Corps simply reenforced the Mississippian's own attitudes.[27]

The War Department continued to oppose increased autonomy or independence but in the early 1930s it grew receptive to the idea of organizing a consolidated air strike force. The Army had used this structure in World War I, operating its offensive aircraft under a single Air Service officer who was responsible only to the commander of the Army field forces.[28] In 1923, based on the recommendations of the Chief of the Air Service, Maj. Gen. Mason M. Patrick, the Lassiter Board called for the creation of an air force of bombardment and pursuit aircraft "directly under General Headquarters for assignment to special and strategical missions, the accomplishment of which may be either in connection with the operation of ground troops or entirely independent of them."[29] The Secretary of War approved the board's recommendations,[30] but the War Department failed to implement them. During the next five years the Army

## ORGANIZATION: 1932-1933

paid mild lip service to the concept of consolidated wartime employment of its air arm. The General Staff's commitment became firm in March 1928, with the publication of the new Army Regulations (AR) 95-10. That document, covering the combat organization and mission of the Air Corps, provided for the air arm to be divided into two segments, that attached to subordinate ground units, and "GHQ aviation." The first of these was to consist of observation units belonging to divisions, corps, and armies; the second would comprise all other combat aviation forces. The regulation explained that "GHQ aviation" would consist of the "air force" and the "air reserve," both commanded by a single air officer responsible solely to the "commander-in-chief" of the Army field forces. The "air force" would conduct a variety of missions, some unrelated to the immediate activities of the ground troops.[31]

Having specifically endorsed the consolidated employment of the air striking force, the War Department refused to reorganize Army aviation under AR 95-10 in peacetime. By 1931 the General Staff had begun to refer to this unified force as the General Headquarters Air Force, but it had done little else. The Air Corps combat squadrons remained under the control of the various corps area commanders. Responsible for technical matters, the Chief of the Air Corps wrote and distributed training doctrines and requirements, but he had no authority to see to it that all units complied. Each corps area commander continued to train the air units stationed in his geographic region according to his own ideas. Having no peacetime GHQ Air Force commander and staff and with segmented control of Air Corps squadrons and groups, the Army air arm was in no position to easily transition into actual combat operations. Peacetime organization was completely askew with wartime employment concepts.[32]

Foulois realized this organizational arrangement was detrimental to combat effectiveness. In the fall of 1931, when the General Staff proposed to further decentralize Army air arm administration by giving over control of most Air Corps schools to the appropriate corps area commanders, the OCAC used the occasion to argue that the wartime-peacetime structural dichotomy was wrong. Since the War Department had asserted that it favored having the Army permanently organized for wartime employment, air officers quite properly asked why the General Staff had not seen fit to remove combat air units from the control of the corps area commanders. War plans based on AR 95-10 gave those individuals no responsibilities for the air fighting units after the onset of hostiliites. The General Staff refused to consider such a change, but on September 29 the Deputy Chief of Staff announced that the plan for more decentralization had been shelved for the time being.[33]

General Staff-Air Corps differences over the peacetime organization of military aviation reflected the two groups' divergent attitudes on the role of the Army air arm. Foulois expressed the Air Corps view before the House Appropriations Committee in January 1932:

> We have always felt that the Air Corps had a bigger mission than just simply carrying out short range operations in direct cooperation with our own ground troops. . . . The Air Force, due to its inherent ability to swiftly cover large areas, must naturally operate more or less independently of ground troops, but always under the supreme military command in the theatre of operations.[34]

He said observation units would give the ground troops continuous support, "whereas the major portion, pursuit, bombardment, and attack are actually employed with ground troops only as military emergencies arise requiring such use."[35] A consolidated GHQ Air Force organization was essential to this concept of employment. If it were achieved in peacetime, the Air Corps would be much more free to perfect the combat methods of independent operations, and would be better situated to resist War Department demands for close cooperation with the ground forces.

Seeing that a peacetime GHQ Air Force controlling all combat air units would encourage the Air Corps to disregard its role as a combat auxiliary, the General Staff was reluctant to establish that organization. The General Staff accepted the need for some independent operations but wanted the air arm to concentrate on its primary task of assisting the land army. The best way to ensure this was to place Air Corps units under the supervision of ground generals for peacetime training.[36] From 1931 to 1935 the air officers waged a continuous campaign to permanently consolidate all Army strike aircraft and crews under the command and control of one person. War Department officials resisted implementing that reorganization, and no doubt the divergent attitudes concerning the air arm's principal role had much to do with both groups' position.

In April 1932 the General Staff briefly considered the wartime strength and composition of the GHQ Air Force. The War Plans Division was reconsidering the RED and ORANGE war plans and was mainly concerned with determining how many aircraft would be needed for each. The planners defined General Headquarters Air Force as a

> continental combat force containing all the bombardment, pursuit, and attack squadrons and in addition a proper portion of observation, transport, and airdrome squadrons with supply, maintenance, and administrative units sufficient to make it a self-sustained unit."[37]

The War Plans Division decided that the GHQ Air Force would need 3,152 planes at the end of the first year of mobilization and agreed with the OCAC's contention that the air arm should be instantly ready for combat at the onset of hostilities.[38] Following this decision, the divisions of the General Staff promptly forgot about the GHQ Air Force for a time.

The Four-Army reorganization plan sponsored by MacArthur in mid-

ORGANIZATION: 1932-1933

1932 eventually elicited some renewed War Department interest. MacArthur had become concerned that the Army was structurally ill prepared to face emergencies. According to the 1920 Army Reorganization Act, each of the nine corps areas was to contain one Regular Army division, two National Guard divisions, and three divisions of the Organized Reserve. However, due to scarcity of funds and public apathy these units never became fully manned. By 1932 the Reserve divisions were paper organizations, and those of the Guard and the Regular Army were well below authorized strength. Further, the corps area structure being only an administrative arrangement, no complete tactical chain of command existed between the General Staff and these field units. If mobilized for field service, the U.S. Army would have consisted of a collection of skeletonized divisions, each responsible to the War Department. To remedy these deficiencies and thereby provide a combat force available for immediate use, MacArthur issued the Four-Army Plan on August 9. The plan created four field armies throughout the United States and gave the Chief of Staff tactical control as commander of all the field forces. He designated the senior corps area commander in each army region the field army commander and established the War Plans Division as his GHQ staff. The Chief of Staff hoped this restructuring would furnish the War Department a force that could carry out limited combat operations without first having to wait for the completion of general mobilization.[39]

When the Four-Army plan was being drawn up, General Moseley, the current Deputy Chief of Staff, recommended that the War Department reorganize the combat air arm at the same time. Moseley proposed a peacetime GHQ Air Force designated as the 1st Air Division. Headquartered in the midwest, it would be commanded by a general officer. During two months out of every year, this individual and his staff would exercise tactical command over the force as it carried out exercises in the nation's various strategic areas. Moseley reasoned this would give the division headquarters experience in handling and moving large air units, and would provide the pilots experience in flying over the nation's vital zones. For the other ten months of the year the division commander was to have no direct control of air units. He would be allowed, however, to travel about inspecting his forces. The Deputy Chief's recommendation was a compromise between the OCAC's desire to have the GHQ Air Force under the permanent command and control of a single leader, and the General Staff's refusal to have a unified air organization in peacetime. Although Moseley's proposal was not adopted, it indicated that the War Department's position was beginning to erode.[40]

When the War Department attempted to couple the Four-Army Plan with elimination of the exempted status for Air Corps schools, the Army air arm again had an opportunity to push for a permanently consolidated

87

air strike force. Between September and December 1932, correspondence passed between the OCAC and the General Staff on the issues of further decentralization and formation of a peacetime GHQ Air Force with centralized control over all combat air units. Foulois and his subordinates adamantly opposed ending the exempted status of installations housing the Air Corps' schools. They likewise proceeded to advocate air arm restructuring, so as to align the peacetime organization with that agreed upon for wartime employment.[41]

Foulois wrote directly to the Chief of Staff on December 3, citing the inconsistency of the present arrangement and the folly of any further decentralization of air arm control. The Chief of the Air Corps used MacArthur's own words to support the creation of a peacetime GHQ Air Force. He said the Chief of Staff had justified the Four-Army Plan as a move to organize the peacetime Army for immediate combat employment. He then asked why the War Department had not seen fit to apply the same philosophy toward the air arm. After all, the existing War Department Mobilization Plan called for the Air Corps "to function immediately, and efficiently, at the very beginning of a major national emergency (M-day)," and to do so in a unified manner. Foulois went on to say:

> This fundamental failure to put into practical effect the War Department's own approved principles and doctrines, regarding Air Corps organization and operation, has, in my belief, been the dominant factor, especially during the past twelve years, which has caused the numerous clashes of opinion between the Air Corps and the War Department General Staff, and resulting investigations by Congress.[42]

Here was clear indication that the Army air arm might become less persistent in seeking independence from General Staff control if a GHQ Air Force were set up. Foulois ended his memorandum by asking that

> the Chief of the Air Corps be designated the Commanding General, of the General Headquarters Air Force, and vested with adequate authority to exercise direct command, control and supervision under the direct orders of the Commanding General, General Headquarters over all Regular Army Air Corps units, stations and establishments.[43]

MacArthur passed the Air Corps Chief's memo to Kilbourne, who, at that time, was still struggling to find a compromise with the OCAC on the issue of air arm employment in coast defense.[44] Kilbourne and his War Plans Division valued a strong, properly organized air force but could not accept Foulois' recommendations for peacetime centralization of the Army air component under the Chief of the Air Corps. Kilbourne wrote MacArthur that the Air Corps had some justification for complaining about the War Department's attitude toward the air arm, for there had been an absence of understanding in the Army of the powers of aviation, "especially of its use as a GHQ Air Force, in which capacity it is a power-

ORGANIZATION: 1932-1933

ful weapon in the hands of the supreme commander to influence the course of the campaign." He opposed tampering with peacetime corps area commander control of flying units, but he recommended the War Department appoint a permanent commanding general for the GHQ Air Force, who would plan for the employment of that force in accordance with the Army's color plans. The commander would work under the supervision of the Chief of the Air Corps to prepare plans and directives for peacetime training, command the GHQ Air Force in annual exercises, and direct it in war. Kilbourne urged that the Assistant Chief of the Air Corps be temporarily appointed commander until the War Department could decide on some other Air Corps line officer.[45] Though still not accepting a centralized peacetime air strike force, the Chief of the War Plans Division was now leading the General Staff to accept the idea of establishing a permanent headquarters for the GHQ Air Force. Pressure applied by Foulois and the OCAC no doubt played an important part in bringing about this attitudinal shift.

After studying the recommendations, MacArthur directed Kilbourne to confer personally with Foulois. Kilbourne wrote the Chief of the Air Corps in late December 1932, enclosing a copy of his memo to MacArthur and emphasizing that the War Plans Division believed in the importance of air power. He told Foulois he wanted to straighten out "such tactical and organizational problems as may be perturbing you at this time."[46] Foulois' reply, coming more than a month later, was an even more fervent demand for centralized peacetime control under a single Air Corps officer. The air chief stressed that the "Air Force" was the one tactical organization actually operated under Army General Headquarters in wartime and that war plans specified employing it as a single unified force: "this unified command and tactical unit, the Air Force, requires coordinated training as a unit, of all its branches, namely observation, attack, bombardment, and pursuit." Unified training was presently impossible, because the Chief of the Air Corps "is not authorized to interfere with the sacred prerogatives of the Corps Area Commanders." Foulois argued that the "control, command, and training of the Air Force should, in peace as well as war, be centered in an Air officer responsible only to GHQ." He found Kilbourne's plan for appointing a commanding general for the GHQ Air Force to be unsatisfactory. It limited that officer to staff work except for certain periods of the year when maneuvers were being held.[47]

During March 1933, Foulois kept up his campaign to win General Staff agreement to a peacetime General Headquarters Air Force and continued to claim the Chief of the Air Corps should be the commander. In a March 13 memo to Kilbourne, the Chief of the Air Corps repeated many of his previous arguments for a unified air strike force. Mentioning that the military principles of "Unity of Command" and "Authority and Re-

sponsibility go hand in hand," he was correct when he wrote:
> These cannot be effectively applied to the Army Air Corps, under the existing system of delegating major authority, to Field Army or Corps Area Commanders, as to the control and supervison of Air Corps Tactical Units, and Establishments, while charging the major responsibilities for their Technical, Tactical, and Administrative efficiency, to the Chief of the Air Corps.[48]

Foulois again made clear that he wanted command and control of the entire Air Corps centralized under his office. He also left no doubt that he disagreed with Kilbourne's proposal to make the Assistant Chief of the Air Corps the commander of the GHQ Air Force. He argued that the Chief of the Air Corps, as senior Air Corps officer, should be responsible directly to the Commanding General of General Headquarters both in peace and war, and should take to the field to direct the GHQ Air Force for the GHQ commander in time of national emergency. The Assistant Chief could be left behind to take care of Zone of Interior responsibilities.[49]

In an answer to a General Staff request for the Air Corps' recommendations on headquarters necessary for initial mobilization, Foulois wrote on March 15 that the air arm required a GHQ Air Force headquarters operationally ready in peacetime. He proposed transferring Headquarters 1st Bombardment Brigade from Langley Field to Washington to serve that function under the command of an Air Corps general.[50] In this instance the air chief was not asking for the "whole load" at once. Perhaps he believed the creation of a functioning peacetime GHQ Air Force Headquarters was a logical first step to eventual air arm centralization. More probably, it was the nature of the General Staff request which limited his response.

Foulois' persistent carping kept the issue before the General Staff, but it won him no friends in the War Department. Kilbourne, who opposed allowing the Chief of the Air Corps expanded command responsibility, recommended to the new Deputy Chief of Staff, General Drum, that Foulois' proposals for a unified, centrally controlled combat air force be given a board hearing "rather than have his entire idea turned down on the recommendation of a [single] Division of the General Staff." Kilbourne also feared any move to further curtail the air chief's powers, such as the proposal to end the exempted status of Air Corps installations belonging to the air arm school system, might not sit well with the House Military Affairs Committee. The committee was beginning new hearings on a bill to create a Department of National Defense and a separate air force.[51]

General Staff officers might continue to consider establishing a GHQ Air Force, but their minds were shut on letting the Chief of the Air Corps command it. Foulois' actions were only partially responsible for this stance. War Department officials believed that, regardless of who was Air Corps' chief, he would be too busy with mobilization duties in a national

## ORGANIZATION: 1932-1933

emergency to properly serve as air force field commander.[52] No doubt Foulois' personal work habits intensified the General Staff's conviction that the air chief was too engrossed in procurement, supply, training, and administration for him to assume additional tasks. He was often away from Washington on inspection trips, and his office had a reputation for slowness in answering War Department correspondence. The Chief of the Air Corps much preferred flying to paperwork. During fiscal year 1933 he flew 310 hours, far more than most tactical squadron pilots accumulated during the period and almost twice that of other senior officers. Love of flying might in part have accounted for his many inspections of Air Corps facilities during the first two years at the Air Corps helm. No doubt it also explained the lack of dispatch with which his office at times treated War Department inquiries and requests.[53] Kilbourne likely mirrored the General Staff's assessment in a memo to Foulois:

> I will be perfectly frank with you without attempting to give offense. Already your activities are so great, and I find you absent so many times that important matters are delayed in your office. Always the drag comes from your office. We can't get ahead with our work. You can't even carry on your work in peace, let alone adding GHQ Air Force to it.[54]

Perhaps Foulois' relentless advocacy of a peacetime GHQ Air Force and

Army Deputy Chief of Staff, Maj. Gen. Hugh A. Drum.

coast defense deployment concepts differing from those established by the General Staff, as well as his congressional testimony in support of air arm independence, also influenced the War Department's attitude.

The Chief of the Air Corps' memos on air arm organization between December 1932 and mid-March 1933 kept the GHQ Air Force issue before the General Staff, but the existence of the Air Corps' mission of aerial coast defense was much more important in the War Department's reevaluation of the need for a centralized air strike force in peacetime. MacArthur's January 3, 1933, policy letter "Employment of Army Aviation in Coast Defense," specifically recognized the GHQ Air Force as a vital element in the continental U.S. defense system, and said: "On or before M-Day, the GHQ Air Force will be concentrated in one or more areas according to plan, to enable it to perform missions assigned." In addition it said this centrally controlled strike force would operate offshore reconnaissance aircraft and gather the intelligence upon which subsequent ground army and air force deployments would be based.[55]

These statements left the General Staff policy of corps area control of all military aviation in peacetime open to attack. Air Corps officers asked how the GHQ Air Force could converge in one area before M-day or fly reconnaissance prior to the actual onset of hostilities, if there were no GHQ Air Force prior to the commencement of general mobilization. The OCAC and the General Staff both agreed that the nation's military forces must be organized to meet the threat of invasion. Air Corps officers deemed a permanent GHQ Air Force essential to that purpose, and during 1933 the War Department gradually approached a similar conclusion.[56]

Two other factors quickened General Staff interest in the GHQ Air Force through the first nine months of 1933: the need to fit the air arm into directives being written to implement the Four-Army Plan, and possible military intervention in Cuba. In February, the War Department circulated a tentative draft containing tables of organization for the Four-Army program. The tables presented the wartime structure and chain of command of the GHQ Air Force, but listed most activities as inactive in peacetime. The headquarters of the GHQ Air Force, however, was described as only partially inactive. According to the draft directive:

> Until the detail by the War Department of a general officer of the line for the purpose, the Chief of the Air Corps will designate a general officer assistant to command the GHQ Air Force. For the time being the necessary staff will be provided by a roster kept in the office of the Chief of the Air Corps and submitted to the Adjutant General when initially completed, and annually on October 1 thereafter.[57]

Consequently, there would be no permanent staff in peacetime.

Foulois' March 15 recommendation that the headquarters for the

## ORGANIZATION: 1932-1933

GHQ Air Force be formed may have done some good. A revised version of the tentative directive for the Four-Army structure, circulated in August 1933, read: "Until the Commander of the GHQ Air Force is detailed by the War Department, the Chief of the Air Corps is charged with the organization of the headquarters of the GHQ Air Force and such mobilization duties pertaining thereto as may be assigned."[58] On August 12 The Adjutant General informed the OCAC that these provisions of the tentative directive were now in force, and new mobilization plans being drawn up would convert Headquarters 1st Bombardment Brigade at Langley Field into Headquarters GHQ Air Force. Apparently the General Staff had now decided a permanent headquarters would be necessary to align the air arm organizationally with the Four-Army Plan.[59]

The prospect of sending a portion of the Army into Cuba must have spurred quicker General Staff consideration of the GHQ Air Force question. Sumner Welles, sent by President Roosevelt as special envoy to assess the internal turmoil in that land, had hinted at military intervention in mid-1933 and actually requested it in September.[60] As a result the War Department in early August began updating its TAN (Cuba) war plan. The August 12 memo also directed Foulois to detail an officer to help revise the TAN plan. So the two issues were interrelated.[61]

A bit bewildered by the order to establish the headquarters, Foulois queried the War Department. He wanted to know if this was a "paper organization to be brought into active being only when the War Department Mobilization Plan is put into effect, or is it to be an *actual, active peacetime organization supervising, controlling and operating* the GHQ Air Force in peacetime so that it will be able to carry out its mission in an emergency?" He was also concerned that the OCAC had not yet received word from the General Staff outlining the part the General Headquarters Air Force would play in the new Four-Army structure.[62] The air chief wanted the headquarters set up under his direct control. Accordingly, he requested that the plan to redesignate Headquarters 1st Bombardment Brigade as the headquarters for GHQ Air Force be held in abeyance. He gave as his reasons the forthcoming Drum Board deliberations and the confusion that would ensue from creating the headquarters away from Washington on an installation (Langley Field, Virginia) controlled by the Commanding General, Third Corps Area.[63]

The Adjutant General apprised the Chief of the Air Corps that, when the directive on the Four-Army organization was eventually released, it would clear up some of his questions concerning the place of the GHQ Air Force. He further conveyed War Department concurrence with Foulois' request to delay the conversion of the Langley Field unit, but cautioned, "the Headquarters, GHQ Air Force (Provisional) for the Tan Plan should be completed promptly."[64] The War Department was obviously still concerned over possible military intervention in Cuba, but its thinking on the GHQ Air Force was in flux.

On August 30, MacArthur made some important decisions concerning the GHQ Air Force headquarters and the Air Corps. The Chief of Staff officially designated the Assistant Chief of the Air Corps the "ex officio" commander of the GHQ Air Force with responsibility for leading the force in peacetime exercises and in war, and supervising its planning and training activities. He directed, however, that all GHQ Air Force correspondence be routed through the Chief of the Air Corps. MacArthur also authorized Foulois to establish GHQ Air Force headquarters in Washington and ordered all consideration of further decentralization of control of Air Corps installations postponed indefinitely. Advised of the Chief of Staff's decisions on September 2, Foulois set about forming the GHQ Air Force headquarters under Westover in the OCAC. Yet he did not abandon the struggle to have the Chief of the Air Corps named the GHQ Air Force commander.[65]

The air chief activated GHQ Air Force headquarters on October 1, but could not secure War Department approval for officer increases in the OCAC to staff the new unit. The Chief of Staff did not want a large headquarters brought into being in peacetime. He desired only a small force to serve as a nucleus for a wartime organization. Consequently, OCAC officers had to absorb the extra workload associated with the formulation of GHQ Air Force training and war plan recommendations. Foulois nevertheless convinced the General Staff to reconstitute Headquarters 1st Bombardment Brigade as Headquarters Squadron, Headquarters GHQ Air Force and to transfer it in February 1934 to Bolling Field, Washington, D.C. This afforded the new headquarters adequate clerical and administrative help.[66]

Slightly over a month after MacArthur authorized the headquarters, the Drum Board submitted its report recommending formation of the GHQ Air Force itself. The board's five officers, originally convened to review the Air Corps' proposal of July 13, 1933, for air arm employment in coast defense, decided it was time for the War Department to organize this force. The members apparently realized the military value of a unified air strike force and concluded that the Army's coast defense responsibilities warranted its creation.[67] Months later, General Drum claimed that the GHQ Air Force had been in the War Department's plans since the time of the 1923 Lassiter Board report, but economic circumstances had stood in the way until 1933. It was not until then, according to the board chairman, that the Air Corps' five-year expansion program had allowed the Army air arm to be formed into a viable strike force.[68] Drum's statement was hardly more than a rationalization for the General Staff's persistent resistance to change during the preceding ten years. After all, the

ORGANIZATION: 1932-1933

Air Corps was little better off in manpower and numbers of aircraft in 1933 than it had been the previous year.[69] It was more likely that pressure for the creation of the organization and War Department perception of its value were great enough to cause the board to decide as it did. The composition of the Drum Board may have been a factor. Generals Drum and Gulick had sat on the 1923 Lassiter Board which had recommended forming a unified bomber and pursuit force directly under Army GHQ. General Kilbourne had previously opposed centralizing control of the air arm under the Chief of the Air Corps, but he was relatively openminded and believed in the importance of military aviation. General Simonds, while Chief of the War Plans Division between 1927 and 1931, had been sympathetic to the GHQ Air Force idea, and Foulois staunchly advocated it.[70]

MacArthur approved the board's report on October 12, making the creation of the GHQ Air Force a matter of War Department policy. The Army finally made the board's findings public in late January 1934:

> Among the decisions reached was a definite conclusion to build up in the Air Corps a homogeneous air unit known as GHQ Air Force, comprising all military elements to aviation and adequate to meet effectively the requirements of all military air and land operations. These operations may be in conjunction with land forces, with naval forces, or at times on distinctly distant air missions. This unit will supply an air force capable of rapid concentration for the defense of our frontiers.[71]

Yet the War Department did nothing between October and the time of the official announcement to bring the organization into existence.

Foulois and his officers were pleased with the Drum Board decison to set up the GHQ Air Force, but they wanted it done at once, with command and control of the force and its installations vested in the Chief of the Air Corps. When General Staff action was not instantly forthcoming, they grew restive.[72] On January 30, 1934, Lt. Col. Jacob E. Fickel, one of Foulois' principal subordinates in the OCAC, wrote directly to Drum and Kilbourne. He pointed out to the Deputy Chief of Staff and the Chief of the War Plans Division that the GHQ Air Force currently contained only a rump staff of OCAC officers, and that all tactical squadrons were still controlled by corps area commanders. "The GHQ Air Force," he emphasized, "should be established immediately with existing units under command of the Chief of the Air Corps. Sufficient personnel should be given the Chief of the Air Corps to establish his headquarters." He also maintained Air Corps appropriations should be increased at the expense of naval aviation, and existing Army flying units should be filled out and new ones created as rapidly as possible. Fickel explained that he had shown the memos to Foulois, but they were not meant to represent the air chief's views.[73] Fickel's comments did represent Foulois' views, but per-

95

haps the Chief of the Air Corps had preferred a lower profile in OCAC-General Staff disputes and thus did not send the memos over his own signature. A relatively cooperative spirit had resulted in the Drum Board report, and maybe Foulois thought it might be beneficial to go on working with the General Staff for now. In any event, the Chief of the Air Corps did not long remain a bystander in the interoffice wars.

In early January 1934 Representative John J. McSwain announced his committee would once more take up the question of the place of aviation in the national defense structure. The congressional air advocate said the committee would seriously consider bills creating a separate air force and/or a department of national defense. McSwain made no secret of his overwhelming support for such legislation.[74] The chairman's announcement may have prodded the War Department to begin positive action to bring the GHQ Air Force to life. On January 21, in executive session testimony, MacArthur briefed the Military Affairs Committee members on the composition and uses of such a force:

> Back of these echelons [the observation squadrons working directly with the ground forces], we have the main striking element of the air—the G.H.Q. force, which is equipped with three types of planes—attack, pursuit, and bombardment. They are used just as you would use a slingshot. They are thrown at the point where they will be the most damaging. For cohesion, coordination, and to prevent their dissipation on minor missions, they are held together as a great general reserve under the commanding general in the field.[75]

The Chief of Staff said the GHQ Air Force could be used in a variety of ways, including "independent missions of destruction, aimed at the vital arteries of a nation." He told the committee that the organization should be composed of five wings of at least two hundred aircraft each.[76] Later in the month the War Department released a synopsis of the Drum Board report to the press and on February 3 sent McSwain a complete copy.[77] Apparently the War Department was seeking to undercut the latest move for air arm independence by furnishing a GHQ Air Force alternative.

As a result of MacArthur's testimony, McSwain invited the Army to submit a bill to provide for the new force. On January 31, Secretary of War Dern sent the War Department's proposal over to Capitol Hill. In a letter enclosed with the bill Dern explained that the Director of the Bureau of the Budget had not as yet given his approval for an increased Air Corps authorization, but that "the expansion of the special Army air organization known as the G.H.Q. Air Force" was extremely important to the War Department.[78] McSwain introduced the Army's bill (H.R. 7553) on February 1. It called for enlarging the aircraft fleet

> to such numbers as will permit the Secretary of War to complete the equipment and organization and to maintain in the Army Air Corps the special Army air organization known as "G.H.Q. Air Force," and our overseas defenses, together with a 25 per centum reserve for such forces.[79]

## ORGANIZATION: 1932-1933

The bill was purposely vague on the total number of aircraft contemplated, but asked that Regular Army personnel strength be raised to that approved in the 1926 Air Corps Act—12,403 officers and 124,990 enlisted men.[80]

Much to the War Department's dismay, McSwain the next day submitted his own bill (H.R. 7601), providing for Air Corps autonomy. McSwain's proposal abolished General Staff control and supervision, and required that the Chief of the Air Corps "report directly to and be the immediate advisor of the Secretary of War on all matters relating to military aviation and shall be charged by the Secretary of War with the planning, development, and execution of the Air Corps program." It stipulated that: "The Chief of the Air Corps shall command such portion of the Air Corps not needed for the Air Service of ground troops." It further specified a separate Air Corps promotion list with set years of service for advancement to the next higher grade (which would have eliminated the existing advancement stagnation), a separate budget, expanded personnel strength, a new five-year expansion program designed to boost the total aircraft inventory to 4,832, and a lieutenant generalcy for the Chief of the Air Corps.[81]

The February 3 issue of the *Army and Navy Journal* reflected the War Department's view on the two legislative proposals. The paper pointed out that the GHQ Air Force would afford

> the benefits of an independently acting Air Force while maintaining unity of command and avoiding the costly duplication involved in providing an autonomous air arm with its own support organizations for supplies, medical attention, subsistence and so forth.[82]

The article also reported that President Roosevelt would likely oppose the McSwain measure and that "Air Corps headquarters in Washington are entirely satisfied with the recognition its arm has received from the General Staff since the practical abolition of the Assistant Secretary of War for Air."[83] The journal may have been correct in its assessment of Roosevelt's stance, but it could not have been more mistaken in its estimate of the OCAC's attitude.

Foulois and his followers remained dissatisfied with General Staff control of the air arm, and the increased authority devolving to the General Staff as a result of the vacant assistant secretary's post only added to that dissatisfaction. Air officers supported the formation of a GHQ Air Force because it appeared the best existing alternative. Yet, they viewed independence or autonomy as the real means of securing an adequate air force for defense of the United States. When Congressman McSwain reintroduced the issue of independence in early January, the Air Corps continued the struggle within the Army to have the GHQ Air Force immediately established. At the same time, it sought an end to General Staff control through congressional action.[84]

In January at McSwain's request, the OCAC staff had secretly drafted H.R. 7601. This was a well-guarded secret and the War Department did not discover the truth until months later. To conceal his office's activity, Foulois went so far as to tell members of the General Staff that he had no knowledge of McSwain's bill until after the congressman introduced it. Caught in this lie a year later, the Chief of the Air Corps tried to justify his earlier statement by saying he had spoken as he did because he had not at the time seen the legislative proposal in printed form—a very lame excuse. In February 1934, Foulois also led the War Department to believe he opposed McSwain's H.R. 7601. This, too, distorted the truth. The air chief may not have been perfectly content with the bill's final form, but he definitely favored the autonomy the measure would have conferred.[85]

On February 1, the day before McSwain introduced H.R. 7601, Foulois was summoned to testify before the House Military Affairs Committee. The Chief of the Air Corps, no longer cooperative with the War Department and noticeably agitated by what he considered the Army's lack of support for aviation, mounted a vocal campaign against continued General Staff control of the Air Corps. Unchanged in his attitudes since the days of his 1919 congressional testimony, Foulois told the committee that the General Staff was the "main obstacle" to the proper growth of military aviation. He opposed the War Department's February 1 aviation expansion bill (H.R. 7553), arguing it was so ambiguous as to allow "the General Staff to do as they blame please." He pleaded for autonomy: "If we are going to advance and build up aviation, we should stand on our own feet. We should have our own budget. We should have our own promotion list." He told the congressmen he wanted "an independent organization that can function without a lot of obstruction" from the various divisions of the General Staff. He protested the bureaucratic red tape entailed in dealing with that body, and he gave examples of War Department decisionmaking on aviation procurement matters in which the OCAC was not consulted, something that did not happen until the post of Assistant Secretary of War for Air was abandoned. Foulois did not ask for instant separation of the air arm from the Army. Nonetheless, he told the committee members that a Department of National Defense embodying a separate Department of Air was the ultimate solution to the problem of defense organization.[86]

The General Staff was quite displeased with McSwain's bill and Foulois' testimony. War Department officers were then contemplating a new five-year expansion program for the Air Corps. Having recently gone on record as favoring a GHQ Air Force, they honestly thought they were treating the air component fairly. They believed that if McSwain's pro-

## ORGANIZATION: 1932-1933

posal became law it would disrupt the entire Army organization.[87] The War Department's concern over H.R. 7601 was reflected in the speed with which the General Staff planned a lengthy booklet, "Information on Aviation and a Department of National Defense," designed to ensure that "divergence of information before Congressional and other committees be avoided" by its officers. Distributed on February 7, the booklet lauded the value of military aviation but was totally opposed to Air Corps autonomy or independence.[88]

On February 21, Secretary of War Dern dispatched a biting letter to McSwain criticizing H.R. 7601 and a second nearly identical bill introduced by the Military Affairs chairman on February 10. The secretary wrote that he was so opposed to removing the Air Corps from General Staff direction that he would refuse to support the War Department's own bill for more GHQ Air Force aircraft until the two offensive proposals were dropped.[89]

In an accompanying statement to the Military Affairs Committee, Dern attacked the air arm's right to independence. The secretary said military aviation was important, but it was just one of several ingredients in a well balanced force. Proclaiming the airplane had "too many limitations to enable it to be decisive alone," he argued that:

> the destruction of armies or populations by projectiles and gas alone is a fantasy of the dreamer. Actual capture of the enemy or the occupation of vital areas is essential before a determined foe can be defeated. An air force alone cannot accomplish these results.[90]

Denying the air advocates' claims to decisiveness in offensive operations, he asserted that neither could military acting alone protect America's coasts: "A fleet can operate at night, in fog, and in weather when airplanes are helpless, if not indeed chained to the ground." Even in good weather it would be difficult to destroy an enemy armada from the air. Thus the air arm possessed no independent mission, and consequently there was no need to constitute an independent Air Force. According to the secretary:

> The most important contribution that an air force can make to success in war is to aid our armies and navies to win victories. Properly directed it is capable of delivering powerful blows, by surprise, at the crisis of an action. It is of utmost value as an agency of harassment for localized destruction and for general observation. It is not an economic substitute for any of the other arms and services in an Army. Regardless of cost, it cannot possibly substitute for the basic elements on the ground.[91]

A senior staff officer could not have expressed the General Staff's view better.

Angered by Dern's blunt words, McSwain refused to give up the fight to free the Air Corps from the Army General Staff.[92] However, the committee chairman's efforts were delayed by the Army air arm's disastrous

99

employment in domestic air mail operations, and the resultant War Department investigation headed by former Secretary of War Baker (all taking place between February and June). These same events also induced the War Department to temporarily suspend its consideration of plans to bring the GHQ Air Force to life.

## CHAPTER IV

## FUNDS, AIRCRAFT, AND PERSONNEL, 1931-1933

The early 1930s were a time of severe financial drought for the armed forces of the United States. Added to the traditional reluctance of Americans to spend large sums for defense in peacetime, the Great Depression caused the Hoover administration to cut military costs to the bone. Hoover believed the country needed an adequate military force to prevent invasion, but "insisted upon a balanced budget as the foundation of all public and private financial stability and of all public confidence."[1] In order to maintain these two principles in the face of declining revenues, the President necessarily defined the term "adequate force" quite loosely. In essence, it came to mean whatever defense the government could buy with the annually decreasing funds made available to the military.[2] Happily the nation faced no immediate external threat, for Hoover erred gravely when he said the Army, as well as the Navy, were being maintained "in a high state of efficiency."[3] In truth, years of parsimonious treatment, topped off by recent extensive budget cuts, had left the Army in no condition to face a determined invader.

War Department leaders accepted the orthodox economic theory that federal expenditures should not exceed revenue. They were therefore hesitant to seek more from Congress than the President had asked for in his annual budget request. However, the General Staff was still quite disturbed by the impact of cost-cutting on military efficiency.[4] MacArthur voiced the Army's concern before the House Appropriations Committee in November 1932:

> In meeting these demands for curtailment successively imposed, everything loose in the Military Establishment has been thrown overboard. Only the naked framework remains. . . . I would be remiss in my duties were I not to point out to you the folly and danger of undoing what we have laboriously accomplished at the expense of blood and treasure. At no time in its history

## FOULOIS AND THE U.S. ARMY AIR CORPS

has the United States had greater need than now for the security of an adequate national defense.[5]

The Army was clearly in a bad way. Although the 1920 Army Reorganization Act authorized 18,000 officers and 280,000 enlisted men, Congress never furnished the funds for this force. By 1931 the Army had for years been down to around 12,000 officers and 118,750 men. Not only was the force small, it was poorly equipped. The funds since World War I were too slim to let the War Department upgrade materiel, so the service relied on the surplus left over from the war. By the early 1930s most of these stocks were used up, worn out, or obsolescent. For example, in 1933 every tank in the inventory save twelve had been built during the war. Most trucks and other vehicles were of the same vintage. Spending only six to seven per cent of the federal budget for the military activities of the Army, the United States could not match the military might of such small nations as Belgium or Portugal.[6] The General Staff, whose job it was to plan and prepare for the defense of the American homeland and overseas possessions, worried over this weakness.

While also suffering in the early 1930s, the Air Corps was much better off than the rest of the Army. The five-year expansion begun by the Air Corps Act of 1926 brought substantial gains in manpower and equipment. The program made filling out the air component a priority War Department policy, so the Air Corps' share of the military activities budget steadily increased from 1926 to 1931. From mid-1928 to July 1932, aircraft inventory shot up from 903 to 1,646. At the same time, officer strength climbed from 1,014 to about 1,300 and the number of enlisted men rose from 9,468 to 13,400. Considerable airfield and housing construction took place. By 1933 MacArthur could report that the United States ranked roughly fourth in the world in land-based fighting planes—at a time when the nation stood seventeenth in organized military strength.[7]

Foulois and his fellow aviators were far from satisfied. Never during the five-year program did the administration ask for, or Congress appropriate, sufficient money to purchase all the aircraft called for by the 1926 Air Corps Act. Ten years after the act's passage, the air arm still did not have 1,800 serviceable planes—a figure that should have been reached in 1931. Officer strength stayed well below the 1,650 authorized, a situation which could not be easily remedied unless the 12,000-officer limit set for the entire Army was lifted. From 1931 to 1935, West Point was the sole avenue to a Regular Army commission. The school's output of pilot training volunteers did little more than replace Air Corps losses, and few officers from the Army's other branches sought transfers to the air arm.

The Air Corps could not make up shortages by assigning more Reserve officer pilot training graduates to extended active duty. In fact,

FUNDS, AIRCRAFT, AND PERSONNEL, 1931-1933

funding and aircraft shortages prevented the War Department from allowing its air component to keep on active duty all of the 550 Reserve officers authorized by the five-year expansion program. The Air Corps, however, received all of the enlisted men called for in the expansion, but at great cost to the rest of the Army. With no increase in appropriations to fund an air arm of 15,000 men, Air Corps enlisted increases had to come through transfers from other branches.[8]

The Office of the Chief of the Air Corps was continually dismayed at having its annual fund requests drastically reduced by the Secretary of War and the Director of the Bureau of the Budget. Adding to the unhappiness of Army flyers, the Navy finished its five-year aviation expansion on time in 1932. Air officers did not care that the Air Corps by 1931 was receiving nearly twenty percent of the Army's total funds for military activities. They saw only that the War Department and the Bureau of the Budget were not asking for enough money to complete their expansion. In March 1931 the OCAC prepared preliminary budget estimates of $54,433,599 for fiscal year 1932. This included money to buy the 859 aircraft needed to bring the Air Corps to 1,800 serviceable planes (2,034 total planes, minus a percentage for depot overhaul).[9]

As in previous years, the Secretary of War slashed the request, approving just $38,390,529. The secretary's action, based on General Staff recommendations, was the result of Bureau of the Budget-imposed limitations on the size of the War Department's overall request. Following established practice, the General Staff suggested to the secretary how the estimates of all War Department branches and agencies should be revised to fit within the ceiling set by the Bureau of the Budget. In this instance, it trimmed the Air Corps' preliminary estimates by over $16 million. When the Bureau of the Budget wound up its own investigation, it sliced the air arm's request another $7 million. Congress rarely tampered with defense funds requested by the administration during the depression years. It approved the bureau's figures almost without alteration, appropriating $31,479,635. Due to depressed prices, the Secretary of War then impounded $1,952,011 of this. With its original estimate of $54,433,599 pared to a final figure of $29,527,624, the Air Corps could buy but 382 aircraft. In view of the nation's sad economic state and the Hoover administration's commitment to a balanced budget, maybe the OCAC was unrealistic in its original request. Nonetheless, air officers thought the extensive reductions imposed by the War Department reflected insufficient support for aviation. In subsequent years the War Department eliminated the need to make such drastic cuts by requiring the OCAC to base its estimates on limitations previously set by the Bureau of the Budget.[10] As a consequence, Foulois and his staff, while still possessing a major voice in determining the types of aircraft to be purchased, found them-

103

Sec. of War
Patrick J. Hurley.

selves in the awkward position of being unable to request adequate funds to expand the Air Corps to 1,800 planes.

MacArthur and the General Staff did not believe the War Department was niggardly in its treatment of the Air Corps. On the contrary, they believed the aviators frequently sought far more than their fair share of Army funds. The Chief of Staff appreciated the value of the airplane and the need for a strong Air Corps. But he also sought to create a balanced combat force and therefore could not allow the air arm to so dominate War Department spending as to cause further decay in the other arms.[11] In August 1931 he wrote Secretary of War Patrick J. Hurley: "An army overstrong in the air would be like an army overstrong in cavalry, able to strike suddenly and to effect great temporary destruction, but

## FUNDS, AIRCRAFT, AND PERSONNEL, 1931-1933

powerless to hold objectives thus gained." MacArthur told the secretary that even though 2,950 planes were warranted for defense, he did not favor raising air strength above that specified in the 1926 Air Corps Act: "In view of the present economic conditions, of the undesirability of further increasing the disproportion of our Air Corps to other arms of the service . . . it is recommended that our aircraft program be stabilized at approximately 1,800 planes gross."[12] Explaining the General Staff view, MacArthur wrote in his 1933 annual report: "To build up and have ready for immediate use a satisfactory air contingent, the War Department has sacrificed much else that is required in a well-balanced program, with the result that no other arm or service of our army is relatively so well prepared as is the Air Corps."[13]

The tight money of the depression years worsened Air Corps-General Staff tensions. Though not intentionally trying to starve the air arm of funds, the General Staff opposed increases for the relatively well-heeled Air Corps that would further shortchange the other arms and services.[14] The Army air arm, however, did not care about the purported need for a balanced military force. Air Corps officers believed military aviation was the decisive instrument in both defensive and offensive warfare. To restrict its development for any reason showed a genuine lack of understanding for air power's military value. Thus Foulois and his OCAC staff felt justified in pushing for more money.

The War Department's fiscal year 1933 budget dropped sharply. During calendar year 1931, Hoover became very concerned over declining federal revenues. In the fall he directed the executive departments, then preparing their budgets for fiscal year 1933, to make all possible cuts. Secretary of War Hurley announced in November that the War Department budget would be $44 million under the 1932 level. In December the Bureau of the Budget forced additional cuts. Under the important "military activities" category, the 1933 War Department appropriations bill would be about $295 million—a sharp decrease from the $334,764,748 available in fiscal year 1932.[15]

The bill requested just $25,482,903 for the air arm as compared to $31,479,625 in the fiscal year 1932 appropriation. Foulois had initially asked for $34.5 million but the War Department reduced this by $4 million. The Bureau of the Budget lopped off another $5 million. This left the Air Corps with a request $9 million below its original estimates and $4 million less than was available during fiscal year 1932 after the Secretary of War's withdrawal of $1.95 million. Congress approved the 1933 request almost without change, enabling the Air Corps to buy only 238 new aircraft—not enough even to replace the year's attrition.[16]

MacArthur defended the proposed budget for fiscal year 1933 as the very minimum needed for national security. In December he told the House Appropriations Committee that all nonessential items had already been removed, and implied that additional cuts would endanger the future security of the United States. The Chief of Staff's testimony would have been even more vehement had he known there was a congressional move afoot to reduce military manpower.[17]

When it came to budgeting, MacArthur and the General Staff considered manpower and training far more important than military hardware. The Air Corps held the opposite view. During his tenure as Chief of the Air Corps, Foulois argued unceasingly that War Department mobilization planning for the Air Corps was faulty because it geared everything to the length of time required to amass a citizen-soldier ground army. He pointed out to the General Staff that, without sufficient supplies of aircraft and associated equipment already on hand, it made no difference how fast civilians could be brought into the Air Corps. For the air arm to expand at the beginning of mobilization, it had to build up its stock of planes during peacetime. Hence, Foulois maintained that materiel must be given priority over manpower in defense spending. Conversely, MacArthur insisted that without sufficient numbers of trained soldiers instantly available, the United States would not be prepared for a hostile attack. Moreover, without a sizable force, the Army could not carry out the peacetime training of the National Guard and Organized Reserve forces, thus allowing America's second line of defense to slip into deeper decay. In January 1932 the MacArthur-Foulois difference in perspective became significant when the air chief testified before the House Appropriations Committee on the fiscal year 1933 military budget bill. Seeking more money for military aviation, Foulois noted that it was more important to put funds into materiel than in manpower. In doing so, he gave direct support to Representative Ross Collins' plan to drastically cut the Army's officer strength.[18]

Collins opened his campaign for reductions in late December 1931 and continued it into July 1932. The Mississippi Democrat had little patience with what he deemed the General Staff's conservative, outmoded notions on manpower. Like his fellow congressman, John McSwain, he looked upon mechanized land forces and air power as the important ingredients in future wars. With better economy and improved military efficiency as his goals, Collins used his position as chairman of the Subcommittee on Military Appropriations in an attempt to cut officer strength, dismantle much of the Reserve training system, and increase Army mechanization. In late December the press reported that Collins was striving to cut the Army's 12,000-man officer corps by as many as 4,000, and that his subcommittee might compromise on a 2,000-officer reduction. In January 1932 the subcommittee went into executive session with Collins and Congressman Joseph W. Byrns, chairman of the full committee, pushing hard for personnel strength cuts.

## FUNDS, AIRCRAFT, AND PERSONNEL, 1931-1933

After Collins told reporters in late January that no worthwhile branch of the Army would be hurt in any cutback, rumors circulated that neither the Air Corps nor the Coast Artillery would lose personnel, while the Cavalry, Infantry, and Field Artillery would fare badly. The subcommittee finished redrafting the appropriations bill on January 29. As expected, the proposal reduced funds for Reserve training, cut officer strength by 2,000, and assessed the cuts as previously rumored—the Cavalry being hardest hit. Despite administration opposition, a defiant Democrat-controlled Appropriations Committee kept the bill in committee until early May.[19]

MacArthur vented his displeasure over the revised bill in a letter to Representative Bertrand H. Snell, the House minority leader. Snell inserted the letter into the *Congressional Record*. The Chief of Staff argued that the Army needed more, not less, manpower. He said that the War Department had often reported to Congress that its minimum manpower levels for military effectiveness should be 14,063 officers and 165,000 men, in lieu of the current 12,000 and 118,750 respectively. MacArthur expressed disgust at not being apprised of the contemplated reductions when he appeared before the appropriations subcommittee. He emphasized that a loss of 2,000 officers would prostrate the already weakened Army.[20]

Regardless of MacArthur's and the Hoover administration's exertions, the House passed the Collins bill on May 21 but not before doctoring it to further protect the Air Corps. McSwain secured special treatment for the air arm by successfully sponsoring an amendment that excluded the Air Corps and the Judge Advocate General's Department from the strength reduction. The Military Affairs Committee chairman explained the Air Corps was already 393 officers below authorized strength. He maintained it was Congress' duty to build up this vital branch of the defense establishment to levels set by the 1926 Air Corps Act, as soon as economic conditions improved. There was no indication that Foulois was clandestinely involved in McSwain's latest venture on behalf of military aviation, but the little general most certainly was pleased with it. The House approved the amended Bill 201-182 and sent it to the Senate.[21]

However, the Republican-controlled upper chamber forced the House to reconsider by refusing to endorse the bill. The Senate's version of the measure, reflecting the administration's position, contained no cuts. The vote of 51 to 16 and the stand of the senators in the conference committee made it evident they would not compromise on the manpower issue. Collins waged a dogged fight in the conference committee and on the House floor, even offering to accept a 1,000-officer reduction, but he was unable to hold his fellow congressmen to their initial decision. On July 12, after the start of the new fiscal year, the House finally approved the Senate's position on the manpower question. On the fourteenth, the President signed the appropriations bill into law. It gave the administration about the same amount of money it had originally requested for War Department military activities.[22]

While the conference committee was mulling over the officer cut, the House and Senate passed the Omnibus Economy Bill and sent it to the President on June 28. Congressional members had been quite concerned over dwindling federal revenues and decided to reduce government salaries. The original House proposal specified eleven percent cuts for all government workers and members of the armed forces making more than $1,000 a year. Hoover countered by asking for a payless thirty-day furlough in place of the direct pay cut. As finally passed, the act froze the pay of all federal employees, including military members, and enacted Hoover's furlough plan for every officer and government worker earning over $1,000 annually. This in effect meant an 8 1/3 percent pay cut.[23]

The act hit the relatively underpaid military officer harder than anyone else. Between 1908 and 1932 the government had increased the pay of civilian federal employees between 25 and 175 percent. The only raise for Army officers since 1908 had come in 1922. Congress at that time increased the annual pay of major generals two percent (from $9,532 to $9,700), and gave an average eleven-percent hike to other officers down through first lieutenant. Unfortunately, second lieutenants had their yearly income lowered two percent (from $2,253 to $2,199).[24]

Promotion stagnation compounded the pay problem. These following factors dampened any prospect of promotion to major before twenty-three years service: a 12,000-officer ceiling and congressional curbs on the number of officers occupying each grade; no mandatory thirty-year retirement; an officer corps composed mostly of men commissioned during or just prior to World War I; and advancement based wholly on longevity. Advancement to full colonel meant an additional twelve years of commissioned service. MacArthur sponsored a bill in 1931 to eliminate the stagnation problem by authorizing additional senior officer billets, but the economy-minded Congress was in no mood to enact legislation requiring more defense funds. The Chief of Staff believed military members deserved sizable pay boosts and better promotion opportunity, but due to the nation's economic woes, he proposed no remedial legislation in 1932 or 1933. With the Omnibus Economy Bill taking effect on July 1, 1932, all Army officers lost their right to paid annual leave. In addition, their salaries were frozen at the July 1 level regardless of subsequent advancement in rank or eligibility for longevity increases. And they were forced to take a month's unpaid furlough during fiscal year 1933, having 2 1/2 days wages subtracted from each month's pay.[25]

## FUNDS, AIRCRAFT, AND PERSONNEL, 1931-1933

Despite these provisions Air Corps officers continued to live rather comfortably in the early 1930s. Base pay may have been low, but flyers received a monthly supplement equal to fifty percent of that figure for risking their lives in airplanes. Further, officers rarely worked long hours. While enlisted men formed up for prebreakfast roll call at 0630 each weekday, officers normally put in their first official appearance an hour later. They began flying at 0800 and continued until 1130, when everyone broke for lunch. Pilots usually relaxed at the club until around 1315, then returned to duty until 1530—the end of the official duty day. Nearly all Air Corps personnel received weekends off and also a half day on Wednesday. Almost no one worked nights. Most important, officers and men had job security at a time millions of Americans were out of work.[26]

Air Corps personnel spent a considerable amount of their off-duty time in various physical fitness activities. General Foulois lent his full official and moral support because he deemed physical training just as important as flying training: "No flying officer can hope to maintain his flying efficiency over a period of years, unless he continually maintains a high standard of physical fitness." During his tenure as head of the air arm, Foulois tried to supply Air Corps stations with athletic facilities and equipment.[27] An accomplished squash player, the air chief believed the game had sharpened his eyesight and therefore urged every pilot to take part in the sport. The result was predictable: interest in the game soared, and a rash of squash-court building hit Air Corps posts across the country.[28]

Army aviators may have lived in comparative comfort, but their work was very dangerous. In fiscal year 1931 the Air Corps accounted for 456 airplane accidents in which 26 people were killed and 75 injured. Fiscal year 1932 proved even more disastrous, with 50 killed and 89 injured in 423 accidents. Since just about 1,900 Regular and Reserve officers, pilot trainees, and enlisted aviators engaged in flying operations, the accident and death rates were quite high. In fiscal year 1932, over two and a half percent of all Army aviators lost their lives in crashes. Most fatalities involved Reserve officers serving one year's active duty after completion of pilot training. The second greatest killer was pilot training itself. Statistics on accidents and deaths showed little change during the rest of the Foulois years. Pilots, whose annual flying time was severely curtailed by the government in the name of economy, continued to push their planes up to, and sometimes beyond aircraft performance limits. Just as regularly, they crashed and killed themselves.[29]

In the early 1930s, Army officers fretted over the promotion stagnation but Air Corps officers had special reason to complain. Advancement depended on length of commissioned service alone. Because most aviators had entered the Army during or just prior to World War I, they stood well down on the Army's single promotion list. In fact the air arm in 1932 had no officers with sufficient service to hold the rank of colonel. Foulois and Westover had jumped from their permanent grade of lieutenant colonel to general officer rank only by virtue of the offices to which they were appointed. The World War hump in the list also posed a problem in the air officer's promotion picture. The hump stemmed from the swift wartime expansion of the officer corps. After the war ended, many of the new officers stayed on, resulting in a disproportionate share with dates of rank within one and a half years of each other. During the war, aviators underwent nine months of training before commissioning as opposed to the three given prospective ground officers. With commissioning dates six months after those of their ground-bound contemporaries, the flyers fell as a group toward the rear of the war hump. Since only a few vacancies occurred each year in the small postwar Army, a difference in date of rank of six months translated into several years waiting time for the next promotion.[30]

As a result of the hump and the relative youth of most air officers, the Air Corps found that it did not have nearly enough field grade officers for all of its command positions. The air arm therefore resorted to filling these posts with officers holding far less rank than called for by the responsibilities involved. Captains and first lieutenants commanded tactical squadrons; lieutenant colonels and majors directed wings. Including the air officers in one common Army promotion list opened this wide gap between rank and responsibility within the Air Corps. To remedy the situation Foulois, like other Army flyers, favored a separate Air Corps list, but the War Department adamantly refused to consider such a step. As a result, flyers went on grumbling about the promotion system until 1935, when a special promotion system took effect to ease the rank-responsibility imbalance.[31]

Air Corps enlisted men faced both promotion stagnation and low pay. The air arm may have received nearly all the troops authorized by the five-year plan, but it did not receive ample upper-level grades for them. With fewer intermediate and senior noncommissioned officer slots in proportion to the size of the force, advancement slowed to a trickle. In fiscal year 1932 the Air Corps conducted no examination for promotion to technical and master sergeant, for the list of those who had previously passed the test was still quite long in comparison with projected vacancies in each of the two grades. Likewise, pay remained low for the enlisted force. The Army private could justifiably complain in 1933 when Civilian Conservation Corps (CCC) workers were given $30 per month while he drew merely $18. The Omnibus Economy Bill of 1932 did not reduce enlisted pay, but it did prohibit raises based on promotion and longevity. This worked some hardships. Even so, job security more than compensated for

## FUNDS, AIRCRAFT, AND PERSONNEL, 1931-1933

problems of pay and promotion during the depression years.[32]

According to the calendar, June 30, 1932 should have marked the end of the Air Corps' five-year expansion program. However, on that date the Air Corps had approximately 1,300 officers, 13,400 enlisted men, and 1,646 serviceable aircraft rather than the 1,650 officers, 15,000 enlisted troops, and 1,800 serviceable planes specified in the 1926 Air Corps Act. The War Department developed plans which would fill out the enlisted complement by June 1934, but the officer strength situation defied solution under existing circumstances. Furthermore, the parsimonious fiscal 1933 budget would not even permit the Air Corps to replace aircraft losses for the year. By June 1933, the Army's airplane inventory had declined to 1,497, not again to reach its 1932 level until just before World War II.[33]

Disregarding aircraft and manpower shortages, from December 1931 onward Foulois argued that the War Department should allow the OCAC to form all of the tactical units set forth in the five-year program. He believed that once these were in being Congress would provide the money and airplanes to bring them up to strength. By June 1932 the Air Corps had organized and activated all but five pursuit squadrons. During the next fifteen months the OCAC brought the five to life, completing at least the unit phase of the five-year program. This gave the Army air arm fifty tactical squadrons—four attack, twelve bombardment, thirteen observation, and twenty-one pursuit—all of which were understrength in manpower and aircraft. It also generated a large organizational overhead that needed to be absorbed by the small Air Corps.[34]

The five-year program required three wings and a separate group in the continental United States, one wing each in Panama and Hawaii, and a composite group in the Philippines. By mid-1932 the wings at March Field, California, and Langley Field, Virginia, contained their full complements of bombardment and pursuit squadrons. Nonetheless, activation of the attack wing at Barksdale Field, Louisiana, was delayed until fiscal year 1935, due to the dearth of funds to complete that new installation. Squadrons for Hawaii and the Canal Zone were the last to be organized because airfield construction also lagged in those localities. The pursuit group at Selfridge Field, Michigan, and the composite group in the Philippines were organizationally complete in 1932.[35]

Lack of funds not only prevented completion of the five-year program, it also hampered the Air Corps training program in 1932-33. In October 1931 the Hoover administration impounded nearly $2 million allocated for flying operations and training. This sharply curtailed the flying done by almost all Air Corps pilots during the rest of the fiscal year, resulting in less than satisfactory training for the members of the combat squadrons. Cancellation of the 1932 air maneuvers further handicapped training by denying flyers experience in large air operations. The single air activity of note for the entire fiscal year was the January emergency resupply of Navajo and Hopi Indians stranded by a blizzard in Arizona. Nine Air Corps planes dropped 30,000 pounds of food in the relief effort. The 1933 budget did not contain significant increases for tactical training, but it did fund May air exercises in California and Kentucky—neither remotely approaching the scale of the 1931 maneuvers. Unit training during the remainder of the year was still on a reduced scale. The commander of the 2d Bombardment Group may have revealed a problem common to all tactical units when he complained that his outfit could not conduct serious gunnery or bombing training due to an ammunition shortage.[36]

Air Corps responsibility for a portion of President Roosevelt's CCC program also complicated unit training in 1933. Colonel Arnold, commander of the wing at March Field, grumbled in August that delivering supplies to CCC camps was about all the training his pilots were getting. Arnold said unit training was impossible with so many of his officers caught up in CCC administration. Lt. Col. Frank M. Andrews, commander of the pursuit group at Selfridge Field, expressed similar complaints in September. This was, of course, a problem common to the entire Army, yet it was another impediment to proper training for air combat operations.[37]

The constant turnover of Reserve officers in the tactical squadrons added a persistent training difficulty. Each year, after intensive screening and testing, the Air Corps Training Center admitted several hundred men direct from civilian life and trained them as military aviators. Since after 1930 there were no vacancies in the Regular Army for any but West Point graduates, the War Department rewarded with Reserve commissions the forty percent skilled enough to get through pilot training. The Air Corps Act of 1926 let Reserve officers serve on active duty from one to two years, and the five-year program developed by the OCAC called for keeping 550 on active duty at all times. Even so, fund shortages kept the Air Corps from bringing its active Reserve officer force to that level. In addition the dearth of funds compelled the OCAC to restrict each Reserve officer to one year of active duty to make room for the next year's training center graduates. Consequently, each tactical squadron was constantly teaching new pilots combat maneuvers and unit employment tactics. Once the Reserve officer became reasonably proficient, his year was up. He would be replaced by an officer fresh from pilot training and the whole process would begin anew.[38]

President Hoover pursued military cost-cutting right up to the day he left office. In December 1932 he presented a fiscal year 1934 budget request for $278.6 million covering War Department military activity expenditures. This was $56 million less than the 1932 appropriation and $16.5 million lower than the current fiscal year. MacArthur was unhappy

# FUNDS, AIRCRAFT, AND PERSONNEL, 1931-1933

Ft. Defiance, Ariz., southern Navajo agency headquarters for the relief of snowbound Indians.

with the $278.6 million request. He was even more unhappy when Congress lopped off another $9 million before passing the appropriation, for he was convinced that $269,673,353 would not provide adequate national security.[39]

The Air Corps shared in Hoover's cuts but not in the congressional pruning. The War Department trimmed the OCAC's original request of $32,068,932 by $2.5 million, but it did not tamper with the Air Corps request for more money to support an average of 200 hours flying time per pilot (a rise of 35 hours over that provided since 1931). When the Bureau of the Budget wrung another $2.5 million from the request, the OCAC reacted angrily. Westover, filling in for the again-absent Foulois, wrote the War Department budget officer in November 1932 that the Bureau of the Budget figure of $26,818,560 was much too small to equip the Air Corps to meet its national defense responsibilities. The Assistant Chief pointed out that the five-year aircraft program, soon to enter its seventh year, was still far from complete.[40]

In December both Foulois and Assistant Secretary of War for Air Davison did their best to convince Congress that the Air Corps needed to have more money. Foulois, who had just published an article on the need for training and preparedness in peacetime, defended the allocation of more flying hours on the basis of safety, arguing that the aircraft fatality rate was related inversely to flying proficiency. He bemoaned the fact the Air Corps could not bestow Regular commissions on training center graduates because of the congressionally-imposed 12,000-officer Army ceiling. He went on to explain how the proposed budget would decrease the number of Air Corps aircraft. Foulois asserted that the administration's request would fund merely 375 planes, while 466 were projected to become worn out or destroyed by June 30, 1934. Davison echoed many of Foulois' remarks and affirmed that the Air Corps would be 389 aircraft short of the 1,800 "serviceable" planes (2,058 total planes) under the administration's budget proposal. The comments of the Air Corps' spokesmen may have had some bearing on the House Appropriation Committee's decisions. More probable, Congressman Collins, chairman of the Subcommittee on Military Appropriations, used his influence in the air arm's behalf. As passed on March 4, 1933, the War Department appropriations bill contained virtually all of the Air Corps funds requested by the President—$26,324,185.[41] Coming at a time when most other War Department requests were taking sizable cuts, this was a clear victory for the air arm.

However, this triumph evaporated quickly. In April the new President clearly indicated he intended to honor his campaign pledge to slash government spending by 25 percent. Franklin Roosevelt ordered the War Department budget for fiscal 1934 cut by $144 million. The Director of the Budget, Lewis W. Douglas, announced that $90 million of this would come from military activities funds. On April 20 the Chief Executive sent a message to Congress seeking authority to curtail flight pay and to furlough officers at half pay, to help achieve the desired War Department reduction in expenditures. The *Army and Navy Journal* reported the President was thinking in terms of 3,000 to 4,000 officers. In the eyes of the General Staff the Director of the Budget began to take on the trappings of a dictator. He talked openly of retiring about 3,000 officers, separating 13,000 enlisted men, and scaling down flight pay for senior officers. Douglas added that the furlough authority asked for by Roosevelt could also be used if a greater cutback was warranted.[42]

MacArthur was most upset over these cost-cutting plans. Vehemently opposed to any personnel cuts, he testified against the bill allowing the President to furlough officers, telling the House Military Affairs Committee that any reductions in officer strength "would wreck the military system set up by Congress in the National Defense Act and leave the country deficient in defense needs."[43] Between April and June the Chief of Staff pressured administration officials to reconsider the tremendous budget

## FUNDS, AIRCRAFT, AND PERSONNEL, 1931-1933

cuts imposed on the War Department for 1934, and took the issue to the public in a series of speeches across the country. He believed the Army had to hold the line against the destructive New Dealers and even threatened to resign if the funds were not restored.[44]

The issue was eventually resolved through compromise. By late May the administration lost interest in the furlough idea, due to its need for large numbers of Army officers to administer the CCC program. In June the Senate voted to kill the measure. The administration also compromised on the $90 million decrease for military activities. Secretary of War Dern supported MacArthur, and Roosevelt ultimately ordered Budget Director Douglas to reconsider the matter. Douglas decided to make $224,905,181 available for military activities in the new fiscal year. Thus nearly half of the suggested cut was retrieved.[45]

The Air Corps' share of the reduction was substantial. Of the $26,321,185 first appropriated, the administration approved the spending of just $11,599,673. Foulois complained to MacArthur that this would require the Air Corps to abandon all aircraft procurement during fiscal year 1934. Sympathetic, the Chief of Staff said he hoped the administration might revert to the original appropriations as the year progressed. He told Foulois to plan on no more than $20.6 million for fiscal year 1935, but asked him to try to work into his fiscal 1935 proposal at least one-fourth of the airplanes originally appropriated for fiscal 1934.[46]

Although Congress did not let Roosevelt furlough officers, it empowered him to restrict flight pay. Foulois worked hard to defeat this measure, and for a time it looked as if he might succeed. He appeared before the Senate Appropriations Committee on May 15 and his testimony, supported by members of the House Military and Naval Affairs Committees, helped convince the Senate to render the bill far less drastic. Foulois, like MacArthur, was no admirer of the New Deal and was very unhappy with Roosevelt's policy of starving the military. He was willing to accept the Senate's version of the flight pay bill for it simply limited the amount an aviator could receive to that currently paid a lieutenant colonel and did not grant the President power to cut it further. However, the Senate's version failed to stand. As it emerged from the conference committee, the bill authorized the President to do away with all or part of military flight pay. Once granted the power, Roosevelt did not use it in a dictatorial manner. Instead, he asked the War and Navy Departments to recommend what should be trimmed. Both departments supported their flyers, reporting that they opposed flight pay reductions for officers below the rank of colonel (Navy captain). If it became necessary to modify the present system, they suggested it be changed only to limit senior officers to the flight pay of a lieutenant colonel (Navy commander). The administration accepted and acted on these recommendations.[47] The flight pay dispute, begun with the presidential request in April, and dragged out until September by the administration's indecisiveness, fomented a great deal of friction but saved little money.

The Roosevelt administration did make large savings in other areas of military pay. In March, while Director of the Budget Douglas was formulating plans to reduce War Department expenditures for military activities, the President requested Congress to repeal the existing one-month unpaid furlough program and institute in its stead a reduction in pay for all government workers, military and civilian, of up to fifteen percent. The administration's bill gave the President authority to determine the exact amount of the cut and power to modify it from time to time, based on fluctuations in the cost of living. The measure restored paid annual leave, but it kept the pay increase freeze and applied cuts of up to 15 percent to all officers and enlisted men regardless of income. Congress dutifully passed the measure in mid-March. The President at once decreed a full 15-percent reduction, saying the cost of living had dropped 21.7 percent since 1928. The War Department was displeased with the measure, but its protests went unheeded.[48]

Foulois and his OCAC staff were unwilling to sit idly by while the Roosevelt administration destroyed the Air Corps' financial base. Between March and August they argued before Congress and within the War Department that aviation resources needed to be greatly expanded rather than reduced. The OCAC's independent spirit and lack of concern for the plight of the rest of the Army annoyed the General Staff, as did the air arm's apparent disregard for economic reality. On March 11—before the new President had set the scope of his military cost-cutting, but after Congress had already slashed the War Department's 1934 budget—Foulois reminded the Deputy Chief of Staff that the five-year expansion program was a long way from completion. Four days later the OCAC sent the General Staff a proposal for an adequate coastal air defense program which called for tremendous expansion of the Army air fleet.[49]

In late March, Foulois took his plea for expansion before the House Military Affairs Committee. On March 29, Chairman McSwain introduced a bill for a single Department of National Defense (H.R. 4318), as well as a second measure designed to raise Air Corps officer strength to the 1,650 authorized by the 1926 Air Corps Act.[50] This second bill required the War Department to award Regular commissions to 100 training center graduates a year until the air arm reached full strength. It likewise prescribed keeping an average of 550 Reserve officer aviators on extended active duty, each eligible for up to three years continuous service. At McSwain's request, Foulois testified before the committee on March 31, but the air chief did not address his comments specifically to the two bills. While endorsing unification of Army and Navy tactical aviation into a

## FUNDS, AIRCRAFT, AND PERSONNEL, 1931-1933

single service and calling for a congressional study of the entire national defense organization, he spent much of his time explaining to the lawmakers how distant the Air Corps was from achieving the aircraft and officer strength levels established by the 1926 act. Foulois juggled definitions during his presentation, asserting that the Air Corps Act provided for 1,800 serviceable *combat* aircraft. This let him discount trainers and transports in his calculations and claim that the Army air arm was currently over 800 planes short of the 1926 authorization. The Air Corps chief stretched the truth with his redefinition, but it served his purpose by dramatizing the Air Corps' needs. Lt. Col. James E. Chaney of the OCAC appeared before the committee one week later and testified that the Air Corps needed a total of 4,181 aircraft in order to adequately protect the United States and her overseas possessions.[51]

The General Staff did not like the Air Corps' solo campaign, especially in a time of shrinking military finances. Any gains won by the air arm were very likely to come at the expense of the rest of the Army. The War Plans Division checked over the figures Chaney used to justify his request for 4,181 planes, and Kilbourne's staff came to the conclusion the Air Corps would need only 2,950 aircraft on the first day of mobilization. The War Plans Division realized its figure was nearly twice as large as the current aircraft inventory, but could see no way to provide the additional planes without causing further deterioration in the other combat arms. By mid-April, when word of the deep defense spending cuts being planned by the Roosevelt administration began to circulate, Kilbourne wrote Westover that he would be unable to support the continuation of the Air Corps' five-year expansion program, even at its present rate, due to the dire financial needs of other important segments of the Army defense system.[52] The War Plans Division chief was not consciously seeking to hinder Air Corps development. He was only attempting to look after the needs of the entire Army during a period of deep financial strain. He and other senior officers of the General Staff opposed further aviation expansion at the time, not because they failed to appreciate the importance of the air weapon, but because the Air Corps was in relatively good shape compared with the other combatant arms.

On Kilbourne's recommendation, the War Department contested McSwain's proposal to build up Air Corps officer strength. Westover, filling in during still another of Foulois' absences, wrote to MacArthur requesting Army backing for the bill. However, Kilbourne's arguments were more persuasive. He pointed out that if one hundred Regular commissions were given to training center graduates each year, there would not be enough vacancies left to commission all of the annual graduates of West Point.[53] The Army leaders, West Pointers almost to a man, shied away from sacrificing one hundred men trained in the ways of the professional

117

soldier at their alma mater for a like number of citizen-soldiers who could pilot airplanes. Besides, at a point when Roosevelt and Douglas were thinking of removing more than three thousand officers from active duty, the General Staff was in no mood to counsel the additional loss of one hundred ground officers a year to the air arm. Accordingly, professional prejudice and the demands of the other branches dictated the War Department's stance on the McSwain bill. Like McSwain's other measures to succor the Air Corps, the bill never got to the House floor.

With the passage of the National Industrial Recovery Act on May 23, 1933, the Office of the Chief of the Air Corps gained a new opportunity to press for more aircraft. This new law directed the spending of $3.3 billion on public works. Showing Roosevelt's ambivalence toward defense spending, it allowed funds for Army housing, aircraft, mechanization, and motorization. Even before the act passed, the General Staff set to work on a request for Public Works Administrtion (PWA) funds. At a May 18 conference, the Deputy Chief of Staff, General Drum, ordered the War Plans Division to furnish him a program for aircraft construction by May 25. Drum wanted the division's proposal to be based on filling out the Air Corps to the eighteen hundred serviceable planes stipulated in the five-year expansion program. Only pursuit, observation, attack, and bombardment aircraft were to be part of the purchase plan.

Somehow misinterpreting Drum's instructions, Kilbourne asked the Chief of the Air Corps for recommendations based upon a total of 2,600 planes. He also asked Foulois to lend him an OCAC officer to help plan the rush program. The air chief responded on May 22 with a plan for buying 1,351 aircraft at a total estimated cost of around $68 million. The OCAC paper broke this amount into five priorities, with the first priority consisting of 628 planes costing $20.1 million. Foulois explained that by spending $68 million in PWA funds, plus gaining the release of the procurement funds previously impounded by the Roosevelt administration, the Air Corps could beef up its inventory to 2,600 aircraft. The total cost would run $79.5 million.[54]

Honoring Kilbourne's request for the loan of an Air Corps officer, the OCAC sent Maj. Leslie MacDill to assist the War Plans Division in its planning efforts. However, MacDill did not function as an official representative of the Chief of the Air Corps, a fact Foulois wanted made clear to Kilbourne when the War Plans Division set up modifying the OCAC proposal. Kilbourne directed MacDill and other staff officers working on the project to eliminate 164 of the 259 coastal patrol planes Foulois had requested and to make a few other modifications. As submitted to the Deputy Chief of Staff, priority one remained essentially unchanged from what the OCAC had proposed, containing the same numbers and types of aircraft at a slightly higher cost. The War Plans Division listed total cost

## FUNDS, AIRCRAFT, AND PERSONNEL, 1931-1933

of the five priority categories at $54.1 million in PWA money plus the $11.5 million of 1934 Air Corps procurement funds that had been withheld by the administration.[55]

This proposal was obsolete when it reached Drum, for on May 27 the Deputy Chief of Staff sent out a notice reiterating his May 18 instructions limiting the aircraft buildup to a total of 1,800 serviceable machines. Kilbourne thereupon instructed his division planners and MacDill to draft an alternate plan consistent with Drum's wishes. MacDill said the Air Corps would need 1,236 new planes to bring the force up to the new limiting figure, and that number became the basis for the alternate program. The planners split their proposal into two priorities. The first provided funds, which would be used in addition to the $11.5 million in withheld Air Corps procurement money, to build the air arm to 1,800 serviceable aircraft by the end of fiscal year 1934; the second furnished money to replace aircraft lost through attrition in 1935. Forwarded to Drum on May 31, the program called for purchasing 415 planes with the withheld 1934 appropriation, 258 planes at a cost of $13 million under priority one, and 563 at $17 million under priority two. While not providing the numbers of the various types of aircraft the Air Corps wanted, the program would have finally completed the five-year expansion so far as quantity of planes was concerned. The War Plans Division listed the total cost, including the $11.5 million in fiscal 1934 funds, at slightly less than $42 million.[56]

Before the aircraft program was approved, Kilbourne received word from Col. Donald H. Sawyer, director of the Federal Employment Stabilization Board and supervisor of public works requests, that he should put in for no more than $10 million for aircraft. At about the same time, General Drum advised Kilbourne to omit primary training, photo, and transport planes from the program. Kilbourne complied with both men's instructions, hurriedly paring the price of the proposal to a total of $39.5 million and redesigning the two priorities. In its final form the plan no longer mentioned the release of the impounded Air Corps appropriation and, under priority one, asked for about $10 million to buy 291 planes. Calling for a total of 1,034 new planes (a reduction of 202 since the first revision), the program now contemplated raising the Air Corps' inventory to a total of 1,800 planes, but with no allowance for the 12 1/2 percent of the fleet undergoing depot overhaul. However, attaining the 1,800 figure was dependent upon PWA funding of both priorities. In light of Sawyer's comments to Kilbourne, this was unlikely. Dern approved the aircraft program on June 3 and forwarded it in early July to PWA authorities, together with the other War Department requests.[57]

Foulois was very angry about the way the War Department had ignored the Air Corps in preparing the PWA aircraft program. The OCAC's

119

only direct input had been the May 22 recommendation. The final product of the War Plans Division bore little resemblance to that plan. Bitter over not being consulted, the air chief and his staff were also disturbed to see the scope of the program steadily shrink, first from 2,600 aircraft to 1,800 serviceable ones, then down to a total of 1,800. The reduction in funds was just as appalling—from $79.5 million requested by the OCAC to $39.5 million approved by the Secretary of War. To make matters worse, the War Department included only $10 million for planes in its top request priority, less than Congress had originally appropriated for Air Corps procurement for 1934. Foulois wrote to Kilbourne on June 8 objecting to the program as approved by the Secretary of War. He asserted that he had had no say in its formulation—a radical change from established practices—and consequently would not accept responsibility for it. The air chief used the opportunity again to urge construction of a force of over 4,000 planes. Kilbourne and the rest of the General Staff were unreceptive to this plea.[58]

Notwithstanding, the OCAC refused to be stilled in its quest for a greatly enlarged aircraft inventory. It continued to hound the War Department throughout June and July, but ultimately to no avail. On June 23, Westover wrote Kilbourne claiming the Air Corps needed 4,241 planes. On July 13, the Assistant Chief of the Air Corps submitted the OCAC's Air Plan for the Defense of the United States. This proposal, responding to MacArthur's request for OCAC air employment plans in connection with the RED, RED-ORANGE, and GREEN war plans, was in essence little more than a justification for expanding the air fleet to 4,459 planes. The General Staff quite properly judged these requests to be unreasonable because of the scarcity of funds and the absence of an external air threat.[59]

The Air Corps' lack of PWA funding was due chiefly to the Roosevelt administration's attitude. Certainly the War Department was not eager to have the air arm receive more than what it considered a reasonable share of the War Department's PWA allotment, but it was willing to approve a program raising aircraft strength to 1,800. Pressure from the administration impelled the General Staff to put only $10 million in the category of most important Army requests. However, Secretary of War Dern made it clear in his July 5 letter to the administrator of the PWA that the Air Corps required the full $39.5 million to finish the long-overdue aircraft phase of its five-year expansion program. Since the intent of the National Industrial Recovery Act was to put people back to work, Dern tried to justify the spending in terms of its usefulness as a job creator in the depressed aircraft industry. Both McSwain and the airplane manufacturers also pressed the administration to provide a large PWA allocation for military aircraft procurement. The President, however, re-

## FUNDS, AIRCRAFT, AND PERSONNEL, 1931-1933

mained unconvinced. In October, after a three-month delay, he approved only $15 million for military aviation, to be split equally between the Army and the Navy. The Army as a whole did not fare much better, receiving $95.4 million of the total $383.7 million requested. Besides the $7.5 million for aircraft, the War Department gave the Air Corps an additional $19.4 million of its allocation for airfield and housing construction. The General Staff ordered the OCAC to use the $7.5 million in aircraft PWA money to buy thirty attack planes, forty-six bombers, and twenty-four pursuit planes. For the second time within six months the OCAC had been largely ignored in aircraft procurement decisionmaking.[60]

In August, while the War Department's PWA request was still pending, MacArthur directed the formation of the Drum Board to review and revise the OCAC's July 13 Air Plan for the Defense of the United States. The board found the Air Corps needed 2,320 planes to meet "worst case" air defense needs, and it acknowledged that the air arm was presently far short of this amount. Yet the board cautioned in its October report: "Congress should make no appropriations toward carrying out the recommendations contained herein for any increase of the Air Corps over 1,800 serviceable planes which will be at the expense of the other arms and branches of the military establishment."[61]

Board members believed 1,800 serviceable planes, while providing no cushion, would allow an adequate air defense. They concluded that the ground Army, rather than the air arm, was the weak link in the defense system. The board therefore refused to recommend Air Corps expansion beyond the levels set in the five-year program until some of the needs of the other combat arms were met.[62]

The Drum Board also concluded that the Air Corps had a faulty distribution of aircraft types. It called for a large increase in combat and long-range reconnaissance planes at the expense of observation and training aircraft. The board prepared a chart comparing the number of various types on hand with the ideal composition in a force of 1,800 planes, as follows:

| Type of Aircraft | Numbers currently on hand* | Recommended number + |
|---|---|---|
| Bomber | 156 | 319 |
| Pursuit | 361 | 410 |
| Attack | 92 | 237 |
| Observation (corps & army) | 503 | 270 |
| Observation (long-range) | 0 | 140 |
| Photo | 13 | 12 |
| Cargo ` | 74 | 105 |
| Training | 486 | 307 |
| TOTAL | 1,685 | 1,800 |

*Includes planes undergoing depot overhaul (12 1/3 percent of the force)
+Does not include allowance for overhaul.[63]

## FOULOIS AND THE U.S. ARMY AIR CORPS

The change in distribution recommended by the Drum Board was wholly in line with Air Corps thinking, except for the types of aircraft to be sacrificed. Foulois and his OCAC staff desired to build up combat aviation and procure long-range reconnaissance planes, but they preferred to do so almost exclusively at the cost of observation, photo, and transport aircraft. The OCAC claimed trainers were essential to pilot production, and, as such, were just as valuable as combat aircraft.[64]

The Drum Board also recommended extensive changes in the number of tactical squadrons organized under the five-year expansion program. Foulois may have influenced this decision, for the air arm favored all of the proposed changes. Reflecting Air Corps interest in bombers and long-range reconnaissance planes, the board report recommended fifteen bombardment, three long-range light bombardment/reconnaissance, and three long-range amphibian squadrons in place of the twelve bombardment squadrons currently in existence. Attack squadrons would climb from the present four to ten, and corps and army observation squadrons would drop from thirteen to eight (the National Guard would still contain nineteen more). In accord with the Air Corps' changing attitudes on the significance of pursuit planes, the board recommended eliminating nine of the existing twenty-one squadrons. Foulois favored making the proposed changes as soon as possible. However, the events of early 1934 interceded and prevented additional War Department and OCAC action on the matter for several months.[65]

The condition of the Air Corps as 1933 came to a close was not much different from what it had been a year earlier. Officer strength still hovered in the vicinity of 1,300 and the enlisted force stood at 14,000. There were 277 Reserve officers on extended active duty (instead of the 550 authorized), and fewer than 180 flying cadets were undergoing pilot training. As of September 30, the Air Corps had 1,409 serviceable planes on hand and 190 more undergoing depot overhaul. With but $7.5 million in PWA funds plus $3 million finally released from impounded fiscal year 1934 procurement funds in late November, the OCAC could strive only to match aircraft attrition. Thus, in all categories, the air arm continued to fall short of the goals set in the five-year program.[66]

By late January 1934, the War Department faced a set of circumstances which forced it to sponsor a bill to give the Air Corps more planes. The Navy was campaigning for legislation to exceed the 1,000-plane limit set in 1936, thus threatening to upset the established 18:10 ratio in Army and Navy air strength. At the same time, Congressman McSwain was again threatening to introduce measures to give the Air Corps independence from the General Staff. Both the OCAC and the War Department were unhappy over the Navy's action. After the House Naval Affairs Committee reported out a bill in January providing for an 1,184 air-

## FUNDS, AIRCRAFT, AND PERSONNEL, 1931-1933

craft increase, the General Staff felt compelled to act. If passed, this measure would cause a severe imbalance in subsequent appropriations for Army and Navy aviation. MacArthur decided that the War Department should at once prepare legislative proposals to counter the Navy's move. This, as well as McSwain's request for a War Department bill to supply the necessary forces for the GHQ Air Force, sparked the hurried drafting and introduction of H.R. 7553 on February 1. The General Staff hoped the measure would placate McSwain and at the same time maintain the current Army-Navy aircraft balance.[67]

The necessity for new aircraft procurement legislation put MacArthur and his staff in a difficult position. They wanted very much to maintain the existing 18:10 plane ratio and thereby satisfy the Air Corps as well as keep the Navy from gaining an excessive share of military aviation funds. On the other hand, they did not want to build up the Air Corps beyond 1,800 serviceable planes at the cost of further starvation to the rest of the Army. It appears the War Department sponsored H.R. 7553 primarily as a tool to deter the passage of the naval air expansion legislation, for the Army could not afford to accentuate aircraft procurement. And, as Kilbourne pointed out, if both the Army's and Navy's bills passed, the United States would have far more military aircraft than it needed.[68]

H.R. 7553 was vague as to the number of aircraft the Army actually desired. MacArthur did not want to be tied to a specific commitment, and the bill fulfilled his wishes.[69] It called for enough aircraft to equip the GHQ Air Force, provide for overseas defenses and a 25-percent reserve, and carry out other Air Corps functions. But it also said, "That of the increase authorized herein not to exceed two thousand serviceable airplanes, including equipment and accessories, shall be maintained at any time during the next five years."[70] This set an upper, rather than lower, limit on expansion and would allow the War Department to build its air arm up to whatever level it desired. Further, the limiting phrase was so vaguely written it could be interpreted as an increase of 2,000 serviceable planes over the existing 1,800 limit or as a ceiling of 2,000 serviceable aircraft, only 200 above existing limits. Apparently the War Department intended it as an increase of 2,000, but Foulois was highly suspicious. Neither was he pleased with the words "not to exceed."[71]

Prior to sending the bill to Capitol Hill, the War Department began to consider a new five-year Air Corps expansion program. Motivated by the Navy's efforts, McSwain's attitude toward Air Corps autonomy, and the findings of the Drum Board, MacArthur told the House Military Affairs Committee the Army would soon undertake such a program. The January 27 War Department publicity release on the Drum Board report said the board had found 1,800 planes to be insufficient for national defense. As a result, the Army was working on a new five-year airplane

123

## FOULOIS AND THE U.S. ARMY AIR CORPS

program to increase the strength of the Air Corps beyond the present statutory limit. However, the General Staff had undertaken no detailed planning by the time H.R. 7553 was introduced. When the War Department began to hurriedly construct a program between January 31 and February 2, it was not with the intention of increasing the aircraft inventory to approximately 3,800 as implied in the bill. Instead, the General Staff wanted a three-priority program: (1) completion of the original five-year aircraft expansion plan; (2) provision for the necessary planes to meet the Drum Board's figure of 2,320; and (3) additional planes that might be required above 2,320, not to exceed a total inventory of 3,104. General Callan, Assistant Chief of Staff, G-4, met with Foulois and other OCAC officers on January 31 and briefed them on these priorities. Callan asked Foulois to furnish the Air Corps' recommendations for the program no later than February 2. In complying, the air chief ignored the General Staff's priority ceiling and recommended creation of a 4,422-plane force.[72]

Events soon overtook War Department planning for the new expansion. McSwain introduced his bill for Air Corps autonomy on February 2, and a week later the President ordered the Army air arm to carry the mail. At about the same time, Congress began probing the War Department's procurement activities. Following the Secretary of War's decision in March to investigate shortcomings in the Air Corps' air mail operations, the General Staff deferred any further action on plans affecting the air arm. On March 27 the Vinson-Trammell Act became law, authorizing the Navy to built up its aviation to 1,910 planes by 1941.[73] The spring of 1934 was not so kind to the Air Corps.

# CHAPTER V

# THE AIR MAIL FIASCO

On Friday morning, February 9, 1934, General Foulois received a telephone call. Second Assistant Postmaster General Harllee Branch asked the air chief to come to the Post Office Building to confer with him on undisclosed aviation matters. Unknown to Foulois, the topic of the hastily called meeting would be the Air Corps' ability to take over domestic air mail service.[1]

Earlier that morning President Roosevelt decided that government mail contracts with commercial airlines had been arranged through collusion and fraud and therefore warranted immediate cancellation. The President's decision was based upon evidence uncovered by a special Senate investigation headed by Senator Hugo L. Black and a companion probe undertaken by the Post Office Department. Both Black and Solicitor of the Post Office Department, Karl A. Crowley, found that President Hoover's Postmaster General, Walter F. Brown, had used his contracting authority between 1929 and 1933 to create virtual monopolies in air mail operations. By altering the competitive bidding procedure he had prevented smaller airlines from gaining contracts and allowed three large holding companies to dominate the lucrative air mail trade. On February 6, Crowley sent his findings to Postmaster General James A. Farley and two days later both men met with Roosevelt and recommended that the apparently illegal contracts be voided. Before taking action, the President sent Crowley's brief to Attorney General Homer S. Cummings for comment. Returning the material the next morning, Cummings advised Roosevelt that the accumulated evidence seemed sufficient to justify cancellation.[2]

Farley recommended Roosevelt announce the contracts would be canceled effective June 1. This would allow the Post Office Department time to advertise for bids and issue new contracts, thus preventing any interruption in service. The President, however, would have none of this. He believed the contracts must be immediately thrown out, for to do otherwise would let the wrongdoers continue to profit from their misdeeds. He apparently made up his mind on the morning of the ninth to give the air mail job to the Air Corps, at least temporarily. Harold L. Ickes, Secretary of the Interior, spoke with the President that day, writing in his diary that Roosevelt even contemplated making the new arrangement permanent. The Commander in Chief seemed supremely confident the Army air arm was up to the task, but before announcing his decision he wanted the Chief of the Air Corps' opinion.[3]

When Foulois arrived at Branch's office shortly before noon, the Second Assistant Postmaster General explained that the purpose of the conference was to discuss the Air Corps' ability to take over domestic air mail operations in the event existing contracts were annulled. Foulois had read in the newspapers that the administration was considering canceling the contracts, so he was not caught completely off guard by Branch's statement. He phoned at once for two of his assistants to join him, and together with Branch and Department of Commerce representatives they reviewed current air mail routes and schedules. Branch explained that the Post Office Department was most concerned over the routes linking the twelve Federal Reserve Bank cities and desired to have the Air Corps initially service these in the event of cancellation.[4]

After almost three hours of study, Foulois announced that he could see "no reason why the Army could not handle the mails and handle them satisfactorily."[5] When Branch asked how long it would take the Air Corps to prepare for such a task, Foulois, not thinking he meant from that moment, answered rather casually: "I think we could be ready in about a week or ten days."[6] Thereupon the air chief and his two assistants returned to his office and spent a short time going over some of the details of the potential takeover. Then, and only then, did Foulois think to inform his superiors of his day's activities.[7]

Before the Chief of the Air Corps could contact General MacArthur or his deputy, General Drum, Roosevelt promulgated an executive order canceling the contracts and directing the Army Air Corps to take over domestic air mail operations effective February 19, for the duration of the "emergency."[8] While Foulois was conferring with Branch, the President and his cabinet were also discussing the air mail situation. The postal officials must have immediately informed Roosevelt of Foulois' comments just after the air chief had ended the meeting with the Second Assistant Postmaster General. Still in the cabinet meeting, Roosevelt turned to Secretary of War Dern and asked his opinion of the Air Corps' capability. With Dern's expression of confidence and Foulois' assurances that the Air Corps could do the job, Roosevelt did not trouble himself to

## THE AIR MAIL FIASCO

consult MacArthur and the General Staff. He immediately issued the cancellation order.[9]

The Chief of Staff was not disturbed by the President's decision. Nor did he appear angry at Foulois for not keeping him properly informed. As yet unaware of the executive order, the air chief arrived at the War Department around four in the afternoon and went to see the Deputy Chief of Staff. Foulois had finished telling Drum about his conference with Branch when MacArthur came into the room and informed them an Associated Press correspondent had just apprised him of the President's decision. Foulois then explained his earlier activities to MacArthur. Thereupon the Chief of Staff called in the members of the press, who were waiting for a War Department statement.[10] Although surprised by events, MacArthur seemed genuinely pleased with the new task just given the Army when he told the reporters:

[T]he Army has the resources and the will do make the mails go through ... The Army has the planes, the pilots and the wherewithal to do what the president has in mind.

I have the utmost confidence the Army will handle the air mail in a magnificent way. I believe it will illustrate again the Army's ability to adjust itself to requirements—as demonstrated by its organization of the CCC. This will be another example of the Army's preparedness to take every call in its stride.[11]

The Chief of Staff, interested in keeping the Army before the public eye in the hope that publicity might further his efforts to secure increased funding, closed the impromptu news conference with the overambitious assertion: "We will start flying the mail a week from today and there will be no delay, no difficulty, and no interruptions."[12] Foulois in effect had offered the Air Corps' services and pledged that the Army air arm could do the job. MacArthur was now supporting that position based upon the circumstances in which he found himself and his air chief's assurances.

Foulois had not given the matter much thought before making his commitment to Branch. He had utmost confidence in the Air Corps, and he welcomed the chance to test its operational readiness and gain national exposure for his poorly funded force. He believed the air arm had to be prepared to respond immediately in event of war and should therefore be rigorously tested in peacetime. Here was the perfect opportunity. Moreover, publicity from the operation might better the chances of receiving needed funds to equip the combat air arm. Foulois deemed flying the mail no more hazardous than normal peacetime training.[13] He did not take the time to discover that air mail operations demanded proficiency in skills his aviators did not possess—night and instrument flying. This oversight would prove very costly.

Foulois' rather hasty reply to Branch was motivated in part by his desire to execute the orders of his Commander in Chief. Everyone present at the conference realized Roosevelt wanted an immediate yes, and Foulois interpreted the President's wishes as a call for action. Deputy Chief of Staff Drum told Senate Appropriations Committee members in March 1934, that he, too, regarded the question put to the air chief on February 9 as a presidential request for action and thus would have felt compelled to respond as had Foulois. Writing years later, General Arnold expressed a similar view.[14] However, another factor also influenced Foulois' quick reply: organizational pride and a desire to further the interests of the Air Corps.

With the announcement of the President's executive order, the OCAC stepped up its planning of the operation. After talking with MacArthur and Drum, Foulois instructed his staff to make an overnight study of the mission as well as the personnel and equipment needed for initial operations. Saturday, February 10, was a busy day for Foulois and his assistants. Early in the day, he formed an emergency headquarters for mail activities within his office and divided the nation into three air mail zones. He designated General Westover to command the overall effort from the Washington headquarters, and selected Maj. Byron Q. Jones, Lt. Col. Horace M. Hickam, and Lt. Col. Henry H. Arnold to run the eastern, central, and western zones respectively. Foulois next asked for and received authority from the Secretary of War to control all Air Corps facilities, personnel, and equipment for the duration of the emergency, and to delegate that authority to the zone commanders as necessary. Later, the air chief met with officials from the Post Office Department and the Department of Commerce to decide which routes would go into service on February 19. Westover and his small staff then set up a rough distribution of resources between the three zones.[15]

On the eleventh, Westover sent radiograms to the zone commanders detailing the routes they would be responsible for and giving them operational control over all Air Corps resources within their zones. The Assistant Chief told the commanders about the equipment they would be furnished from outside their zones, and directed them to organize their manpower and aircraft to carry out their route assignments. Since the operation appeared to be a short-term undertaking, Foulois and Westover decided to rely on tactical units and detachments assigned to train the Reserve components for the necessary personnel and aircraft. This ensured the uninterrupted function of the pilot training center and other Air Corps schools, but also it kept many of the more highly skilled pilots out of the first phases of the operation. The tactical squadrons and Reserve training detachments yielded a pool of 481 Regular officers, 242 extended active duty Reserve officers, and 6,912 enlisted men. Jones, Hickam, and Arnold hurried to organize these resources, creating headquarters in New York, Chicago, and Salt Lake City.[16]

## THE AIR MAIL FIASCO

Foulois set to work arranging funding for the operation. The General Staff advised him at the outset that no War Department funds would be available. He and the Army's Chief of Finance met with Harllee Branch on Saturday, February 10, and the Second Assistant Postmaster General agreed to make $800,000 available as soon as possible. He and Foulois agreed that this money should be used to cover all maintenance, operation, and storage costs for aircraft involved in the air mail project as well as salaries for additional employees, per diem of $5 per day for military personnel away from home stations on mail duty, and rental costs for office space and airfield facilities. The air chief wrote the Postmaster General on Monday asking that a check for $800,000 be sent at once to the War Department. The same day the OCAC finance officer and the Army Chief of Finance prepared a draft executive order authorizing the transfer. With the approval of the Post Office Department, it was delivered to the White House on February 13. However, the Comptroller General of the Post Office Department announced the same day the discovery that fiscal 1934 appropriations legislation for his department had been so worded as to disallow the proposed transfer of funds. New legislation would be needed, and, at the request of the Post Office Department, the War Department submitted the necessary bill to the House Post Office Committee on February 14. Until Congress could act, the Air Corps—and the War Department—would have to find another way to finance the operation. And it soon became apparent that the lawmakers would be in no hurry.[17]

Facing the prospect of congressional delay, Foulois suggested the War Department seek the release of a portion of the Air Corps' impounded fiscal 1934 funds. The air chief met with Drum on February 17 and requested $800,000 to cover the first weeks of air mail activity. The War Department approved only $562,500, and the Bureau of the Budget reduced that figure by almost half, approving on February 19 the release of $300,000 to finance the operation until March 1. Foulois protested this skimpy allocation but to no avail. When Congress had still not acted on the fund transfer bill by early March, the Bureau of the Budget, at War Department urging, released an additional $1,431,655 to defray expenses through the end of the month. This, however, like the $300,000 before it, did not include per diem funds for the officers and men on air mail duty away from their home stations. Congress finally approved the bill on March 27, and the Post Office Department promptly transferred $2,541,500 to reimburse the War Department for costs to date and to fund operations for the month of April. In accordance with the new law, this amount included payment of past and future per diem. Thereafter, the Post Office Department transferred funds monthly to cover air mail expenses until mail service was again turned over to the

129

private contractors.[18]

When Foulois assured Branch that the Air Corps would have no trouble handling the air mail operation, he was assuming all the airports and airways facilities through the United States used by the commercial operators would be made available to the Army air arm. The Department of Commerce placed its weather and airway personnel under Air Corps control for the duration, but the Post Office Department initially opposed the air arm's use of airfields either owned or operated by companies that had just had their contracts canceled. As the Air Corps worked to ready itself for mail duty, the significance of this restriction became quite apparent.[19] Foulois pointed out the difficulty in a February 13 letter to Branch:

> [A] number of essential stations are either owned and operated exclusively by one of the companies or concerns whose air mail contract has been annulled by the Government, or are municipal fields at which all necessary facilities for successful operation of the air mail are owned or controlled by such air line companies. . . . At many stations the office space and the Postal, Communications and Weather Service facilities are provided under existing contract by an air mail company whose air mail contract was annulled.[20]

He asked Branch to seek Postmaster General Farley's permission for the Air Corps to negotiate directly with the companies in question for the use of these important fields and facilities.[21] Farley honored the request, since strict compliance with the Post Office Department restriction would have required the air arm to find suitable alternate landing fields which contained adequate supplies of fuel as well as hangar and office space, and establish its own terminal weather forecasting and reporting system. (The Department of Commerce weather system did not, in itself, provide coverage for all of the airfields involved in the air mail route structure.) This did not solve all of the Air Corps' basing problems, for many of the companies were, for obvious reasons, less than eager to assist the Army flyers. However, in time, the Air Corps was able to establish workable, though not completely adequate, arrangements all across the country.[22]

Between February 11 and 19 the officers and men assigned to air mail duty expended a tremendous effort preparing the force to carry out its new task. Plans called for initially assuming fourteen of the airline's twenty-six mail routes, using 200 pilots, 340 enlisted men, and 122 planes; Foulois would later add 50 more men and 26 additional planes. This small air fleet needed to fly 41,000 miles daily to fulfill the modified schedule. Air officers optimistically believed this would just be the beginning and planned to expand the operation to encompass more of the original routes by the end of February. Pilots and ground crews worked around the clock configuring the planes for air mail duty and deploying them to their predetermined staging bases. Westover and Foulois wanted all aircraft and personnel in place by February 16 to give flyers time to familiarize them-

## THE AIR MAIL FIASCO

selves with their assigned routes. This was not always possible due to the time-consuming tasks of removing weapons, extra seats, and other detachable equipment; and installing flight instruments, radios, and mail containers.[23]

Army planes as a rule carried no "blind flying" instruments or radios, but these items were absolutely a must for air mail operations. Military aviators prized lightness and maneuverability in their planes and thought primarily in terms of combat operations in good weather during daylight hours, when the enemy could be located. Flying the mail was essentially a nighttime job requiring pilots to navigate across great stretches of the country in all kinds of weather with only the aid of the Department of Commerce's airway system. This government system included lights and radio beacons spaced along the route structure. Foulois, who had experimented with new flying instruments in his own plane over the past few years, ordered each mail plane equipped with a directional gyro, artificial horizon, and at least a radio receiver. This equipment would enable the Army pilots to fly at night and in bad weather, navigate by radio beacons, and monitor weather broadcasts.[24]

Complying with Foulois' directive was no easy job. As of February 10 the Air Corps owned only 274 directional gyros and 460 artificial horizons, and very few of these were mounted in airplanes. Instead, the poorly funded Air Corps was saving most of them for use in future aircraft. Further, at the start of operations the air arm had but 172 radio transmitter-receivers, too few to equip all of the mail planes for two-way communications. These, like the Air Corps' receiver sets, were neither channelized for easy tuning (as were the airlines' radios) nor usable at ranges greater than thirty miles. The commercial carriers' high-powered equipment had nearly three times this range. Mechanics installed the instruments and radios as rapidly as they became available, frequently having to first remove them from aircraft not assigned to air mail duty. In their haste, the airmen often mounted the instruments in difficult-to-see locations, using bailing wire to hold them in place. Lacking an adequate supply of vibration-dampening instrument panels, the mechanics installed the sensitive directional gyros and artificial horizons on the solid panels already in the planes where engine and aircraft vibrations soon rendered them inoperative. Sometimes working around the clock, the ground crews had the air mail fleet equipped in compliance with Foulois' directive and the planes on their way to assigned operating locations prior to the February 19 start of actual mail carrying.[25]

The disposition of Air Corps instrument-flying equipment prior to February 10 provides a clear indication of the air arm's existing state of weather flying proficiency. The Air Corps had worked for years developing instrument flying and landing equipment and procedures, but due to fund shortages and the stress on daytime fair-weather combat operations, the OCAC gave instrument and night training relatively low priorities. All student pilots received some instrument practice at the training center, but little recurring training took place in the tactical units. In 1933 the OCAC published its first instrument-training directive, requiring all tactical pilots with low instrument-flying proficiency to take a ten-hour refresher course. The order provided, however, that those who had already taken a similar course or could demonstrate basic instrument skills, needed to accomplish only five hours of instrument flying per year. In October 1933, the Air Corps opened navigation schools at Langley Field, Virginia, and Rockwell Field, California, to afford additional instrument training for a limited number of tactical pilots to better prepare them for the coast defense mission. One class of thirty-eight officers had completed the six-week program, and another, of forty-one aviators, was in the middle of the course when the President ordered the Air Corps to assume responsibility for the air mail.

Still, weather-flying proficiency stayed extremely low. An incident in September 1933 underscored the Air Corps' inability to operate under nighttime adverse weather conditions. Late in the evening, a squadron of seven planes from Mitchel Field, New York, encountered fog over New York City. The crews of three of the planes bailed out, and of the four remaining aircraft only two successfully located and landed at their home field. The other two ran low on fuel and made emergency landings at civilian airports.[26] Lt. Col. Frank M. Andrews, writing about his own unit, touched on the problems common to most tactical organizations in February 1934:

> This station has not a single directional gyro or artificial horizon, and never has had one as far as I know. . . . All recent graduates of the Training Center are given, as you know, a certain amount of training in instrument flying, but have not been able to keep up that training effectively with this Group.[27]

On February 16, three days before the Army planes began transporting the mail, Foulois claimed in testimony before the House Post Office Committee:

> We have assigned to this work the most experienced pilots in the Army Air Corps. We have had a great deal of experience in flying at night, and in flying in fogs and bad weather, in blind flying, and in flying under all other conditions. We have not had the actual experience of flying over these scheduled routes, but we feel that after three or four days of preliminary flying over these routes we shall experience no difficulty in maintaining the regular schedules.[28]

In making this statement, Foulois was either misinformed or was seeking to mislead the congressmen. Because the OCAC, in organizing the operation had turned to tactical squadrons in which there were many one-year Reserve officers, 140 of the approximately 262 pilots actually flying

## THE AIR MAIL FIASCO

the mail had less than two years flying experience. The great majority of these officers were second lieutenants; just 1 aviator above the rank of first lieutenant flew any of the mail missions. Only 31 of the pilots had more than fifty hours of night flying, and merely 2 had that much instrument time. The vast majority, 214, had less than twenty-five hours of weather or simulated weather time to their credit.[29] It was possible that due to inadequate recordkeeping Foulois did not know how poorly trained his pilots actually were for the task at hand. Apparently, the Department of Commerce had some inkling of the gravity of the problem, for The Washington Post reported on February 14:

> Lack of pilot experience and instruments for night and blind flying, both highly important factors in handling the air mail, may prevent the Army from ever successfully carrying the mail to the point of efficiency maintained by commercial airlines, Department of Commerce officials said today.[30]

Besides lacking instrument training and equipment, the Air Corps did not possess the kinds of aircraft suitable for hauling heavy mail loads. Pursuit, observation, and attack planes, used extensively because of their availability and speed, could carry only between one hundred and five hundred pounds of mail rather than the eighteen hundred to two thousand pounds regularly transported by the commercial aircraft. Mail bags had to be crammed into vacant rear cockpits or stuffed around the pilot in single-seat planes. The added weight frequently shifted the plane's center of gravity enough to make takeoff and landing quite difficult. Further, most of the aircraft used by the Air Corps were open-cockpit models, which were extremely uncomfortable on long-distance, cold-weather flights.[31]

The air arm was thus entering the air mail business with extensive disadvantages. In training and equipment for the job as well as familiarity with air mail routes, the Army pilots were decidedly inferior to their airline counterparts. Commercial pilots averaged nine hundred flying hours per year to the military aviators' two hundred. Flying the same routes over and over, they were familiar with the terrain, weather conditions, and available navigation aids. Air Corps pilots were fortunate if they were able to scan their routes more than once before beginning actual mail flights. Commercial mail planes were tailored for all-weather day and night operations and provided for the comfort of the normal two-pilot crew. More important, commercial aviators trained extensively in instrument flying while Army pilots did not.[32] As Maj. Clarence L. Tinker, commander of the 17th Pursuit Group, explained:

> There are no radio beams or lights to show [the military aviator] where the enemy is. . . . The Army pilot is used to flying in formation, to bombing, to fighting ships in the air, to pursuit and attack. . . . If the weather is bad, there is no object to sending an army plane up. In war we must see our objective.[33]

## FOULOIS AND U.S. ARMY AIR CORPS

Shortly after Roosevelt issued his executive order, a number of individuals raised their voices to protest the unfairness of the move and question the Air Corps ability to fill in for the commercial lines. On February 11, Charles A. Lindbergh, who worked as a technical adviser for one of the affected companies, released the text of his telegram to the President in which he attacked the cancellation order. This was the first sign of a growing public debate on an issue that would soon take on bitter partisan political overtones.[34] The following day Will Rogers, humorist and experienced air traveler wrote:

> [Y]ou are going to lose some fine boys in these army flyers, who are marvelously trained in their line, but not in night cross-country flying in rain and snow.
>
> I trust an air line, for I know that the pilot has flown that course hundreds of times. He knows it in the dark. Neither could the mail pilots do the Army flyers' stunts and their close formation flying.
>
> I do wish they would prosecute the crooks, but. . . . I hope they don't stop every industry where they find crookedness at the top.[35]

Eddie Rickenbacker, World War I ace and airline executive, joined those

Will Rogers (right), humorist and aviation enthusiast, shown with Sec. of War Patrick J. Hurley, expressed his apprehension over the Army's flying the mail.

## THE AIR MAIL FIASCO

who questioned the military aviators' abilities to carry the mail, telling a New York Times reporter on February 21: "Either they are going to pile up ships all across the continent or they are not going to fly the mail on schedule."[36]

When the press gave wide coverage to such adverse comments, Air Corps officers knew they were on the spot, yet they reacted with enthusiasm to the challenge. Major Jones, commander of the eastern zone, told reporters on February 15: "We'll carry the mail—don't worry about that—unless an elephant drops on us. If it does, we'll cut it up and ship it out as mail." Colonel Arnold, western zone commander, responded to the question of whether Air Corps aviators could match the skills of the airline pilots by saying of the commercial pilots: "Look them over. You'll find that 90 percent of them were trained in the Army."[37] The Army aviators may have known they did not have the same equipment and instrument flying experience as their airline counterparts, but they refused publicly to admit they might have difficulty with the task at hand.

Foulois did not want his pilots, in their enthusiasm to impress the public with the Air Corps' abilities, to take unnecessary chances. On February 11 he sent an order to the three zone commanders requiring pilots to continue complying with peacetime flying regulations. This prohibited the aviators from taking off at night if the ceiling was less than 1,000 feet and required at least a 500-foot ceiling for daytime operations. Foulois followed this up with a radiogram on February 16:

> In conduct of air-mail operations, zone commanders will govern their operations with a view to safeguarding lives and property at all times, even at the sacrifice of mail service. Before clearing any scheduled trip, careful consideration will be given to experience of personnel, suitability of aircraft, night-flying equipment, and blind-flying equipment. Steps will be taken to inculcate all personnel engaged in air-mail operations with the above principle.[38]

Shortly after this message was dispatched, the Washington mail operations headquarters got word that three Army pilots on air mail training flights in the western zone had just died in crashes. Two of the victims, Lts. Jean D. Grenier and Edwin D. White, Jr., had been flying a night familiarization mission over the Cheyenne-to-Salt Lake City run when their A-12 attack plane crashed in a snowstorm. The other fatality, Lt. James Y. Eastman, was flying a training mission on the Salt Lake City-to-Seattle route when his twin-engine B-7 bomber ran into fog and crashed during an attempted emergency night landing at Jerome, Idaho. None of the three officers had been rated pilots for more than a year. Bad weather and low instrument-flying proficiency were the primary causes of both accidents. Eddie Rickenbacker immediately labeled the deaths "legalized murder" and predicted even higher casualties if the Army went ahead with its plans to carry the mail.[39]

135

Foulois' reaction was to furnish his zone commanders more explicit safety instructions on February 17:

> If weather conditions are uncertain, instruct your pilots they must stay on the ground, even if this interrupts the mail schedules for several days. The safety of pilots, mail, and planes is of more importance than keeping of air mail schedules. Drill these instructions into your pilots daily until they thoroughly understand the safety-first policy of the Air Corps.[40]

In addition the Chief of the Air Corps ordered instrument-training planes and instructors sent to the three zone headquarters to give pilots more instruction before the February 19 start of mail service. This training continued during three and a half months of the operation, with instructors from the now defunct schools at Langley and Rockwell Fields moving about the route structure so that all Air Corps mail pilots could benefit. This, however, proved too little and too late to rapidly improve the force's instrument flying proficiency. Because of poorly installed instruments and their inexperience in bad-weather flying, most Air Corps pilots were loath to trust their fate to the gauges, preferring instead to go low in an attempt to stay in visual flying conditions.[41]

On February 18, Jones, Hickam, and Arnold confirmed that all aircraft and personnel were in place and ready to begin operations. Even so, some planes were still being fitted with radios and instruments. Logistics, maintenance, and basing arrangements at numerous operating locations continued in a makeshift state for weeks afterward.[42] The officer organizing the unit at Port Columbus Airport in Columbus, Ohio, complained that a few days prior to the February 19 start date he had pilots, planes, and maintenance men, "but no tools, supplies, or office equipment."[43] At Byrd Field in Richmond, Virginia, the sole available office space was in the ladies restroom at the Richmond Air Transport and Sales Company hangar. Furnished with a small coal stove and two folding field desks, the room became headquarters for three weeks. Through the rest of February, various locations suffered a shortage of shops, hangars, office space, supplies, and tools. At places like Cheyenne and Chicago, planes had to be left out in the open and worked on in subzero weather.[44]

As the Air Corps stood by to take over the air mail service, Eddie Rickenbacker and other airline officials prepared a parting publicity stunt to show the public how efficient the commercial carriers were. Rushing a new Douglas DC-2 aircraft to completion, the World War I ace and two other pilots took off from California on the evening of February 18. Carrying a partial load of mail, the plane raced eastward, passing up some of the regular air mail stops and staying barely ahead of a winter storm. It arrived at Newark, New Jersey, at ten in the morning on the nineteenth, setting a new cross-country record of thirteen hours, four minutes, and

## THE AIR MAIL FIASCO

twenty seconds. The trip appeared even more dramatic because immediately after Rickenbacker arrived bad weather moved into the Newark area, grounding the Air Corps before it could get its first official mail flight airborne from the eastern zone headquarters.[45]

Thus, very poor flying weather heralded the shift of the air mail system from commercial to Air Corps control. The storm that hit the east spread snow, rain, and dense fog from Ohio to Virginia and north into New England. Nine inches of snow fell on New York City and fifteen inches blanketed the Boston area. In the Rocky Mountains states, storms and icy gales prevailed throughout the day, making air travel impossible. Bitter temperatures, high winds, and snowstorms gripped the area east of the Mississippi River for the rest of the month.[46] First it was equipment, training, and organizational problems—now it was bad weather.

During the first day of mail operations, eager Air Corps pilots remained grounded along the eastern seaboard, from Virginia north. Several flyers on the west coast took off, but severe weather halted them at the Rockies. Airmen in the southern states transported mail on schedule, and by evening Air Corps pilots were attempting to fly most of the routes west of New York. One military aviator even managed to struggle through to Newark with his load of mail from Cleveland. Flying in the open cockpit of an old B-6 bomber in subzero temperatures, he coaxed his charge down safely despite a dead battery and a frosted instrument panel. This typified the spirited approach of the aviators to their new job. Many scheduled runs were canceled and others flown late the first day, but this was not due to lack of tenacity on the part of the Army flyers.[47]

Persistent bad weather and a tremendous increase in mail volume compounded problems during the first week of Air Corps operations. The government had introduced special cancellation stamps to show that the air mail was carried by the air arm. As a result, philatelists deluged post offices throughout the country with huge bundles of letters. This completely upset the original sortie rate plans based on the daily volume of mail carried by the commercial airlines. To handle the huge increase, the Air Corps added planes to supplement those originally scheduled. This, in turn, exposed many more pilots to the dangers and discomfort of flying in open cockpits during biting cold and stormy weather.[48]

Air mail activities went more smoothly for the next two days, but on February 22 disaster struck. Possibly due to faulty navigation equipment, Lt. Durward O. Lowry strayed nearly fifty miles off course and died in a nighttime, fog-shrouded crash not far from Deshler, Ohio. Another Air Corps pilot was killed that same evening while on a training flight in Texas. His engine quit at two hundred feet, and he and the plane plummeted to the ground. A third flyer, Lt. Harold L. Dietz, narrowly escaped death as he lost his way in fog and darkness on the mail run from Newark to Richmond. Afraid to rely on his flight instruments, he fractured his skull in a crash-landing attempt. Before the night was over, one more pilot became lost in a snowstorm near Fremont, Ohio, and bailed out. A fifth flyer made an emergency landing at Woodland, Pennsylvania. On February 23 an Air Corps officer en route from New York to Langley Field, Virginia, to pick up an air mail plane, drowned when the plane in which he was a passenger made a forced landing in the Atlantic. By now the Army air arm had suffered six fatalities and about a dozen crackups since beginning familiarization flights a little more than a week before. The press increased the Air Corps' embarrassment by giving the various accidents front-page coverage.[49]

Foulois knew this disastrous situation stemmed from the continued poor flying weather and pilot overeagerness to accomplish the mission. He ordered his zone commanders on February 24 to tighten up safety restrictions:

> Pilots will not be on flight duty more than a scheduled 8 hours in any 24 hour period and shall have 24 consecutive hours' relief from all duty in each four-day period. Only pilots of more than 2 years' service in the Air Corps will be used on air mail operations involving night flying unless weather conditions all along the route to be flown are excellent. After take-off on a night air mail run no pilot will proceed on his flight unless the flight instruments are working satisfactorily and he has received proper reception on his radio. Pilots on night runs will not commence flights into unfavorable weather conditions nor will they continue flights into unfavorable weather conditions.[50]

The directive also forbade flights into known icing conditions and required station control officers to inspect all aircraft before releasing them for flight.

The air mail issue had partisan political overtones from the outset. Republicans were unhappy over Roosevelt's summary cancellation of airline contracts and disliked the inference that Hoover's Postmaster General Brown had been engaged in illegal activity. The disasters of February 22 and 23 handed them an ideal opportunity to attack the President's action on the basis of the Air Corps' apparent inability to safely fly the mail. Debating the air mail funding bill on February 24, Republican congressmen repeated Rickenbacker's earlier charge of "legalized murder." They stoutly condemned the administration's decision to risk the Army flyers' lives in what they termed inadequate and unsafe equipment. McSwain and a few other Democrats defended the Air Corps, but most members of the majority party were quite worried over the national reaction to the six deaths.[51]

The President also was disturbed by the turn of events. With the Republicans making political hay and the press focusing on Air Corps' accidents, he was on the spot. While publicly proclaiming continued confidence in the air arm, he secretly ordered plans drawn for the swift re-

## THE AIR MAIL FIASCO

turn of the air mail to the private operators. Apparently Roosevelt had not considered the possibility of numerous deaths resulting from his February 9 decision. He was dissatisfied with the Air Corps' performance but at present could do nothing without seeming to admit he had been wrong in his original decision. He blamed Foulois for misleading him about the Air Corps' capabilities, and willingly honored the air chief's request to give a radio address aimed at blunting public criticism.[52]

Foulois spoke over a Columbia Broadcasting System radio hookup on the evening of February 27. He described the zone organization, route structure, and instrument equipment used in the operation, and then talked at length about flying safety. He cautioned his listeners that "the flying of military aircraft designed primarily for combat purposes is recognized as inherently hazardous under all conditions, and accidents increase when flying activities are carried out on a large scale." He pointed out that only one of the six fatalities had taken place on a scheduled air mail run and explained that "no attempt has been made by the Air Corps to maintain a high percentage of mail schedules regardless of the hazards involved." Foulois reviewed his previous safety instructions "to give assurance to the families of the pilots who are flying the air mail as well as the public at large, that every possible precaution has been and is being taken in the interest of their welfare." Striking back at the critics, he asked the public "to discount as untrue, unfair and unfounded recent accusations and headline seeking phrases which have reflected not only against the efficiency of the Air Corps personnel, but also against the present administration." He branded these derogatory statements as partisan propaganda and praised the abilities and dedication of his flyers. According to Foulois, the pilots were quickly learning their new duties, and mail operations would soon be running smoothly and efficiently. He warned, however, "that no matter how experienced a pilot may be, or how efficient and modern his aircraft equipment, frequent accidents will still occur."[53]

Despite the public criticism and poor living and working conditions in the field, the morale of Air Corps personnel remained high. Faced with the nagging problems of expanded mail volume and bad weather, the pilots and ground crewmen worked hard to prove the Air Corps could do the job. The flyers complained of the poor instrumentation in their planes, but this did not deter them from taking excessive chances (in violation of Foulois' safety instructions) to get the mail through. Overworked, constantly short of necessary supplies, and operating aircraft ill-suited for the task at hand, the officers and men of the air arm were out to prove the critics wrong.[54] The stresses endured by the pilots were tremendous. As one flyer explained:

> Picture an Army aviator flying at night in subzero weather. He is flying in the open with a biting wind passing him at 100 miles an hour or more. He is

> trying to follow a map. He is trying to navigate his ship. He is trying to operate his radio. He must hang on to the controls. His necessarily heavy clothing and gloves hamper him. He is sitting in a tiny cockpit with hardly enough room to move.[55]

Ground crewmen also suffered as they struggled to repair planes in the open in cold and stormy weather, often without the proper tools or clothing.[56]

Living conditions for the officers and men based at civilian flying fields were frequently deplorable. Forced to subsist on the local economy, they received no extra compensation for the added expenses. Foulois won acceptance of $5 per diem from postal officials on February 10, but the money was unavailable until Congress acted. Meanwhile, officers and men went into debt to buy food and lodging. Enlisted men were particularly hard pressed since some of them made as little as $21 a month. The financial strain compelled many men to sleep in hangars and prepare their own meals as best they could. Officers oftentimes helped out with loans, but on company grade pay there was usually little left over after the officers covered their own expenses. By the third week in March, numerous troops were destitute. Foulois was not insensitive to their plight. In response to congressional footdragging, he sought other ways to secure per diem funds, but the War Department refused to cooperate. When the money finally became available on March 27, the air chief and the General Staff worked in concert to speed backpayments to the men in the field.[57]

Through the last week of February and the first week of March, the Air Corps canceled more air mail sorties than it flew, but no more pilots lost their lives. With only minor crashes to report, the operations ceased being front-page news. Foulois as well as others thought the worst was at last over. The air chief optimistically reported to a House Military Affairs Subcommittee on March 1 that the Air Corps was as well fitted as the commercial airlines to handle the mail.[58]

In a move to bolster the experience level of the air mail force, the War Department at Foulois' request called fourteen former commercial air mail pilots to active duty on March 8. These men were Reserve officers who had lost their jobs due to the cancellation order and had volunteered for active duty. The Air Corps assigned them to their former routes. By mid-April the air arm was employing fifty such officers plus five civilian airline pilots who had been out of work. At the time Roosevelt canceled the contracts Air Corps officials had considered calling up these specially qualified Reserve officers, but neither the OCAC nor the Reserve officer airline pilots were anxious to go forward with the scheme.

On February 12, Foulois had begun a series of conferences with rep-

THE AIR MAIL FIASCO

resentatives of the Airline Pilots Association, but he did not seem sincerely interested in instantly calling the commercial pilots to active duty. He appreciated the administration's desire to offer jobs to men put out of work by the President's action, but a February 23 note from his office to the General Staff explained the Air Corps already had sufficient pilots to fly the mail. Perhaps pressure from Roosevelt after the accidents of February 22-23 and the growing number of volunteers for active duty caused Foulois to modify his position. He sent word to his zone commanders on February 26 to start accepting applications at once. Colonel Hickam, central zone commander, used the Reserve volunteers but objected to the program. He pointed out to Foulois on March 15 that these individuals were not as safe as Air Corps pilots because they were used to flying in aircraft with the best instruments and radio equipment. The air chief never thought the Air Corps needed the help of seasoned air mail pilots. Many years later, he rather cynically mentioned that the eleventh aviator to lose his life in the operation was one of these experienced individuals.[59]

Foulois' February 27 speech and the Air Corps' better safety record failed to placate congressional critics. Republicans continued to fault the air arm for not affording consistent and accident-free service. House Speaker Henry T. Rainey, a Democrat, joined this chorus on February 28, stating that Air Corps pilots were poorly trained. Other Democrats increasingly insisted the air arm's shortcomings were due to deficient equipment. McSwain still defended the military flyers but sponsored a resolution calling for the investigation of all War Department procurement, especially that of the Air Corps. The House approved the resolution on March 2. Intent on shifting the blame for the current debacle from the party and the administration, the Democrats probably hoped and believed the investigation would reveal the culprits in the military establishment who were responsible for the Air Corps' inadequacies. Passage of McSwain's resolution in no way slowed the efforts of such Republican stalwarts as Representatives Hamilton Fish, Jr., and Edith N. Rogers, who continued to press for the immediate return of the air mail service to the commercial airlines.[60]

On March 9 the Air Corps furnished its detractors a host of new ammunition. Headlines in *The Washington Post* told the story: "CRASHES KILL FOUR MORE FLYERS IN ARMY MAIL SERVICE, TOTAL 10."[61] The first fatal accident happened in the early morning hours near Cleveland, when a veteran pilot flew into the ground during a snowstorm. A few hours later, a crewmember on a B-6 bomber died when both of the plane's engines failed and it smashed into the woods adjoining the airport at Daytona Beach, Florida. That night two more flyers died when their aircraft crashed on takeoff from Cheyenne, Wyoming. Three other Air Corps planes crash-landed in bad weather on the night of

# FOULOIS AND THE U.S. ARMY AIR CORPS

Above: Foulois explains air routes covered during Air Corps' operation of air mail in 1934; left: radio station at Las Vegas, Nev., used during air mail runs.

In the air mail venture, various Air Corps planes delivered their sacks from coast to coast. On the adjacent page (top), a pilot is about to embark in a Boeing P-12 Pursuit plane from March Field, Calif.; center: an air mail truck transfers his dispatches to a Thomas Morse O-19 at Denver, Colorado; bottom: though not used regularly, even the Curtiss B-2 Condors were pressed into service.

# THE AIR MAIL FIASCO

March 9-10, one each in Iowa, South Carolina, and Pennsylvania. The air mail operation was again page one news.[62]

Republican members of Congress used the new rash of disasters to apply more pressure on the President for rapid reversion to commercial air mail operations. Representative Rogers asked for immediate consideration of a resolution to halt Air Corps mail activity. In the Senate the Republican whip from Ohio, Simeon D. Fess, renewed the charges of "legalized murder." Even some Democrats were hedging toward open advocacy of a change in the present arrangement. Roosevelt was on the spot. In light of the spate of recent accidents, he could no longer ignore the rising tide of hostile public opinion and partisan political rhetoric.[63]

On March 10 the President acted. He ordered MacArthur and Foulois to report to the White House in midmorning and administered the two officers a severe tongue lashing. Blaming Army officials for the adverse publicity the administration was receiving from the numerous accidents, Roosevelt asked Foulois when the air mail killing was going to stop. The air chief responded: "Only when airplanes stop flying, Mr. President."[64] Roosevelt showed MacArthur and Foulois a letter to Secretary of War Dern he had just dictated and then dismissed them with a curt wave of the hand.[65]

The letter set forth the President's new policy, and his office promptly released it to the press. In it Roosevelt acknowledged that persistent bad weather blanketing the country had been a major contributing factor in the ten air mail fatalities, but he went on to say:

> [T]he continuation of the deaths in the Army Air Corps must stop.
>
> We all know that flying under the best of conditions is a definite hazard, but the ratio of accidents has been far too high during the past three weeks.
>
> Will you therefore please issue immediate orders to the Army Air Corps stopping all carrying of air mail, except on such routes, under such weather conditions and under such equipment and personnel conditions as will insure, as far as the utmost care can provide, against constant recurrence of fatal accidents.
>
> This exception includes of course full authority to change or modify schedules.[66]

The letter also explained that the present emergency would end as soon as the necessary legislation could be enacted and new contracts obtained, and Roosevelt let it be known that he was immediately seeking such legislation. Clearly the Commander in Chief wanted to expedite the return of the air mail to commercial airline hands.[67]

Roosevelt blamed Foulois and the Air Corps for his predicament and desired to direct the public's attention to the air arm's responsibility. He claimed his decision to cancel the contracts and turn the air mail over to the Army was based upon assurances given him that the Air Corps could handle the job. When this turned out not to be true, he felt justified in

## THE AIR MAIL FIASCO

diverting blame for the entire situation.[68] An article written by Elliott Roosevelt for *The Washington Herald* may have revealed his father's attitude toward the Air Corps: "The Army failed to 'deliver the goods' as a commercial aviation organization because the Army Air Service was undertrained, poorly equipped, and hamstrung with obsolete regulations and ancient red tape."[69] The President took steps to see that he was not held accountable for the flying equipment deficiencies. On March 10 he asked Congress for an additional $10 million to purchase Army aircraft and related aviation facilities. This action, coupled with his letter directing the Air Corps to attempt only what military aviation leaders determined were safe flying operations, insulated the White House against charges of responsibility in the event of future disasters in the air mail operation.[70]

Foulois tried to comply immediately with instructions contained in the President's March 10 letter to Dern. His radiogram to zone commanders the same day advised them of Roosevelt's stand and authorized them to cancel any and all flights deemed necessary to prevent additional accidents. On March 11 he ordered a temporary halt to all air mail flights until safer schedules could be worked out. Previous to this, he and his staff began a series of meetings with Post Office Department officials to organize the new schedules. Postal officials did not want to eliminate all of the night missions, because without them there would be no special advantage to shipping mail by air. Late on March 11, Foulois and Post Office representatives worked out a compromise which the air chief believed could be put immediately into effect. It reduced the daily total miles flown from 40,821 to 25,628 and cut the number of night trips (each of which might involve more than one airplane) from 38 to 14.[71]

The Chief of the Air Corps wrote MacArthur the next morning requesting approval of the new schedule. He assured the Chief of Staff that Air Corps planes and flying equipment were adequate, and added that he had recently ordered zone commanders "to use only their most experienced pilots on all trips." Foulois asserted that the revised schedule eliminated the most dangerous routes but cautioned that "operations during the next two or three months, even over the routes which are planned to be kept in operation, will still be hazardous, and I expect some casualties to occur." The air chief realized he could not guarantee there would be no deaths, although this was what Roosevelt appeared to want. Trying to mitigate the conflicting presidential demands that the Air Corps efficiently conduct air mail operations while avoiding additional fatalities, Foulois advised the Chief of Staff:

> If the proposed new schedule of operations continues to result in casualties which are considered to be excessive, all remaining night trips should be cancelled. If this latter action does not produce the desired result, then it is believed that the operation of the air mail by the Army Air Corps should be

suspended, at least in the northern section of the country, until weather conditions have cleared.[72]

Secretary of War Dern approved the revised schedule on the twelfth, but with such qualifications as to still hold Foulois responsible for any further fatalities. The secretary sanctioned renewed operations if

> the specific instructions of the President [in his March 10 letter] . . . are observed in every particular and detail. The commanders of the air mail zones and local commanders of personnel on air mail duty will be directed by you to use every precaution and care to insure that no flights are ordered or authorized which will in any way depart from the specific instructions contained in the President's directive.[73]

Dern had conveniently covered himself and the administration. The choice was now up to Foulois.

The Chief of the Air Corps resolved to leave operations suspended for the time being and took off on an inspection trip to satisfy himself that the air mail operation could be safely resumed. Before departing Washington he instructed his zone commanders to ensure that airplanes used on future mail sorties were up to the job, and that only the most experienced pilots flew future night and hazardous day runs. He insisted they recheck all planes for proper installation of radios and instruments and make sure planes used for night operations contained operable two-way radios. Foulois then traveled to Mitchel Field, New York, and met with Jones. From there he journeyed to Chicago to confer with Hickam and Arnold. The zone commanders used the standdown period to comply with the chief's instructions. Enlisted men busily reworked the original hasty installation of flight instruments, this time mounting the delicate apparatus on vibration-proof instrument panels. They also overhauled a number of the planes and inspected radio equipment. As a result the Air Corps eventually resumed flying the mail with equipment in better shape than at the inception of operations in February.[74]

Foulois was not happy with either the heavy public criticism heaped on the Army air arm or the Roosevelt administration's apparent buck-passing. Reflecting the feelings of his officers and men, he was humiliated by what he considered to be the unjustified lack of confidence expressed in the President's March 10 letter. He realized pilot overeagerness had contributed to the air arm's recent poor safety record, but he believed the chief cause was unusually severe weather. While visiting Mitchel Field, Foulois told members of the press that air mail fatalities had not been excessive. He cited casualty statistics for the past two fiscal years to prove his point: For fiscal years 1932 and 1933 the Air Corps had experienced fifty and forty-six flying accident deaths, while thus far in fiscal year 1934 there had been thirty-nine.[75] With permission from the War Department and the President, he released a statement to counteract the public's criti-

## THE AIR MAIL FIASCO

cism of the Air Corps' safety record. The air chief avowed that the air mail operation was a useful combat readiness test and asserted: "The hazards involved in carrying the Air Mail are not, in my belief, as great as those normally encountered annually by the Army combat pilots in the normal performance of their duties."[76] However, only a reduced casualty rate, rather than words, would silence those who assailed the Air Corps.

On March 17, Foulois notified Dern from Chicago that the Air Corps would be ready to resume operations on March 19.[77] Westover relayed the secretary's response: "You are authorized to use your own judgment in the matter, bearing in mind the general limitations of the President's instructions and those issued by the Secretary of War supplemental thereto."[78] When Roosevelt received word of this he wrote Dern on March 18: "I cannot approve this order unless you have received definite assurances from responsible officers of the Air Corps that the mail can be carried with the highest degree of safety." The President would condone no more deaths. The day before, the Air Corps had recorded its eleventh fatality when a recently activated Reserve officer crashed while on a training flight near Cheyenne. Thus the President wrote Dern:

> I wish you would issue new instructions to the Air Corps. In these instructions, please make it clear that, if on any route, on any day, the conditions of weather, personnel or equipment are such as to give rise to any doubt as to the safety of moving the mails, that is from the standpoint of human safety, the mails shall not and will not be carried.[79]

The secretary issued the directive on the evening of March 18. Foulois responded with assurances that the Air Corps could carry the mail safely. The administration therefore gave the Army air arm the green light for its planned resumption on March 19.[80] However, the President and the Secretary of War had so ordered the ground rules that the Chief of the Air Corps alone would bear direct responsibility for any new disasters.

With improved weather and equipment as well as increased pilot experience and instrument-flying proficiency, the Air Corps did a much better job of moving the mail after the March 10-18 interlude. Operating just nine routes, or about forty percent of the mileage formerly flown by the commercial air mail carriers, the Army air arm's mission cancellation rate decreased to almost half of what it had been prior to the standdown. More important, the Air Corps suffered only one additional air mail fatality between March 19 and the end of operations on June 1. Having no deaths to report, the press lost interest. Aside from the improved weather, the continuing program of instrument training and the strictly enforced safety regulations were perhaps the key reasons for this remarkable improvement.[81]

In late March the administration took steps to speed the return of the air mail to the commercial airlines. Since Congress had not as yet passed legislation establishing a new contracting system, Roosevelt and postal officials decided to let temporary three-month contracts. The government advertised for bids on March 28. The commercial lines began taking over the routes on May 7 and by May 17 were operating all but one. The Air Corps turned over the remaining run on June 1.[82]

On May 7, the last day the Air Corps was responsible for the coast-to-coast route, the Army flyers replied in kind to Rickenbacker's February 18-19 show of commercial aviation superiority. Using new Martin B-10 bombers, military aviators flew from San Francisco to Newark in approximately fourteen hours. This was not far short of Rickenbacker's record time, yet the total distance had been 279 miles farther and the Army flyers had made three additional stops for mail. The headlines announcing the May 7 accomplishment afforded the much-maligned officers and men of the Air Corps a moral victory.[83]

Foulois may have harbored mixed feelings as the operation came to a close and flying units reverted once more to control of the corps area commanders. The Air Corps had endured twelve deaths and sixty-six crashes while carrying the mail and had been the target of widespread public and congressional criticism. The air chief's charges had done well after the temporary halt in March, but the overall record was not good. The Air Corps' completion rate for scheduled sorties was 65.83 percent, well below that of the commercial lines for the same months in previous years. The operating costs of seventy cents per mile flown almost doubled the thirty-eight cents per mile of commercial air mail operations.[84]

Yet there had been benefits. Pilots gained valuable training and instrument-flying experience which they otherwise would have been denied. As Foulois had emphasized, the operation proved to be an excellent test of the Air Corps' abilities and shortcomings. Hence, it helped air leaders prepare the force for the future. Further, it kindled public and government interest in the problems of the Army air arm and led to the creation of two investigative bodies—the Baker Board and the Federal Aviation Commission—whose work enhanced the organization and capabilities of military aviation.[85] Foulois overstated the positive results of the air mail experience when he wrote in 1954 that "the President and Congress were, in my opinion, forced to reverse the then existing policy of starving National Military Preparedness, and divert some of the taxpayers' dollars to National Military Air Preparedness."[86] Congress appropriated no more for the Air Corps for fiscal 1935 than it had the year before, but the mail operation did serve to point out to the administration that an adequately prepared air arm required proper financial support. Roosevelt did not again impound Air Corps funds, and from fiscal year 1936 on he requested and received sizable increases in Army air arm appropriations.[87]

## THE AIR MAIL FIASCO

The air mail experience vividly highlighted the deficiencies of the Air Corps' instrument and night-training programs and produced a dramatic change in the air arm's attitude toward the need for all-weather capabilities. In March 1934, the OCAC organized a course to teach pilots how to make landings without outside visual references, using those trained in the program as instrument-landing instructors at their home stations. The Air Corps also purchased trucks and equipment for portable instrument-landing ground stations, and bought more advanced aircraft flight instruments. Starting in 1934, all new planes purchased came with two-way radios. Before the air mail operation ended, Foulois ordered an additional thirty-five hours of instruction in instrument flying and navigation for each training center student. In April 1935, he issued a directive greatly increasing the amount of instrument and night training required for all Air Corps pilots. In the past, flyers in tactical units needed to log no more than five to ten hours of instrument flying per year and fifteen to twenty hours of night time. Now, they had to annually fly twenty to thirty hours on the gauges and accrue twenty-five to forty-two hours in the air at night.[88]

Foulois erred when he told Branch on February 9 that the Air Corps could operate the nation's air mail system, for the air arm lacked the necessary night and instrument-flying equipment and training. Yet these deficiencies would have been less critical had the weather not turned and remained extremely bad.[89] Postmaster General Farley seemed undisturbed by the Air Corps' mediocre showing. In a May 18 speech he discounted much of the politically motivated criticism directed at the flyers and praised Foulois and his men for their determination and willingness to handle the difficult air mail task in the face of "perhaps the worst and most prolonged season of bad flying weather ever encountered in this country." Farley went on to point out "that not a single pound of mail was lost during the time the Army has flown the mail."[90] Unfortunately for the Air Corps, this was its only outstanding achievement in the operation.

# CHAPTER VI

# PROCUREMENT TROUBLES, 1933-1935

Hauling the air mail was not the Air Corps' only problem. In February 1934, Congress became keenly interested in apparent materiel shortcomings and began to pry into the methods used to secure new planes. All purchases under the $7.5 million PWA grant were held in abeyance as the investigation progressed. Subcommittee Number 3 of the House Military Affairs Committee conducted the probe. Its interim report in May condemned the manner in which the Air Corps attempted to expend the $7.5 million and accused Foulois of violating those sections of the 1926 Air Corps Act dealing with quantity aircraft purchases. The subcommittee contended that competitive bidding must be used to pick contractors.[1]

Army aviators disagreed. They claimed negotiated agreements between selected airplane manufacturers and the War Department were not only legal but better served Air Corps' interests. Military aviators were not completely opposed to competition, but they desired to buy the best planes available at the most reasonable cost. Since passage of the 1926 act they had exclusively used negotiated contracts for the purchase of all aircraft. This method enabled them to keep fairly close control of prices, and to select the manufacturer they thought best able to produce the types of equipment needed. Given the rapid strides in aviation technology, Air Corps officials deemed it wise to rely on proven firms that had the capacity to produce advanced designs and turn them into functioning aircraft. Assistant Secretary of War for Air Davison used the analogy of a man choosing a surgeon for an operation. He argued that the prospective patient would not call for competitive bids from all interested practicing physicians, but would go instead to the doctor he knew could best do the job. Foulois judged competitive bidding acceptable for standardized items such as boots and potatoes, but not for airplanes, which were in a contin-

PROCUREMENT TROUBLES, 1933-1935

uing state of development.[2]

Air Corps officers presumed the competitive system would compel them to award contracts to less credible companies that could come up with aircraft designs but not turn them into functioning planes having the designated performance characteristics. They further felt open competition would lead to steeper costs. Airplane manufacturers were aware the Air Corps stressed quality over price and also knew what competing companies were capable of producing. Consequently, Army air arm officials feared a firm that knew it had the best plane available would submit it at a higher bid price than could be arrived at under the negotiated system. Likewise, a purely negotiated system afforded air officers latitude in distributing contracts in such a way as to keep a number of qualified companies in business during an economic decline, thus building a more acceptable base for expanded production in time of national emergency.[3]

The Air Corps Act of 1926 covered aircraft procurement in detail, but it was not completely clear on the competitive bidding versus negotiated contract issue. Portions of Section 10 of the act specifically required aircraft design competitions, but they also authorized the Secretary of War to negotiate with the owner of the winning design for quantity production. Or if a satisfactory price could not be agreed upon, the secretary could allow other manufacturers to bid on the production contract. Section 10(k) sanctioned the purchase of experimental aircraft and designs without competition. Section 10(q) permitted the Air Corps to buy aircraft existing at the time of the act, as well as subsequent modifications of those planes, through direct negotiations with the producers. Section 10(t) authorized the secretary to award competitive contracts to "the lowest responsible bidder that can satisfactorily perform the work or service required to the best advantage of the Government," and specified that such contracts were not reviewable except by the President and federal courts.[4]

Air Corps officials realized it was Congress' intent in writing the 1926 law to foster competitive procurement. However, they continually ignored this intent and selectively applied only those provisions allowing negotiated contracts. After The Judge Advocate General ruled in 1927 that the Air Corps did not have to buy its planes and equipment solely under the provisions of the act, officers turned to AR 5-240 when necessary to justify negotiated quantity purchases. Based on an older law, this directive permitted procurement without competition if the articles desired were made by only one manufacturer and had no counterpart available from other sources. This allowed the Air Corps to bypass the undesirable procedure of awarding production contracts to the winners of paper design competitions. Instead, it could buy experimental planes under Section 10(k) of the Air Corps Act, test them, and then negotiate the purchase of numbers of the most successful model calling them test aircraft under 10(k), or make a large quantity buy using AR 5-240.

The Judge Advocate General rendered an opinion in 1929 that quantity procurement under Section 10(k) was illegal unless based upon competitive bidding. Even so, he went on approving all contracts based on 10(k) and AR 5-240 down to 1934. Each purchase agreement also received the approval of the Secretary of War and the responsible assistant secretary.[5] An Air Corps staff officer warned Foulois in May 1932 after reviewing the Air Corps' methods of buying planes: "I feel we are skating on exceedingly thin ice insofar as procurement of aircraft in quantity by negotiation is concerned."[6] But the air chief believed in the correctness and legality of the existing system and could see no reason to alter a method that had War Department sanction.[7]

Over the years since 1926, the Army air arm developed an intricate procurement procedure. Purchase action got under way with a directive issued by the Chief of the Air Corps. Based on the recommendations of various Air Corps agencies, the directive told the Materiel Division in general terms what the chief desired to buy. The division would next make studies on the proposed plane, draw up a document containing the aircraft's desired characteristics, and send copies to selected companies judged competent to produce the aircraft. Other firms could request this information from the division. Manufacturers were given a specified length of time to submit drawings and specifications for the proposed aircraft, after which the Materiel Division would select the one or two that seemed most likely to meet or exceed the performance characteristics. With the approval of the Chief of the Air Corps, the Materiel Division would offer the winning company or companies a cooperative contract to build an experimental model of the plane. In these joint ventures, the Air Corps supplied certain equipment and material while the manufacturer shouldered all other development costs. During the experimental aircraft's construction, the air arm would negotiate its purchase from the producer, contingent upon the plane's passing the Materiel Division's flight test.

Other companies were always free to build and submit their own test planes. However, they would have to cover the full cost of the venture and had no guarantee the Air Corps would buy them. If funds were available after the successful completion of the flight-test phase, the Chief of the Air Corps would convene the Procurement Planning Board, composed of the OCAC and Materiel Division officers, to consider quantity production and the numbers to be bought. With the approval of the Assistant Secretary of War, Materiel Division officials would negotiate a quantity aircraft purchase, obligating funds previously allocated for this purpose in the Air Corps budget.[8]

Air Corps officials believed companies developing acceptable aircraft

PROCUREMENT TROUBLES, 1933-1935

should be rewarded, but they also wanted to curb excessive profits. As corporate earnings from military aviation business soared in the late 1920s, the Air Corps started to closely monitor the manufacturers' finances. Beginning around 1930, Materiel Division officers audited producers' costs for the experimental models before negotiating the quantity purchase contracts. Using the manufacturer's expenses for the test plane as a gauge, they would usually add an estimated fifteen percent profit. This became the Air Corps offering price per plane. At the end of the production run the Materiel Division would again scrutinize the manufacturer's books. Excessive profits as well as losses incurred through no fault of the contractor, were noted and applied in adjusting later contracts with the same firm. In one instance even before the full implementation of the audit system, Air Corps officers pressured Consolidated Aircraft Corporation into selling the Air Corps fifty $6,000 planes for $1 each to make up for huge profits on 1927-28 contracts.[9]

Foulois and his assistants labored to preserve the health of the nation's aircraft industry but opposed dealing with companies that could not build what they designed. With the concurrence of The Judge Advocate General, the Air Corps kept an "approved list" of manufacturers deemed able to produce acceptable planes, engines, and aircraft accessories. From the list the Materiel Division sought to establish two supply sources for every type of equipment used by the air arm, thus maintaining a stronger industrial base for wartime expansion. During these times when funds were so scarce that just one producer could be given a quantity contract for a particular type of plane, the Air Corps tried to negotiate a contract for an experimental aircraft of the same type with another manufacturer. Foulois, however, gave short shrift to companies that could merely design planes. He insisted that firms receiving Air Corps business have proper engineering staffs, sound financial backing, and the expertise to turn their paper designs into functioning aircraft.[10]

In early December 1933, the OCAC prepared to spend the $7.5 million in PWA funds allocated for aircraft procurement. The General Staff and Chief of the Air Corps finally agreed to use the money to purchase thirty attack planes, forty-six bombers, and twenty-four pursuit aircraft, complete with radios and spare engines and parts. Since PWA money was supposed to be used to promptly put people back to work and because the Air Corps wanted to immediately buy planes for its understrength tactical squadrons, Foulois and his staff decided to negotiate the purchase of additional numbers of the best existing aircraft rather than go through the lengthy procedure of first contracting for new experimental models. They selected the Northrop, Glenn L. Martin, and Boeing companies respectively to build the desired attack, bombardment, and pursuit aircraft.[11]

Assistant Secretary of War Woodring prevented the Air Corps from completing the plan. He believed in competitive contracting and had apparently been concerned for some time over the failure to fully comply with the 1926 Air Corps Act. When word circulated in the autumn that PWA funds would soon be made available, his office received a number of complaints from airplane manufacturers of unfair exclusion from government business. Most of the complainants were small operators without the means or experience to build acceptable combat planes. However, on December 7, Burdette S. Wright, a representative of Curtiss-Wright Corporation (a large and reputable aircraft firm) visited Woodring and criticized Air Corps procurement policies. He had earlier been to see Foulois and Westover and asked how the PWA funds would be spent, but they refused to give him any information. Wright and other corporation officials thought Foulois was prejudiced against their firm, and was seeking to deny it a share of the PWA pie. The Curtiss-Wright spokesmen probably mentioned this to Woodring during their talk. Charging Foulois with bias was hardly justifiable, for in fiscal years 1931 through 1933 Curtiss-Wright had received over $12.6 million in Air Corps business. Wright's comments nevertheless must have had some effect on Woodring, for on the afternoon of December 7 the assistant secretary informed the OCAC that no negotiations for new aircraft would be undertaken until he, Woodring, gave his personal approval. He instructed the OCAC to resubmit its purchase proposal to his office for further review.[12]

On December 8, Woodring resolved not to approve the OCAC request to buy planes through negotiated contracts. He arranged a conference for December 21 with OCAC officials to establish a system of competitive bidding for the PWA fund expenditure. Generals Foulois, Westover, and Brig. Gen. Henry C. Pratt from the Materiel Division attended the conference. They were not pleased with Woodring's stand, contending that competitive bidding might mean accepting untested and inferior planes. They asserted that the Air Corps should not be put in the position of having to accept bids on planes not previously approved by the Army. The assistant secretary explained he had no intention of forcing the purchase of inferior aircraft but felt that competition would yield lower prices. He gave Foulois three days to submit a plan by which the air arm could procure satisfactory planes through competitive bidding.[13]

Foulois and several assistants met the next day with Lt. Col. James K. Crain, Woodring's executive officer. Together they tried to comply with the assistant secretary's directive. The Air Corps officials told Crain that the three manufacturers formerly picked for PWA-funded contracts each produced a plane superior to others of its kind. If the performance specifications of these aircraft were used in invitations to bids, it would exclude other bidders. Similarly, if minimum specifications were watered down to let more firms compete, and these firms came in with the lowest

## PROCUREMENT TROUBLES, 1933-1935

bids, the Air Corps might be forced to buy less advanced planes. Foulois and Crain eventually agreed in the end that: the Air Corps would accept bids only on airplanes already tested and approved by the Army; contracts would be awarded under Section 10(t) of the Air Corps Act, which gave weight to performance as well as to price; and the interval between the invitation for bids and their opening would be fifteen days. Woodring approved this plan without delay.[14]

Over the next several days, Materiel Division officers hammered out the details of the bid invitations. This necessitated reducing speed, range, and load specifications so that at least two companies could bid on each type of aircraft. Since there were very few modern bombers, attack, and pursuit planes which had previously been approved by the Air Corps, these reductions were extensive. In one instance the planners had to reduce the required speed for pursuit planes from 230 miles-per-hour (the original Air Corps standard) to 176.5 miles-per-hour. Although Woodring did not personally decrease aircraft performance requirements, his order on competitive bidding did exactly that. To broaden competition, Air Corps officials recommended that bids also be accepted on planes previously tested and approved by the Navy. Woodring approved this change along with an OCAC proposal to extend the time between invitations and bid openings from fifteen to twenty days. Foulois and his staff may not have liked the change to competitive contracting, but they did their best to forge a workable system under Woodring's directive.[15]

On January 3 the assistant secretary told the OCAC to proceed with the expenditure of the $7.5 million in PWA money under the new procurement procedure. On the same day Woodring approved the use of a portion of the $3 million recently released from impounded fiscal 1934 Air Corps procurement funds in negotiated contracts for experimental aircraft.[16] In both instances he was seeking to strictly comply with the Air Corps Act of 1925:

> Under . . . authority [of the act] certain experimental purchases are made from the designer of a specific type of aircraft without competition. Such purchases are few in number, however, and procurement of airplanes in quantity will be made under the provisions of sub-paragraph (t) of Section 10 of the Act . . . after competitive bidding and evaluation of the airplanes submitted.[17]

Prodded by the War Department to get PWA-funded procurement under way, the Air Corps issued invitations for bids soon after getting the go-ahead from Woodring. Harold L. Ickes, director of the PWA, was threatening to abandon projects not yet begun, and the General Staff passed this negative encouragement on to Foulois. The contractors responded with their bids by the January 25-26 deadlines. Air Corps officials weighed the merits of each one and declared the three companies originally selected for negotiated contracts the winners. Foulois recommended Woodring immediately award the contracts, but the assistant secretary delayed. The House Military Affairs Committee was beginning a probe into War Department procurement, a Woodring responsibility. Personally involved in the investigation and finding the committee particularly interested in aircraft purchasing procedures, the assistant secretary was not about to make a decision that might place him in jeopardy.[18]

There were several reasons for fresh congressional interest in Air Corps procurement policies during February 1934. A federal grand jury in Washington was investigating charges of collusion in sales of surplus government property and purchases of PWA-funded motor vehicles. This served to arouse suspicion on Capitol Hill of a wider range of War Department procurement wrongdoing. Coupled with this were revelations in early February before the House Naval Affairs Committee that aircraft manufacturers had reaped huge profits on government contracts. Rear Adm. Ernest J. King, Chief of the Bureau of Aeronautics, reported to the committee that one firm garnered a fifty-percent profit on a $10 million plane order, and had maintained a thirty-six-percent profit level for seven years.

On February 6, William E. Boeing, chairman of the board of United Aircraft and Transport and founder of Boeing Airplane Company, admitted to Senator Black's special committee investigating air mail contracts that his companies had made big profits selling airplanes and engines to the Army and Navy. Boeing mentioned that they kept a six-man lobby of ex-military officers in Washington to seek government contracts. At this time, Congressman McSwain was about to open hearings before the Military Affairs Committee on his Air Corps autonomy bill and on the War Department proposal to authorize additional planes to equip the GHQ Air Force. The disclosures of undue profits and hints of misconduct induced him to add aircraft procurement to the committee's agenda.[19]

Opening hearings on February 8, the House Military Affairs Committee called Billy Mitchell as its first witness. The ex-general told the congressmen the Air Corps was in terrible shape because aircraft companies had regularly overcharged and turned out inferior planes. With his characteristic flare for the dramatic, he labeled the major producers "profiteers" and accused the past two administrations of letting them "plunder the Treasury." Mitchell's unverified charges reinforced the views of some congressmen and heightened the committee's interest in exploring Air Corps procurement practices.[20]

On the ninth, McSwain called Woodring and General Pratt to explain both the profits made by Air Corps contractors and the Army air arm's procurement methods. Pratt admitted there were a few examples in past years where large profits had been realized on Air Corps contracts, but he pointed out that the OCAC instituted recovery action as soon as such

## PROCUREMENT TROUBLES, 1933-1935

situations were uncovered. Pratt could feel secure as he spoke, since Air Corps audits confirmed that no company realized more than sixteen-percent profit during the past three fiscal years. The Materiel Division chief next explained the pre-December procurement methods employed by the Air Corps. Apparently for the first time, the committee learned that the Army aviators had been relying exclusively on negotiated rather than competitive contracts.

Mcswain, a great proponent of competitive bidding, was aghast. He asked Pratt on what authority the air arm had sidestepped the 1926 Air Corps Act. The general replied as best he could, citing Army Regulations 5-240 and the benefits of negotiated contracts. Committee members were not pleased with the Air Corps' methods. Forsaking the pending bills, McSwain announced the committee would proceed with an investigation of Army aviation procurement.[21] After confronting the congressmen, Pratt was so concerned that he wrote Foulois: "In my opinion we will never be able to submit to the Military Affairs Committee or anybody else a study on this subject which will properly justify our belief in the utilization of negotiated contracts."[22] His assessment as it related to the Military Affairs Committee was correct.

Woodring's testimony simply reinforced McSwain's decision to investigate further. A week or so before, rumors had circulated that the War Department, in order to aid certain contractors, had altered Air Corps specifications for aircraft to be purchased with PWA funds. When the assistant secretary outlined the competitive bidding system being used to expend the $7.5 million, the congressmen confronted him at once with charges that the new procedure had resulted in reduced aircraft performance criteria. Representative William F. (Frank) James and Paul J. Kvale argued that the War Department had imposed the reductions on the air arm and asserted that this would lead to the purchase of inferior planes. Some Air Corps supporters on the committee branded Woodring's revised purchasing system as one more instance of inept War Department control of military aviation and wanted to examine the situation more deeply. The assistant secretary denied any part in altering the specifications, but this failed to soothe the committee.[23]

MacArthur had taken steps in late January to convince the Military Affairs Committee that the General Staff was responsible for neither the existing condition of Air Corps aircraft nor changes in airplane performance requirements. He told committee members:

> Up to the present the General Staff has had nothing whatsoever to do with the planes that have been purchased. This is a matter that has been entirely in the hands of the Assistant Secretary of War for Aviation, acting with the immediate advice of the Chief of the Air Corps. Under the arrangement as now set up the General Staff still has nothing to do with the actual purchase

of planes, this being a function of the Air Corps under the supervision of the Assistant Secretary of War.[24]

He explained that after abandonment of the post of Assistant Secretary for Air, the General Staff, with the advice of the Chief of the Air Corps, had acted only to determine the numbers and types of planes purchased. He maintained:

> If up until the time this new arrangement went into effect, any errors and mistakes have been made in the procurement of Army aircraft, they can be attributed only to the air elements themselves, since the General Staff has had nothing to do with such questions.
>
> Statements have recently appeared in the press or been made over the radio that the General Staff has forced the purchase of slower types than those desired. Such statements are fallacious and without foundation.[25]

The comments made by congressmen during Woodring's February 9 testimony show that MacArthur's statements fell short of convincing some members of the Military Affairs Committee.

Testimony by Pratt, Woodring, and Foulois before the House Appropriations Committee on February 14 furnished further clues to the Military Affairs Committee that all aspects of Air Corps procurement needed thorough review. The Chief of the Materiel Division again described the procedures for purchasing aircraft prior to December, this time going into greater detail. Woodring recounted the changes he had made, but during the course of his testimony, committee members expanded on the ease with which aircraft company executives had gained access to him for discussions. This aroused the suspicion that the procurement changes and the accompanying lowering of specifications might have been meant to give selected inferior manufacturers a chance to win contracts.[26] Foulois' testimony fueled this suspicion. His poorly worded answers to subcommittee chairman Ross A. Collins' questions left the impression that Woodring was directly responsible for the specification changes:

> Mr. Collins: But before bids were invited on these three types of planes, with those particular accomplishments as set in late November as a minimum, a change was made, was there not?
>
> General Foulois: Yes, sir.
>
> Mr. Collins: Who made that change?
>
> General Foulois: The change was made by the Assistant Secretary of War.
>
> . . . . . . . . . . . . . . . . . . . . . . . . . .
>
> Mr. Collins: Now, will you give us a copy of the papers, whether specifications or whatever they may be called, that listed performance, as they were originally drafted in your office, also the same information after they were altered in the office of the Assistant Secretary of War?
>
> General Foulois: Yes, sir. We will give you all the documents. . . .[27]

## PROCUREMENT TROUBLES, 1933-1935

Three weeks later Foulois explained to a subcommittee of the Military Affairs Committee that when he said the Assistant Secretary of War made the change he was referring only to the change in procurement procedure. His answer of "yes, sir" to the other question was simply to signify the documents would be delivered as requested. For the time being, however, Woodring was in trouble. Reports appeared in the press that he might soon resign.[28]

Testimony by two aircraft firm executives before the Military Affairs Committee added to the evidence that something was wrong with Air Corps procurement practices. On February 9, Reuben H. Fleet, president of Consolidated Aircraft Corporation, explained how the Army air arm forced his company to produce fifty $6,000 planes for $1 apiece as a result of the Air Corps' decision that his firm had made excess profits on past business. To secure additional orders, Consolidated had allowed the Air Corps to fix prices in subsequent contracts, and thereby had suffered a net loss of $250,000.[29]

James V. Martin, president of Martin Aircraft Company of New Jersey, appeared on February 13 and charged the Air Corps and major aircraft corporations with collusion: "Every contract is let secretly and conclusively in violation of law; no independent manufacturer is present at conferences where planes are purchased." He claimed the companies receiving all of the business had paid agents in the Air Corps, but when asked could not come up with any names.[30] Martin was something of a crank. Because his name and that of his company resembled those of respected aircraft manufacturer Glenn L. Martin and his firm, James Martin's words often got more attention than they deserved. In fact, his company had never produced anything of worth to military aviation. It lacked engineering talent and had a poor record in aircraft design and development. For these reasons, and Martin's penchant for backdoor politics in his quest for contracts, the Air Corps wanted nothing to do with him or his company.[31] Yet Martin's timely testimony impressed the Military Affairs Committee members.

The Air Corps' poor early showing in the air mail venture was the final link in the chain of events that caused the Military Affairs Committee to seek, and the House to grant permission for, an expanded investigation of Air Corps procurement. On February 20, after three crewmembers had already died, McSwain's committee approved and sent on to the full House a resolution, drafted by the chairman, calling for the probe.[32] As introduced on the floor, House Resolution 275 called for a broadened inquiry into other facets of the War Department's business dealings, but Air Corps procurement remained the central issue. The resolution stated the investigation was required because

159

> allegations and charges of a serious nature have been made relative to profiteering in military aircraft and aircraft engines purchased by the War Department; the leasing of public property by the War Department to private concerns under terms and conditions alleged to be contrary to public interest; profiteering in the purchase of War Department property; the awarding of contracts without competitive bidding, and methods of purchase of military aircraft under which the aircraft purchased is inferior in performance to the military aircraft of other world powers, and to requirements of national defense.[33]

During the ten days between the introduction of the resolution and its eventual passage, Congressman William N. Rogers' Military Aviation Subcommittee pursued the Military Affairs Committee's review of Air Corps procurement. On February 19 the subcommittee ordered Woodring to hold up the PWA-funded contracts and to furnish copies of all specifications and bids bearing on the intended purchases. Rogers told reporters the Military Affairs Committee was not satisfied that the methods used to select contractors for the $7.5 million aircraft purchase ensured open, competitive bidding as specified in the 1926 Air Corps Act. He and his subcommittee colleagues definitely believed deeper probing would turn up proof of collusion in Air Corps contracting. On February 21 he called upon the War Department to supply the names of all Army aviators who had left the service or were on leaves of absence and had taken jobs with aircraft manufacturers. This "fishing trip" produced nothing. Evidence of corruption and graft were illusive. Yet, Rogers claimed on February 24 that the Air Corps' negotiated procurement system—probably operated by some individual or group for personal gain—was the culprit in the air mail disasters.[34]

Other congressmen also linked the air arm's poor showing in the mail operation with equipment and procurement deficiencies. During the March 2 debate on House Resolution 275, they constantly spoke of this relationship. The numerous deaths and crashes of the past weeks could not be dismissed lightly. Some Air Corps supporters blamed bad weather instead of inadequate aircraft, but a large bipartisan majority felt there was ample evidence to the contrary to warrant an investigation. The House adopted the resolution and four days later appropriated ten thousand dollars to finance the probe.[35]

The procurement portion of the investigation fell to Congressman Rogers' Military Aviation Subcommittee (the Military Affairs Committee's Subcommittee Number 3). Public hearings began on March 7 with Woodring testifying again. The previous day's *Washington Post* had commented on Foulois' badly framed answers to questions put to him on February 14 by Congressman Collins, claiming that the Chief of the Air Corps said Woodring had lowered the initial performance specifications

## PROCUREMENT TROUBLES, 1933-1935

drawn up for the PWA-funded purchases in order to ensure competitive bidding. A second article in the March 7 edition said Foulois told the Appropriations Committee that Curtiss-Wright and Consolidated Aircraft officials pressured the assistant secretary to alter the specifications. This was an outright distortion of what the air chief had said, but it interested members of the subcommittee nonetheless.[36]

Facing the subcommittee on the seventh of March, Woodring was quizzed on Foulois' remarks. The assistant secretary was on the defensive, but he patiently reviewed his earlier testimony, explaining that he had changed the procurement procedure in order to make the Army air arm comply with the 1926 Air Corps Act. He again denied responsibility for altering aircraft performance criteria. He assured the members he had no desire to dictate technical considerations but only wanted to institute competitive bidding procedures. He therefore allowed the Air Corps to stipulate that bids could only be submitted on planes already approved by the Army and the Navy. Subcommittee members argued that this provision nullified competitive bidding. Trying to shift the congressmen's displeasure away from himself and toward the Air Corps, Woodring said that he agreed but he had felt compelled to accept the stipulation because Army aviation officers had insisted that without it they would be compelled to buy unsafe planes. He admitted he had erred in this decision and had not gone far enough to enforce competitive bidding. The assistant secretary further advised the members that The Judge Advocate General had just ruled invalid the invitations for bids sent out in January because they did not inform the competing firms of the relative weight given price and performance in the evaluation process. Woodring said he concurred completely in The Judge Advocate General's findings. The anxious assistant secretary was doing all in his power to place himself in the subcommittee's good graces.[37]

When queried about the air chief's February 14 remarks, Woodring produced a message he had just received from Foulois which branded *The Washington Post* articles of March 6 and 7 as complete distortions of what he had really said. Apparently Foulois did not grasp the implications of his responses to Collins' questions until *The Washington Post* reported on them weeks later. Why he waited until the day after the initial article to explain the matter to Woodring is a mystery.[38]

Subcommittee members were shocked by the Foulois memorandum. They apparently were looking for a whipping boy on whom to heap the blame for the Air Corps' reputed poor condition, and Woodring had been their prime candidate. His testimony and the arrival of the message from Foulois caused them to reevaluate their position. The Chief of the Air Corps rapidly replaced the Assistant Secretary of War as their most likely prospect. The congressmen adamantly believed competitive bidding under the 1926 act would secure the best possible aircraft. Foulois, as they knew, was a leading proponent of negotiated contracts. It did not occur to the members that the time constraints imposed by the PWA would make it impossible to buy better quality planes with a competitive system than through direct negotiations.

After Woodring read the memorandum to the congressmen, they voted to send a clerk to search out Foulois and bring him in for a full explanation. Subcommittee members put the same construction on the air chief's February 14 testimony as had *The Washington Post.* So when Foulois entered the hearing room an hour later, Rogers treated him as if he were a defendant being cross-examined in a court of law. The chairman read Foulois' disputed testimony back to him very slowly. He followed with a battery of biting questions concerning why Foulois had spoken as he did if he had not meant to imply Woodring was responsible for specification changes. Foulois was noticeably shaken by this reception. Somewhat fatigued by the strain of the air mail operation and the numerous appearances before congressional committees over the past few weeks, he explained the misinterpretation of his previous testimony and corroborated Woodring's contention that the assistant secretary had not changed the specifications.[39]

Subcommittee members then attacked the Air Corps' use of negotiated contracts and its January competitive bidding procedure. Congressman Edward W. Goss argued that The Judge Advocate General had rendered opinions in the past branding negotiated quantity purchases illegal. Foulois angrily retorted:

> You have indicated that he says it is illegal. I am not certain of that. . . . every contract we have ever signed has gone to the Judge Advocate General, and has come back legally sufficient. Is that the interpretation that the Judge Advocate General, himself, is illegally approving these contracts?[40]

The air chief said he was no lawyer and therefore did not think it was his place "to question the Judge Advocate General of the Army; as long as those contracts were declared legally sufficient, and they came back ready to be put in effect, I saw nothing wrong with them." This explanation failed to satisfy the subcommittee members. They believed the Air Corps had violated the law and wanted to make certain it did not happen again.[41]

In succeeding weeks the Military Aviation Subcommittee concentrated on the issue of negotiated versus competitive contracts. It could find no evidence of collusion in the Air Corps' past procurement activities, so in its quest for an explanation for the Army air arm's purportedly deficient equipment, the subcommittee blamed the Air Corps' contracting system. Committee members did not try to find out if the planes were in truth inferior. Having been authorized by the House to investigate charges

## PROCUREMENT TROUBLES, 1933-1935

of corruption, profiteering, and procurement practices that led to the buying of second-rate aircraft, the members apparently felt they had to establish some duplicity or wrongdoing. The Air Corps' support for negotiated contracting, still evident in January despite Woodring's call for competitive bidding, was all that was available to them.

The subcommittee went into executive session the day following Foulois' appearance and held no further open hearings. Rogers called representatives of the aircraft industry to testify during March and April. The major airplane manufacturers were nearly unanimous in their support for negotiated contracting. Even Thomas A. Morgan, president of Curtiss-Wright, while complaining over what he considered an inequitable share of Air Corps business, generally endorsed the Army air arm's recently superseded procurement system. However, Burdette Wright, one of Morgan's business associates, told the subcommittee he believed the Air Corps had structured its January competition as to exclude Curtiss-Wright. He explained his company had the best attack plane available but could not bid on it because of the stipulation that all aircraft submitted must have been previously tested and approved by the Army or Navy. Morgan backed him up in this assertion. Spokesmen for Boeing and Douglas testified in support of the Air Corps' negotiated contracting procedure, but executives of some of the smaller firms claimed the Air Corps used this procurement system to discriminate against them. Subcommittee members agreed with the latter view.[42]

The probe of the Air Corps altered the attitudes of subcommittee members who in the past had championed the air arm. Congressman Goss told an *Army and Navy Journal* reporter in April:

> The military committee, you know, has always been very much pro-Air Corps. Now, however, I believe that any proposal for a separate department, a separate budget, or any other separation would have no chance. Many of the members who have been sitting in the Rogers subcommittee have completely turned around in the matter.[43]

Rogers clarified this new outlook, saying that the Air Corps had violated procurement law and giving the Army aviators more authority was hardly the proper remedy.[44] Subcommittee members who had previously favored McSwain's February 2 bill (H.R. 7601), to establish an autonomous air arm and promote the Chief of the Air Corps to lieutenant general opposed the legislation and branded Foulois the chief offender in the air arm's illegal procurement actions.

As the closed-door investigation continued, the Air Corps could not spend the $7.5 million in PWA money or the $3 million in formerly withheld fiscal 1934 aircraft procurement funds. Woodring asked The Judge Advocate General on February 23 if the January invitations for bids were legal. Maj. Gen. Arthur W. Brown responded on March 5 that the ad-

163

vertisements did not afford adequate competition because they failed to say how the Air Corps would judge the entries. He also reaffirmed a 1929 judgment that quantity procurement under Section 10(k) was illegal without competitive bidding.

With Congress probing into Army aviation procurement, The Judge Advocate General was being far more careful in evaluating the legality of Air Corps purchase agreements. He undoubtedly did not want his office caught up in the investigation. Woodring sent word to Foulois on March 10 that all bids had been thrown out, and the Air Corps would have to readvertise. He suggested that the new bids drop the requirement that aircraft must have been previously approved by the Army or Navy, make minimum specifications as general as possible, and specify the relative weights of performance and cost in the evaluation process. Air Corps officers disliked these recommendations, for they had originally hoped to design for the competition ground rules that would let them buy from the manufacturers of the best planes available—the firms Foulois had initially designated for negotiated contracts.[45]

To iron out differences on the new invitations for bids, the Assistant Secretary conferred on March 15 and 17 with Air Corps and Judge Advocate General officials. Westover and Pratt represented the air arm and presented various plans. Pratt first tried to convince Woodring that he should authorize negotiated contracts in order to obtain the best planes at a reasonable price in the shortest time. Woodring refused. Another proposal called for limiting competition to aircraft the Air Corps could inspect and test before the bids opened. Though mildly receptive to the idea, Woodring pointed out this would rule out all planes not actually in being. Fearing that the Rogers Subcommittee would spurn any plan not open to every prospective bidder, he took no action. Foulois wrote him on April 14 to protest The Judge Advocate General's decision that advertisements must specify the weights used to determine contract winners. The air chief contended this requirement would erase the discretion extended by Section 10(t) of the Air Corps Act of 1926, and reduce to a mathematical formula the decision on what planes to buy. Foulois said The Judge Advocate General's opinion was wrong and he wanted Woodring to disregard it.[46]

Rogers worked to release a preliminary report of his group's findings in early April in order to clear the way for the expenditure of the procurement funds. The congressman submitted a draft proposal to the subcommittee on April 3 praising Woodring's efforts to foster competitive bidding and accusing Foulois and other Air Corps officers of violating the law. Rogers based his condemnation of the aviators on The Judge Advocate General's March 5 opinion. Members of the subcommittee were strongly in favor of endorsing competitive bidding and taking the Army

## PROCUREMENT TROUBLES, 1933-1935

air arm to task for its past reliance on negotiated contracts. At first, however, they were reluctant to sign a document wholeheartedly endorsing Woodring while accusing Foulois and some of his subordinates of misconduct. The subcommittee eventually worked out its differences on the report and informed Woodring on April 19 that he could proceed with aircraft purchases so long as there was open competition for contracts.[47]

Rogers received added ammunition for the interim report from Comptroller General John R. McCarl. The subcommittee chairman had requested McCarl's opinion on the January advertisements for bids. The Comptroller General's May 2 reply condemned them as well as the Air Corps' past practice of negotiating quantity purchase orders. He explained that the Army aviators had been able to get away with using the illegal negotiated method because the 1926 Air Corps Act had withdrawn aircraft purchases from his jurisdiction by vesting in the Secretary of War the final approval authority on all airplane contracts. McCarl agreed with The Judge Advocate General's opinion on the invitations for bids sent out four months previous, asserting they did not specify on what basis the competing planes would be judged and therefore restricted competition.[48]

Subcommittee Number 3's report, made public on May 7, held only one surprise. It fixed full responsibility for the Air Corps' procurement system on Foulois:

> Your subcommittee finds unanimously that every action taken in connection with this $7,500,000 allotment by Assistant Secretary of War Woodring was deemed by him required and fully justified, while the actions of the Chief of the Air Corps, Major General Benjamin D. Foulois, are in our opinion and in the opinion of the Judge Advocate General of the Army and the Comptroller General of the United States in clear violation of existing law.[49]

Foulois was the spokesman for institutionalized Air Corps procurement views rooted in the mid-1920s.[50] By attacking him the subcommittee was damning these views. It was patently unfair to condemn only this one individual, but it served the members' purpose. Their aim was to inform the Air Corps and War Department that the subcommittee would condone no further restriction of open and equitable competition in quantity aircraft contracting. From now on, the Air Corps would have to rely on competitive bidding as provided in the Air Corps Act of 1926.

The Air Corps still did not consider its past actions illegal, but it had to bend to the subcommittee's will. It did not matter that some members of Congress openly advocated negotiated contracting as the best means of procuring quality aircraft, or that the major producers liked this method.[51] Power to decide the issue rested in the hands of the eight members of Subcommittee Number 3, and they considered a competitive system mandatory under the law.

It was curious that while one congressional committee was taking the

Air Corps to task for negotiated contracting, another committee was exonerating the Navy's use of the same system. The procurement provisions of the Air Corps Act applied to both services, and the Navy had continually sidestepped the restrictions on quantity aircraft purchases much as the Air Corps had. The House Naval Affairs Committee began hearings on aircraft profiteering in late January, and Navy officials immediately revealed to committee members that they favored and were using negotiated contracts. Admiral King said the Navy opposed competitive bidding on quantity buys. It relied instead on agreements with firms that had created test models of planes the sea service desired. This "sole source" buying of a specific piece of equipment was nearly identical to the Air Corps' methods.[52]

After listening to many witnesses in open session, the committee reported in March that "the policy pursued by the Navy Department since the adoption of the Aircraft Procurement Act of 1926, is a practical and prudent one, and should be followed until a better plan is proposed." The committee was favorably disposed toward competitive contracting but recognized "negotiated contracts are necessary until the aeronautical art becomes more stabilized."[53] The divergent opinions of Subcommittee Number 3 of the Military Affairs Committee and the Naval Affairs Committee showed that the question of the legality of negotiated purchases was a relative one.[54]

The Navy went ahead and spent its $7.5 million in PWA aircraft funds through negotiated contracts. But by summer, at the Comptroller General's insistence, it too was forced to adopt competitive bidding. The Secretary of the Navy wanted new legislation clearly authorizing negotiated quantity aircraft purchases. Until it could be passed, however, he ordered the Navy to use open competition. Like the Army air arm, the Navy wanted to keep the old negotiated system.[55]

Once the Rogers subcommittee permitted the Air Corps to proceed with aircraft procurement, the OCAC swiftly set up a system reasonably acceptable to all concerned. New advertisements explained that bids would be evaluated solely on performance characteristics (with no consideration given to price) and spelled out minimum desirable performance criteria. In addition, all competitors were required to submit a sample airplane. The assistant secretary had convinced Subcommittee Number 3 that the sample was necessary to limit bidding to bona fide manufacturers. Since the expenditure of PWA funds had to be expedited, the May 4 advertisement for new bombers stipulated that bids would be opened one month later. Woodring knew this tight deadline narrowed competition to firms with planes in being, but he agreed this was necessary in order to obtain aircraft meeting the Air Corps' needs without undue delay. However, he directed the Air Corps to advertise for planes to

## PROCUREMENT TROUBLES, 1933-1935

be bought with fiscal year 1935 and 1936 funds far enough in advance so manufacturers would have time to design and build their entries before bids were opened.[56]

With War Department approval the OCAC did not buy any pursuit planes with the PWA money, applying the entire $7.5 million to bombers and attack aircraft. When bids for bombardment planes were opened in June, the Air Corps announced that the Glenn L. Martin Company (its original choice) was the only firm to submit a proposal. Consequently, it received the contract. The Materiel Division sent out a call on May 28 for bids on attack aircraft; these were opened on October 9. On the basis of the Materiel Division's evaluation, Woodring awarded the contract to the Northrop Corporation (another of the three companies with which the Air Corps had sought to negotiate in December).[57]

Subcommittee No. 3 continued the Air Corps probe beyond May, but took no further action on the procurement issue apart from passing on the acceptability of the advertisements for bomber and attack planes. Instead, the subcommittee turned its attention to Foulois and his supposed misdeeds. Rogers released an additional report of findings in mid-June which spoke of the air arm's procurement law violations only in so far as they contributed to the subcommittee's case against the air chief.[58]

In late May 1934 Comptroller General McCarl replaced Subcommittee No. 3 as the major antagonist to Air Corps procurement policy. He wrote Secretary of War Dern that an Air Corps contract with the Boeing Corporation for 111 P-26A aircraft, signed January 11, 1933, was illegal. As a result he would allow no further charges against appropriated funds to complete the purchase until the War Department had made a full report to his office. Apparently the political climate prompted McCarl to take action on this old contract. The agreement with Boeing had been made under AR 5-240 rather than the Air Corps Act, thus preserving the Comptroller General's reviewing authority. Finally recognizing this fact, McCarl was now exercising that authority. The Air Corps had originally purchased a few of the P-26s for test purposes under section 10(k) of the 1926 act and then placed the quantity order on the basis of Boeing being the sole manufacturer of a specific item that was not procurable from other sources. Woodring, who did not favor the Air Corps' past methods but thought they were legal, wrote to McCarl in July describing the procedure used by the air arm and claiming there was nothing improper about the contract. McCarl replied two weeks later asserting that competitive contracting would be strictly applied in all aircraft contracting. He refused to exempt the P-26 purchase from this requirement.[59]

Woodring then consulted The Judge Advocate General for an opinion. General Brown replied in November that the Air Corps' actions under AR 5-240 were legal but recommended the assistant secretary seek the

# FOULOIS AND THE U.S. ARMY AIR CORPS

The P-26, which figured in some of Foulois' procurement trouble. This aircraft represented a major breakthrough in fighter aircraft design. It marked the historic change from wood and fabric to an all-metal monoplane fighter.

## PROCUREMENT TROUBLES, 1933-1935

view of the Attorney General. Brown thought it unnecessary and absurd for the War Department to advertise for bids when seeking to purchase an item produced by only one supplier. At Dern's request Attorney General Homer S. Cummings rendered an opinion on January 12, 1935. Cummings wrote that competition for quantity purchases was required unless there was a need for immediate delivery or in cases in which competitive bidding was impossible or impractical. This supported the War Department position and caused the Comptroller General to reverse his stand on the use of funds for the 1933 contract.[60]

McCarl also protested the procedure used to purchase aircraft with PWA funds. He wrote Dern in October objecting to the requirement that competitors submit aircraft along with their bids. He claimed the stipulation discriminated against companies not having models in production and was therefore illegal. After an extensive exchange of correspondence between December 1934 and February 1935, the Comptroller General dropped his objections. Two actions prompted this change of heart: Dern's assurance that future advertisements would provide ample time for all interested companies to construct a plane and Congressman McSwain's plea to McCarl to allow the purchases to proceed.[61]

The Rogers subcommittee had contended that competitive bidding was the single way to ensure the Air Corps would get the highest quality aircraft. Two other investigative bodies disagreed. The Baker Board had been appointed in 1934 by the Secretary of War to examine the condition of the Air Corps and its performance in the air mail operation. The Federal Aviation Commission had been created by the Air Mail Act of June 12, 1934, to investigate all facets of American aviation. Both bodies concluded that negotiated quantity purchases were needed. The Baker Board report, released in July, stated that "we are unanimously of the opinion that if existing law does not authorize procurement by negotiated contracts, in the discretion of the Secretary of War, immediate efforts should be made to secure amendments giving that authority."[62] The Federal Aviation Commission's report of January 1935 endorsed negotiated contracting even more strongly: "We find it impossible to accept the normal process of competitive bidding and award to the low bidder as being calculated to give the government the best value for its money." The commission recommended that the armed services be given the power to buy the best aircraft available directly from its originator. The report asserted that the 1926 law, as it concerned competitive bidding, was presently being too strictly enforced.[63] Roosevelt, however, agreed with the construction placed on the act by the Rogers Subcommittee and wanted no changes instituted that would reduce competition.[64]

Woodring was pleased with the results of the competitive system during fiscal years 1935-36, but the Air Corps was never completely satisfied.

169

## FOULOIS AND THE U.S. ARMY AIR CORPS

The assistant secretary credited the new bidding procedure with great advances in aircraft design and performance—assertions very hard to prove or disprove. Air officers still liked the old negotiated system which allowed them the latitude to force a contractor to modify his test aircraft to make production models more acceptable to Air Corps needs, and to more closely control price. They were unhappy with the long leadtimes imposed on quantity purchases under the new system, for this reduced the number of new planes immediately entering the inventory to offset large attrition losses. Further, air officers scorned the requirement to write lengthy justifications for every contract awarded to counter the protests of the losing competitors. Yet for the time being the Air Corps was stuck with competitive quantity procurement; Foulois and his subordinates worked to make the best of the situation.[65]

# CHAPTER VII

# THE CHIEF IN TROUBLE, 1934-1935

Subcommittee No. 3's animosity toward General Foulois in the spring of 1934 had its origins in the Air Corps' purported use of illegal procurement methods, but as the Rogers Subcommittee continued its probe it reached the conclusion the Chief of the Air Corps was guilty of far more than simply negotiating contracts. Foulois' ill-conceived testimony implicating Woodring as the initiator of specification changes and the air chief's later denial that he had intended to give such an impression caused the subcommittee to suspect the general's credibility. Foulois' assurances to committee members on March 1 that the Air Corps was well fitted to handle the air mail job,[1] coupled with renewed accidents and deaths one week later, fed this suspicion. Committee members reasoned the air chief was intentionally trying to mislead Congress and decided to look for additional evidence in his February 1 testimony before the House Military Affairs Committee on the War Department's GHQ Air Force aircraft bill.

Foulois had appeared on that date at the short-notice request of Chairman McSwain and had employed his traditional approach of campaigning for increased Air Corps autonomy by damning General Staff control of military aviation. Just as in 1919 and in the early 1920s, the air chief lashed out, freely mixing opinion with fact. The committee was in executive session when he arrived, and McSwain encouraged him to speak his mind, telling Foulois: "This testimony which is being taken will be for our information only. It will not be printed. We want to assure you that so far as lies within the power of this committee, you are to be absolutely protected in what you say." The air chief, pleased that his remarks would not go beyond the committee and the War Department, cautioned his listeners that "any statements I make here are my own personal opinion." He then proceeded to criticize the General Staff on a number of specific

## FOULOIS AND THE U.S. ARMY AIR CORPS

issues.[2]

Foulois' open hostility toward the War Department had two immediate causes. The first of these was his bitterness over the General Staff's exclusion of his office from the planning of the aircraft procurement project sent to the PWA in 1933. Contrary to normal practice, the General Staff had allowed the Air Corps almost no voice in arriving at the numbers and types of planes to be purchased with PWA funds. Once the War Plans Division finished its many revisions in early June, the Assistant Chief of Staff, G-4, took over completely, even testifying before the PWA on behalf of the desired allocation. The OCAC was allowed to suggest the numbers of attack, bombardment, and pursuit planes to be purchased with the meager $7.5 million eventually furnished by the PWA, but only after the General Staff had barred all other airplane types from the buy. The War Department, however, still had the final say on aircraft numbers.[3]

The second and more immediate cause of his seething hostility was the War Department's wording of its February 1 bill to fill out the GHQ Air Force. Two days before, MacArthur had called Foulois in to work with Drum on a legislative proposal to keep the existing 18:10 ratio in Army and Navy aircraft.[4] The bill they came up with made no mention of an exact number of planes. It did specify that enough be bought to equip the GHQ Air Force, together with a twenty-five-percent reserve and such other planes as were necessary for national defense. The proposal provided: "That this program shall be carried out in such annual increments as will preserve the air ratio between Army and Navy aviation."[5] MacArthur approved the draft and told Foulois to present it informally to Congressman McSwain, which he did on the evening of January 30. The next night the Chief of Staff called the air chief in again, and showed him a second bill that said nothing about maintaining the Army-Navy ratio. This one had been written by the General Staff's legislative branch and was the proposal McSwain introduced on February 1 at War Department request (H.R. 7553). Foulois was nettled that he had not been consulted on the second bill. Although apparently not revealing his anger to MacArthur, he stood ready to attack. His targets were the shortcomings of the bill and General Staff duplicity in substituting it for the January 30 draft.[6]

Warmed by McSwain's encouragement on February 1, the Chief of the Air Corps told of the air arm's efforts to build up military aviation over the past twenty years. In his view, "the main obstacle—the main blocking element—in the War Department has been the War Department General Staff." He singled out the Drum Board report as the only step taken by the General Staff in the previous two decades to strengthen the air component. Foulois made it clear he was not attacking the integrity of

## THE CHIEF IN TROUBLE, 1934-1935

War Department staff officers, only their ignorance of military aviation. Such individuals, he said, should not be in control of airpower development. The air chief denounced the War Department's bill for its vagueness, and related how the General staff had bypassed his office when writing it. He recounted a conversation he had with an unnamed General Staff officer a few hours before coming to the hearing room. The officer told him that the War Department had deleted the ratio provision on purpose, setting an upper rather than a lower limit on the number of aircraft to deliberately make the bill fuzzy. He then asked angrily: "Who are they trying to fool? You? Me? Or someone else?" He asserted that, with only an upper limit, the General Staff would be free to buy as many or as few planes as it wanted. He did not say so at the time, but Foulois also feared the bill allowed only a total of two thousand aircraft rather than an addition of two thousand to the planes on hand. He brought out this point in corrections to his testimony which he sent to the committee a short time later.[7] The air chief was not alone in interpreting the poorly punctuated legislative proposal in this way, for *The New York Times* expressed it in those terms on February 2.[8]

The Chief of the Air Corps ardently campaigned for autonomy before McSwain's committee. Faulting the General Staff as slow and unresponsive to aviation needs, he argued for a separate budget and promotion list for the Air Corps. He recounted for the committee how his office was ignored in PWA project planning and pointed out that this would never have happened had there been an Assistant Secretary for Air. Foulois also deplored the arrangement that gave other segments of the Army control of the pay for Reserve officers on extended active duty with the Air Corps, and of ammunition, weapons, and radio equipment procurement. He complained that others controlled these Air Corps resources yet he was held responsible for the outcome:

> It is the Chief of the Air Corps that has the responsibility for building up the Air Corps and he is not allowed to make recommendations, or if he does make recommendations, no attention is paid to him, he is never called in to defend the requests for amounts of money, either before the Budget Director or before Congress. Yet when the money is allotted, it is usually allotted regardless of his own recommendations, and in the end he is harnessed with a responsibility to get the thing done.[9]

Foulois, a poor extemporaneous speaker, must have known that this statement could be taken to mean he was forbidden to speak in support of the Air Corps' direct appropriations—which in fact he was not. In the corrected version of his testimony he amended the passage to read: "He is never called in to defend, before the Director of Budget, or before Congress, funds estimated for by other branches for Air Corps purposes."[10]

While deeming the Drum Board report a positive step, the air chief

173

## FOULOIS AND THE U.S. ARMY AIR CORPS

said:

> There are a lot of things in there that I disagreed with; there are a lot of things in there that I agreed with in the interest of harmony, and also to the fact that five members of that board—and I was often the minority member on lots of things that had to happen and that were discussed— there were a great many things that I was voted down on in handling the parliamentary procedure in working up that report.[11]

This, like many of Foulois' other comments that day, was imprecise. He had not meant to leave the impression that he disagreed with the workings of the board or its report, but that is exactly what he had done.[12]

The Chief of the Air Corps' hastily conceived testimony of February 1 was replete with generalizations and personal opinions. His remarks would become a wellspring of trouble for him when Subcommittee Number 3 took time to check them against other sources, and against the general's own written corrections furnished the Military Affairs Committee. Foulois did not knowingly lie to the committee. He simply clung to his approach of years standing, stating the case against the General Staff in the worst possible terms. In doing so, he handed the Rogers Subcommittee more alleged evidence to prove he was seeking to mislead Congress.

Before making a detailed check of his February 1 testimony, Subcommittee Number 3 found other information pointing to Foulois' misconduct. During his March 7 appearance before the Rogers Subcommittee, the air chief, in effect, admitted he had knowingly broken procurement law. When Congressman Goss accused him of violating Army regulations requiring competitive buying with the January 1934 invitations for bids, Foulois responded testily and without much forethought: "That is perfectly all right. I have overlooked the Army regulations and broken them hundreds of times in the interest of the Government, and I will break them again."[13] This statement did not cause a stir at the time, for the subcommittee had not yet decided to build a case against the air chief. Once the members did make that decision, the reply became one more piece of convenient supporting evidence.

Assertions by Curtiss-Wright executives in April before the subcommittee afforded evidence that Foulois had acted unethically. Thomas A. Morgan charged the Chief of the Air Corps with prejudice against Curtiss-Wright, and with keeping Air Corps business away from the Curtiss Company (the aircraft manufacturing portion of the corporation): "I think the record will show that Curtiss has not received an order for planes from the Air Corps in about three years, except when it went over General Foulois' head." As previously mentioned, Burdette S. Wright of Curtiss-Wright claimed that Army aviators had purposely written the January bid invitations for the PWA-funded aircraft purchase to exclude the corporation from competition.[14]

## THE CHIEF IN TROUBLE, 1934-1935

When the subcommittee wrote its interim report in May, it was not yet ready to press for a full indictment of Foulois. It charged him only with responsibility for the Air Corps' use of allegedly illegal procurement procedures to buy planes with PWA funds. The report's findings were actually ridiculous. While praising the actions of Woodring, the man who had approved the use of the January invitations, the subcommittee condemned his military functionary who had to carry out the procedure. No doubt the members looked upon Foulois and his staff as the chief architects of the advertisements, but they overlooked completely the part played by the assistant secretary's office or by Woodring himself. In attacking Foulois, the subcommittee was striking at the Air Corps' deep belief in the worth of negotiated contracts. However, the vigor with which the May report damned the air chief suggested that the eight subcommittee members had, by this time, convinced themselves that Foulois was guilty of much more than just leading an organization that wholly embraced negotiated contracting.

Quite naturally, Foulois was angered by the May 7 report. A few days later, he struck back in a public statement proclaiming his innocence. He explained that the planes he had originally recommended for negotiated purchase were "the best known models in existence." In opting for negotiation, he was following a procedure used by the Air Corps for many years, which "has always been approved by higher authority." The statement recounted how Air Corps personnel had cooperated with the assistant secretary, once he had chosen competitive bidding for the PWA-funded purchase. It pointed out that Woodring had praised the way the Army air arm had carried out his directive to institute competition. Foulois concluded:

> The implication of the press reports of the subcommittee findings is that the Air Corps officers drew up these circular proposals in a manner known by them to be illegal. This is erroneous and wholly unfair to me and the other officers of the Air Corps who participated in this transaction.[15]

This plea did not dissuade the Rogers Subcommittee. It went ahead with its investigation of Foulois, rechecking the air chief's February 1 testimony by calling senior Army officers to comment on his remarks, and by contrasting them with Foulois' edited version. The Chief of the Air Corps had written, expanded, and corrected his statement, for McSwain had told him this was perfectly permissible. The revision changed nothing of substance. Foulois merely modified some of his ambiguous comments to clarify them and qualified the harsher words and phrases used to describe the General Staff's alleged ineptness in handling military aviation. Notwithstanding, the subcommittee pounced on the revision as positive proof the air chief was deliberately trying to mislead members of Congress.[16]

## FOULOIS AND THE U.S. ARMY AIR CORPS

In May and early June, Rogers summoned the four generals who had recently served with Foulois on the Drum board—Kilbourne, Gulick, Simonds, and Drum. They were to testify on the accuracy of the air chief's February 1 remarks and on his fitness to serve as Chief of the Air Corps. From the nature of the questions put to these officers, it was clear the subcommittee members had already reached a verdict on both issues. For their part, the generals were predisposed to portray Foulois in rather negative terms. The pioneer aviator had openly advocated autonomy for the Air Corps just at the time McSwain was fomenting concern in the War Department with his bill to achieve this change. Further, Foulois had spoken ill of the General Staff before Congress and had put the War Department on the spot by failing to deliver on his assurances to postal officials that the Air Corps could adequately handle domestic air mail service. For these reasons and because of his past clashes with General Staff members and his unyielding advocacy of Air Corps interests over those of the rest of the Army, the four generals presented testimony most uncomplimentary to Foulois.[17]

Simonds, Kilbourne, and Gulick appeared together before the subcommittee. Rogers set the tempo of the proceedings by reading excerpts from Foulois' February 1 testimony and asking the three officers to comment. With encouragement from subcommittee members, Simonds asserted there was no basis in fact for the air chief's charges that General Staff officers knew nothing about military aviation and were unresponsive to Air Corps needs. Kilbourne voiced a like view. All three men were shocked when told that Foulois said he had been hampered by parliamentary procedure during the Drum Board deliberations. Parliamentary procedure had not been used. Foulois had worked harmoniously within the group, disagreeing merely on a few minor points. They also denied that the War Department's bill, introduced on February 1, had been designed to "fool anyone."

Twisting the air chief's testimony, Congressman James told Gulick that Foulois had contended he was never called upon to defend Air Corps estimates before the Bureau of the Budget. Gulick commented that this was "absolutely without foundation." Committee members next asked Kilbourne to assess Foulois based on the air chief's February 1 remarks. The Chief of the War Plans Division replied: "For a man to come up here and make such statements as he has made to you, which are easily capable of being refuted, it looks like he is crazy." Kilbourne volunteered that Foulois had been very uncooperative with the General Staff and was often not around when important matters needed his coordination.[18] Without saying so, the three witnesses probably conveyed the impression that Foulois was unfit to continue as Chief of the Air Corps.

General Drum's testimony on June 5 corroborated that of Simonds,

# THE CHIEF IN TROUBLE, 1934-1935

Brig. Gen. George S. Simonds.

Brig. Gen. Charles E. Kilbourne.

Maj. Gen. John W. Gulick.

Gulick, and Kilbourne. The Deputy Chief of Staff countered Foulois' charge that the General Staff was the greatest obstacle to the advancement of military aviation: "My opinion is that the War Department General Staff has exerted special efforts to build up the Air Corps from the period of the war to the present . . . I believe there had been preferential treatment given to the Air Corps, rightly, and should have been." He branded the air chief's comments on the General Staff "an inaccurate statement . . . [which] does not represent the actual conditions." Congressman Joseph Lister Hill led the witness to exclaim that Foulois had been given every chance to make his views known on Air Corps-related procurement of such items as radios and armament, managed by other segments of the Army. Drum did not mention that the air chief was never invited to speak in support of appropriations for these items before the Bureau of the Budget and Congress.

The Deputy Chief of Staff produced a letter from the War department budget office, indicating Foulois was actively involved in planning and defending his own budget. This, however, was irrelevant, for the Chief of the Air Corps had never made claims to the contrary, save in the case of the PWA aircraft project from which he was in fact excluded. When asked why Foulois had given inaccurate information to the House Military Affairs Committee on February 1, Drum offered that the air chief was acting under the "conception that Congress could be persuaded to bring about . . . a separation of the Air Corps by leading them to believe that the Air Corps was hamstrung and blocked by officials of the War Department." The Deputy Chief of Staff wound up his testimony with a wholly unfavorable appraisal of Foulois:

> My personal opinion is that he is not a fit officer to be Chief of the Air Corps; and I come to that opinion not only in view of these misrepresentations that have been presented to me, but from the state of affairs in the Air Corps. The management of the Air Corps, in my mind, has demonstrated that he is not fit for it.[19]

The subcommittee now had the opinions of four high-ranking officers with which to refute Foulois' February 1 opinions.

The question remains: Why did the subcommittee single out Foulois and build an extensive case against him? There were probably three chief motivating factors. First, the subcommittee wanted to find some guilty party to justify the undertaking of the procurement investigation. Second, there was its firm conviction that negotiated contracts were illegal. And finally there was the embarrassment felt by some of the members who, believing the Chief of the Air Corps' assurances that the air arm could carry the air mail, had made statements to that effect on the House floor. Several of Foulois' actions made him a sitting duck for the eager congressmen—advocacy of negotiated contracts; blunders in testimony

## THE CHIEF IN TROUBLE, 1934-1935

before the House Military Affairs Committee on February 1, the House Appropriations Committee on February 14, and Subcommittee Number 3 on March 7; and overoptimistic assurances regarding the Air Corps' abilities in the air mail operation.

Subcommittee members needed to find a guilty party. They began their probe with charges of corruption in aircraft procurement swirling in the press, and they realized they must uncover someone responsible for the Air Corps' alleged poor condition. Investigations that turned up no misdeeds soon lose the publicity on which politicians flourish. When the members of Subcommittee Number 3 could find no collusion in aircraft procurement, they shifted to the system the Air Corps used to buy planes. But blaming the system for the air arm's plight was no substitute for a guilty party. So Subcommittee Number 3 resolved that Foulois, by virtue of his position as the leading advocate of the unacceptable practice of negotiating contracts, would be its candidate.

Members of the Rogers Subcommittee were convinced that negotiated aircraft contracts were illegal and resulted in the purchase of poor quality planes. They were shocked to learn that the Air Corps used this unacceptable procedure and that Foulois championed it. Congressman Paul J. Kvale of Minnesota claimed the procurement issue chilled his former warm regard for the air chief: "The reason for the change of opinion was solely in connection with the P.W.A. $7,500,000 airplane procurement program where it was developed that the General had been disregarding the Air Corps Act of 1926."[20] Other members apparently felt the same way, but this in itself was not enough to trigger an inquiry into other possible wrongdoings by the Chief of the Air Corps.

It was Foulois' unfulfilled assurances on the air mail issue that led the subcommittee to delve deeper into his activities. He had told the members on March 1 that the Air Corps was properly trained and equipped to carry the mail. Based upon these words, Congressmen Rogers and Hill had defended the Army aviators against charges to the contrary on the House floor. On the day after Foulois' appearance, Hill told the members of Congress:

> The reason we had these deaths, gentlemen, was not due to any lack of equipment, was not due to any lack of training, but because the pilots ran into that unusual, that extraordinary, cruel weather we had during those nights.
> . . . . . . . . . . . . . . . . . . . . . . . .
> I want to say, further, that all this talk we have heard on the floor of the House about legalized murder is a lot of political claptrap.[21]

As the accidents continued, subcommittee members who had defended the Air Corps were left out on a limb. They easily concluded that Foulois had purposely lied to them about Air Corps capabilities. Angry over being

179

## FOULOIS AND THE U.S. ARMY AIR CORPS

made to look foolish and keen to find a scapegoat for the persisting air mail debacle, Foulois was the obvious choice.

Evidently the air chief had given the subcommittee members some grossly inaccurate data on March 1. Hill reported Foulois told him that all pilots flying the air mail had a minimum of three years of active duty. According to Rogers, the Chief of the Air Corps said under oath that Army pilots carrying the mail averaged fifty to sixty hours of night-flying experience. The subcommittee checked the statistics on those pilots who had died during the mail operation and found that the overwhelming majority of them had fewer night-flying hours than Foulois had claimed.[22] Unhappy over being deceived, the members screened the air chief's February 1 testimony for more lies. Once the process started, the subcommittee latched onto every inconsistency, every biased opinion and overgeneralization, and even the fact that Foulois had revised his testimony, as conclusive proof he was seeking to mislead Congress.

Concern over the air chief's deceptiveness, rather than his entanglement in negotiated contracting, became the driving force behind the continued investigation. Subcommittee members who had previously supported Foulois and his hopes for air arm autonomy turned against this individual whom they believed had practiced illegal procurement procedures, and lied to them about the Air Corps' abilities and General Staff treatment.[23] Congressman Kvale explained the change in the committee's perception:

> General Foulois gave the [Military Affairs] committee the impression that the General Staff and everybody outside of the Air Corps were doing everything possible to injure the Air Corps.
>
> We started out to investigate the General Staff and Mr. Woodring to find out why they had compelled General Foulois to purchase planes thirty to fifty miles slower. I started out very strongly prejudiced against the Chief of Staff and the General Staff and Mr. Woodring, figuring they had compelled him to purchase planes thirty to fifty miles slower. After a few days I came to the conclusion that we were investigating the wrong people; that General Foulois had lied to us—deliberately lied to us.[24]

Congressman Rogers put it this way: "General Foulois has had a splendid record, a long record as a soldier of distinction. Every man on that committee was his friend until he came before us and lied and perjured himself time and time again."[25]

Subcommittee Number 3 issued a report of its findings on June 15, charging Foulois with procurement violations, deliberately seeking to deceive and mislead Congress, and mismanagement and inefficiency in the air mail operation. The report accused the air chief of "deliberate, willful, and intentional violations" of procurement law. As evidence to support this charge, it quoted Foulois' comment that he had broken Army regulations in the past and would do so again.[26] This was an utterly unjust

## THE CHIEF IN TROUBLE, 1934-1935

statement of the air chief's position. Neither Foulois nor his subordinates believed they were doing anything illegal, and the subcommittee's contention that negotiated quantity purchases violated the law was very much open to question. The report refrained from mentioning that in certain cases AR 5-240 permitted purchases without competitive bidding, or that The Judge Advocate General had cleared all contracts before they went into effect. Likewise, it made no comment on the House Naval Affairs Committee's views on the 1926 act or on Woodring's assertion before Subcommittee Number 3 on June 14 that he did not think the Air Corps had broken the law with its past practices. In summary, this section of the report presented a weak case against Foulois.[27]

The report marshaled slightly better evidence to support the charge that the Chief of the Air Corps had sought to deceive and mislead, but even here the subcommittee could not prove intent. To document their case, the members placed portions of Foulois' February 1 testimony alongside his later corrections. This paralleling proved the air chief had subsequently softened much of the belligerent language used to describe how unsuitable General Staff control was.[28] Still, as General Simonds pointed out months later, both columns of testimony conveyed "the same general impression."[29] Foulois had not changed the substance of the remarks, so the comparison was meaningless.

The opinionated, overgeneralized, and poorly worded comments made by Foulois on February 1 were far more useful to the subcommittee's case. The report specifically mentioned his claim that he had no control over Air Corps-related items administered by other War Department agencies. Using portions of Drum's June 5 testimony and copies of General Staff correspondence, the report showed that Foulois was afforded ample opportunity to make recommendations on these items. Evidence in the report verified that the Chief of the Air Corps was responsible for formulating his own budget request and defending it before the Bureau of the Budget and Congress, facts that Foulois had not contested except in the case of the development of the PWA aircraft purchase program. But neither Drum's words nor the War Department documents refuted the air chief's contention that he was never called upon to defend requests before the Budget Bureau or Congress for Air Corps-related items administered by other agencies. The report was on more solid ground when it attacked Foulois' comments on Drum Board procedures. The subcommittee turned to the testimony of Kilbourne, Simonds, and Gulick to show that the Drum Board had not used parliamentary procedure, and that Foulois had not been voted down on a number of issues (as he had claimed).[30]

To further confirm its charge that he had knowingly tried to deceive the Rogers Committee, the report recounted Foulois' March 1 assurance that the Air Corps was adequately trained and equipped to handle the air mail. It contested information on pilot night-flying experience he had given the subcommittee with statistics on some of the fliers killed in the operation. The report disclosed that none of the nine pilots named had near the fifty to sixty hours of night experience that the Air Corps chief asserted was the average for those engaged in mail activity.[31] In this instance Foulois had misled the subcommittee, but he could have done so unknowingly for the Air Corps had only recently started keeping track of night-flying time. Further, Foulois knew students did a good deal of night flying at the training center, and regulations required all tactical pilots to receive about twenty hours of night experience each year. It was quite likely the air chief, fully believing the Air Corps was equal to the air mail job, based his statement to the Rogers Subcommittee on the above considerations without bothering to carefully check the forces' actual night-training experience. It was also possible that the subcommittee's figures for the dead pilots omitted the hours flown at night while students at the training center.[32] Writing in 1935, General Simonds perhaps expressed the true nature of Foulois' misstatement: "I do not believe, however, that it was a case of willful misrepresentation . . . I do not believe General Foulois knew very closely what the true state of affairs was, although he may have believed he did."[33]

The third charge leveled by Subcommittee Number 3, that of inefficiency and mismanagement in the air mail operation, was based in part upon Foulois' February 9 statement to Harllee Branch that the Air Corps could be ready in ten days. The report declared that the air arm was ill prepared for the venture and that Foulois made a grave mistake when he told Branch otherwise. The subcommittee also denounced the air chief, as well as his assistant, for not properly preparing for the welfare of Air Corps personnel engaged in air mail work. The report cited the problems of "per diem allowances, working conditions, and the availability of hangars" to support this charge. No doubt Foulois showed poor judgment in telling the Second Assistant Postmaster General the Air Corps could operate the air mail system, but the charge of not looking after his men's welfare was absurd. Forces beyond his control dictated what facilities could be used in the operation as well as when per diem funds would become available. Foulois struggled to gain extra money for the troops, and he sought to keep his pilots from taking chances. The report may have demonstrated that Foulois used bad judgment on February 9, but it did not bear out the allegation of "mismanagement and inefficiency."[34]

House Report 2060, which also charged Foulois with "gross misconduct" and "unreliability and dishonesty," concluded by saying:

> We find it necessary to report that we are most firmly convinced from the evidence and records submitted that before any substantial progress in the up-

## THE CHIEF IN TROUBLE, 1934-1935

building of the morale and the materiel of the Army Air Corps can be attained; Major General Benjamin D. Foulois must be relieved from his position as Chief of the Air Corps. We unanimously recommend that the Secretary of War take such action without delay.[35]

Foulois reacted at once to news of the report. He angrily attacked the subcommittee's reliance on secret sessions and the manner in which it quoted only extracts from the hearings in its report rather than publishing the entire proceedings. In a statement released June 17 he explained:

> I have no fear of the ultimate outcome of any fair and impartial investigation of my acts, or my service in connection with my administration of the Army Air Corps, especially when all the facts and conditions surrounding Army Air Corps affairs are fully known.
>
> I consider that the accusations . . . are most unfair and unjust and I am ready and willing at any time to meet my accusers in open court.[36]

The crux of the air chief's rebuttal was that the eight subcommittee members had tried him in secret. He now demanded every shred of evidence supporting the subcommittee's decision be brought into the open for public scrutiny.

The secrecy shrouding the investigation was perplexing. In March, Westover had been unable to get a copy of his own testimony from the subcommittee. Yet at the end of that month, a reporter handed him a transcript of the proceedings containing his as well as other individuals' remarks. When members of the Baker Board requested copies of Foulois' and Westover's testimony, Rogers wrote the board that the subcommittee was unanimous in opposing the release of any information gathered in executive session. However, the congressmen seemed to have no qualms about printing portions of Foulois' February 1 statements, which McSwain had guaranteed were for committee use only.[37]

On June 18, in a verbal attack on Foulois on the House floor, Rogers claimed the air chief had no right to criticize the subcommitte's use of closed hearings. He contended: "Major General Foulois himself came before our committee and asked that they be kept secret and executive."[38] This was a grave distortion. When the Chief of the Air Corps appeared before Subcommitte Number 3 on March 7, he willingly testified in open session. The only recorded instance of his having inquired if his remarks would be open to the public was on February 1, before the full Military Affairs Committee. On that occasion the committee had already been sitting in executive session. There is no evidence that he asked the full committee to hear other witnesses in secret, or ever mentioned the subject of executive proceedings to Subcommittee Number 3.[39]

Rogers said something in his June 18 speech that he later regretted. He told his fellow congressmen all of the evidence substantiating the charges against Foulois was in the record: "It is available to him, it is available to anyone; and if our veracity is doubted, I am sure we will be glad to open them [sic] up to the world and let them see the nature of the testimony."[40] The Chief of the Air Corps responded at once by asking Rogers for a complete transcript of the hearings, which Foulois believed he must have to adequately refute the charges against him.[41] After some delay Rogers replied that it "was not my purpose to imply that testimony given strictly in executive session with the understanding it would be held in strict confidence would be made available to you or any other person at this time." The subcommittee chairman said he personally would be willing to give Foulois the full transcript, but that the majority of subcommittee members opposed doing so.[42] By going back on his June 18 pledge, Rogers furnished the air chief and his press supporters with ammunition for a counterattack.

Many of the nation's leading newspapers and military and aviation journals protested both the subcommittee's findings and its secret methods. An editorial in the *Washington Evening Star* gave the gist of this press criticism:

> The House Subcommittee on Military Affairs did not content itself with merely making to the Secretary of War a report of its findings. It tried—if it can be called a trial—General Foulois, found him guilty, and, acting as judge and jury, sentenced him to be dismissed, and called upon Mr. Dern to carry out the sentence. This appears, at best, to be a high-handed proceeding on the part of a subcommittee of a House committee. . . . A trial conducted behind closed doors, with the prosecutors acting as both judge and jury, is certainly repugnant to all ideas of American justice.[43]

The paper also asserted it did not appear that Foulois had actually violated any laws or regulations.[44] A number of editorials argued that a full transcript of the subcommittee's hearings should be made immediately available to him. In commenting on the charges, *U. S. Air Services* went overboard proclaiming Foulois' virtue: "It is a savage attack on a man who has worked for the Air Corps the way Joan of Arc worked for France, the chief difference between them being that the General has smoked a pipe." The editorial continued: "Call Gandhi a well-dressed man, call Grant garrulous, say that Lee loved not Virginia, but don't be an ass and assert that Foulois is dishonest."[45]

The subcommittee erred badly when it called Foulois' honesty into question. The Chief of the Air Corps was a man of integrity who had never used his position for personal gain. Unlike some senior Air Corps officers, who apparently did not believe small gifts or favors from aircraft contractors compromised their honor, Foulois followed a strict policy of accepting nothing from anyone while in office. He returned even trivial items such as a picture of a B-10 bomber and a box of cigars because he did not want to feel obligated to businessmen and politicians.

The *Army and Navy Journal* took the subcommittee to task for charging the air chief with dishonesty and called for it to publicly apolo-

## THE CHIEF IN TROUBLE, 1934-1935

gize to Foulois. The trade journal said there was a tremendous difference between the accusation the eight congressmen had made and the charge of dishonesty of expression they had probably intended to make.[46] Congressman Kvale acknowledged the subcommittee's error in early July, insisting that by dishonesty the report meant only that Foulois had deliberately sought to mislead the committee. He added that the subcommittee members "have failed to uncover one single instance of any financial dishonesty on the part of any officer in the Air Corps, or in any of the transactions jointly involving the corps and the aviation industry in procurement affairs." Kvale also admitted that while the subcommittee found that Foulois had deliberately violated the law, he believed the air chief did so "sincerely believing that he was acting in the best interests of the Air Corps."[47]

On June 18, Rogers wrote to Roosevelt officially informing him of the subcommittee's report and asking the President to promptly remove Foulois from the post of Chief of the Air Corps. Dern took charge of the matter for the administration and, in accordance with normal War Department practices, referred the report to the accused for comment. Subcommittee members wanted the secretary to quickly carry out their wishes, threatening to withhold action on all Air Corps-related legislation until he did. But Dern could not be hurried. During the next six weeks, Foulois worked on his rebuttal and continued to seek the release of the hearings transcript.[48]

The Chief of the Air Corps was deeply disturbed by the subcommittee report. He felt helpless to defend himself against charges based on concealed evidence and testimony. He sincerely believed he could easily clear his name if the basis for the subcommittee's accusations were brought out—but this Subcommittee Number 3 would not allow. Justifiably angry, he wrote a statement for the press (never released) attacking the subcommittee members for the "unethical" way they had used his February 1 testimony. He complained they had violated the pledge given him that his statement would not be made public, unfairly attacked his revisions, and printed just those portions of his remarks in the June report that could be twisted to support the subcommittee's contentions. He could not understand how Rogers and his cohorts could deny him the right to see the transcript of proceedings when they had broken their trust and printed part of his executive session remarks.[49]

Foulois refuted the report's charges in a written statement to the Baker Board in early July. The board, wrapping up its investigation, had not concerned itself with the workings of the Rogers Subcommittee nor the alleged wrongdoings of the Chief of the Air Corps. Foulois, however, felt constrained to give his fellow board members his side of the story. He realized he was a poor extemporaneous speaker and told the board that

185

the subcommittee had taken unfair advantage of this defect. Claiming he had never knowingly made false statements in his testimony, he explained that his "mental makeup as a flying man" caused him to develop "a habit of rapid speech, often unconnected and incoherent, and generally requiring considerable verbal repetition on my part, in order that my real thoughts and ideas may be clearly and accurately expressed." He also reviewed for the board members the multitude of evidence, including the recent findings of the House Naval Affairs Committee, to confirm the legality of negotiated contracting.[50]

On August 10, Foulois submitted a statement on the subcommittee report to the Secretary of War. The air chief began the paper by reviewing his extensive correspondence of the past month and a half with McSwain and the eight subcommittee members, in which he had sought to secure a transcript of the hearings. Foulois told Dern how the subcommittee had violated "the solemn promises" given him concerning his February 1 testimony. He contrasted the methods and outcome of the Naval Affairs Committee's procurement probe with those of the Rogers Subcommittee. In an effort to persuade the secretary that the Chief of the Air Corps was now a cooperative member of the War Department team, and thus worth saving, Foulois pointed to his "loyal, sincere, and wholehearted support and cooperation" during the Baker Board investigation. In closing, he affirmed that to prepare a proper defense, it was "absolutely essential" he be allowed to see the elusive hearing transcripts. He asked Dern to suspend action in the case until the subcommittee made its records available to him.[51] Dern was probably not swayed by Foulois' efforts to portray himself as a member of the War Department "team," but he did believe in the air chief's right to see the evidence used against him. Moreover, he had little love for McSwain and his Military Affairs Committee.

The secretary sent Foulois' statement and one of his own to Congressman Rogers on August 21. Dern's message criticized the subcommittee's methods, but did so diplomatically:

> A most difficult problem now confronts me, the solution of which involves some of the fundamental precepts of our system of jurisprudence embodying many of the most sacred rights of American citizenship.
>
> Had the report of the committee been confined to an indictment or charges against Major General Foulois, the situation would have presented no difficulty. In such event I could have followed the regular procedure prescribed for the determination of such matters by referring the case to a military tribunal for adjudication. Instead, however, the report is not limited to an indictment, but in effect finds the accused guilty, fixes the sentence, and calls on the Secretary of War to execute it.[52]

Dern explained that if he now referred the case to a military tribunal "for the determination of the precise matters which your committee already has adjudged," it might look as though the secretary were questioning the

THE CHIEF IN TROUBLE, 1934-1935

subcommittee's findings. "Such a suggestion I desire most scrupulously to avoid."[53]

Dern claimed:

> had the report and recommendation of the committee been based on a full and complete hearing wherein the constitutional rights of the accused were assured, even though the procedure was somewhat unusual, I would have felt constrained to comply with the mandate of the committee. But such was not the case.[54]

He stressed that Foulois had appeared before the subcommittee only as a witness—not as a defendant—and had been given no chance to hear or cross-examine those who testified against him or to offer evidence in his own defense. Nor had Foulois been permitted to be represented by counsel at the hearings. "All of these rights are sacred to every American citizen and are guaranteed by the Constitution." Dern wrote that under the present circumstances he could not in clear conscience act against the Chief of the Air Corps:

> I feel that the only step now open to me is to transmit to the committee the partial statement of Major General Foulois to the end that the committee may consider whether he should not now be permitted to have full access to the evidence against him and then appear before the committee to present his defense.[55]

The secretary thus dumped the issue back into the subcommittee's lap.

The members of Subcommittee Number 3 were very upset with Dern's statement and his inference that they had violated Foulois' constitutional rights. Rogers responded for the group in late September, reiterating to reporters the subcommittee's demand that Foulois must go. He also said the members would formally consider the air chief's request for access to all of the records in the investigation as soon as the fall elections were over. He again claimed he had always favored giving the information to Foulois, and believed the subcommittee would turn over to the air chief whatever he wanted when it reconvened.[56]

Press reaction to Dern's stand probably prompted Roger's accommodating attitude. Editorial comment overwhelmingly supported the secretary's position. This pleased Foulois, for it put the subcommittee on the defensive. MacArthur told the subcommittee in December that ninety-nine percent of the papers commenting on the issue agreed the air chief should have access to all of the testimony and be allowed to defend himself before the eight congressmen. The Chief of Staff personally endorsed this solution. Other events interceded, however, and the subcommittee never did release the documents to Foulois.[57]

During MacArthur's December 7 appearance, he and the subcommittee members aired their differing perspectives on the Foulois case. The congressmen defended their action, saying all the charges against the Air

## FOULOIS AND THE U.S. ARMY AIR CORPS

Corps Chief came from his own testimony. Countering, MacArthur contended that Foulois had spoken to the subcommittee as a witness and not as a defendant. In off-the-record comments the previous June, the Chief of Staff had implied to the congressmen that he questioned Foulois' fitness to command, possibly due to the air mail fiasco. But on December 7, MacArthur let the members know in very certain terms that the air chief deserved to see all of the evidence and be given a chance to properly defend himself before Subcommittee Number 3: "I can say very frankly for myself, I am amazed that the committee did not call the man and listen to him and hear his evidence. I cannot understand it." Congressman Hill volunteered that the subcommittee had expected Dern to convene a court of inquiry upon receiving its June report. He said the congressmen had merely been functioning as a grand jury and would not have been offended if a resulting War Deparment investigation disagreed with the subcommittee's findings. MacArthur replied that he thought the secretary's action would have been different had the subcommittee not recommended the punishment in the case. He explained that if the subcommittee wanted Dern to investigate Foulois, the secretary would probably do so at once, if the members turned over the evidence used to support the original charges.[58]

MacArthur's icebreaking offer of a War Department probe, coupled with other factors, caused the Secretary of War, after consulting with subcommittee members on December 13, to order The Inspector General to look into the charges against Foulois. This was not an outright capitulation on Dern's part, for the subcommittee promised to turn over its records to the investigators. Perhaps the secretary was influenced in his decision by subcommittee hints to MacArthur on December 7 that some Air Corps officers had voiced complaints against Foulois at the spring hearings. Likewise, the members may have revealed additional pieces of evidence against the air chief during the December 13 meeting which impacted upon Dern. Then, too, the Rogers Subcommittee was probing other facets of War Department business activity and desired an Inspector General investigation of seven additional Army officers in December. This may have inspired the secretary to dispose of the allegations facing Foulois at the same time he was dealing with the charges against the other men.[59]

Foulois liked neither Dern's decision nor the way the investigation progressed. On December 27, he wrote Col. Thorne Strayer, the individual conducting the investigation, requesting that the eight subcommittee members be required to sign their list of allegations against him. Strayer informed him the signatures were not needed since the Secretary of War had ordered the probe. Foulois was suspicious when The Inspector General suddenly removed Strayer from the case around January 20 and replaced him with Col. Walter L. Reed. Strayer had earlier taken testimony from Drum and Kilbourne and apparently had ruffled the Deputy Chief of Staff's feathers with his attitude. A coded message in Foulois' files reveals Strayer's version of his removal: Drum had visited Congressman McSwain and asked him to put pressure on The Inspector General to remove Strayer from the case because the investigator appeared to be hostile toward Drum and in support of Foulois' position. McSwain then phoned The Inspector General and threatened to call Strayer before the Military Affairs Committee if he were not replaced. Thereupon The Inspector General assigned Reed to carry out the investigation. Reed threw out the testimony thus far taken and began anew. Foulois did not trust the new investigator. During the four and a half months of the inquiry Reed gave him the feeling that he was on trial before a court-martial. Unnerved by the whole process and fearful of a War Department plot to oust him, the Chief of the Air Corps defended himself as best he could.[60]

Reed gathered statements from the four Army generals who had testified before Subcommittee Number 3—Drum, Gulick, Kilbourne, and Simonds—and allowed Foulois to see their comments and cross-examine them by means of written questions given the investigator. Drum repeated much of what he had said before the Rogers Subcommittee, including the claim that Foulois was unfit to be the Chief of the Air Corps. His reasons for reaching this conclusion were quite curious. To show the air chief's shortcomings as a strategic thinker, he mentioned Foulois' sponsorship of the 1933 plans for the air defense of the United States. This was a potentially valid point, but Drum spent most of his time attacking the Chief of the Air Corps' lack of expertise in aeronautical engineering. The deputy chief based this stand on Foulois' dearth of formal education, an entirely inadequate gauge when applied to a man who had begun modifying and repairing airplanes in 1909. Undoubtedly the main reason Drum judged Foulois unacceptable was the latter's stiff resistance to War Department control: "My own personal opinion is that the Chief of the Air Corps should be of that type man that he can lead his Corps into a state of mind whereby they loyally support the policies of the Secretary of War and the Chief of Staff."[61]

Kilbourne went well beyond his May testimony, telling Reed: "I agree that General Foulois should be relieved." He said Air Corps officers no longer had confidence in their chief and that Foulois had never tried to cooperate with the General Staff. He cited Foulois' anti-General Staff testimony of February 1 and recalled how the OCAC had secretly drafted McSwain's February 2, 1934, bill to extend autonomy to the Air Corps.[62]

Simonds was much kinder to the Chief of the Air Corps. He faulted Foulois for being too harsh in his February 1 criticism of the General Staff and for frequently relying on biased opinions and thus distorting the facts. However, he did not think the air chief was intentionally trying to be dishonest in his remarks to the Military Affairs Committee and Subcommittee Number 3. Simonds believed the air chief was only giving his views and seeking to win the committee over. Though not directly calling for removal, Simonds told Reed "doubts have arisen in my mind" whether Foulois is suited to the job.[63]

The charge of giving false and misleading information to Congress was the prominent issue in Reed's investigation. Foulois could say he believed he was acting legally when he used negotiated contracting. He could contend he was using his best judgment when he told Branch the Air Corps could handle the air mail. But it would be far more difficult to explain away his February 1 remarks on the General Staff's treatment of the Army air arm.

Reviewing a copy of his testimony, Foulois realized how easily his overgeneralizations and poorly worded, opinionated comments could be misconstrued. He admitted this to Reed, but insisted he had neither intentionally lied to the House Military Affairs Committee nor sought to malign the General Staff. He may have been sincere about his desire to be honest with the committee, but his remark about the General Staff is hard to believe. As a general defense for the entire February 1 episode Foulois claimed he had been ill and emotionally upset that day, and "[d]ue to my abnormal physical and mental condition, coupled with loss of my temper on several occasions . . . I undoubtedly, on several occasions, used words which were incoherent, unrelated, and misleading."[64] Foulois made no mention of his February 1 illness to the Baker Board or in other correspondence prior to the beginning of the inspector general probe. His personal records do not show he was sick in January or February 1934. Perhaps his illness was the product of reflective thinking.

To bolster his case, the air chief solicited testimonials in his behalf from numerous congressmen and aircraft manufacturers. Many congressmen and senators responded, among them the Speaker of the House, the chairman of the Senate Military Affairs Committee, and four members of the House Military Affairs Committee. Most of them told The Inspector General that the printed record of Foulois' February 1 testimony contained no evidence of false statements or willful intent to deceive. Aircraft company executives wrote to attest to the Chief of the Air Corps' technical abilities, counteracting Drum's assertions.[65]

By April 1935 the House Military Affairs Committee had become impatient with the slow pace of the investigation. It voted to give the Secretary of War until May 1 to make a report. The committee threatened to summon The Inspector General for an explanation if Dern did not comply. Committee members further implied they would sit on all pending War Department legislation to encourage the speedy conclusion

## THE CHIEF IN TROUBLE, 1934-1935

of the probe. Reed had not completed his work by the congressional deadline, but he sent a partial report that temporarily placated McSwain and the other committee members.[66]

A month and a half later, on June 14, Dern released The Inspector General's final report. According to the Secretary of War:

> The Inspector General found with regard to these allegations, first, that the evidence adduced did not establish that General Foulois violated existing laws in the purchase of airplanes and aircraft materials; second, that there was no cause for censure in General Foulois' opinional statements with regard to the capacity of his corps to fly the air mail; and third, General Foulois did depart from the ethics and standards of the service by making exaggerated, unfair, and misleading statements to a Congressional committee.[67]

In a letter to McSwain, Secretary Dern expanded on the one area of confirmed guilt. He said Foulois had made statements on February 1

> which were not only unfair and misleading to the committee itself but which also seriously reflected upon the integrity of his brother officers, and that in general, during his appearance before your committee, he evinced a lack of team spirit and a tendency to make exaggerated and inexact statements.[68]

For these minor misdeeds, Dern sent Foulois a letter of reprimand.[69]

In the letter to the Chief of the Air Corps, the secretary listed the specific portions of the February 1 testimony Reed had probed and the findings in each instance. On many of the issues the investigation concluded that Foulois' remarks, when placed in the proper context, represented the general's opinions and were not necessarily exaggerated or misleading. The Inspector General found only two instances when the air chief had made false or unjustified statements deserving of censure. One was his charge that War Department officers were trying to deceive the committee with their February 1 bill. The other was Foulois' vague statements on his lack of opportunity to present Air Corps needs to the Director of the Bureau of the Budget and Congress. Reed concluded that Foulois' statements to the effect that the General Staff had hindered the Army air arm were exaggerated and unfair, but they "were largely expressions of his own opinions or conclusions and were not, therefore of such character that they may be properly classified as false."[70]

Both Foulois and the Rogers Subcommittee considered The Inspector General's conclusions tantamount to an acquittal. The general was pleased and relieved. He had spent a great deal of time over the past year defending himself rather than running the Air Corps. He now thought the ordeal was over. Rogers was livid, for he and other subcommittee members believed the affair would end in Foulois' court-martial and the subcommittee's vindication. Roger's June 15 remarks on the House floor blasted what he called the "slap on the wrist" administered by Dern to a "liar and perjurer."[71] Most of the members of the Military Affairs Committee were also dissatisfied with the Secretary of War's refusal to remove Foulois. On

191

June 19 the committee wrote Dern demanding to see The Inspector General's report. Rogers told newsmen:

> I am determined to go through with this fight because I know it is right. If it is necessary to go to the White House, I am in favor of doing that. Secretary Dern has admitted that General Foulois gave false testimony to the committee, and that should be reason enough to end his usefulness as head of the Air Corps.[72]

Full of vindictiveness, the subcommittee chairman did not abandon his campaign to oust the air chief until Foulois announced in August that he would retire in December, at the end of his four-year tour as Chief of the Air Corps. Rogers' attacks and the attitude of the Military Affairs Committee, not pressure from within the War Department, spurred Foulois to opt for retirement and to request terminal leave effective September 25. He had come to the conclusion that the committee members' feeling toward him might jeopardize future Air Corps legislation. Frustrated and disheartened by the relentless pressure for his removal, Foulois decided to depart quietly. He did not want to hinder the organization for which he had fought so hard over the past two decades.[73] What had begun in early 1934 as an investigation of Air Corps procurement procedures came to a close in August 1935, amid vicious attacks on the Chief of the Air Corps for the manner in which he had spoken about the General Staff to members of the House Military Affairs Committee.

## CHAPTER VIII

## ORGANIZATION, 1934-1935: THE GHQ AIR FORCE

General Staff-Air Corps relations were unsettled during the first months of 1934. In addition to the War Department's embarrassment over air mail operations and tensions generated by Subcommittee No. 3's early efforts to prove the Air Corps' alleged materiel shortcomings, the General Staff was deeply concerned over what appeared to be a favorable atmosphere in Congress in February and March toward autonomy for the Army air arm.[1]

Foulois' remarks of February 1 on the inappropriateness of ground officer control of military aviation initially fell on receptive ears. The following day McSwain introduced his bill (H.R. 7601) to cut the Air Corps free from the General Staff. For the next six weeks there were rumors of growing support on Capitol Hill for such a reorganization. The many crashes and deaths associated with air mail activities and the charges of inferior aircraft led some congressmen to conclude that the Army was doing a poor job of administering its air component. Representative Rogers reported: "Sentiment in the Congress for a separate air force, largely independent of the War Department, is strong and is all the time growing stronger."[2]

It was in this atmosphere and as a direct result of the Air Corps' poor showing in the air mail operation that Secretary of War Dern resolved to appoint a special committee to study and report on the condition of the Army air arm. He told Roosevelt on March 11 that the group would include the members of the Drum Board plus a few civilian authorities on aviation. Dern promptly asked Charles A. Lindbergh, Orville Wright, and Clarence D. Chamberlin to take part in the probe. Lindbergh, who believed Roosevelt had no right to cancel the air mail contracts and to use the Air Corps in the first place, refused the secretary's

# FOULOIS AND THE U.S. ARMY AIR CORPS

President Wilson's Sec. of War, Newton D. Baker, was selected to chair a group convened to investigate the Air Corps in 1934.

request on principle. Wright declined due to poor health. With just ex-Army officer Chamberlin at his disposal, Dern decided to delay the study and invite five more civilians to join the committee. Newton D. Baker, Wilson's Secretary of War, agreed to chair the enlarged group. He and the other members were ready to begin work on April 17.[3]

Dern told the Baker Board they were being convened to conduct "a constructive study and report upon the operations of the Army Air Corps and the adequacy and efficiency of its technical flying equipment and training for the performance of its mission in peace and war."[4] He added:

> It appears that the experience of the Army Air Corps in carrying the mail has raised doubts about the general efficiency of our Army Air Force. These doubts have been emphasized by the utterances of critics whose competence the public cannot evaluate. Many of our citizens are bewildered. They do not know whether we have a good military air force or not. If we have, the public ought to know it and be reassured. If, on the other hand, we are deficient in equipment, personnel, or training, we want your best judgment as to what should be done to bring us up to a satisfactory standard.[5]

The group immediately began hearings and compiled 4,283 pages of testimony over the next two months. It devoted twenty-five days to taking testimony from 105 witnesses, and also considered comments sent in by over five hundred Air Corps officers. Members briefly reviewed the findings of fourteen earlier military aviation investigations. They visited Air Corps installations in Texas and Ohio to better grasp the air arm's workings and problems. Studying everything from procurement practices to

## ORGANIZATION: 1934-1935

training, equipment, policy, and relations with the General Staff, the Baker Board conducted a very thorough probe.[6]

The General Staff, however, was quite careful to see that the investigators did not reach faulty conclusions. It knew that military aviators appearing before the board would surely press for autonomy and that such a change had the support of some very vocal congressmen. Senior staff officers therefore organized the probe so as to ensure their views would prevail. The very makeup of the board gave them a clear-cut advantage. Of the five general officer members, Foulois alone was a flier. Moreover, Chairman Baker had opposed greater air arm independence in 1919, and his attitude had not changed since. Of the other five civilian members, only James H. (Jimmy) Doolittle could be regarded as a supporter of the Air Corps' view.

For added insurance the vice chairman, General Drum, appointed Maj. Albert E. Brown of the General Staff to act as recorder and direct the questioning of witnesses. Brown guided the testimony, asking leading questions or switching the line of inquiry according to General Staff interests. He also set the agenda and with Drum won board agreement to use the Morrow Board's conclusions and the Air Corps Act of 1926 as a proper point of departure for the probe. This sidestepped the problem of discussing in detail the findings of committees that had favored increased air arm independence prior to 1926. As a final guarantee that War Department views would prevail, Drum saw to it that he, General Simonds, and one civilian member would draft the board's final report.[7]

Brown argued for excluding the separate air force issue altogether, since the question had not been included in the Secretary of War's instructions to the board. When Foulois objected, Baker decided to allow discussion on the subject. Brown thereupon called numerous ground officers to testify on the correctness and military benefits of keeping the Air Corps in its present status. The General Staff was prepared to organize the GHQ Air Force along the lines recommended by the Drum Board, but that was as far as it was willing to go. Kilbourne told his fellow members that the War Department was about to bring the GHQ Air Force to life when McSwain introduced his "disruptive" bills and Subcommittee Number 3 commenced its investigation. He claimed that except for these interferences and the air mail operation, the GHQ Air Force would now exist. The General Staff aimed to undercut the proponents of air arm independence/autonomy by committing itself completely to creating this new force.[8]

The Baker Board gave Air Corps officers ample opportunity to air their views, and the flyers rushed to campaign for control of their own institutional destiny. In a unified effort the aviators testified before or wrote letters to Baker's group, vigorously advocating freedom from War Department control. Maj. Walter H. Frank from the OCAC expressed an attitude that the board found prevalent throughout the Air Corps. Frank told the investigators that "the military mind of the ground officer traditionally had tied air operations down to the movement of ground troops"—negating much of air power's worth. The War Department had inhibited the growth of military aviation, and to leave this vital military element in the hands of those who did not understand it was foolish:

> In the commercial world they do not select a civil engineer to perform their surgical operations, nor do they select medical specialists to give them legal advice. . . . Yet, the operation of a system which functions just like this is what the Air Corps is subjected to under General Staff procedure at this time.[9]

Frank wanted independence for the Army air arm but was willing to accept a separate budget, separate promotion list, and the removal of air matters from General Staff control as a compromise. He told the board: "In the Office of the Chief of the Air Corps I think there is only one man who has views to the contrary of these that I have expressed."[10] Other Air Corps officers appearing before the Baker Board wholeheartedly endorsed Frank's views.

Shortly after opening hearings, the board instructed The Adjutant General to inform all Army aviators that it would consider any constructive suggestions they might care to make. The response surprised and angered the investigators. Apparently unknown to Foulois, Air Corps officers in the field organized a coordinated letter-writing campaign. The flyers at Maxwell Field, Alabama, put together and signed a single letter of response, and Maj. Follett Bradley, from the OCAC, circulated it to other Air Corps installations while on his air mail inspection trips. Those bases not visited by Bradley got a telegram from the Maxwell Field officers. It contained the recommendations in the Maxwell letter and a request that other officers make similar replies to the board's request.[11] The letter made the following "constructive suggestions" to the Baker Board:

> First, that the Air Corps be reorganized as a separate and independent branch of our national defense coequal with the other military services.
>
> Second, that it be charged with the responsibility of providing for the air defense of the United States.
>
> Third, that it may or may not include naval aviation.
>
> Fourth, that it present its requirements to Congress through the medium of a separate budget.
>
> Fifth, that in effecting this separate and independent organization it is of no vital moment whether it be accomplished through a separate Department of Air or by reorganization of the War Department, provided the military head of the Air Force is made responsible directly to the Secretary of War in the same manner as is the Chief of Staff of the Army.[12]

As a result of the campaign, 516 Air Corps officers signed similar letters and sent them to the board.[13]

The board members were incensed at this apparent collusion. They hastily ordered aviators to Washington to explain the group response but

## ORGANIZATION: 1934-1935

could uncover no evidence of pressure being applied to force flyers to join in the campaign. Maj. Harvey Burwell,* one of those who had refused to take part, informed the board that Foulois' OCAC staff had nothing to do with the letter-writing scheme; instead, officers in the field "have an honest unanimity of thought on that subject, that each one, individually, I believe, without pressure of any papers which have been prepared on it, have honest convictions on that subject."[14] The board, revealing the General Staff's strong influence, refused to be swayed by the written pleas for increased autonomy. The members believed the "unanimity was influenced by action of those formerly advocating complete separation" and claimed "the manner in which these written opinions, generally identical in expression, were gathered tends to support this belief and to weaken greatly the effect of the testimony."[15]

General Foulois assumed an innocuous stance during the investigation. Realizing he was in trouble with Subcommittee Number 3 and that he had enemies among the military members of the board, he denied any knowledge of the letter-writing campaign and refrained from commenting on the Air Corps' quest for autonomy. Perhaps he knew that nothing he could say would influence the board to go against the General Staff's wishes. More likely he feared making his own situation worse and felt he should be as cooperative as possible. The air chief asked the board to recommend that the War Department continue to give the Air Corps funding priority until the five-year program could be completed and argued for a unified GHQ Air Force exempt from corps area control. But apart from this, he bent to the views of the General Staff.[16] The degree of Foulois' surrender was evident in a July 10 written message he delivered to the board:

> The agitation for separation of the Army Air Corps from the rest of the Army will quickly subside provided prompt and adequate steps are taken to build up the Air Corps as now contemplated in the proposed recommendations of this Committee to the Secretary of War.
>
> However, in order to insure that each and every individual officer and enlisted man in the Air Corps fully understands that the Air Corps shall remain an integral part of the Army for sometime to come, this Committee should clearly and unanimously recommend to the Secretary of War its views to such effect, with the hope that a positive and conclusive pronouncement covering the question may also be made by the President.[17]

Due to his troubles, or a decision to work only within the realm of the possible, Foulois was accepting formation of a GHQ Air Force in lieu of

---

*Full name, Henry B. S. Burwell.

autonomy. Most other Air Corps officers would soon follow suit.

As it related to organization and doctrine, the Baker Board report issued in mid-July did little more than restate the Drum Board findings. It concluded that military aviation was valuable in both offensive and defensive operations, but could not replace other elements in the national defense structure. The report claimed that within the present limits of technology, air power could not independently affect the outcome of war and thus should stay an integral part of the Army. Maintaining that the Air Corps, with its own Assistant Secretary for Air, "has virtually been independent since its inception," the board was "convinced that the time has arrived for the Air Corps to become in all respects a homogeneous part of the Army, under General Staff control, and be subject to military coordination, study, influence, and operation." The report lauded the principle of "unity of command" and underscored that the board "is not greatly impressed with the several imputations against the General Staff." After all, "control is always repressive when misunderstood or inimical to personal interests." However, it called for more Air Corps officers on the General Staff, "with the object of more equitable representation and the inculcation of a broader understanding."[18]

The report recommended that a GHQ Air Force, consisting of all combat units and their auxiliaries in the continental United States, be formed at once. The GHQ Air Force commander—a suitable air officer—was to report directly to the Chief of Staff in peace and to the theater commander in war. The board maintained this commander's jurisdiction should extend to all questions related to his force's organization, maintenance and operation of technical equipment, maneuvers, and unit training. Again reflecting the General Staff's touch, the report said "the air fields and their maintenance outfits could remain under corps area commanders." It suggested leaving procurement, supply, development of training doctrine, and Air Corps schools to the Chief of the Air Corps. Thus, while championing unity of command, the Baker Board called for a three-way split in the control of the tactical portion of the Air Corps. The GHQ Air Force commander would have operations and training; the corps area commander, the installations and housekeeping forces; and the Chief of the Air Corps, the administration of supply and procurement and the development of doctrine. While the board did not explicitly prohibit the Chief of the Air Corps from commanding the GHQ Air Force, the report certainly implied this.[19]

Besides recommending a GHQ Air Force, the Baker Board endorsed the Drum Board's call for a force of 2,320 aircraft and the manpower specified in the Air Corps Act of 1926—"but not at the expense of the rest of the Army." It also advocated a number of improvements not mentioned in the 1933 study, such as increased instrument and night training;

## ORGANIZATION: 1934-1935

use of the provisions of the 1926 Air Corps Act which authorized temporary promotions for officers to make rank commensurate with responsibiltiies; a rise in flying hours per pilot to three hundred a year; and the removal of tactical training from control of the corps area commanders.[20]

The report did not pass judgment on the air mail operation. The board was content to comment that Air Corps equipment was suitable for combat operations, but "not easily adaptable to air mail work." Flyers trained for military missions "could not be expected in the beginning to perform . . . as efficiently as experienced air mail pilots." Pointing out that bad weather compounded the Air Corps' problems, the report praised the work of the Army aviators and added that the operation gave the air arm an excellent readiness test.[21]

The Baker Board report, reflecting the General Staff's views on every major issue, was signed by each of the eleven members. Doolittle alone mildly objected to the findings. He appended a reservation to the report saying the nation's future security depended on an adequate air force that could best be developed if the air arm was organized as a separate service. Although offering autonomy as an alternative, Doolittle agreed to accept the report's proposals since they represented the views of the full committee.[22]

The War Department was quite pleased with the report. It undercut the claims of airpower advocates and recommended more—not less—General Staff control of military aviation. Its comprehensive program to improve the Air Corps could be used to dissuade the recently formed Federal Aviation Commission from tampering with the existing order. In addition, the report offered an alternate to autonomy—the GHQ Air Force, a combat organization that the aviators prized highly. This force could carry out all the missions contemplated for an independent air arm. Hence, it was bound to placate most Air Corps' officers at least temporarily.[23] With Dern's and Roosevelt's approval, the War Department promptly began to put into effect those board proposals not requiring legislation.[24]

Foulois was willing to accept the board's recommendations and wanted OCAC personnel to be as helpful as possible to General Staff planners preparing programs based on the proposals. Westover described Foulois' position in a July memo to the Plans Division of the OCAC:

> General Foulois desires me to inform you that it is his intention to have the Air Corps comply wholeheartedly and efficiently in carrying out the recommendations of the Board. He considers that the Baker Board report constitutes the first comprehensive outline of War Department policy with respect to military aviation that the Air Corps has ever had. He, therefore, desires the Air Corps to carry out such policy in a thoroughly cooperative and sincere endeavor in order that the greatest possible progress may be accomplished toward upbuilding the Air Corps to meet the needs of national defense.[25]

## FOULOIS AND THE U.S. ARMY AIR CORPS

The air chief's cooperative attitude stemmed from both his troubles with the Rogers Committee and from his desire to see the GHQ Air Force finally brought to life. Some Air Corps officers disagreed with him and went on seeking freedom from General Staff control. However, by virtue of his position and personal influence within the Army air arm, his acquiescence had a decided effect on the attitudes held by most Air Corps officers toward the Baker Board recommendations.

While the General Staff and OCAC worked during late summer to implement the recommendations, the Federal Aviation Commission prepared to launch its investigation of all phases of American aviation. After passage of the Air Mail Act in June, Roosevelt appointed Clark Howell, editor of the *Atlanta Constitution*, chairman of the five-member commission. Untainted by General Staff prejudices, these individuals commenced at once to gather background information. Howell journeyed abroad to study the status of aviation and government administration of aeronautics

Clark Howell, selected by Roosevelt to chair the Federal Aviation Commission.

## ORGANIZATION: 1934–1935

in four leading European countries. Other members traveled throughout the United States and the Caribbean on a similar mission. The five civilians opened public hearings in late September, taking the testimony of 102 witnesses over the next six weeks. The commission then went into executive session to hear 89 witnesses on issues relating to national defense. Howell announced at the outset of the probe that his group would conduct a completely independent study. He did, however, tell reporters the commission would review the Baker Board report along with those of other past investigations. In light of ambivalent public opinion on the issue of a separate air force and the favorable disposition of McSwain and some members of his committee toward one, the General Staff was deeply concerned over Howell's independent stand.[26]

The War Department did not want the Federal Aviation Commission to undo its Baker Board handiwork, and it took steps to prevent this from happening. Secretary Dern appointed Kilbourne the single War Department contact for the commission. Deputy Chief of Staff Drum in turn directed that all personnel having business with the Howell group go through the War Plans Division chief. This move was designed to foster unity of opinion. Kilbourne believed the Federal Aviation Commission would probably be the last committee reporting on military aeronautics in the near future and that its recommendations would carry great weight with Roosevelt and Congress. He deemed it imperative that the War Department voice its views as convincingly as possible. MacArthur agreed, and all General Staff agencies and the OCAC set about building a brief in support of the Baker Board's findings. In early August, Kilbourne sought the Navy Department's cooperation in establishing a common line of testimony. Earlier, Gen. George Van Horn Moseley, a personal friend of Howell, attempted to convince the commission chairman of the correctness of the War Department's views of military aviation. The General Staff was leaving nothing to chance.[27]

The War Department statement submitted to the Federal Aviation Commission in late August was nothing more than a defense of the Baker Board program. It explained that the Army had adopted the board's recommendations of the July report and was putting them into effect: "The conclusions of that Committee present fully the views of the War Department." The paper underscored the General Staff's opposition to any further reorganization. It said the War Department "sees no advantage in any change and cannot surrender any functions to the control of another agency." Freely quoting the Baker Board's recommendations throughout the eighty-six-page statement, the General Staff held:

Unless the conclusions of the War Department special committee [Baker Board] on the broad questions of organization and utilization of Army aviation can be accepted, it will be necessary to present, in closed session, considerations that must govern those responsible for the national defense but which cannot be made public.[28]

The War Department went all out to control the testimony of Army officers before the commission. MacArthur required them to review the statement sent to the commission before appearing. He admonished those testifying as War Department representatives to refrain from venturing opinions contrary to the set policy in their official presentations.[29] After Foulois' office queried the General Staff on the right of witnesses to voice their personal views, Kilbourne wrote that

> it appears inevitable that, in questions by the Commission, personal views will be asked and must be given. The only requirement, in case such opinion is at variance with the approval policy of the War Department, is that the witnesses call attention to the fact, as well as the fact that these policies have been formulated after consideration of testimony from all available sources.[30]

Kilbourne likewise reviewed drafts of official testimony officers were to present and called those who went to make official statements together for a discussion before they testified. The War Plans Division chief or one of his assistants then sat in on all hearings in which Army officers spoke before the commission.[31]

The General Staff was not alone in its efforts to influence the Howell Commission. A number of Air Corps officers, still clinging to the goal of autonomy, did their best to win the commission's support. One airpower advocate took it upon himself to try to sway Howell during his visit to Great Britain.[32] Others strove to make their views known in testimony before the commission. Foulois continued to maintain an innocuous stance, but he allowed his OCAC subordinates to design presentations for Westover and himself that affirmed the independent decisiveness of air power and argued the need for aircraft in excess of the number recommended by the Baker Board. The paper prepared for Foulois claimed the United States and Japan were the only two major nations in which all military aviation activities were not unified in one department. It asserted that "the trend is definitely toward a unified Air Corps under a Minister of Air."[33]

Kilbourne strenuously objected when he saw the drafts of Foulois' and Westover's proposed presentations. He took the air chief to task for letting his subordinates dwell on controversial questions and suggested that Foulois rewrite his statement to delete the objectionable comments. The Chief of the Air Corps complied, expunging all references to the decisiveness of aviation and independence. The result was a bland presentation on the noncontroversial needs of the Army air arm. Kilbourne protested remarks in Westover's paper which implied that long-range overseas bombing missions were not only possible but probable. The Chief of the War Plans Division contended the Assistant Chief of the Air Corps should

ORGANIZATION: 1934-1935

emphasize in his testimony the tremendous difficulties inherent in such operations.[34] This Westover agreed to do, but he also told the commission:

With constantly increasing ranges, speeds, and carrying capacity, we must be prepared to defend against, as well as retaliate in kind against, air attacks launched from great distances. There seems to be no doubt that it will only be a matter of a few years before operating ranges of 3,000 to 4,000 miles for bombardment aircraft will be entirely feasible.[35]

This statement called into question the conclusion of the Drum and Baker Boards that the United States was invulnerable to air attack. In doing so it advanced the Air Corps' claim that an independent air mission existed, which could be used as the rationale for a separate air force.

Some Air Corps officers openly advocated separation from General Staff control before the commission, but many offered that they were prepared to give the GHQ Air Force an extended trial before asking for further changes. Those most adamantly against the present order were Air Corps Tactical School instructors. The Howell Commission had invited them to discuss the role of air power, and they eagerly jumped at the chance to vent their views.[36] The ACTS officers played upon the danger of air attack on the United States and the need for a separate air force to discharge the important air defense mission. Maj. Donald Wilson and Capt. Harold L. George stressed the decisiveness of offensive air operations. They extolled air power as a new method of warfare that could crush the enemy's will to resist without first defeating his field forces or occupying his territory. George warned that "so long as we have an air force subordinate to and controlled by officers whose entire experience has been had in ground warfare, we will find that the Air Force is considered only in connection with other branches of the ground Army." To prepare military aviation for its proper offensive and defensive missions, George insisted it must be given independence from the rest of the Army. His fellow instructors echoed George's views.[37]

The Federal Aviation Commission was quite sympathetic to the needs of military aviation. However, in the face of adamant Army and Navy resistance to organizational change and in light of the findings of the Baker Board, the commission decided not to recommend any immediate institutional alterations. The members in their January 1935 report did affirm that "aircraft have now passed far beyond their former position as useful auxiliaries, and must in the future be considered and utilized as an important means of exerting directly the will of the Commander in Chief." Hinting that the commission favored increased Air Corps independence but that it was deterred from advocating it by the War Department's plans to organize the GHQ Air Force, the report stated that "until this solution has had an adequate trial we prefer to refrain from comment." It explained:

> We have no doubt that there will be a progressively greater measure of independent action of aircraft in military operations as the capacities of aircraft increase. We interpret the present proposals [of the Baker Board] as a step towards provision for such increased independence. . . . Further steps may in due course become necessary.[38]

This, the report said, may dictate "further organizational changes." The commission suggested that the GHQ Air Force experiment be fully carried out to check its validity and called upon the Army and Navy to study continuously "the employment of the air force as an independent striking unit." The report said the creation of a separate air force did not seem to be the required remedy for the current lack of coordination between the War and Navy Departments, but it advised that "the whole problem of military organization and inter-service relationships be made the subject of extended examination by some appropriate agency in the near future."[39]

So the commission, though recognizing the growing importance of military aviation, could not bring itself to make recommendations contrary to those of the Baker Board. It mattered very little that Howell wrote to the House Military Affairs Committee three months later advocating a separate Department of Aviation.[40] Air Corps officers were pleased with the commission's appreciation for the value of air power. Still they were disappointed that its January report did not come out unequivocally in support of independence from the General Staff.

While the Federal Aviation Commission was carrying out its investigation, the War Department was developing plans to bring the GHQ Air Force to life. The General Staff gave the OCAC a major role in the planning, and officers of the two agencies worked fairly well together. In line with earlier Air Corps thinking, they decided that each GHQ Air Force installation would have three types of units: combat squadrons, mobile service squadrons, and a station complement. The service squadrons were to travel with the combat units to forward areas and take care of aircraft maintenance and other support functions in the field. Station complements would contain those personnel necessary to operate the home bases, irrespective of the location of combat and mobile service squadrons. This would enable GHQ Air Force installations to be immediately available as training bases when the fighting units deployed to forward combat areas. This would trim mobilization time for follow-on Air Corps forces in the event of war. Planners believed that service squadrons would make the GHQ Air Force more mobile and flexible.[41]

The OCAC differed with the General Staff on but two principal points. Foulois wanted station complements as well as GHQ Air Force installations exempted from corps area control and given over to the

Organization of the GHQ Air Force as it was established following the recommendations of the Baker Board.

AS OF MARCH 1ST, 1935.

\* = INACTIVE

## G.H.Q. AIR FORCE
**HEADQUARTERS LANGLEY FIELD, VA.**

---

### SERVICE SQUADRONS
- 56TH SERVICE SQUAD. — SELFRIDGE
- 57TH SERVICE SQUAD. — SELFRIDGE
- 58TH SERVICE SQUAD. — LANGLEY
- 59TH SERVICE SQUAD. — LANGLEY
- 60TH SERVICE SQUAD. — BARKSDALE
- 61ST SERVICE SQUAD. — MITCHEL
- 64TH SERVICE SQUAD. — MARCH
- 69TH SERVICE SQUAD. — HAMILTON
- 70TH SERVICE SQUAD. — HAMILTON
- 71ST SERVICE SQUAD. — BARKSDALE
- 76TH SERVICE SQUAD. — ROCKWELL
- 100TH SERVICE SQUAD. — BOLLING

---

### 21ST AIRSHIP GROUP
- HEADQUARTERS — SCOTT
- 9TH AIRSHIP SQUAD. — SCOTT
- 19TH AIRSHIP SQUAD. — LANGLEY

---

### 1ST WING
**HEADQUARTERS, MARCH FIELD**

#### 19TH BOMBARDMENT GROUP
- HEADQUARTERS — ROCKWELL
- 30TH BOMB. SQUAD. — ROCKWELL
- 32ND BOMB. SQUAD. — ROCKWELL
- 93RD BOMB. SQUAD.* — ROCKWELL

#### 7TH BOMBARDMENT GROUP
- HEADQUARTERS — HAMILTON
- 9TH BOMB. SQUAD. — HAMILTON
- 11TH BOMB. SQUAD. — HAMILTON
- 31ST BOMB. SQUAD. — HAMILTON

#### 17TH ATTACK GROUP
- HEADQUARTERS — MARCH
- 34TH ATTACK SQUAD. — MARCH
- 73RD ATTACK SQUAD. — MARCH
- 95TH ATTACK SQUAD. — MARCH

- 86TH OBS. SQUAD. L.R.AMPH. — BROOKS
- 38TH OBS. SQUAD.L.R.B. — *ROCKWELL
- 89TH OBS. SQUAD.L.R.B. — *MARCH

---

### 2ND WING
**HEADQUARTERS, LANGLEY FIELD**

#### 2ND BOMBARDMENT GROUP
- HEADQUARTERS — LANGLEY
- 20TH BOMB. SQUAD. — LANGLEY
- 49TH BOMB. SQUAD. — LANGLEY
- 96TH BOMB. SQUAD. — LANGLEY
- 54TH BOMB. SQUAD. — DET. FROM G.H.Q.AIR FORCE TO TACTICAL SCHOOL

#### 9TH BOMBARDMENT GROUP
- HEADQUARTERS — MITCHEL
- 1ST BOMB. SQUAD. — MITCHEL
- 5TH BOMB. SQUAD. — MITCHEL
- 99TH BOMB. SQUAD. — MITCHEL
- 14TH BOMB. SQUAD. — BOLLING

#### 8TH PURSUIT GROUP
- HEADQUARTERS — LANGLEY
- 33RD PUR. SQUAD. — LANGLEY
- 35TH PUR. SQUAD. — LANGLEY
- 36TH PUR. SQUAD. — LANGLEY
- 37TH ATT. SQUAD.(ATT) — LANGLEY

#### 1ST PURSUIT GROUP
- HEADQUARTERS — SELFRIDGE
- 17TH PUR. SQUAD. — SELFRIDGE
- 27TH PUR. SQUAD. — SELFRIDGE
- 94TH PUR. SQUAD. — SELFRIDGE

- 21ST OBS. SQUAD. L.R. AMPH. — BOLLING
- 18TH OBS. SQUAD. L.R. AMPH. — *MITCHEL DET. TEMP. FROM G.H.Q. AIR FORCE TO A.C. ADV. FLY. SCH. TO BE MOVED TO LANGLEY.
- 41ST OBS. SQUAD. L.R. AMPH.

---

### 3RD WING
**HEADQUARTERS, BARKSDALE FIELD**

#### 3RD ATTACK GROUP
- HEADQUARTERS — BARKSDALE
- 8TH ATTACK SQUAD. — BARKSDALE
- 13TH ATTACK SQUAD. — BARKSDALE
- 90TH ATTACK SQUAD. — DET. FROM G.H.Q.AIR FORCE TO A.C. TACT. SCH.
- 51ST ATTACK SQUAD.

- 42ND BOMB. SQUAD. — DET. FROM G.H.Q. AIR FORCE TO THE ADV. FLYING SCHOOL
- 40TH ATTACK SQUAD.
- 43RD PUR. SQUAD.
- 48TH PUR. SQUAD. — DET. FROM G.H.Q. AIR FORCE TO THE A.C. TECHNICAL SCHOOL.

#### 20TH PURSUIT GROUP
- HEADQUARTERS — BARKSDALE
- 55TH PUR. SQUAD. — BARKSDALE
- 77TH PUR. SQUAD. — BARKSDALE
- 79TH PUR. SQUAD. — BARKSDALE
- 87TH PUR. SQUAD. — DET. FROM G.H.Q. AIR FORCE TO A.C. TACT. SCH.

## FOULOIS AND THE U.S. ARMY AIR CORPS

GHQ Air Force commander like the combat and mobile service units. He and his staff also lamely advocated making that commander responsible to Chief of the Air Corps. The air chief wrote the General Staff in August and again in November saying the Baker Board had meant for all GHQ Air Force installations and personnel to be under the GHQ Air Force commander. The War Department disagreed, contending that the board had desired to create a highly mobile force unfettered by ground functions or duties. Drum settled the matter in late September. He said corps area commanders should have the same responsibilities under the new setup as they had now. The War Department turned down "exempt status" for GHQ Air Force bases when the new organization was formed in March 1935, but the issue was far from being permanently settled.[42]

The brief skirmish over the Chief of the Air Corps' right to supervise the GHQ Air Force commander was due in part to Foulois' hurt feelings. Newspapers had been implying that the proposed reorganization, excluding the air chief from operational control, was an intentional slap in the face for Foulois, brought on by his apparent recent misdeeds.[43] This was untrue. Senior War Department officers had resolved in 1933 that the Chief of the Air Corps should not be responsible for GHQ Air Force operations. Foulois realized the new arrangement would not appreciably diminish his powers, yet press reports to the contrary disturbed him. He and some of his staff officers also feared that the Baker Board proposal would result in a segmented, uncoordinated force. They thought it foolish to vest in one officer responsibility for supply, procurement, and training at Air Corps schools, while giving another officer tactical control over combat units. Foulois' protested this arrangement, but to no avail.[44]

By January 1935 the General Staff and OCAC worked out the major details of the new organization. The GHQ Air Force commander was to establish his headquarters at Langley Field, Virginia, and exercise control over the force through three tactical wing commanders. The War Department picked Lt. Col. Frank M. Andrews to lead the GHQ Air Force. A highly respected aviator, Andrews had served in the OCAC and as commander of the 1st Pursuit Group before coming to Washington in 1934 to join the General Staff. The War Department ordered him to take over tactical command of the Air Corps' combat forces effective March 1. He was furnished a small staff of officers and the enlisted force that had previously been constituted as the GHQ Air Force headquarters squadron at Bolling Field. A General Staff directive made Andrews directly responsible to the Chief of Staff or theater commander for the GHQ Air Force's effectiveness in peace and war, but it gave him no authority over his force's installations, station complements, or procurement and supply. Nevertheless, he did have complete control of Army combat aviation except those observation units which did not belong to the GHQ Air Force.

ORGANIZATION: 1934-1935

This in itself was a vast improvement, as far as Air Corps officers were concerned, over the past system of segmented control under the corps area commanders. The War Department directed Andrews to conduct a one-year test to find out if the new arrangement would work. His preliminary report was due on October 1, 1935.[45]

The GHQ Air Force was a compromise between the extreme positions of those airpower advocates who wanted to free the Air Corps completely from Army control and the conservative ground officers who demanded that military aviation be tied to the advance of the surface forces. Because the new organization was capable of independent air missions as well as close support of ground troops, it offered something to both groups. Army aviators praised it because it enabled both concentrated employment of air power under a single Air Corps commander and standardized unit training, unhindered by the whims of the various corps area commanders.

Foulois labeled the decision to create the GHQ Air Force "the most important and forward looking single step ever taken to secure a military unit of adequate striking power to insure to the United States a proper defense in the air."[46] The General Staff also liked the decision. It preserved War Department authority over its air component and soothed the restless aviators. It also provided a very useful tool for combat operations. A War Department press release in December 1934 described it as "the most important and evolutionary step toward modernization of the forces of the United States that had been taken since the World War."[47] MacArthur said of the new force:

> The GHQ Air Force could be used as a great deciding factor in mass combat and for rapid reinforcement at distant threatened points, such as at outposts in Panama and Hawaii. It could be used on independent missions of destruction aimed at the vital arteries of a nation.[48]

In his annual report for 1935, he used the existence of the new organization to discourage further consideration of a separate air arm, saying the GHQ Air Force must be given at least five years to fully develop.[49]

With the activation of this consolidated strike force on March 1, 1935, campaigning by Air Corps officers for service autonomy all but ceased. This did not mean the aviators had put aside their long-held goal. Rather, it indicated they believed the GHQ Air Force was a step in the right direction and were now willing to give it a chance before renewing the old struggle. Editorials favoring a separate air force continued to appear in aviation magazines, but senior Army flyers ceased to champion this approach before Congress or in the media. When Congressman McSwain began hearings on a bill to create a separate Department of Aeronautics in April 1935, Generals Arnold and Westover and Lt. Col. Follett Bradley testified against the measure, saying they were satisfied

## FOULOIS AND THE U.S. ARMY AIR CORPS

Ass't. Sec. of War, Harry H. Woodring, formally presents the appointment as Chief of Staff to Gen. Malin Craig.

with the existing arrangement. Just one Air Corps officer, a captain, came out before the committee in favor of immediate independence.[50] Other factors, such as War Department approval of research and development funds for a long-range bomber and the introduction of a special promotion system, helped shape this new attitude. But creation of the GHQ Air Force was far and away the leading cause. Foulois and other Air Corps officers were genuinely enthusiastic about their new unified strike force and wanted to prove its value as an instrument of national defense.[51]

Gen. Malin Craig, who replaced MacArthur as Chief of Staff in October 1935, wanted to ensure the air arm's cooperative attitude continued. In November he wrote to Andrews and Acting Chief of the Air Corps Westover, stressing his need for loyalty and cooperation from all echelons of the Air Corps. Craig told the two air leaders that he expected their help in keeping the Air Corps a satisfied part of the Army team.[52] The new Chief of Staff seemed more distrustful of the aviators and less understanding of military aviation than his dynamic predecessor. This came through in his note to Andrews: "I shall expect that discussion or criticism of the G.H.Q. Air Force organization or operations be confined to the military service, which should adjust within itself its differences with a view to presenting a united front when we appeal to Congress for legislation or supporting appropriations."[53]

Westover believed in proper channels of military authority. He mirrored Craig's attitude on loyalty and Army team spirit. With Foulois on terminal leave, he now used his position as Acting Chief to insist that all Air Corps officers refrain from giving their personal views to Congress or to the public. In a letter to all commissioned personnel he said:

> The Air Corps as a whole has suffered in the past not alone from a lack of full understanding of its many and varied problems and from delays in the com-

## ORGANIZATION: 1934–1935

pletion of definite approved programs for its development and equipment, but also undoubtedly from the aggressive and enthusiastic efforts of some of its personnel in seeking remedial measures which have not perhaps always been directed along the proper line to attain the results desired.[54]

He assured his fellow aviators that constructive criticism through channels was welcomed, but he stressed that when higher authority found it necessary to take no action or disapprove of recommendations

> it should be understood by all concerned that such decisions are backed by cogent reasons, the knowledge of which is vested in higher authority. In such-cases, it is encumbent upon every member of the military establishment to conform wholeheartedly to such decisions. . . . Honest differences of opinion are recognized but their expression to persons outside the military service should be avoided.[55]

Andrews' reaction to Craig's letter is unrecorded. Since his attitude toward military aviation resembled that of Foulois, it is doubtful that he responded by ordering quiet obedience.[56]

Soon after the GHQ Air Force's activation, Andrews discovered his most serious problem was the "divided responsibility and control inherent in the . . . exempted status responsibility of Air Force stations."[57] The corps commanders controlled his installations and station complements and exercised court-martial jurisdiction over all officers and men who were not part of his headquarters. The Chief of the Air Corps' authority over supply, procurement, and tactics development confused the situation even more. However, during Foulois' tenure the OCAC and Andrews' staff worked together harmoniously. Yet the three-way division of power made for a perplexing work environment for GHQ Air Force unit commanders. In August, Andrews wrote the new Deputy Chief of Staff, General Simonds, asking that the control of corps area commanders be done away with. Simonds was unsympathetic and informed Andrews that the Chief of Staff opposed any immediate radical departures from the present structure.[58]

The air strike force chief renewed his plea in his October GHQ Air Force progress report. He explained that the basic concept of the GHQ Air Force was quite sound, but not the division of responsibility between the commander of the force and the corps area commanders. "Lines of demarcation are not clearly defined. . . . Such overlapping is definitely interfering with GHQ Air Force operations and training, and therefore, makes it difficult to determine and establish a proper organization based upon sound operating principles." Andrews again recommended that "all Air Corps stations, at which GHQ Air Force units are garrison, be on an exempted status, under command of the senior Air Corps flying officer assigned to duty thereat." He argued: "It is essential to sound planning and legal jurisdiction that the Air Force Commander exercise complete control, jurisdiction and command over all elements of the base, and not

## FOULOIS AND THE U.S. ARMY AIR CORPS

be dependent upon lateral coordination and cooperation."[59] Andrews repeated his call for exempted status in a February 1936 GHQ Air Force progress report.[60]

Six months before, he had won General Staff approval for a survey of station complements to see if any changes were needed in the current organization at the base level. The Browning Board, named after Col. William S. Browning of The Inspector General's Office who headed the study, reported in January 1936 that it favored ending the three-way split of authority. The board recommended exempting GHQ Air Force installations from corps area control and putting the complete air organization under the Chief of the Air Corps. In March and April Andrews requested Craig grant exempted status as called for by the Browning Board report, with the provision that the bases be placed under the commander of the GHQ Air Force rather than the Chief of the Air Corps.[61]

Andrews' request reflected the growing tensions between his organization and the OCAC once Westover had succeeded Foulois. Westover believed a cleavage had developed within the Air Corps due to the division of responsibility between his office and the GHQ Air Force. Maintaining that the Browning report provided an excellent solution to the problem, he advocated to the Chief of Staff in April that he be given control over the entire Army air arm. The War Department, however, sided with Andrews and ordered that on July 1 the leader of the GHQ Air Force would assume command of all permanent GHQ Air Force stations and assigned personnel. In August the General Staff allowed Andrews to abolish the mobile service squadrons and provide flying units with their own maintenance force. At the same time, he changed the name of the stations' complements to air base squadrons.[62]

Thus, in 1936 the General Staff brought an end to interference by corps area commanders in the affairs of the Air Corps tactical units. This had been a goal of Foulois and other Army flyers for many years, but it came to pass only after the aviation pioneer had retired. However, not until 1939 did the War Department act to solve the other hindrance of air arm unified control—its refusal to let the Chief of the Air Corps supervise the GHQ Air Force.

Benjamin Foulois can probably be held partly responsible for this turn of events. His demands for Air Corps priority in spending, his advocacy of autonomy, and his style of leadership convinced the General Staff in 1933 that he should not be permitted to command the GHQ Air Force. Not until March 1, 1939, did the General Staff finally decide to eliminate the division of responsibility and give the Chief of the Air Corps jurisdiction over the air striking arm. Unfortunately for the Air Corps, in 1940 the War Department reversed itself on this decision as well as its 1936 decision allowing GHQ Air Force bases exempted status. On the eve of

ORGANIZATION: 1934-1935

World War II, air arm installations and air base squadrons reverted to the control of corps area commanders, and the three-way division of responsibility for the air strike force was reinstated.[63]

# CHAPTER IX

# DOCTRINE, MISSION, AND EMPLOYMENT CONCEPTS, 1934-1935

The War Department's pre-Baker Board decision to create the GHQ Air Force pleased Air Corps officers. The Army's commitment to bring the force to life meant that the air arm would be organized in peacetime in accordance with wartime employment concepts. This would enable the Air Corps to better prepare itself to meet the threat of hostile invasion, and, as airpower advocates realized, it also provided the air arm with a unified strike force that could conceivably be used in strategic bombing operations against the enemy.

In early 1934 the General Staff acknowledged the advantages the GHQ Air Force would provide in coast defense operations, but it continued to deny the decisiveness of air power in warfare. A February position paper praised the GHQ Air Force's capacity to rapidly concentrate a strong air armada in any threatened area of the nation and to furnish valuable distant reconnaissance. It claimed the existence of this organization, with its abilities to prevent strategic surprise and destroy much of the enemy seaborne force before it reached American beaches, would deter hostile attacks on the United States. Asserting the importance of air superiority, the War Department paper maintained: "It is doubtful whether an enemy fleet convoying troop transports would approach our coasts even in the absence of the fleet unless the commander was reasonably sure that he could secure at least temporary control of the air." But the paper went on to say that, due to poor flying weather during half of each month, "the air force alone cannot be depended upon for coast defense." Instead, the General Staff insisted, this was a coordinated function of the entire Army. Repeated was the War Department's traditional stand on avi-

## CONCEPTS, 1934–1935

ation's ability to independently influence the outcome of war: "Only by defeat of the enemy's armies can his morale be broken and vital areas occupied, thus forcing him to consent to yield." The ground generals still viewed the air arm as an auxiliary, though a most useful one.[1] Their position would not change down through World War II.

A War Plans Division study in late spring 1934 fully examined the question of how the GHQ Air Force should be employed. The General Staff was preparing for September command post exercises in which a paper unified air strike force would take part for the first time. Before the maneuvers began, it wanted to fill the doctrinal void on how this force would be used in land warfare. On June 12 Kilbourne submitted a draft statement listing four primary operations for the force: "Bombardment of enemy establishments and installations beyond the range of artillery . . . pursuit action to counter enemy air operations . . . long-range reconnaissance . . . [and attack of] critical targets in the battle area." Close air support, which the War Department had so prized over the years, wound up behind the other three activities on the list. No doubt this pleased the officers in the OCAC. Kilbourne's draft followed established Air Corps doctrine in naming bombardment aircraft as "the most important element of the GHQ Air Force," because they were capable of inflicting damage on the enemy's Zone of Interior—"which no other weapon can do." Kilbourne suggested two ways for Army GHQ to use the air force. It could outline the campaign plans to the GHQ Air Force commander and "then permit him to undertake such operations which he considers will best further the objectives of the plan of campaign." Or it could designate certain objectives from time to time against which the air strike force would be directed.

The War Plans Division chief said that regardless of the method used, the actual conduct of operations should be left entirely to the GHQ Air Force commander. Kilbourne tilted toward the second alternative as "normally the more satisfactory method, probably the only method applicable in decisive periods of a campaign, and unless our Air Force is greatly superior should be used throughout the campaign." This would "insure the cooperation of the Air Force with the ground units" and would make certain that the air strike force "will be directed against those objectives which will further the operations of the ground forces and the general plan of campaign."[2] Kilbourne's June 12 statement still tied the GHQ Air Force to the advance of the infantry, but it went further than any previous General Staff paper toward accepting the Air Corps' views on combat employment.

Westover, the acting commander of the yet-to-be-activated GHQ Air Force, responded to the War Plans Division's proposal, recommending what he and Foulois believed to be a better method of GHQ control over air operations. He suggested that the Army theater commander should "outline the plan of the campaign to the G.H.Q. Air Force Commander, calling for his recommendations" on how the force should be used "to further the objectives of the plan of campaign." Westover declared that the Air Force commander could then come up with a proposal for GHQ approval or modification. He stressed that the GHQ should seek updated proposals from the commander of the GHQ Air Force as the combat situation changed and rely on him to do all of the basic planning of air operations throughout the campaign.[3]

MacArthur further clarified the War Department's view on the issue in August. He said there were really three ways to use the GHQ Air Force. The first was to assign the GHQ Air Force a broad general mission and give its commander the latitude to carry it out as he saw fit. This approach would be used before ground troops came in contact and during lulls in the campaign. The second was to assign the air strike force commander special missions against major objectives. This would be the procedure in the period between contact of opposing ground units and the actual beginning of the battle. The Chief of Staff said that during periods of ground combat the third means, that of employing "the striking power of the G.H.Q. Air Force for decisive attacks in conjunction with ground forces," would apply. This would be done "by assignment of specific missions to the G.H.Q. Air Force Commander for execution under direct control of GHQ, or by directing the G.H.Q. Air Force Commander to support specific operations of an army in accordance with the instruction of said army's commander." MacArthur's contention that the third approach "ensures the maximum development of air power in battle" made it clear he would forbid the air arm to free-lance once ground troops were actively engaged.[4]

MacArthur stated that the situation, as developed for the September command post exercise, required the GHQ Air Force to be employed solely under the second and third methods. As a result, Westover was given little freedom of action, causing some Air Corps bitterness. Air officers could not understand why the directors of the exercise refused to use the GHQ Air Force to oppose the mock invasion and instead employed it merely for close support of ground troops once the enemy was ashore. This served to confirm the beliefs of airpower advocates that the General Staff neither understood the full value of military aviation nor knew how to employ it. The aviators evidently did not realize that those running the exercise purposely allowed the fictitious enemy to land in order to provide training for all of the Army's field forces.[5]

Air Corps officers were not shy about voicing their views before the Baker Board on the proper offensive and defensive uses of air power. Lt. Col. John F. Curry, Air Corps Tactical School commandant, testified in

CONCEPTS, 1934-1935

May 1934 that the air arm's chief mission in coast defense was to destroy the enemy's aviation by bombing his carriers and land-based flying installations. He reiterated the Air Corps' position on support of ground troops, claiming the air strike force should be used to stop the flow of men and materiel to the front rather than in close air support: "As we all know, that if all is lost you employ everything you have, even cooks in your company, but our normal plan is that it [the air force] is not a field weapon. It is a strategical weapon [that should be used] against a logistical air target." Curry did not speak on the value of strategic bombing operations. Arnold mentioned it, however, to prove the United States needed a strong and well-organized air defense structure. He asserted that once an air force gained air superiority, it could "wreck havoc" by demolishing industrial centers, transportation facilities, and water supplies. Such strategic air operations could destroy a peoples' morale and "cause them to conclude that it will be cheaper to pay than to fight."

Other Air Corps officers made similar statements, but the Army aviators did not speak with one voice on the existing threat and the advantages of strategic bombing. One flyer summed up for the board the plight of those advocating this type of warfare: "We might take a 2,000-pound bomb to Europe, but that is all. We would have to come back and get another one."[6] The state of technology simply did not support the arguments that the United States was in imminent danger or that strategic bombing could win wars.

This lack of airpower credibility, together with General Staff influence, had its effect on the Baker Board. Its July 1934 report concluded that military aviation was not a decisive weapon and that the nation need not fear attacks from the sky. The report admitted that air power was an important factor in warfare but went to great lengths to point out its "vital limitations and inherent weaknesses." Restating time-honored War Department views, the report faulted military aviation for its inability to take and hold territory, its need for good weather, the inability of existing aircraft to strike distant targets with large loads of ordnance, and the airplane's lack of staying power. The board claimed the United States was safe from air attacks launched from overseas bases and that aviation alone could not stave off air strikes on the American homeland:

> To date no type of airplane has been developed capable of crossing the Atlantic or Pacific with an effective load, attacking successfully our vital areas, and returning to its bases. . . .
> The "air invasion of the United States" and the "air defense of the United States" are conceptions of those who fail to realize the inherent limitations of aviation and to consider ocean barriers. Aircraft in sufficient numbers to threaten serious damage can be brought against us only in conjunction with sea forces or with land forces which must be met by forces identical in nature and equally capable of prolonged effort.[7]

215

## FOULOIS AND THE U.S. ARMY AIR CORPS

Foulois' aviators were undeterred by the Baker Board's doctrinal pronouncements. They spoke before the Federal Aviation Commission of the importance of air superiority as well as the decisiveness of strategic bombing. The Air Corps Tactical School proceeded to preach that offensive air operations offered the most direct avenue to victory. The ACTS faculty taught its 1934-35 class that "loss of morale in the civilian population is decisive" in war and that air power alone could directly affect this key factor. The instructors played down the advantages of population bombing because international sentiment opposed this method and because air officers believed destruction of an adversary's industrial base, raw materials, transportation system, and energy supplies would be a more efficient way to induce peace. The ACTS's "Air Force" text was a bit uncertain whether the foe's air force should be wiped out before launching a campaign against his economy, but it eventually resolved that if the hostile air arm was a threat it must first be neutralized. The text nevertheless made it clear there were no air missions more important than these two in bringing about the enemy's defeat. Responding to the Baker Board report, it denied that the air arm was just an auxiliary. Offensive air action would obviate the need to seize or hold portions of an enemy's territory. Ignoring technological limitations, the ACTS faculty maintained "the air force should be the principal arm in future warfare" for it alone could directly attack "the roots of a nation's power."[8]

ACTS course materials in 1934-35 devoted far less space to defensive operations than to strategic bombardment. The "Air Force" text mentioned ground force support and coast defense as GHQ Air Force tasks but placed them below counterair operations and strategic bombardment in its list of missions.[9] This arrangement of priorities was not in line with War Department policy, for the General Staff still asserted in 1934 that the main function of the Air Corps was "to operate as an arm of the mobile Army." The War Department deemed all other air activities secondary, including coast defense. The General Staff's written statement to the Federal Aviation Commission in August 1934 did not even mention strategic bombardment in its list of Air Corps missions.[10]

The Air Corps Tactical School's obsession for offensive operations against the enemy's heartland did not mean the Air Corps had lost interest in its coast defense mission. Army flyers still believed that the GHQ Air Force's foremost task at the outbreak of war was to defeat the foe's air force before it could unleash attacks on America's economic structure. They said this called for the GHQ Air Force to be a highly mobile strike force. Only then could it be swiftly deployed to any area of the United States or its possessions at the first threat of invasion.[11]

In July 1934, at Foulois' request, Arnold led a squadron of B-10s from Washington, D.C., to Alaska to test and demonstrate the air arm's capacity to rapidly move units to distant areas. Ten planes took part in the 8,290-mile round-trip exercise. The force lifted off Bolling Field on July 19 and touched down at Fairbanks on July 24, compiling a total 25 1/2 hours flying time while covering about 4,000 miles. After mapping parts of Alaska from the air, the squadron began its return trip, and on August 17 flew the 990 miles from Juneau to Seattle nonstop. Just one minor accident marred the operation. During activities in Alaska, an engine failed on one of the planes and the pilot ditched his craft in Cook Inlet near Anchorage. The sturdy B-10 was towed ashore, quickly repaired, and returned to duty. Foulois was well pleased with the mobility exercise.[12]

Soon after the GHQ Air Force came into existence in March 1935, Andrews and his staff began to sort out their thinking on coast defense. Relying on the three phases of employment in MacArthur's policy letter of January 1933 as a guide, the planners asserted that during the first, or independent employment, phase the GHQ Air Force would attack enemy aircraft carriers and landing fields to neutralize the hostile air threat. Next, it would assault the adversary's other naval forces and chokepoints in his lines of communications. In accord with traditional Air Corps thinking, the GHQ Air Force leadership claimed strategic bombing of the enemy's war industries would also be part of the first phase of coastal air defense operations.[13]

Advocating distant strategic operations in the name of coast defense was absurd, unless both the enemy and his industrial facilities were located in Canada or Mexico, which was highly unlikely. Existing aircraft were incapable of mounting powerful long-range raids. Furthermore, undertaking strategic bombings in the first phase of operations would violate the Air Corps' own frequently voiced principle of concentrated employment—at a time when the GHQ Air Force would need all of its resources to prevent an invasion force from landing in the United States. However, this linking of strategic and defensive missions serves to point out that the Army aviators were not satisfied with a purely defensive wartime role. They believed in the importance of defending the nation against hostile air attack and invasion, but at the same time they were convinced that the doctrine of offensive bombardment was the proper way to bring a war to a speedy and decisive conclusion.

MacArthur and his staff held a different view. They thought the GHQ Air Force would be a valuable tool for immediate use in an emergency, and they conceded that in land campaigns and coast defense activities "there would undoubtedly be occasions . . . when air operations beyond the immediate theatres of land and sea forces will be desirable."[14] But the Chief of Staff remained unconvinced by the aviators' assertions that strategic bombing was decisive. He remarked in his annual report for

# FOULOIS AND THE U.S. ARMY AIR CORPS

Top: Lt. Col. "Hap" Arnold, commanding the Alaskan Flight of 10 Martin B-10s; center: one of the aircraft obtains reconnaissance photos for mapping the territory between Fairbanks and Anchorage; bottom: Col. Arnold receives the key to the city of Fairbanks.

## CONCEPTS, 1934–1935

Right: Sec. of War George H. Dern and Maj. Gen. Foulois greet Col. Arnold upon his return from Alaska on Aug. 20, 1934, at the Bolling Field flight line (below).

1935 that "so far as tactical and strategic doctrine is concerned, there exist two great fields for Air Force employment; one fully demonstrated and proved, the other conjectural." In the proven category, MacArthur put those tasks involving direct cooperation with the ground forces: close air support, interdiction, observation, reconnaissance, transportation, and air cover. He said "the more conjectural use of the Air Force involves its employment against unarmed centers of population and industry," and affirmed that "the sentiment of this country . . . will always repudiate and forbid the unprovoked initiation of this kind of war by our own forces." Even so, he judged the GHQ Air Force suitably organized to efficiently carry out strategic bombing if needed to safeguard the nation.[15]

The War Department's formal commitment to establish the GHQ Air Force quickened the Army-Navy debate in 1934 over which service would have primary responsibility for aerial coast defense. The Navy stepped up its campaign to gain control of all overwater military air activity. The Air Corps and the General Staff continued to claim Army dominion over coast defense activities and all combat air operations originating from land. Adm. William H. Standley, Chief of Naval Operations, spoke quite firmly to the Baker Board: Unless Air Corps pilots were acting under Navy control, "they have no business doing bombing at sea." He claimed that overwater air patrols were the job of the sea service and that the GHQ Air Force's bomber fleet should conduct no strikes out at sea unless directed to do so by the Navy.[16]

Standley had rescinded Pratt's naval air operating policy of November 1930 and replaced it with a more expansive aviation policy statement in May 1934. Among the naval air functions set forth in this new document were: "Provision of timely information of the approach of an enemy in sea areas both of the continental United States and of overseas possessions" and "protection of commerce on the high seas, in coastal zones and in sea lanes." Naval air units based ashore now had as one of their missions the "operation of aircraft for protection of commerce in coastal zones and sea lanes, by means of patrol and scouting over the sea and offensive action connected therewith."[17]

Admiral King, Chief of the Bureau of Aeronautics, stirred Air Corps concern in early 1934 when he advocated the building of a large force of long-range patrol planes. These "patrol-bombing-torpedo seaplanes" could work with the fleet, but their principal usefulness lay elsewhere. According to King, such aircraft would make possible "powerful striking forces" that could be used "as protective patrol and scouting units along our coasts and at our outlying bases."[18] He warned the General Board that although "such planes and their employment fit directly into the Navy's mission, . . . unless the Navy takes advantage of this force, there is no question but that the Army, already realizing the tremendous possi-

CONCEPTS, 1934-1935

bilities of such a force and its appeal to popular imagination, will beat the Navy to its development." The consequences would be serious, for "a highly important naval force with untold future possibilities may pass partially or totally from under naval control." Admiral King pleaded for vocal Navy support for his proposal. He believed a well-organized and "properly publicized" Navy air patrol force "will go a long ways in maintaining the control of air operations over the sea in naval hands."[19] The bureau chief kept the issue alive through 1934, but he received only mild Navy Department support. The aircraft in question were too costly to purchase in the quantities King desired (approximately six hundred). Yet the Navy did make plans for both a smaller buy and the expansion of naval aviation facilities ashore.[20]

Air Corps officers feared the Navy was bent on stealing the coastal air defense mission. In early 1934, Foulois pressed the General Staff to support the air arm's claims to responsibility for overwater reconnaissance activities. He argued that GHQ Air Force distant patrol operations were essential to prevent the enemy from making air attacks on the United States. While unaware of King's plans for a large force of long-range patrol planes, Foulois and other Air Corps officials were suspicious of the Navy's earlier decision to buy additional medium-range, shore-based patrol aircraft with fiscal 1935 money. In May 1934 they protested the proposed purchase to MacArthur, asserting that it would supply the sea service with planes that duplicated a portion of the Air Corps' coast defense function. Thus the purchase would violate the MacArthur-Pratt agreement. Foulois and his cohorts would have been outraged had they known of King's struggle to secure a large force of long-range flying boats. OCAC officials also worried over possible Navy-Coast Guard collusion that might jeopardize the Air Corps mission. They even went so far as to suggest to the Chief of Staff that he arrange for the Air Corps to absorb Coast Guard aviation and communications nets in time of war. Justifiably concerned over the sea service's ambitions, the Army aviators wanted the War Department to thwart the Navy's efforts to assume control of aerial coast defense operations.[21]

The General Staff opposed the Navy's purported encroachment on the coast defense mission, but it did not want the Air Corps to intensify the conflict. The War Department banned publication of an article Foulois had written titled "Air Power in Defense of Our Sea Frontier," because of its inflammatory statements on long-range, antifleet air operations. It also worked to secure a clear division of air responsibilities between the two services. The War Department concluded that the Air Corps' right to reconnaissance and combat operations at extreme distances from the shore, sanctioned in MacArthur's policy letter of January 3, 1933, was the root of the Navy Department's refusal to formalize the MacArthur-Pratt agreement. It therefore set about redefining the limits of the GHQ Air Force's coast defense duties in a manner acceptable to the sea service.[22]

During discussions in August 1934, Kilbourne and Drum tried to get naval officials to agree that patrol of coastal shipping lanes and other Navy air functions not related to fleet operations were secondary missions. The General Staff officers further wanted the sea service to accept the findings of the Drum and Baker Boards as they related to the use of the GHQ Air Force in coast defense. In exchange, the War Department willingly acknowledged that the Navy had paramount responsibility for locating the enemy and reporting on his approach to American shores. Kilbourne and Drum assented to the use of both land-based and carrier-borne naval aircraft for such reconnaissance activity. Navy Department leaders eventually agreed to accept the Drum and Baker reports as the basis for GHQ Air Force air defense employment, but they refused to reclassify the sea service's close-to-shore air functions as secondary.[23]

The General Staff submitted a draft of the Army-Navy agreement to the Joint Board. After making some minor changes, the senior service representatives signed it on September 26 and sent it to the Secretaries of War and Navy for final approval. MacArthur issued it as a War Department policy statement on October 17.[24] Titled "Doctrines for the Employment of the G.H.Q. Air Force," the agreement quoted statements from the Baker and Drum reports denying the Army air arm's abilities to independently protect the United States from hostile attack. Bowing to the Navy's wishes, it stated that the "organization of the G.H.Q. Air Force within the Army does not contravene any of the existing policies relating to the primary and secondary functions of the Army and Navy." This prevented the Air Corps from seizing the sea service's antisubmarine and antisurface raider missions in coastal waters. The Joint Board paper contained the essentials of the MacArthur-Pratt agreement, but with qualifications asserting the Navy's right to control overwater operations if the fleet were present:

> The Army is responsible for the direct defense of the coast. This responsibility and the possibility that naval strategy may demand the presence of the fleet in another theater, require that joint plans for coastal frontier defense be drawn without counting upon the assistance of the fleet.
>
> . . . . . . . . . . . . . . . . . . . . . . . . . . .
>
> When the fleet, as distinguished from local naval defense forces, is strategically present and free to act, paramount interest in operations at sea rests with the Navy. If the G.H.Q. Air Force joins in such operations, it will be in conjunction with and under the temporary command of the naval commander. In the absence of the fleet, the primary responsibility of securing information of hostile fleet movements rests with Naval District forces supplemented by Army Air Corps units. However, in either situation the G.H.Q. Air Force

retains the responsibility for such reconnaissance as is essential to its combat efficiency.[25]

The agreement listed the three phases of Army air arm employment in coast defense operations that, under MacArthur's January 1933 policy letter, were to be undertaken in the absence of the fleet. But no longer was there a permissive phase allowing Army aviation to operate to the limit of its range. Instead, the explanation of the first phase called for "the conduct of reconnaissance over the sea approaches to the coast and . . . the attack of enemy elements." While not drawing a definite line beyond which GHQ Air Force operations would be forbidden, the paper implied that Army air activity would be kept close to the shore. In two instances the agreement casually mentioned that GHQ Air Force "operates along the coast."[26]

The Joint Board paper achieved very little. It was so vaguely worded and full of qualifying conditions that it failed to clearly define air defense responsibilities. Moreover, the paper did not deter the Air Corps or the Navy from seeking to expand the scope of its coast defense responsibilities. Army aviators may have been dismayed by the implied restriction on the distance from the shore the GHQ Air Force was to operate, but they refused to publicly acknowledge this limitation and continued to claim responsibility for overwater air operations within the cruising radius of Army aircraft.[27] The Navy went on asserting the right to control all air combat and reconnaissance beyond the coastline. In its report to the Federal Aviation Commission, the Navy Department argued the Army should cease training pilots and procuring planes for overwater operations. The report maintained that the sea service should be made strong enough to protect the United States and its possessions without assistance from Army aviation. Calling long-range, shore-based patrol aircraft "an indispensable part of the Navy's Air Component," it insisted the Navy needed more of these aircraft and fields from which to operate them. Then it could properly discharge its mission of patrolling and protecting America's sea approaches. The Navy held that the GHQ Air Force should perform solely those functions that "will enable the Army to protect the continental and overseas possessions of the United States from an enemy engaged in land-warfare."[28]

The General Staff was pleased with the Joint Board agreement. War Department officers had gotten the Navy to admit coast defense was an Army mission. In exchange the General Staff sacrificed the Air Corps' right to distant overwater operations. Restricting the air arm to close-in tasks, accepting the sea service's paramount interest in anti-invasion operations when the fleet was present, and giving naval aviation the responsibility for coast defense reconnaissance held an additional advantage for the War Department. These limitations drew the GHQ Air Force's combat responsibilities into line with what the General Staff regarded as the air arm's primary function—support of the mobile army.[29]

During 1935 Air Corps officers continued to fret over the Navy's drive to assume a greater share of the coastal air defense mission. Reports circulated in the fall that Standley was planning to build a big, land-based air strike force, composed of King's proposed long-range, patrol-bombing-torpedo seaplanes. The news prompted Andrews to ask the new Chief of Staff, General Malin Craig, to do what he could to head off this program.[30] The GHQ Air Force chief had only sketchy details on the Navy's intentions. In fact King and Standley were acting to forestall what they thought was an Air Corps incursion into a purely Navy mission. As the Chief of the Bureau of Aeronautics saw it, GHQ Air Force operations beyond the immediate vicinity of the coastline were unwarranted. The Navy, with its patrol-bombing planes and other resources, had sole responsibility for protecting the sea and air approaches to the United States and its possessions.[31]

King and his Navy associates were signaling their intent to take charge of all overwater operations, a move that would put an end to the Air Corps' only politically acceptable semi-independent mission. Army aviators were not going to take this lying down. Andrews resolved in 1936 to treat the naval threat as a challenge: "When it comes to a final showdown on this function of air defense, the air branch of our National Defense which has the most airplanes, with best performance, best trained crews, and the proper base set-up, is going to have the strongest arguments to get this Air Defense."[32] He worked to perfect the GHQ Air Force accordingly.

The Army and Navy attempted to further define coast defense responsibilities and air missions in a 1935 update of the official pamphlet, "Joint Action of the Army and the Navy." The revision stated that the chief role of the Army air component was "to operate as an arm of the mobile Army, both in the conduct of air operations over the land in support of land operations and in the conduct of air operations over the sea in direct defense of the coast." The two services thus acknowledged the importance of the Air Corps' coastal air defense mission by raising it from its previously designated secondary status. The pamphlet named operations in support of the fleet as the primary mission for the naval air arm.[33] The new agreement produced only a slight erosion of the Navy's position, for the sea service defined "direct defense of the coast" to mean close-in defense. The Navy's long-range seaplanes, having the primary function of supporting the fleet, could still be used for coast defense operations beyond this close-in area.

In addition the Joint Board document reiterated the September 1934 coast defense agreement, and tried to establish a clean-cut division of air

CONCEPTS, 1934-1935

defense responsibilties. It charged the Navy with patrolling the coastal zone and accepted that service's dominance in operations against enemy forces still outside of "Defensive Coastal Areas." The Army was to repel actual attacks against land frontiers and would take over anti-invasion activities when it became apparent that the enemy force meant to attack "a shore objective." To muddy the issue the pamphlet said: "In operations within a Defense Coastal Area, paramount interest will be vested in the Army, except when it is apparent that the objective of the enemy force is shipping within the Coastal Zone."

The document went on to say that when the fleet was on hand the Navy would run all operations at sea. GHQ Air Force units joining in the action were to fall under naval control. If the fleet were not present and "enemy forces approach close enough to threaten or launch a direct attack against our territory . . . paramount interest shifts to the Army and the function of the Navy is to support the Army." Under this setup the Navy would still have charge of defensive actions beyond the "Defensive Coastal Areas" even if the fleet were absent—if it was not certain the enemy planned to assault land positions. However, another section of the pamphlet implied that the Army could carry out overwater air operations in the event the fleet was absent and stated that coast defense plans should be based on the assumption that naval surface forces would not be available.[34]

The Joint Board's division of responsibilities was far too ambiguous to furnish a workable air defense program. With "paramount interest" shifting back and forth and neither service eager to simplify the arrangement for fear of further sacrificing its own institutional interests, the American air defense system remained confused through December 1941. Both the Navy and the Air Corps believed they were capable of independently protecting the nation and its possessions from hostile attack. In truth, neither could do the job alone. Both assumed the other would cooperate if the need arose. Yet neither took steps to define how this cooperation would be carried out. Consequently, the United States paid the price in Hawaii in 1941 for the ambiguity the military services created in 1935.[35]

After adopting the September 1934 Joint Board agreement on GHQ Air Force employment, the General Staff attempted to create an air doctrine statement that would be acceptable to the entire Army. The War Department realized the existing regulations on Air Corps employment were completely outdated and had resolved shortly after acceptance of the Drum Board report to revise them. The General Staff was chiefly concerned with Training Regulations (TR) 440-15: *Employment of the Air Forces of the Army*, for the current (1926) edition was not consistent with MacArthur's policy letter of January 3, 1933, and the Drum report.

However, the convening of the Baker Board and the Navy's reluctance to formalize the MacArthur-Pratt agreement delayed the revision.[36]

After listening to Air Corps witnesses before the Federal Aviation Commission, Kilbourne became convinced that War Department air doctrine was confused. He suggested to Drum that the War Plans Division draw up and circulate a draft doctrinal statement which could be used as a departure point for creating a single coherent air doctrine. Following MacArthur's approval, on December 21, 1934, Kilbourne sent copies of the draft, "Doctrines of the Army Air Corps," to the other General Staff divisions and to the Air Corps.[37] In the cover letter he said this was a very rough outline and asked for comments and criticisms. Kilbourne explained:

> The desire is to prepare a study that will eventually present to the service the adopted principles for the utilization of air power and the doctrines that should govern its personnel. This [is being done] with a view to [creating] a broader understanding of the Air Corps' place in the scheme of national defense and in expectation of doing away with the misconceptions and interbranch prejudices that have prevented the Army from reaching a common understanding and presenting a united front on the subject.[38]

The War Plans Division chief hoped to have the statement of doctrine in final form by March 1, 1935, so it could be issued to the service on the day the GHQ Air Force came into being. He planned to then use it as the basis for revising the outdated regulations.[39]

"Doctrines of the Army Air Corps" tried to chart a middle course between the traditional Army conception of aviation as only an auxiliary and the claims of independent decisiveness voiced by airpower advocates. The paper said military aviation was very important in modern warfare but claimed that military operations could best be carried out if aviation remained an integral part of the Army. It maintained:

> the GHQ Air Force will meet the demands for the application of air power beyond the sphere of influence of surface forces, thus ensuring to us the advantages of a powerful striking force for independent air operations, without the disadvantages inherent to an organization in which the aviation is in a separate department.[40]

The War Plans Division paper admitted that military aviation acting alone could control "weak and poorly organized peoples." But air power's ability to break the will of a well-organized nation "has never been demonstrated and is not accepted by members of the armed services of this nation." To win wars a nation must occupy the enemy's territory, a task that could be "greatly assisted" by military aviation.[41]

The paper spelled out MacArthur's three methods for controlling the operations of the GHQ Air Force and enumerated the following combat missions for that force: "(1) Operations beyond the sphere of influence of ground forces. (2) Operations in immediate support of the ground forces

CONCEPTS, 1934-1935

in campaign. (3) Operations in defense of the coast and/or land frontiers. (4) Operations in defense of rear areas." By placing independent operations ahead of ground support, Kilbourne was either seeking to placate the aviators or was acknowledging the importance of this mission.

"Air Doctrines of the Army Air Corps" stated that the destruction of enemy aviation was the primary objective in operations beyond the range of ground troops, but it also listed lines of communications and troop concentrations, enemy munitions factories, refineries, powerplants, and other utilities as acceptable targets. The paper called for long-range reconnaissance and mentioned attacks on population centers in reprisal for similar enemy action.[42] By advancing this target list, the War Plans Division was all but endorsing the Air Corps' concept of strategic bombardment. This was quite a departure for a branch of the General Staff.

The draft doctrinal statement took a more conservative stance toward the ground support and coast defense missions. While including enemy aviation, lines of communications, supply areas, and troop concentrations as acceptable ground support targets, it also called for attacks on hostile forces in frontline positions, something the Army aviators had persistently opposed. Likewise, the statement reaffirmed that "success on the battlefield . . . was the decisive factor in war." The paper's position on coastal air defense was for the most part a rehash of the September Joint Board agreement. It left distant overwater reconnaissance to the Navy and conceded the sea service's dominant interest in combat operations beyond the coast, if the fleet were present and free to act. The draft pointed out, however, that in the absence of the fleet, the Army would be in charge of anti-invasion operations. The War Plans Division paper further said that the Air Corps should "in periods of positive threat," fly surveillance out to a distance equal to twelve hours steaming time for the hostile fleet. Also, it allowed the Army to assume "paramount interest" in overwater reconnaissance opposite a threatened land area if the Army commander in that area judged the Navy to be incapable of properly performing that function.[43]

While permitting the GHQ Air Force to venture farther out to sea than had been the apparent intent of the September Joint Board agreement, the paper still stressed close-in operations:

In general, the closer the enemy approaches the coast, the more favorable is the situation for the attack by the General Headquarters Air Force. With respect to raids from the sea, surveillance should normally be left to Naval District forces.[44]

However, the draft did call for immediate GHQ Air Force reconnaissance and combat operations against a hostile carrier force if the enemy attempted air raids with shipborne aviation.[45]

Foulois and most OCAC officers were not displeased with the War

Plans Division draft. The Chief of the Air Corps circulated it for comment within his office and asked the Air Corps Tactical School for its views. Nevertheless, he was not disposed to accept any radical alterations of what appeared to be a reasonable compromise doctrine. Perhaps this attitude could be traced to his troubles with Subcommittee Number 3 and the impending investigation by The Inspector General. Still, some airpower advocates wanted to use the opening provided by Kilbourne to press for War Department acceptance of their points of view. One such individual, Lt. Col. Walter R. Weaver, prepared a paper that stressed the importance of destroying the enemy's air resources and morale, and that completely eliminated support of ground forces as an air arm mission.[46]

An ACTS study criticized parts of the December 21 draft. The tactical school paper said the absence of a united Army position on air policy matters stemmed from prejudices held by the older branches that were

> occasioned by a natural psychological reaction against a new method of warfare that disturbed time-worn ideas and theories . . . and . . . challenged the dominant position in warfare that ground forces have enjoyed since the dawn of history.[47]

Sent to the OCAC on January 31, 1935, the study debated the contention in Kilbourne's draft that air power could not bring about a decision in war and contended that the GHQ Air Force could best support Army field forces by defeating the enemy's air arm. It demanded that all references to use of the air strike force in direct support of troops in contact be deleted. After all, neutralization of the foe's air force would make it impossible for hostile ground units to concentrate for combat.

The ACTS went on to attack the War Plans Division paper for its murkiness on coast defense operations. It declared that the GHQ Air Force should be charged with all offshore aerial reconnaissance and be authorized to control all counterinvasion operations in the absence of the fleet. The study affirmed that counter-air force activities comprised the major mission of the GHQ Air Force, but cautioned:

> This, it must be realized, is [only] applicable for that period of time during which the radius of action of aircraft is less than that required to reach vital strategical objectives in other parts of the world from United States territory. . . . There is no intention anywhere in these comments of not conveying the thought the principal and all important mission of air power, when its equipment permits, is the attack of those vital objectives in a nation's economic structure which will tend to paralyze that nation's ability to wage war and thus contribute directly to . . . the disintegration of the hostile will to resist.[48]

The ACTS for the first time in years had aligned its doctrine with technological reality. In doing so, it had taken a position less hostile to the War Plans Division paper than would have otherwise been the case.

The OCAC reviewed the tactical school study but integrated few of its proposals in the Air Corps' response to the General Staff. Foulois

CONCEPTS, 1934-1935

made but minor changes to Kilbourne's December 21 draft, to accent slightly the importance of air power. He submitted it on February 27 along with a proposal that it be used as the basis for revising TR 440-15. The General Staff was very responsive to Foulois' suggestion and circulated his paper for comment. Brig. Gen. John H. Hughes, Assistant Chief of Staff, G-3, was impressed both with the Chief of the Air Corps' suggestion on the training regulations and his changes in the original draft. Andrews was also enthusiastic. Other General Staff divisions suggested minor revisions that caused the proposed directive's final form to stress the air arm's responsibility to the overall Army mission. As it was published, however, TR 440-15 varied little from the OCAC's original revision of the Kilbourne draft. The War Department completed work on the air employment directive in April. But to avoid problems with the Navy, it delayed releasing it until after the Joint Board completed the revision of Joint Action of the Army and the Navy in September.[49]

The new TR 440-15 came into effect on October 15, 1935, giving the Army air arm an updated doctrine to match its new combat organization. Reflecting the OCAC's desires, the regulation no longer mentioned defense of rear areas as a GHQ Air Force mission. Revealing the input of General Staff ground officers, it explained that "air operations beyond the sphere of influence of the ground forces are undertaken in furtherance of the Army Strategical Plan." TR 440-15 contained no other changes of substance save in the realm of coast defense. The directive did not try to sort out the GHQ Air Force's responsibilities from those of the Navy. It simply stated that aerial coast defense operations would be based on the recently completed Joint Action of the Army and the Navy.[50]

The upshot of Kilbourne's work in December 1934 was a formal air doctrine acceptable to both ground and air officers. Very few statements in TR 440-15 offended airpower advocates. No doubt some objected to the way the directive continued to tie military aviation to ground force actions and to deny the decisiveness of the air weapon. But according to Major Follett Bradley, a leading advocate in 1934 of Air Corps independence from General Staff control, TR 440-15 "spelled out for the first time an Air Doctrine to which most Air Corps officers could subscribe." The 1935 regulations remained in force until 1940.[51]

The year 1935 was a banner one for the Air Corps. Not only did the air arm receive a new doctrine and a combat air organization, it also tested its first aircraft capable of strategic bombing operations. Aviators wanted long-range bombers to bolster coast defense and to conduct strategic air warfare. They had convinced the General Staff of the bomber's primacy, but until the development of the B-17 prototype in 1935 the flyers lacked an adequate instrument for distant destruction of the enemy fleet and for strategic bombardment. The Air Corps believed in the im-

229

portance of both of these missions. Coastal air defense, however, was more in accord with national policy, and the War Department was reticent about air attacks on the enemy's economy. Hence, the aviators used the nation's air defense needs as the rationale in arguing for long-range bombers.

Very much in favor of long-range aircraft development, Foulois set about selling the mildly receptive General Staff on the idea. Air Corps officers were enthusiastic over the design and performance advances incorporated in the B-10. In March 1933 the air chief sent a questionnaire to his pilots seeking their recommendations on future bomber development. Responses were quite varied, but the trend ran distinctly toward large, four-engine aircraft capable of carrying large bombloads over great distances at high altitude and able to attack both sea and land targets. In July the Materiel Division began a feasibility study to see how far a four-engine plane could carry 2,000 pounds of ordnance. The result showed that a range of 5,000 miles at a speed of 200 miles per hour was quite possible. Foulois accordingly submitted Project A (a request to procure such a plane) to the War Department in December.[52]

The Chief of the Air Corps explained that money was available for the project since the administration had recently released $3 million of previously withdrawn procurement funds. He and Westover dwelt on the defensive features of the new plane. In notes to the General Staff, they said the aircraft could instantly reinforce either coast as well as Panama, Hawaii, and Alaska. Foulois was surprised to find that the War Department tentatively approved $609,300 for long-range bomber development on December 19 and in February 1934 accepted the proposed project "in principle." With MacArthur's approval, in May the Secretary of War authorized the Air Corps to proceed with the purchase.[53]

Though not overly enthusiastic about the proposal, the General Staff was willing to allow the Air Corps to develop the plane. Kilbourne could see no need for an aircraft with a 5,000-mile range. He thought it might be more practical to use the money to buy a large number of the existing type of bombers, stationing them in Hawaii, Panama, and on both coasts of the continental United States. He maintained that reconnaissance planes of 1,000-1,500 miles range were the air arm's greatest present need. If this reconnaissance requirement was already being taken care of, however, he was willing to endorse the Air Corps' proposal "purely for its general value in the development of aviation possibilities in military planes."[54]

MacArthur was relatively open minded on the long-range bomber issue, but events in Washington during early 1934 may have influenced his decision to go forward with the project.[55] Rumors were circulating that the General Staff had badly managed its air resources. In light of this and

## CONCEPTS, 1934-1935

McSwain's threats to sponsor air autonomy legislation, Subcommittee Number 3's investigation, and the Army air arm's poor showing in the air mail operations, the Chief of Staff was probably reluctant to take any step that could be construed as a curb on military aviation development.

Foulois had initially hoped to negotiate contracts with the Boeing and Glenn L. Martin companies for the construction of two prototype aircraft. The General Staff approved this course of action. A change in the program became necessary, however, when the two manufacturers informed the Air Corps in June that the development cost for each plane would be well above the $609,300 available for the whole project. Foulois decided it would be best to have a design competition between the two firms, with the Air Corps paying each producer $75,000 for his work. The company producing the winning design would be awarded a contract to build an experimental plane. The War Department agreed. Boeing was the eventual winner and started constructing its XB-15 bomber in 1935.[56]

The plane did not fly until 1937 and subsequent flight tests showed it was too large for engines available at the time. Project A was nonetheless very beneficial. It produced advances in aeronautical technology that enabled the United States to build excellent heavy bombers during World War II. More immediate, Boeing's work to develop a four-engine aircraft with increased range and bomb load enabled that company in 1935 to produce the prototype for the B-17.[57]

Project A was kept secret from the public as was the follow-on program authorized by the War Department in October 1935. Project D called for developing a plane that could carry 2,400 pounds of ordnance 8,000 miles or a 10,000- to 12,000-pound bombload 3,000 miles. The resulting Douglas XB-19 was not completed until 1941, but the General Staff's acceptance of the project lent encouragement to airpower advocates.[58]

During June 1934 the Air Corps distributed invitations for bids on a quantity order for new bombers. The circular gave the competitors until August 1935 to deliver a sample plane for testing. It specified the following performance criteria: 2,000-pound bombload; minimum top speed of 200 miles-per-hour, 250 miles-per-hour desired; 1,020-mile range required, 2,200 miles desired. The OCAC anticipated an order for up to 220 planes for the winning firm. Three companies responded to the Air Corps invitation. The Glenn L. Martin Company entered the B-12, a revised version of its B-10. The Douglas Aircraft Company submitted a newly designed plane, the XB-18, powered by two engines like the Martin entry. Only the Boeing Airplane Company departed from this conventional approach by building a large, four-engine aircraft.[59]

The Boeing 299 (later designated the XB-17) impressed both the press and Air Corps officials. In August 1935 it flew the 2,100 miles from Seat-

231

The Boeing XB-15 (above) served as a stepping stone in aeronautical technology for the Douglas XB-19 pictured on the adjacent page.

tle to Dayton nonstop at an average speed of 232 miles-per-hour. The feat clearly demonstrated that the Boeing entry far outclassed its two competitors. Besides tremendous speed, the XB-17 could carry 2,500 pounds of bombs 2,260 miles and could attack closer targets with up to 9,000 pounds of ordnance. Army aviators were overjoyed at the prospect of purchasing a plane that would make strategic bombing a reality. Even before the competition was complete, Foulois and his staff decided they wanted this plane. Its higher costs would mean fewer aircraft could be purchased, but air officers were more than ready to make this tradeoff. The air chief made his views known to the War Department on October 1. He said if the aircraft evaluation board picked the XB-17, he wanted to buy sixty-five of the planes with fiscal 1936 funds, a portion of which had already been earmarked for other aircraft.[60] The OCAC viewed the purchase of the XB-17 as a logical step in the development of the Army air arm

> in that it will serve as the most powerful offensive bombardment weapon that can be obtained at this time, and serve to train crews and the Air Corps for the adoption of the 5,000 mile Project A ship which is visualized as the backbone of a fighting air force.[61]

Foulois and his subordinates were no longer interested in long-range amphibian planes. They saw the future of the Air Corps in land-based heavy bombers.[62]

## CONCEPTS, 1934-1935

A fatal accident upset the Air Corps' procurement plans just as the Materiel Division was about to conclude the evaluation of the XB-17 and two other planes. Boeing's chief test pilot and two Army flyers had unknowingly tried to take off in the XB-17 on October 30 with the gust locks still engaged on the elevators and rudder. The plane became airborne and then went into a steep climb, stalling at about 300 feet above the ground. One military flyer died in the crash that totally destroyed the only existing copy of the Boeing bomber. Even though an investigation proved the pilot was at fault, the Air Corps was forced to exclude the XB-17 from the competition because the accident had occurred before completion of the formal evaluation. Consequently, the Douglas XB-18 was declared the winner, and the Army air arm ordered ninety of these aircraft.[63]

Disturbed over the disqualificaton, Air Corps leaders quickly took steps to secure at least a few XB-17s. Andrews was a prime mover in this action. He wrote Westover the day of the accident to point out that the air arm could, by designating the plane as experimental, still make a small quantity buy under Section 10(k) of the 1926 Air Corps Act. The GHQ Air Force commander wanted no fewer than thirteen of these advanced bombers so he could form at least one combat squadron.[64] The Acting Chief of the Air Corps took up the issue with Woodring and the General Staff. He stressed that "it would be a serious set-back to aviation progress if, as a result of this unfortunate accident, the remarkable aeronautical development should be lost to the War Department."[65] In December the War Department approved the purchase of thirteen planes under Section 10(k).[66]

## FOULOIS AND THE U.S. ARMY AIR CORPS

In many respects, the future looked bright for the Air Corps at the close of 1935. It had an ongoing program of long-range bomber development and would soon receive its first B-17s. It appeared that in short order the Air Corps would have the tools to both carry out strategic air warfare and bolster its claim to the coastal air defense mission. However, this proved to be an illusion. Under General Craig's leadership, the General Staff was reluctant to buy additional B-17s. As of September 1939, the Air Corps still owned only thirteen of the planes. Moreover, Craig undermined the Army air arm's claim to distant overwater operations. He made a personal agreement with the Chief of Naval Operations in 1938, limiting the Air Corps to operational flights of no more than one hundred miles from the shore. This killed one of the chief reasons for having the long-range bomber. MacArthur's successor seemingly disregarded the distant air operations and coast defense activities set forth in TR 440-15 as he worked to attach the air arm more firmly to its third mission, support of the Army field forces.[67]

Doctrinally, the Air Corps at the end of 1935 was well on its way to forging the offensive employment concepts with which it would fight World War II. Air officers believed at the conclusion of the Foulois years that the aim in war was the destruction of the enemy's will. This could best be accomplished by defeating the adversary's air force and destroying the vital elements within his nation through a well-coordinated strategic bombing campaign. Army aviators were unsure of the role of pursuit aviation. Most of them tended to agree that the vastly increased range and speed of the modern bomber rendered existing pursuit planes unacceptable for escort duty and inadequate for air defense. Some Air Corps officers proposed developing large, fast, multiplace fighters for bomber protection, while others held that the bombers could get through to their targets unescorted.

By the end of 1935, the Air Corps Tactical School had not come out unequivocally in favor of precision, high-altitude, daylight bombing. The school did lean heavily in that direction, however. Generally, the Army air arm rejected the Douhet-Mitchell theory of area bombing and sought instead to strike specific industrial and military targets whose destruction would bear directly on the enemy's capacity to wage war. Advances in bombsight design during the early 1930s by the Norden and Sperry companies, along with persistent public hostility to the concept of indiscriminate terror bombing, facilitated this approach. So, too, did the Air Corps' appreciation that it would not have many bombers available at the start of the next war. Precision bombing promised tremendous results even when done by a fairly small force; effective area saturation raids required a huge fleet of bombers.[68]

The first half of the 1930s had yielded a unified strike force, a rea-

## CONCEPTS, 1934-1935

sonably well-defined doctrine for its offensive use, and the beginnings of a vehicle to carry out that doctrine. The age was not so kind to the Army aviators in terms of manpower and numbers of aircraft—vital ingredients if the Air Corps was to become an effective offensive and defensive force.

Douglas Aircraft's newly designed bomber, B-18A.

## CHAPTER X

## FUNDS, AIRCRAFT, PERSONNEL, AND BASES, 1934-1935

For a number of years the Air Corps had been slowly building up its aircraft strength, but beginning in fiscal 1933 this trend reversed. During each of the next four years, the government failed to provide sufficient funds to replace aircraft losses, and, as a result, the Air Corps' inventory shrank from a high of 1,646 planes in July 1932 to 855 in June 1936. In June 1934, the Army air arm possessed approximately 1,300 aircraft of which less than one-third were combat types. Due to the long procurement lead times required by Assistant Secretary of War Woodring as part of his new competitive contracting system, the Air Corps received just forty-one new planes during fiscal 1935. This was the smallest number since passage of the 1926 Air Corps Act, producing a net aircraft decrease of 223. By December 1934 most tactical squadrons were operating with less than fifty percent of authorized aircraft strength.[1]

Both the OCAC and the General Staff were concerned over the shrinking force structure and attempted to remedy the situation with the fiscal 1935 budget. Foulois requested the War Department to ask for enough money to immediately fill out the Air Corps to 1,800 planes and submitted an estimate for $36 million to cover the cost of the proposed purchase. The General Staff was in the process of preparing a request for $314 million to fund military activities—$90 million more than the President had made available in the current fiscal year. It was therefore willing to include a large portion of the funds needed to complete the Air Corps' five-year program, since the money would not have to come at the expense of the other arms. As a result, the War Department asked for $34 million for the Air Corps in its budget request. In September 1933, the Director of the Bureau of the Budget returned the War Department's estimate and demanded it be cut to $248 million. This forced the General

## FUNDS, AIRCRAFT, PERSONNEL, AND BASES, 1934-1935

Staff to limit the Air Corps to $25.5 million, a figure that would not buy enough planes to make up for predicted losses through attrition. The Bureau of the Budget later slashed this inadequate amount another $1 million.[2]

Congress approved the administration's initial military spending package. It did not, however, fully honor Roosevelt's March 1934 request—at the height of the air mail fiasco—to give the Air Corps an additional $10 million. Congress voted only half that amount, providing the air arm a total of around $30 million for fiscal 1935. Apparently the legislators' budget decisions were not affected by the Air Corps' poor showing in the air mail operation or by Foulois' explanation of the five year program's current status. Nor were they swayed by MacArthur's statement during the appropriations hearings that Congress was chiefly responsible for the Air Corps' plane shortage. The Chief of Staff had taken the congressmen to task for creating the expansion program with the 1926 Air Corps Act and then not coming up with the money to carry it out. He argued that by relying year after year on the spending ceilings set by the Bureau of the Budget, the lawmakers had been delinquent in their duties. Due to continually rising prices and the need to spend most of its procurement dollars on more expensive combat planes, the Air Corps could let contracts for merely 215 planes in fiscal year 1935.[3]

The War Department's commitment to expand the number of planes in the Army inventory, as signaled in the February 1, 1934 bill to equip the GHQ Air Force, faltered during the turmoil of the next few months. MacArthur urged a new five-year expansion program before the House Military Affairs Committee in February, but it soon became obvious that the General Staff desired simply to complete the old one. As War Department officials tackled the 1936 budget in April 1934, they told Foulois to base Air Corps preliminary estimates on what would be necessary to attain the 1,800 serviceable aircraft called for in the 1926 act. In May the Army announced a program to spend $50 million over three years for new planes, and MacArthur admitted a short time later in his 1934 annual report that the air arm desperately needed more aircraft. The War Department, however, was thinking in terms of 1,800 machines as specified in the 1926 act rather than the tremendous increases referred to in the February bill.[4]

The Baker Board report stimulated the General Staff to seek more aircraft for the Air Corps. As it had on most other issues, the Baker group endorsed the Drum Board's conclusion that the Army had to have 2,320 planes and decried the current shortages. The July 1934 report noted the Drum Board's recommendation that the number of aircraft not be increased above 1,800 at the expense of the other combat arms, but it called for going ahead with the 2,320-plane program. The War Department was anxious to adopt all of the Baker Board recommendations. This would prove it was responsive to the air arm's needs and thereby undercut criticism by members of Congress and by Army flyers testifying before the Federal Aviation Commission. MacArthur suggested that a three-year program be set up at once to give the Air Corps a total of 2,320 planes. Underlining the urgency of the matter, Dern asked Roosevelt to support MacArthur's plans.[5]

During the summer of 1934 the General Staff and the OCAC worked together on the three-year program. Prior to the Chief of Staff's decision to stretch the increase over three years, Foulois had proposed that the War Department include 1,000 new aircraft in its 1936 appropriations request. Ever eager to rapidly flesh out the air fleet, he reasoned that this would fulfill the Baker Board recommendation in one shot. The General Staff was hesitant. The Director of the Budget had already told MacArthur that 1936 War Department estimates were to be kept very low. The Chief of Staff eventually ordered Foulois to prepare a study on what should be bought annually to reach a total of 2,320 planes in three years. The air chief responded on August 24 with a plan based on the distribution of aircraft types recommended by the Drum Board. Spreading the buy as MacArthur desired, the plan called for procuring about 800 planes a year with 500 of them to be replacements for obsolete and worn-out machines.

The General Staff liked the proposal but held off implementing it in the coming fiscal year for fear the administration and Congress would refuse to provide the needed funds. Further, MacArthur wanted to make sure the War Department purchase program balanced the needs of all combat arms. He did not want big increases for the Air Corps at the expense of the rest of the Army. In January 1935 the General Staff drafted legislation covering the three-year 2,320-aircraft program, but the War Department did not send the bill to Congress until 1936. The delay dismayed Foulois and his subordinates.[6]

Convinced that the three-year program should be put into effect at once, Foulois forwarded a preliminary estimate for the fiscal 1936 budget containing enough money to buy 800 planes. The General Staff tentatively approved the estimate in late 1934, making it part of an enlarged fund request sent to the Bureau of the Budget in defiance of early instructions to hold down costs. The budget bureau reacted by making large cuts throughout the Army estimate and authorizing the War Department to ask for only 547 planes. The administration had thus shaved $6 million from the Air Corps' request, paring it to $48 million. This amount was still a steep increase over the $30 million appropriated for the current year.[7]

Congress did not tamper with Roosevelt's fund request for military

## FUNDS, AIRCRAFT, PERSONNEL, AND BASES, 1934–1935

aviation, appropriating just what the Bureau of the Budget had approved. However, the lawmakers departed from their set pattern of accepting the administration's overall ceiling on defense spending. After MacArthur told them how the Bureau of the Budget had slashed the War Department's original requests, the congressmen voted to restore funds for more manpower and equipment modernization in the nonflying branches. The resulting improvement in the Army's material condition made the War Department more sympathetic to the three-year aircraft expansion program. Unfortunately, because of higher production costs and the Air Corps-General Staff decision to buy greater numbers of larger and more expensive bombers, the funds for airplane procurement in fiscal 1936 once again did not cover losses due to attrition.[8]

By mid-1935 the Air Corps' declining resources quickened the concern of air officers. Instead of being equipped with 980 aircraft—as called for by the Drum Board—the GHQ Air Force had only about 450, of which fewer than 175 were relatively modern. In May the Chief of the Air Corps urged the General Staff to institute the three-year program as soon as possible. He and his staff regarded the situation as very serious and wanted the Secretary of War informed in the hope that some special action might be taken at once.[9]

Foulois did not realize it, but MacArthur, Dern, and Woodring were already sold on the need for extra funds to buy additional planes. When it appeared that more PWA money might be made available to the War Department in 1935-36, MacArthur went before the House Military Affairs Committee in February and, to the delight of McSwain, asked for around $90 million to procure aircraft. Congress, however, forbade further spending of PWA money for military hardware. Undeterred, Assistant Secretary of War Woodring appeared before the Rogers Aviation Subcommittee on May 7 and appealed for an immediate supplemental appropriation of $30 million for new planes. He had just returned from surveying Air Corps resources and was quite taken with the aircraft situation. The next day, Woodring conferred with Andrews on GHQ Air Force shortages. While the two men were talking, Rogers phoned to say his subcommittee was impressed with the assistant secretary's presentation. He added that, with the full committee's approval, he and Woodring would see Roosevelt about releasing the desired funds from the unexpended portion of the fiscal 1935 PWA appropriation.[10]

After some delay, the House Military Affairs Committee took up the question in mid-June. At the insistence of McSwain and members of the Rogers Subcommittee, the committee called War Department officials for their views a few weeks later. Dern, MacArthur, Woodring, and Westover testified on the Air Corps' current deficiency in planes, pointing out the procurement appropriation for fiscal 1936 would not cover expected

239

losses. The four officials fully endorsed a proposal before the committee to release an extra $40 million for aircraft purchases. The War Department presentation convinced the congressmen to seek the additional funds. Since the fiscal 1935 PWA money was no longer available, the committee members agreed that the quickest way to secure the funds was to win Roosevelt's support for a supplemental appropriation. The committee appointed Rogers and three other members to present the issue to the President. Rogers wrote to Roosevelt on July 23, but the Chief Executive refused to act. The project accordingly came to nothing, and the Air Corps was left to do the best it could with shrinking resources. In October Andrews complained to the Chief of Staff that the GHQ Air Force was down to 346 planes of which only 168 were standard combat types.[11]

MacArthur's support for the proposed $40 million supplemental appropriation did not represent a dramatic shift in his attitude toward military aviation. The Chief of Staff had for years appreciated the need for an adequate air component but had persistently refused to build up the Air Corps at the expense of the other arms. He also believed manpower was more important than equipment and opposed purchases that might require offsetting reductions in personnel. Notwithstanding, by 1935 the Army's situation had changed. Congress not only approved funds for additional Army equipment as part of the fiscal 1934 PWA program and furnished more modernization funds in the 1936 regular appropriation, but it also authorized additional manpower.

With these basic needs in the process of being fulfilled, MacArthur felt less constrained on the issue of aircraft increases. Further, he knew the extra $40 million in Air Corps funds would not result in reductions in the programs of the other arms. With Congress more willing to spend money for defense, the Chief of Staff and his War Department subordinates apparently believed it was now also safe to sponsor the legislation for a continuing aircraft expansion program. In his 1935 annual report MacArthur proposed that Congress act without delay to strengthen the Air Corps. Calling for a continuing program to buy eight hundred planes a year, he now claimed the nation needed a balanced force of twenty-five hundred aircraft.[12]

Secretary of War Dern went even further. He recommended in his 1935 report to Roosevelt that the government immediately begin a five-year expansion program to purchase eight hundred planes of all types annually. This, he said, would make available by 1941 a force of three thousand combat aircraft of modern design, plus a considerable number of trainers and transports. Dern insisted: "A sound preparedness policy . . . dictates that we should at least equip ourselves with enough of the most modern fighting planes to repel an invader at the outbreak of hostilities. At present our air force is far short of its reasonable requirements."

## FUNDS, AIRCRAFT, PERSONNEL, AND BASES, 1934-1935

He pointed out that he had endorsed a three-year expansion program as a result of the Baker Board report, but now believed a program of longer duration was in order.[13] Foulois, persona non grata on Capitol Hill and out of favor with many senior General Staff officers, was delighted over this newfound War Department support for the Air Corps.

Until his death in 1936, Dern worked hard to win additional funds for aircraft procurement and to gain congressional acceptance of his expansion plan. In June 1936, Congress passed a bill authorizing an increase in aircraft strength to 2,320, but over Dern's protests the administration refused to allow the Air Corps enough money in its fiscal 1937 appropriations request to begin the buildup. In succeeding years, however, Roosevelt paid more attention to the Army's aviation needs. Even so, not until the eve of World War II did the government provide enough money to equip the Air Corps with the number of planes called for by the Baker Board in 1934.[14]

While 1934 and 1935 may have been difficult years for aircraft procurement, they did usher in some improvement in the Air Corps' personnel situation. In mid-1934 the air arm was still about 350 officers short of the 1,650 specified in the Air Corps Act of 1926. However, the War Department appropriations bill passed for fiscal 1935 indirectly helped the air arm make slight gains in commissioned strength. It required the Army to have no more than 11,750 officers with commissioning dates prior to June 1, 1934. By continuing the 12,000-officer ceiling it had imposed in the past, the law left room for 250 new second lieutenants. Since West Point yielded too few graduates to fill all of these vacancies, the Air Corps was again able to grant Regular commissions to a few Reserve officers and enlisted men who had completed pilot training. After holding examinations in the spring of 1935, and with War Department approval, the Air Corps commissioned 42 such individuals in July. Foulois was pleased with Congress' action and the resulting officer increase for the Army air arm.[15] He had written Senator Morris Sheppard, chairman of the Senate Military Affairs Committee, in March 1934 explaining that:

> the *shortage of Regular officers* can only be overcome through an increase in the present authorized total commissioned strength of the Regular Army, or through *separating* from the Active List of the Army enough Regular Army officers to provide vacancies for Second Lieutenants of the Air Corps.[16]

The air chief may have not been instrumental in getting Congress to insert the 11,750-officer restriction in the 1935 appropriations bill, but he certainly backed that move.

The 1936 appropriations act benefited the Air Corps and the Army as a whole by raising enlisted strength to 165,000. Since 1930 the War Department had pressed for a minimum force of 14,000 officers and 165,000 men, and MacArthur had campaigned vigorously over the past years for the increases. While the Roosevelt administration continued to oppose personnel increases in 1934, and forbade the War Department to make them part of the formal appropriations request for fiscal 1936, MacArthur argued for the force enlargement before the House and Senate Appropriations Committees. The lawmakers, more willing than in the past to disregard the President's wishes on military funding and showing fresh interest in a sound national defense system, responded to the Chief of Staff's plea by voting funds for 165,000 enlisted men. This provided an increase of nearly 47,000 troops, of which the Air Corps received 1,442. As a result, the air arm surpassed the enlisted levels set in the 1926 act, having nearly 16,000 troops assigned during fiscal 1936.[17]

For the Air Corps, however, the enlisted shortage had never been as acute a problem as low officer strength. One way to partially relieve the Regular officer pinch was to put more Reserve officers on extended active duty. Since 1931, Foulois had annually urged the General Staff to seek appropriations to maintain 550 active duty Reserve pilots, but limited funds continued to prevent more than about half that number from serving with the Air Corps each year. As a result, the Air Corps chief sponsored a plan in mid-July 1933 that would furnish additional pilots without expanding the number of active Reserve officers. He proposed that instead of commissioning new pilots upon their graduation from the training center, they could be assigned to tactical units in flying cadet status for one year, after which they could serve an extra year as Reserve officers. Since cadet pay was far lower than that of second lieutenants, this would give the Air Corps twice the number of Reserve aviators with only a slight increase in cost. In addition, the plan would enable the citizen-soldiers to become better tactical pilots before their active duty period ended, enhancing their value to the Air Corps. Following General Staff approval, Foulois implemented the program in February 1934.[18]

The OCAC wanted the authority and money to keep Reserve officers on active duty beyond the two years specified in the 1926 Air Corps Act. The Baker Board endorsed this view in mid-1934. The General Staff agreed that in order to get a proper return on their training, three years should be the minimum active duty tour for Reserve pilots. The War Department was also willing to support the OCAC's request for more Reserves to partially offset Regular officer shortages, but only if they could be had at no cost to the rest of the Army. Congress finally acted on the Reserve issue in June 1936, authorizing the War Department to call a maximum of 1,350 Reserve officers to active duty with the Air Corps for five years. But the lawmakers were less free with appropriations to support this force; they provided just enough money in fiscal 1937 to keep 300 Reserve officers on extended active duty.[19]

In 1934-35 Foulois was interested in securing additional Reserve pi-

## FUNDS, AIRCRAFT, PERSONNEL, AND BASES, 1934-1935

lots, but his chief personnel concern was the continuing scarcity of Regular officers. The Air Corps had neither the seasoned leaders nor the commissioned strength to fill out all of the tactical units formed over the past few years, and this put an undue strain on individuals assigned to those units. Reserve officers and aviation cadets were only of marginal value. By law, they could not be charged with responsibility for property or funds, and their limited experience kept them from filling technical and administrative positions.

Some Air Corps officers considered it foolish to maintain the large overhead required to keep all of the understrength units in being. Foulois disagreed. He still held—as he had at the time he became Chief of the Air Corps—that the way to alleviate a portion of the shortage and leadership problem was to pare the number of aviators in service schools and on detached duty. He told the Baker Board in 1934 that he desired his veteran flyers to man the tactical units and had therefore asked the General Staff many times to trim the number of Air Corps officers assigned to the Army school system. The air chief was perturbed over the War Department's lack of cooperation. He complained to the board that the General Staff's response was to detail more flyers to service schools. Agitated by Foulois' comments, Drum defended the school system and detached duty as important to meeting the Army's needs. He reminded Foulois that the Air Corps belonged to the Army and pointed out that aviators had to complete Command and General Staff School to make them eligible for General Staff duty.[20]

The Air Corps chief's thinking on the school program was at odds with that of many of his subordinates who eagerly sought additional professional training. Yet, in light of the Air Corps' shortage of experienced aviators, Foulois' position was understandable. By 1935 combat squadrons in the United States averaged fewer than three Regular officers each. A 1934 report revealed that out of a total force of 1,305 Regular officers, 147 flyers were currently attending either a service school or civilian university, while 42 others were on detached duty with the Reserve forces. The air chief placed the pressing needs of the Air Corps above the desires of his aviators and worked, mostly without success, to prevent large numbers of them from gaining assignments to Army school billets. He did not appear to realize that he might be depriving Air Corps officers of administrative and managerial skills of future benefit to the air arm.[21]

During the GHQ Air Force's first year of operation, the officer deficit was very real. Tables of organization called for 1,245 pilots, but Andrews found only 257 Regular officers on hand when he organized his command in February 1935. Counting Reserve pilots and a few more Regular officers later removed from other activities by Foulois, the force numbered 555 pilots upon its activation. The GHQ Air Force grew to 623

## FOULOIS AND THE U.S. ARMY AIR CORPS

flyers by October, but in the next eight months it gained just 17 more. Andrews struggled to build up the Regular component of his organization and asked that priority be given it when making officer assignments. By June 1936 the GHQ Air Force had 409 of the Air Corps' 1,350 Regular officers. This represented some improvement, but it also indicated that a high percentage of the air arm's officers was still being allocated to nontactical functions.[22]

Congress finally acted in August 1935 to bring the Air Corps to its authorized strength of 1,650 officers. After having considered similar legislation over the past two years, the lawmakers voted to give the Secretary of War authority to grant Regular commissions to fifty training center graduates a year for the next ten years. Since the new statute supplied no funds, the War Department had to defer the program's start until fiscal 1937. The General Staff supported the new law because it did not require the War Department to withhold commissions from West Point graduates in order to make vacancies available to the citizen-aviators.[23]

The 1934-35 period not only witnessed a moderate rise in the number of Air Corps personnel, but it also brought changes that materially affected the members of the air arm. Overriding Roosevelt's veto in March 1934, Congress restored one-third of the fifteen-percent pay cut of the previous year and ended the freeze on pay raises associated with promotions. The lawmakers restored another one-third on July 1, 1934, and one year later the President completely ended the economy measure, making service members again eligible for longevity pay boosts. Though grateful for these actions, senior War Department officials still groused that military pay was much too low.[24]

Even more important to Air Corps officers was the sunnier promotion outlook during the last two years of Foulois' term of office. Sympathetic congressmen had for years sponsored bills calling for a separate promotion list for the Army air arm. Foulois and his fellow aviators were persistent advocates of such legislation. The air chief had proposed a promotion system apart from the rest of the Army on many occasions before congressional committees. In early 1934 he allowed the OCAC to secretly draft legislation for McSwain containing this provision. The War Department stoutly resisted the 1934 bill as it had earlier ones, and by July 1934 Foulois was sure that a separate promotion system was out of the question. A board of Air Corps officers looking into the issue had reported that the opposition of the other service arms would stave off congressional acceptance of the measure. Moreover, the persistence of the OCAC to get a separate promotion bill would likely rule out better promotion laws for the whole Army. Perhaps swayed by his troubles with Subcommittee Number 3, Foulois decided to honor MacArthur's wishes and present a common front on behalf of a promotion proposal being readied

## FUNDS, AIRCRAFT, PERSONNEL, AND BASES, 1934–1935

by the General Staff.[25]

The Baker Board's recommendations also played a part in the air chief's changed attitude toward a separate promotion list. The board noted that the rank of Air Corps officers was generally inconsistent with their assigned duties. It called upon the War Department to remedy the situation by implementing the sections of the Air Corps Act which provided for temporary promotions, and in doing so to interpret these provisions as widely as possible so that a great number of officers might profit. The report also noted the promotion stagnation existing throughout the Army and advocated immediate action to speed promotions. The Federal Aviation Commission fully endorsed these two recommendations when it met a few months later. The War Department adopted the Baker report as its aviation policy and was thus committed to the temporary promotion proposal as well as the previously established Army policy of seeking promotion relief. Foulois had resisted the use of the temporary promotion provisions of the 1926 act because inequities could arise. Now he felt it might be best for the air arm to give the expanded temporary system, as advocated by the Baker Board, a try.[26]

OCAC officials had never used the temporary promotion authority contained in the Air Corps Act because they believed it would benefit only a few officers while creating dissatisfaction among the remainder. The wording of the act seemed too narrow. It said officers could be advanced solely if the Chief of the Air Corps certified there were no officers of permanent rank available for the duty requiring the higher rank. Further, the act excluded from temporary promotion those officer serving with the General Staff or the OCAC, for it specified that increased rank could go only to officers assigned to flying commands and schools, commanders of key air stations, and to the staffs of the commanders of troops. Air Corps officials feared this would drive qualified officers away from OCAC and General Staff assignments. Accordingly, the Chief of the Air Corps recommended in 1926 that no use be made of the promotion provisions of the law. The Assistant Secretary of War for Air made an informal agreement to that effect with the House and Senate Military Affairs Committees. The OCAC reviewed this 1926 decision in later years, but up to the time of the Baker Board hearings, it opposed using temporary promotions.[27]

After lengthy haggling between the General Staff and the OCAC over which duty assignments would be eligible for temporary promotions, the War Department put the new system into effect in early 1935. The OCAC developed new tables of organization specifying the appropriate rank for each position of responsibility throughout the Air Corps. It then recommended that temporary promotions be extended only to the more important command and staff posts. General Hughes, Assistant Chief of Staff,

G-3, wanted an even narrower application of the system, but the War Department carried it down to the lowest tactical levels, promoting 616 of the Air Corps' 1,333 Regular officers. GHQ Air Force personnel benefited most from the program. Two of the three wing commanders became brigadier generals while the third took the rank of colonel. The post of Commanding General, GHQ Air Force, became a major general's billet. Lieutenant Colonel Andrews, however, took over the position as a brigadier general because the Air Corps Act restricted temporary promotion to two grades above a person's permanent rank.[28]

An opinion of The Judge Advocate General in mid-January 1935 eased administration of the temporary promotion procedure. The 1926 act required the Chief of the Air Corps to certify that no officers of applicable permanent rank were available to fill a given post before temporary promotion could be authorized for a lower ranking officer. The word "available" had troubled the OCAC since the act's passage. The Judge Advocate General gave the word a very broad construction, interpreting it to mean professionally qualified and administratively available. The decision permitted the Air Corps to apply the temporary system without having first to resort to numerous personnel transfers, and it freed the air arm from the requirement to put officers in posts for which they were not qualified. This gave the Chief of the Air Corps wide latitude in designat-

Brig. Gen. Frank M. Andrews, promoted from Lt. Colonel to become Commanding General, GHQ Air Force.

# FUNDS, AIRCRAFT, PERSONNEL, AND BASES, 1934-1935

ing those who, by virtue of their jobs, were eligible for promotion.[29]

While Foulois was willing to give the new system a try and to work with the War Department in support of new promotion legislation, in early 1935 some Air Corps officers wanted to go on fighting for a separate promotion list. The War Department was in the process of drafting its Army-wide promotion proposal when McSwain introduced a bill on January 21 calling for a separate Air Corps promotion system. Realizing that McSwain's offering, if passed, would probably ruin chances for the Army bill, the professional associations of the other combat arms sent resolutions to the House Military Affairs Committee condemning the chairman's legislative proposal. Army ground officers suspected the Air Corps was backing the McSwain bill, but this was not the case. Some OCAC officers suggested that the air arm work for the measure's passage, but Foulois steadfastly refused. In May he wrote MacArthur, who had just found out that the OCAC had secretly drafted a similar bill for McSwain in 1934. Foulois said he was squarely behind the Army's promotion measure and wanted nothing to do with the Military Affairs Committee chairman's proposal. The air chief's stand apparently stemmed from his ongoing troubles and his earlier conclusion that separate promotion legislation stood no chance of passage. He also realized that the Army's bill held the prospect of at least some relief from the Air Corps' promotion drought.[30]

The Senate began hearings on the War Department's bill in early February and passed it about six weeks later. The House Military Affairs Committee held off considering it until mid-June, awaiting the outcome of The Inspector General's investigation of Foulois. The lower chamber finally passed the measure in early August. The new law raised the percentages of promotion list officers authorized in the grades of major through colonel. It also provided for advancement to first lieutenant after three years service and to captain at the completion of ten years of active duty. Field grade hikes depended on specified years of commissioned service and a vacant slot. An officer was eligible for promotion to major after fifteen years, to lieutenant colonel after twenty, and to colonel upon completion of twenty-six years of commissioned service. The statute provided for the following changes in the percentages of the field grade officer force:

| Grade | Old law | New law |
| --- | --- | --- |
| Major | 16.5 | 25 |
| Lieutenant Colonel | 5.5 | 9 |
| Colonel | 4.5 | 6 |

## FOULOIS AND THE U.S. ARMY AIR CORPS

The higher percentiles translated into 158 additional colonels, 364 more lieutenant colonels, and 890 additional majors.

The law also authorized retirement, with the approval of the President, any time after completion of fifteen years service. Under the old statute, officers were required to serve thirty years to apply for presidential approval for retirement and needed forty years' service to retire without the Chief Executive's consent. The August law delighted the War Department; the statute gave immediate advancement to nearly half of all Army officers below the rank of colonel, and brought the remainder eight years closer to promotion.[31]

Although Air Corps officers benefited from the act, they fared worse than ground officers because as a group they occupied lower positions on the single promotion list. Only eight Air Corps lieutenant colonels, thirty-two majors, and forty-one captains were high enough on the list to be promoted at once. The law permitted 6 percent of all Army line officers to hold the rank of colonel, but merely 1.2 percent of all aviators held that grade as of late August 1935. Less than 4 percent were lieutenant colonels compared to 9 percent throughout the service. A skimpy 7 percent were majors as opposed to 25 percent of all Army officers. Air Corps second and first lieutenants, however, profited tremendously from the act. Based on years of service, more than 330 of them were promoted at once to the next higher grade.[32]

Congressman McSwain was annoyed that the new law resulted in barely twelve percent of all Air Corps officers holding field grade rank when the overall Army average was forty percent. He therefore introduced a bill on August 14 that called for the Secretary of War to right the imbalance. The secretary was to make such temporary promotions as would be necessary, based on seniority, to place five percent of the Air Corps officers in the grade of colonel, eight percent in the grade of lieutenant colonel, and eighteen percent in the rank of major. The bill provided that the promoted officers would hold the temporary rank until they were advanced to it permanently under the Army promotion law. McSwain said this would give the Air Corps a little over thirty-percent field graders, which was still less than in any other Army branch. The OCAC did not support the proposal. Congress, having recently passed the Army promotion bill, was cool to the Military Affairs Committee chairman's request for another law.[33]

During the spring and summer of 1935, numerous Air Corps officers began to express distaste for the temporary promotion procedure growing out of the Baker Board recommendations. As a result, Foulois set to work seeking to have the program abolished. Even those who had benefited from the system complained that it was unfair. Arnold claimed it was destroying morale; other senior aviators agreed. Officers in important

## FUNDS, AIRCRAFT, PERSONNEL, AND BASES, 1934-1935

posts that were not on the approved list for temporary promotions were extremely dismayed when other officers, some junior to them on the promotion list, received advancements of up to two grades. Likewise, officers getting the temporary promotions were upset when individuals of higher permanent rank arrived in the units they commanded, for it meant they would have to surrender their temporary promotions as well as their leadership positions. Since officers in the OCAC were ineligible for temporary promotions, they were nearly unanimous in their opposition to the system.[34]

Foulois had doubts about the program from the start. In August he recommended the General Staff end all temporary promotions, except for that of the GHQ Air Force commander, effective October 1. The air chief explained that if the War Department disagreed with this proposal, he favored, as an alternate solution, limiting the program to positions of equal or greater importance to that of wing commander. The G-1 division of the General Staff reached a similar conclusion in August. It recommended that only the commanders of the GHQ Air Force and the combat air wings be eligible for temporary promotion. Regardless of these proposals, the General Staff did nothing to change the system until mid-1936. At that time Congress passed a law broadening the categories for temporary promotion and providing that advancement be made in order of seniority.[35]

Adopting the temporary promotion procedures of the Air Corps Act was just one of the many Baker Board recommendations acted upon by the War Department during 1934-35. Like that of the Drum Board before it, the board's July 1934 report had also called for the development of adequate GHQ Air Force airfields in all strategic areas of the United States. This prompted the General Staff to direct a special board of officers to study the air arm's basing needs for a suitable air defense. Foulois and his staff had been advocating the creation of air bases in the nation's vital zones since July 1932, when the air chief had won the Harbor Defense Board's endorsement of the OCAC's proposal on frontier air defense. Air Corps officers believed quite strongly in strategically located air installations. They deemed them essential to keep a hostile power from successfully invading the United states or carrying out bombing attacks on the economic fabric of the nation. In response to the Drum report and at the behest of the War Department, the OCAC began a preliminary survey of strategic areas in the spring of 1934. The aim was to find out what civilian fields were presently available for Air Corps use in an emergency and what other fields might be needed. The aviators seemed to be in no hurry to complete this task, and had made very little progress by the time the Baker Board rendered its report.[36]

## FOULOIS AND THE U.S. ARMY AIR CORPS

After the General Staff created an airdrome board in August in response to the Baker Board recommendations, the Air Corps slacked off on its own basing survey. Foulois and his staff reasoned that it would be best to suspend judgment on the issue until the airdrome board completed its more detailed probe. This stance displeased the War Department, for there were clear signs that Congress would study Air Corps needs for strategically located bases in early 1935. Since the airdrome board was not expected to finish its work before June, the General Staff needed the Air Corps' survey to prepare itself to deal with the forthcoming congressional action.

In a December 21 memo to Foulois, Kilbourne criticized the OCAC's inaction. Five days later, the General Staff ordered the Air Corps to render a report by January 10 showing the availability of suitable civilian airfields and the need for additional facilities in the nation's strategic frontier areas. The OCAC complied, forwarding a paper that reviewed the airdromes situated in the seven strategic zones designated in the Drum report. It stressed, in accord with Kilbourne's opinion, that New England should receive the first priority in air base construction. The report was a bit skimpy and, as an OCAC staff officer admitted in an accompanying memo, it had been prepared rather hurriedly.[37]

Air Corps footdragging on the landing-field survey did not signify that the aviators had lost interest in setting up bases in strategic frontier areas. OCAC officials testifying before the Federal Aviation Commission in November 1934, recommended that three large installations with extensive facilities be constructed on each coast and that additional ones be built in Alaska, Panama, Hawaii, and the Philippines. Congressman James M. Wilcox (Democrat—Florida) had been weighing the Air Corps' air defense needs for some time and was impressed with the air arm's continuing stand on airfield development. In mid-November he took it upon himself to organize the National Air Frontier Defense Association, a pressure group to support the OCAC's proposal before the Federal Aviation Commission. In December he proposed a bill for the construction of a number of frontier defense air bases. Wilcox probably coordinated his activities with OCAC officials, for James Fechet, Foulois' predecessor as Chief of the Air Corps, helped the congressman form the association and worked closely with him on the air base question.[38]

By making the Baker Board report its air policy, the War Department was committed to the building of air installations within the nation's strategic frontier zones. Even so, the General Staff did not want Congress to pass an expensive base construction bill. Kilbourne attended the first meeting of the National Air Frontier Defense Association and pledged to the many influential businessmen and politicians present that the War Department approved of the group's goals. However, he cautioned them not

## FUNDS, AIRCRAFT, PERSONNEL, AND BASES, 1934-1935

to campaign for increases in the Air Corps that might come at the expense of the rest of the Army. He also asked that site selection for future air bases be left to the War Department.[39]

Wilcox introduced his bill (H.R. 4130) on January 17, 1935. The proposal called for building ten "frontier defense bases," each of which was to be capable of normally accommodating one wing of 132 aircraft. All of the new bases were to have numerous landing fields and servicing facilities so that 1,000 planes could operate from each of the ten new installations in times of emergency. The bill authorized the Secretary of War to select the sites of the new bases, but it required that one be located in each of the following regions: New England, the Southeastern Atlantic States, along the Gulf of Mexico, Southern California, Northern California, the Pacific Northwest, the Great Lakes area, Panama, and the Rocky Mountain area. (Wilcox did not perceive the Rocky Mountain base as a deterrent to future Indian uprisings, but as a backup for the West Coast installations.) His bill set a ceiling of $19 million per base and authorized $190 million for the total package.[40]

The War Department did not like Wilcox's bill. The General Staff favored immediate construction of one small Air Corps station in New England, Alaska, the Southeast, and in the Pacific Northwest, but it did not want large sums of money spent to build the mammoth bases called for by Wilcox. Kilbourne informed MacArthur that some auxiliary landing fields around the permanent stations could be developed through local interest and initiative. He maintained any additional facilities needed could be built after the outbreak of war.

Reacting to the Wilcox bill, the War Plans Division, the airdrome board, and the OCAC jointly drafted a substitute proposal. It omitted all mention of appropriation of funds and gave the Secretary of War permissive authority to establish new bases as needed. The War Department bill required that at least one base be located in the Northeast, Southeast, Northwest, Great Lakes, Gulf of Mexico, and Rocky Mountains regions as well as in Alaska. Each new installation was to accommodate a minimum of one three-squadron group.[41] Foulois supported the bill, but he emphasized to the General Staff that "to create new stations without creating additional equipment, units and personnel therefor would have the effect of further weakening, if not destroying, our already over skeletonized Air Corps tactical units."[42]

Kilbourne convinced Wilcox and the House Military Affairs Committee members to substitute the new bill for the original one. The bill became law on August 12, 1935. Besides the above provisions, it allowed the Secretary of War to build depots and intermediate supporting bases in rear areas and to enlarge existing Air Corps stations. The War Department now had the authority to construct a complete network of installations for the new GHQ Air Force, but at its own request, it had no money to carry out this task.[43]

During the hearings on the War Department bill, very sensitive information was released to the press which caused a stir with the Canadian government. Kilbourne had told the House Military Affairs Committee in secret session on April 28 that the United States must prepare itself to repel a possible attack from the north. So as not to upset relations with Canada, he said he had used "camouflaged" wording in the bill, calling for "intermediate stations" when the General Staff meant bases along the Canadian border. The day before, Andrews had made similar remarks before the committee, implying that Canada could be a potential enemy in a future war. Through oversight both officers' remarks were released to the press. The embarrassing situation elicited a greater response from Roosevelt than from the Canadian government. The President swiftly censured the committee. He announced publicly that Kilbourne's and Andrews' statements did not represent official policy and that the United States held only warmest regards for its neighbor to the north. Canadian authorities noted the two officers' remarks, but seemed unruffled by the General Staff's desire to strengthen American air defenses in the north.[44]

With passage of the bill in August, the War Department appeared anxious to get base construction under way in the strategically most important regions. The airdrome board reported on August 26 that the GHQ Air Force immediately required one base each in New England and the Pacific Northwest, an air depot in the Rocky Mountains area, and two small air stations near Miami, Florida, from which long-range reconnaissance aircraft could operate. A few days earlier, the War Department appointed a new special committee to do a study, based on the airdrome board's findings, to determine what facilities were needed in each strategic area and to arrange a priority list for new construction. Lt. Col. John D. Reardan, the Air Corps' officer who had chaired the previous board, was designated to head the new group.

The special committee reported in December that the Army could not afford to instantly build big installations with numerous auxiliary fields in all of the strategic zones. The report recommended that the War Department act at once to set up one small installation in New England, the Northwest, and Florida as a nucleus for larger bases to be established in the future. The General Staff was willing to pursue this course, but the administration would not request the necessary funds. As a result, by the end of 1936 the GHQ Air Force still lacked strategic bases in many of the nation's vital areas from which to operate against a hostile force.[45]

Using the Baker Board report as its guide, the War Department, in cooperation with the OCAC, achieved a number of other improvements in 1934-35 that were beneficial to the Air Corps. The General Staff raised

## FUNDS, AIRCRAFT, PERSONNEL, AND BASES, 1934-1935

the number of aviators on the General Staff from five to nine, and it required all West Point cadets to receive at least twenty hours of flying experience to help acquaint them with the capabilities and problems of military aviation. The War Department revitalized the all-but-defunct Air Corps Board by ordering Foulois to assign officers to that body permanently. The board had been established years before to study and report on any subjects referred to it by the Chief of the Air Corps. Collocated with the Air Corps Tactical School, in the past it had relied upon the temporary services of faculty members on the infrequent occasions the air chief had assigned it projects. The War Department also encouraged the Air Corps to rewrite its training regulations to include greater annual requirements for night, instrument, and navigation training. Wholly in accord with Foulois' desires, the Army likewise secured funds that enabled Air Corps pilots to fly an average of three hundred hours per year and allowed the GHQ Air Force to conduct limited exercises throughout the United States.[46]

Foulois backed all these changes and did his best to help the General Staff achieve them. Indirectly he was responsible for this flurry of War Department reform, for had he not volunteered the air arm for mail duty there would have been no Baker Board. And without this board's recommendation, it is doubtful that the War Department would have taken the

Maj. Gen. Oscar Westover, appointed Chief of the Air Corps, upon retirement of Foulois.

## FOULOIS AND THE U.S. ARMY AIR CORPS

initiative to sponsor or would have accepted the numerous beneficial changes. Due to his continuing troubles with Subcommittee Number 3, however, Foulois played a reduced part in bringing the Baker Board proposals to fruition. Defending himself for the better part of a year against the subcommittee charges consumed a great deal of his time. This compelled him to rely more heavily on his subordinates for decisionmaking and the day-to-day administration of the Air Corps. His personal predicament also made him more amenable to General Staff views and caused the OCAC to become a more compliant junior partner in General Staff-Air Corps discussions of air matters. Yet, Foulois did not cease working for the Air Corps' material interests during his last year in office. He continued to argue for increased funding with which to expand the air arm's dwindling aircraft resources. Even when on terminal leave in the fall of 1935, he made a number of speeches in support of air preparedness and took time to write a magazine article highlighting the need to strengthen the GHQ Air Force.[47] As in the previous three years, Foulois spent his last year as Air Corps chief working to complete the initial five-year expansion program. Blame for his failure could not be attributed to lack of effort or to War Department hostility to aviation. It lay at the door of the administration and Congress, who were unwilling to supply the funds needed to equip the Air Corps with eighteen hundred serviceable aircraft.

When Foulois quietly retired in late December 1935, he passed from the scene almost unnoticed. During his three months of terminal leave, he rarely interfered with the workings of the OCAC and generally allowed Westover to direct the affairs of the Air Corps. Once the aviation pioneer announced his impending departure, Congressman Rogers stopped hounding him and the press lost interest. Perhaps Foulois considered Westover too anxious to please the General Staff, for before leaving office he tried to have Hap Arnold designated his replacement. The commander of the west coast wing was an excellent administrator, a diplomatic yet dynamic airpower advocate, and the Air Corps' senior active pilot. In Foulois' eyes he was the right man for the job. The War Department, however, rejected his recommendation and elevated Westover instead. Arnold got the Assistant Chief's post.[48]

Although Foulois could be proud of the Army air arm's progress during his four years at the helm and must have been pleased by the complimentary articles appearing in military and aviation journals after his August announcement of retirement, he left office full of bitterness. He declined Westover's offer of a farewell party, and on December 31, 1935, signed out of the Air Corps without ceremony.[49] Upset over his treatment at the hands of the Rogers Subcommittee and embittered by the low regard senior General Staff members had for him, Foulois would

## FUNDS, AIRCRAFT, PERSONNEL, AND BASES, 1934-1935

later complain: "I was sick of the system that would allow a man to be vilified publicly when his only crime was dedication to the cause of air power."[50] The man who had flown with the Wright brothers and had just led the Air Corps through a period of tremendous transition was once again a private citizen.

# CHAPTER XI

# AN AGE OF TRANSITION

The years 1931-35 were formative in the development of military aviation. Prior to that period the Air Corps had no specific mission or clearly defined doctrine. It was not organized for unified employment or trained for all-weather operations, and its wood and fabric aircraft were incapable of traveling great distances with large ordnance loads. By 1936 all of this had changed. The Army air arm was now charged with the responsibility for coastal air defense, organized into a GHQ Air Force, committed to offensive strategic bombardment operations as the most direct avenue to victory in war, and possessed for the first time a powerful plane that could bomb distant targets. These and other changes during the first half of the 1930s strengthened the Air Corps as a combat force and better prepared it to meet the challenges of World War II.

General Foulois played an instrumental part in this transition. As Chief of the Air Corps, he set the tempo for the Army air arm's efforts and led its campaign for change. No doctrinal innovator, he firmly believed in the importance of military aviation and worked to place it in a position of prominence in the nation's defense structure. He persistently campaigned to free the Air Corps from General Staff control until mid-1934, when his problems with Subcommittee Number 3 required him to temper his advocacy. He supplied the continuing pressure on the War Department which resulted in formation of a coherent air defense employment doctrine and the creation of the GHQ Air Force. Foulois struggled throughout his tour as air chief to complete the manpower and aircraft goals of the five-year expansion progam. He badgered the General Staff to provide the Air Corps with the necessary funds, and frequently complained to Congress over what he considered ground officer neglect of military aviation needs. He encouraged the War Department to approve long-range bomber development and stressed the need for frontier defense bases. He also pressed the General Staff to accept the Air Corps' offen-

## AN AGE OF TRANSITION

sive employment concepts, thus stimulating the War Department to write a more acceptable version of TR 440-15.

During his first two and one-half years as Chief of the Air Corps Foulois lacked tact in dealing with the General Staff. Reflecting the view dominant in the Air Corps, he continually emphasized the importance of military aviation and made demands for increased aircraft strength that were inconsistent with existing defense needs and economic reality. His avid campaigning for an extensive coast defense organization and the immediate creation of the GHQ Air Force did nothing to endear him to senior General Staff officers. He further irritated them by running to congressional military committees with his gripes against the War Department, speaking openly in behalf of Air Corps autonomy. The General Staff was probably quite pleased to see its nemesis attacked by Subcommittee Number 3.

The Rogers Subcommittee's treatment of Foulois was entirely unfair, but it caused a striking change in his attitude and actions toward the General Staff. The Subcommittee used Foulois as a scapegoat, blaming him for both the supposed materiel shortcomings arising from the Air Corps' practice of negotiating aircraft purchases and the air arm's poor showing in the air mail operation. The congressmen were certain he had knowingly lied to them and developed a case against him based upon his February 1 comments on General Staff control of aviation. Foulois had prefaced his remarks that day by saying he was giving his personal opinions, but in its haste to find him guilty, the subcommittee did not consider this. The air chief's poor speaking ability and harsh criticism of the General Staff made it easy for the congressmen to misinterpret his remarks. Foulois had meant to persuade the Military Affairs Committee that the General Staff was inhibiting the development of military aviation and that the Air Corps consequently deserved autonomy, but he had not intended to deliberately lie to the congressmen.

Foulois was shaken by the subcommittee's indictment and The Inspector General's investigation which followed. He also knew that Roosevelt was displeased with him over the air mail fiasco and that he had few friends on the General Staff. Hence he became a much more cooperative War Department team member. No longer did he openly advocate autonomy or take an extreme stand on General Staff-Air Corps issues. During his last year and a half in office the air chief supported compromise solutions, using his position and influence to spread quietude throughout the Air Corps.

Senior General Staff officers did not care for Foulois, but they were not insensitive to the need for a viable air arm. However, they approached the subject from a different perspective from that of the aviators. While Foulois and his subordinates insisted that military aviation was a new and decisive military force in offensive and defensive operations and therefore should be given priority, War Department officials were intent upon building a balanced combat force of which the air arm was but one component. The General Staff valued the support military aviation could provide to the ground army, but was not convinced that the air arm could be decisive when acting alone. Two key principles guided the War Department's aviation policy during the first half of the 1930s: do not allow the Air Corps greater freedom from General Staff control; and do not allow it to increase its resources at the expense of the rest of the Army.

The War Department went to great lengths to carry out the first of these principles. It systematically opposed all congressional proposals calling for any degree of autonomy for military aviation, and it so rigged the Baker Board investigation that it was impossible for that body to reach conclusions contrary to the outlook of the General Staff. By wholly embracing the Baker report, War Department officials also tried to deter the Federal Aviation Commission from proposing unacceptable changes. The General Staff believed that an independent Air Corps would neglect air support of the ground forces and would gain greater aviation appropriations at the expense of the other army components. Accordingly, it was adamant in opposing any such organizational change.

The War Department believed that, since passage of the 1926 Air Corps Act, it had been more than generous to the Army air arm. The General Staff wanted no further sacrifice by the other combat branches for the benefit of military aviation. By the early 1930s, the Air Corps was receiving twenty percent of the Army's funds for military activities. The five-year expansion program had boosted the air component's strength—though not up to the proposed levels—while the surface forces deteriorated. Roosevelt's budget restrictions during the depression years accentuated the imbalance. Quite naturally, MacArthur, Kilbourne, and other responsible War Department leaders, believing that wars were still ultimately won on the ground by the infantry, desired to improve the lot of the surface forces before pumping more money into the Air Corps for additional expansion. The General Staff officers realized the air arm was understrength; they also were aware it was in better shape than any other segment of the Army.

Foulois and other aviators denied the need for a balanced combat force. They argued that the Air Corps alone, if properly organized and equipped, could prevent an attack on the United States. Moreover, by 1934-35, many air officers were convinced that the shortest path to victory was to destroy the enemy's economy and warmaking capacity through a coordinated strategic bombing campaign. As a result, they viewed the General Staff's refusal to spend more than twenty percent of the budget on military aviation as proof of the War Department's lack of

## AN AGE OF TRANSITION

proper concern for air power. Foulois stressed time and again during his four years as Air Corps Chief that completion of the five-year program deserved priority in the Army's budget.

The bulk of General Staff-Air Corps disagreements between 1931 and 1935 flowed from different perspectives on the place of military aviation in the defense system. Neither the aviators nor the ground officers grasped the other's viewpoint. The General Staff resisted change because the existing arrangements kept the air arm subservient to the needs of the ground forces. Foulois and his fellow aviators fought for change because they believed the present order did not adequately provide for air power nor permit its proper use. Thus the air chief constantly showered proposals on the General Staff to create the GHQ Air Force, to forge a strong coast defense force with an established doctrine of employment, to attain financial autonomy, and to achieve a number of other alterations. After the Chief of the Air Corps or congressional airpower proponents generated enough pressure on a specific issue, the War Department would review its position. Bargaining would then usually ensue between the Air Corps and the General Staff, with compromise frequently the outcome.

The creation of the GHQ Air Force was a prime example of this interplay. The War Department had first accepted the need for such a force in 1923 when it adopted the findings of the Lassiter Board. Yet reluctance to accept change caused the issue to languish until the early 1930s. The General Staff agreed that the GHQ Air Force would be formed in time of war, but it refused to sanction the removal of tactical air units from the control of corps area commanders in peacetime. During 1932-33, Foulois repeatedly raised the Air Force issue, underscoring the necessity of having the air component organized under accepted wartime concepts. Eventually the General Staff reexamined its stand in light of current defense needs, and in the fall of 1933 agreed to form a GHQ Air Force. Delayed by the events of early 1934, after reendorsement of the unified air strike force by the Baker Board the War Department moved to bring the new unit to life. The eventual solution was a compromise, for the step was taken to deter the aviators from persisting in their campaign for autonomy and, as finally instituted, the corps area commanders continued to control tactical air installations and station complements.

The General Staff's endorsement of the Air Corps' coast defense mission and the development of an air defense employment doctrine are other examples of the bargaining/compromise procedure. After MacArthur and Pratt reached their 1931 agreement, the War Department was in no hurry to expand upon the Air Corps' new responsibilities. Action came only after Foulois prodded the General Staff with the 1932 Harbor Defense Board-approved air defense plan. After months of bargaining, MacArthur issued a policy letter on the subject on January 3, 1933. While not giving the aviators all they had asked for, the Chief of Staff did approve independent air action during the first phase of counterinvasion operations and sanctioned long-range reconnaissance activities.

There were many other instances during 1931-35 in which the War Department was jarred from its initial stand by Air Corps persistence and congressional pressure and eventually resolved issues through compromise. The activities of the Drum Board stemmed from a General Staff-Air Corps disagreement over air defense employment concepts and the number of planes needed for national defense. The War Department's quick acceptance of all of the Baker Board findings was prompted by a desire to compromise away the Air Corps' quest for additional change. The General Staff's approval of the long-range bomber development program was another case in point. It came at a time when the Air Corps was pressing the issue and the War Department was being accused by congressmen of doing too little for aviation development. The 1935 revision of TR 440-15 also grew out of General Staff-Air Corps interplay. It was an attempt to bargain away current differences on air employment doctrine. By applying pressure on various specific issues, Foulois and the Air Corps were thus able to win numerous concessions which served the air arm's interests. Although the aviators rarely swung the War Department completely to their point of view, the bargaining/compromise procedure certainly helped the Air Corps.

The conclusion that in the first half of the 1930s the General Staff was composed of reactionaries, who were unconcerned with the needs of military aviation and sought to stymie its broader applications, is unacceptable. Both MacArthur and Kilbourne valued air power. They wanted to see it expand but not to the detriment of the rest of the Army. They believed the Air Corps' principal mission was to support the land force, but by 1935 they were willing to admit that strategic bombing operations could be of value. At times Foulois did not have to lobby very hard before the General Staff was willing to readjust its position. In 1935, when it seemed that Congress had become more generous with defense funds, MacArthur recommended a new aircraft expansion program. The year before he affirmed that the GHQ Air Force would as a rule be employed independently in both offensive and defensive operations before ground troops became engaged in battle. The general acceptance of strategic bombardment in Kilbourne's draft air doctrine of December 1934 was one more example of the relatively open-mindedness of these two prominent War Department officers.

In the 1920s the General Staff may have misunderstood the worth and flexibility of Army aviation and, during the post-1935 period, Malin Craig evidently worked to draw the Air Corps closer to its ground support task. But the years MacArthur and Kilbourne served in the War Depart-

# ORGANIZATION CHART

Office of the Chief of the Air Corps

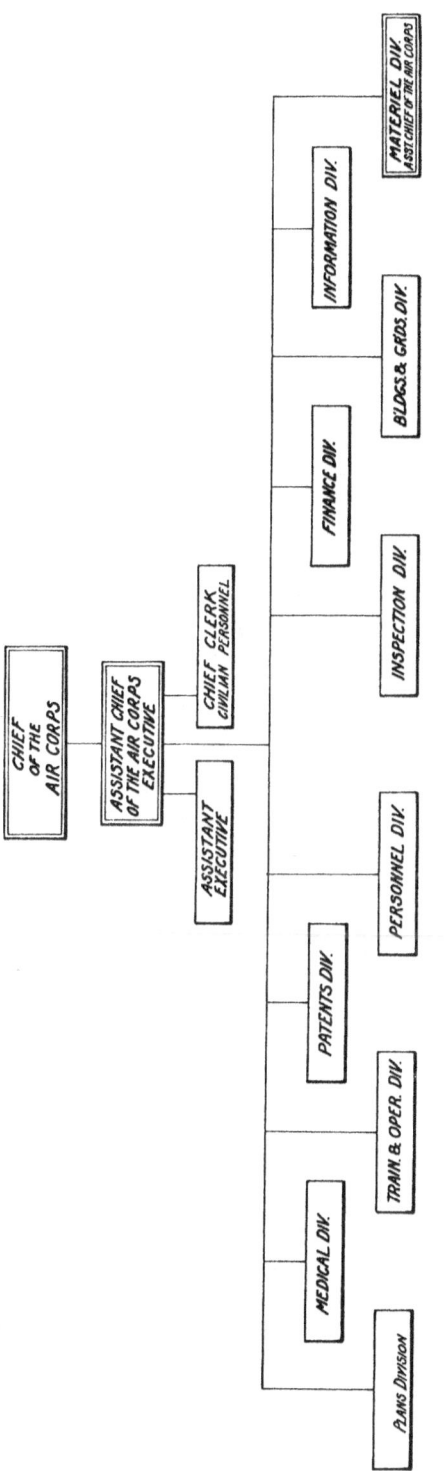

ment were a different story. The General Staff cooperated—if at times reluctantly—with the aviators in defining the air arm's mission in broader terms and in improving air power resources.

Neither Hoover nor Roosevelt did much to benefit the Air Corps during the Foulois years. Unconcerned over the threat of hostile invasion, both Presidents wanted to keep defense costs down. Consequently, the entire Army suffered from inadequate appropriations. Small relief came when Roosevelt released PWA funds to the Army in fiscal 1934, but not until fiscal 1936 did the Air Corps get its first real boost under the New Deal. Hoover and his successor were not swayed by the claims of airpower advocates nor were they interested in strategic air doctrine. Both men rejected any military reorganization that might increase defense costs.

Until 1935, members of Congress generally followed the administration's lead in defense funding and organization. McSwain and a few other congressional airpower advocates frequently raised the specter of autonomy for the Air Corps. Although they lacked the needed support to accomplish this change, they frightened the General Staff. MacArthur and Foulois might expound at length on the needs of the ground forces and air arm during congressional hearings, but the lawmakers consistently voted for what the President wanted. In 1935, however, Congress temporarily ceased acting as a rubber stamp. Against the wishes of Roosevelt, it appropriated funds to expand the enlisted strength of the Army to 165,000. It also passed the new promotion law, the Wilcox Frontier Defense Bill, and legislation authorizing the Secretary of War to commission 50 training center graduates a year for the next ten years. In 1936 the legislators authorized the Air Corps to expand to 2,320 aircraft and to keep 1,350 Reserve officers on active duty for five years. Nevertheless, Congress proved less willing to come up with the money to immediately carry out all of these Air Corps-related projects.

During the Foulois years the Navy blocked the Army air arm's bid for universal acceptance of its coast defense responsibilities. The sea service objected to the Air Corps' claim that it necessarily had to operate far out to sea to prevent hostile air attack and invasion. In fact the Navy did not want the Army aviators flying beyond the coasts at all, unless they were under the control of the naval defense force commander. It seemed quite clear by 1934-35 that the Navy was seeking complete control of the overwater coastal air defense task, thus depriving the Air Corps of its only publicly acceptable semi-independent mission.

The sea service's actions worried the Army aviators. So did the War Department's post-1933 absence of support for the GHQ Air Force's responsibility for distant overwater operations. The coastal air defense mission was not a front to enable the Air Corps to perfect its strategic bombing force. Army aviators fully accepted the coast defense mission in its

## AN AGE OF TRANSITION

own right and did not want to lose this important task to the Navy. Unfortunately, the issue of responsibility for overwater counterair operations remained muddled down to the time the Japanese attacked Pearl Harbor in 1941.

By the early 1930s the Air Corps had become committed to a unique approach to air defense. Recent aeronautical advances had yielded bombers so speedy that it seemed pursuit interceptors were no longer useful. The Air Corps therefore adopted the bomber as its primary air defense weapon. Air officers believed bombers could render the enemy's aviation striking power impotent by hitting his carriers, land-based airfields, support installations, and aviation-related industries. Far different than the method used by the British in 1940, this approach dovetailed nicely with the Air Corps' strategic bombing doctrine. Even so, it seems doubtful that B-17s employing high altitude bombing techniques could have defeated a determined carrierborne air assault on the United States or its possessions as Army aviators asserted.

By 1935 Air Corps officers had suspended their struggle for freedom from the General Staff and had set to work forming and perfecting the GHQ Air Force. The War Department's new TR 440-15 gave the unified air strike force a temporarily acceptable doctrine, and the B-17 offered the flyers a vehicle which they thought would make strategic bombing a reality and reinforce their claim to responsibility for distant overwater coast defense operations. Foulois and his associates were pleased that Army aviators now were receiving increased instrument and night-flying training and that the Army air arm for the first time had the money to make three hundred flying hours per year available to every pilot. Air Corps leaders were likewise heartened that the new organizational arrangement kept corps area commanders from meddling in the tactical training program. The aviators were concerned over the dwindling number of aircraft in the inventory, but they could be cheered by the War Department's endorsement of an expanded procurement program. In most every way the Air Corps of late 1935 was a vast improvement over what it had been five years previous. The air arm's strategic bombardment doctrine would undergo minor revisions and clarifications in the future, but in most respects the changes in doctrine, organization, and aircraft capabilities brought about between 1931 and 1935 laid the groundwork for the World War II Army air effort.

General Benjamin Foulois, unfairly maligned by the Rogers Subcommittee and disliked by General Staff members, played a key role in bringing about these changes, for he supplied the pressure that started the negotiation/compromise process. Foulois was not a dynamic leader like Mitchell. Moreover, his preference for flying and dealing directly with his people and their problems, his disdain for office routine, and his short-

# FOULOIS AND THE U.S. ARMY AIR CORPS

Top: B-17 developed for strategic bombing in the late 1930s; left: Maj. Barney M. Giles, pilot of the first B-17 to land at Langley Field, Va., is greeted by Maj. Gen. Frank M. Andrews.

## AN AGE OF TRANSITION

comings as a public speaker made him only a fair administrator. Sincerely believing that the nation's security required a strong air arm, he did an excellent job, however, of representing Air Corps' interests before the War Department and Congress. Foulois made mistakes in judgment during his tenure as Chief of the Air Corps, as in the decision that his organization could operate the air mail system, but such errors were usually the result of his deep convictions on the worth of military aviation. The years 1931-1935 were a time of progress for the Air Corps, and Foulois deserves a great deal of the credit for this.

# Notes

## Chapter I

### Foulois and the Air Arm, 1908-1931

1. *Air Corps Newsletter* XVIII (Dec 15, 1935), l; Benjamin D. Foulois, "Early Flying Experiences," *The Air Power Historian* II (Apr 55), 18; Benjamin D. Foulois and Carroll V. Glines, *From the Wright Brothers to the Astronauts: The Memoirs of Major General Benjamin D. Foulois* (New York, 1968), pp 7-13.
2. Foulois, "Early Flying Experiences," 18; Foulois, *Memoirs*, p 15.
3. Foulois, *Memoirs*, pp 24-25. Also see: *Army and Navy Journal* LXVIII (Jul 18, 1931), 1093; "Extract of Personal Service Record of Major General B. D. Foulois," MIL C-2e, Box 42, Foulois Papers, Library of Congress [hereafter cited as LC].
4. Foulois, "Early Flying Experiences," 19-20. Also see: *Air Corps Newsletter* XVIII (Dec 15, 1935), 2; *Army and Navy Journal* LXVIII (Jul 18, 1931), 1093; Foulois, *Memoirs*, pp 42-47; Foulois Interview, Jan 20, 1960, p 1, Foulois Files, U.S. Air Force Academy Library [hereafter cited as AFAL].
5. Prior to that time the Army had worked with captive balloons but was just beginning to experiment with airships. It neither owned nor had experimented with airplanes.
6. Foulois, *Memoirs*, pp 62-63; Foulois Interview, Jan 20, 1960, pp 1-3, 42, Foulois Files, AFAL; Oral History Interview 766, Albert F. Simpson Historical Research Center, Maxwell AFB, Alabama [hereafter cited as AFSHRC]: "Extract of Personal Service Record of Major General B. D. Foulois," MIL C-2e, Box 42, Foulois Papers; Foulois Interview, Apr 20, 1965, AFSHRC 105-105.51-4; Foulois, "Early Flying Experiences," 20-25. Foulois, five feet six inches tall, only weighed 126 pounds at the time of the July 1909 tests.
7. Foulois, *Memoirs*, p 63.
8. *Ibid.*, pp 66-69; Foulois, "Early Flying Experiences," 25-27; Foulois Interview, Jan 20, 1960, pp 7-9, Foulois Files, AFAL; Foulois Interview, Apr 20, 1965, AFSHRC 105.51-4.

9. Lieutenant Lahm was relieved from duty with the Signal Corps under the provisions of the so-called "Manchu" law which required line officers to return to duty with troops of their own arm of the service after having spent four years in a staff assignment. Lieutenant Humphreys was ordered back to his branch of the service, the Corps of Engineers. Foulois, "Early Flying Experiences," 27.
10. Quoted in Foulois, *Memoirs*, p 2. Also see: President's Aircraft Board, *Hearings before the President's Aircraft Board* [hereafter cited as *Morrow Board Hearings*] (Washington, 1925), p 477; and Foulois, "Early Flying Experiences," 27-31.
11. Foulois Interview, Apr 20, 1965, AFSHRC 105.51-4; Fred J. Wilkins, "One-Man Air Force," *Army Digest* XXV (Mar 70), 38-41; Foulois, *Memoirs*, pp 80-84; *Army Air Forces Historical Studies: No. 39: Legislation Relating to the Air Corps Personnel and Training Programs, 1907-1939* (Washington, 1945), p 2.
12. *Morrow Board Hearings*, p 477. Also see: Foulois, "Early Flying Experiences," 29-35.
13. Foulois, *Memoirs*, p 80. Also see: Benjamin D. Foulois, "Early Flying Experiences—Part II," *Air Power Historian* II (Jul 55), 45-47.
14. Wesley F. Craven and James L. Cate, eds, *The Army Air Forces in World War II*, Vol I: *Plans and Early Operations, January 1939 to August 1942* (Chicago, 1948), 6-7; *Historical Studies: No. 39*, pp 7-8; *Morrow Board Hearings*, p 477.
15. This was due to the "Manchu" law—the same one that had affected Lahm and Humphreys earlier.
16. Foulois Interview, Jan 20, 1960, pp 14, 21-22, Foulois File, AFAL; Foulois, *Memoirs*, p 112; "Extract of Personal Service Record of Major General B. D. Foulois," MIL C-2e, Box 42, Foulois Papers.
17. *Morrow Board Hearings*, p 478.
18. Martin Caidin, *Air Force: A Pictorial History of American Airpower* (New

York, 1957), p 9. Also see: Foulois Interview, Jan 20, 1960, pp 22-28, Foulois Files, AFAL; "Extract of Personal Service Record of Major General B. D. Foulois," MIL C-2e, Box 42, Foulois Papers; Foulois' comments on *The Army Flies the Mails*, Mar 25, 1954, p 3, Box 15, Foulois Papers.

19. Craven and Cate, *Army Air Forces in World War II I*, 6-7. *Air Corps Newsletter* XXVIII (Dec 15, 1935), 5, puts the total number of aircraft delivered to the Army between 1909 and 1916 at 142. Anytime the author uses the term "aircraft," unless otherwise specified, he is referring only to airplanes.

20. "Extract of Personal Service Record of . . . Foulois," MIL C-2e, Box 42, Foulois Papers; Oral History Interview 766, p 1, AFSHRC.

21. Foulois Interview, Apr 20, 1965, AFSHRC 105.51-4. Also see: Oral History Interview 766, pp 2-3, AFSHRC.

22. Foulois Interview, Oct 23, 1956, Foulois Files, AFAL. Also see: *Morrow Board Hearings*, p 478.

23. Foulois, *Memoirs*, pp 156-59.

24. Robert Frank Futrell, *Ideas, Concepts, Doctrine: A History of Basic Thinking in the United States Air Force, 1907-1964* (Maxwell Air Force Base, Ala., 1971), p 20. Also see: Craven and Cate, *Army Air Forces in World War II*, I, 10-11.

25. Quoted in Craven and Cate, *Army Air Forces in World War II*, I, 11.

26. Futrell, *Ideas, Concepts, Doctrine*, p 20.

27. Alfred F. Hurley, *Billy Mitchell: Crusader for Air Power* (New York, 1964), pp 33-34; Oral History Interview 766, pp 40-42, AFSHRC; Foulois, *Memoirs*, pp 167-176.

28. For impressions of Foulois' style and personality see: letter from Maj Gen Haywood S. Hansell, Jr., USAF, Ret, Feb 11, 1975; letter from Lt Gen Ira C. Eaker, USAF, Ret, Jan 22, 1975; letter from Maj Gen Orval R. Cook, USAF, Ret, Mar 10, 1975; letter from Maj Gen Eugene L. Eubank, USAF, Ret, Apr 4, 1975. For Foulois' own comparison of his outlook and approach with that of Mitchell see: Oral History Interview 766, pp 55-56, AFSHRC; Foulois Interview Oct 23, 1956, Foulois Files, AFAL. Foulois had a good sense of humor and enjoyed having a drink with his friends throughout his life. General Hansell reports that the last time he saw General Foulois the ex-Chief of the Air Corps was carrying a typewritten note signed by the Chief Flight Surgeon of the Air Force which read: "General Foulois is eighty-four years old. He must have two martinis before lunch." Quoted in letter from Gen Haywood S. Hansell, Jr., Feb 11, 1975.

29. Craven and Cate, *Army Air Forces in World War II*, I, 9-14; Futrell, *Ideas, Concepts, Doctrine*, pp 20-24; Foulois, *Memoirs*, p 178.

30. Craven and Cate, *Army Air Forces in World War II*, I, 9-10; *Army Air Force Historical Studies: No. 25: Organization of Military Aeronautics, 1907-1935* (Washington, 1944), pp 32-33, 37. The President's executive order actually established two separate aviation organizations: the Bureau of Aircraft Production, under civilian leadership; and the Division of Military Aeronautics within the War Department. During the latter part of 1918 a civilian Director of Air Service exercised supervision and control over both agencies. However, after the end of the war, the military took charge of both aircraft procurement and operations.

31. *Historical Studies: No. 39*, pp 14-15; R. Earl McClendon, *The Question of Autonomy for the U.S. Air Arm, 1907-1945*, (Maxwell AFB, Ala., 1950), p 72; Hurley, *Billy Mitchell*, p 41. Also see: Foulois' comments on *The Army Flies the Mails*, Mar 25, 1954, p 4, Box 15, Foulois Papers.

32. *USAF Historical Studies: No. 89: Development of Air Doctrine in the Army Air Arm, 1917-1941* (Maxwell AFB, Ala., 1955), pp 14-16; McClendon, *The Question of Autonomy*, pp 72-73. Also see, for example, U.S. House of Representatives, Committee on Military Affairs, *Hearings on a United Air Service*, 66th Cong, 2d sess, 1919, p 119.

33. McClendon, The Question of Autonomy, pp 74-79, 87-88; *Historical Studies: No. 89*, pp 20-21.

34. *Historical Studies: No. 25*, pp 41-43; *Historical Studies: No. 89*, p 22; McClendon, *The Question of Autonomy*, pp 72-73, 84-87.

35. Foulois, *Memoirs*, pp 184-86; Foulois Interview, Oct 23, 1956, Foulois Files, AFAL.

36. Upon his return to the United States Foulois reverted to his permanent grade of captain in the Infantry. Shortly thereafter he was given the temporary rank of major in the Air Service. Foulois, *Memoirs*, p 185.

37. Letter, Foulois to Chief of Air Service, Jun 7, 1919, G R & P l-C, Box 36, Foulois Papers; "Extract: Statement of Major B. D. Foulois before the House Committee on Military Affairs, October 7, 1919," p 2, Foulois File, AFAL.
38. Quoted in *Historical Studies: No. 39*, pp 17-19.
39. "Extract: Statement of Major B. D. Foulois before the House Committee on Military Affairs, October 7, 1919," p 4, Foulois File, AFAL; U.S. Senate, Committee on Military Affairs, *Hearings on Reorganization of the Army*, 66th Cong, 2d sess, 1919, p 1262.
40. "Extract: Statement of Major B. D. Foulois before the House Committee on Military Affairs, October 7, 1919," pp 3-4, Foulois Files, AFAL.
41. *Ibid.*
42. U.S. Senate, Committee on Military Affairs, *Hearings on Reorganization of the Army*, 66th Cong, 2d sess, 1919, pp 1257-1260.
43. U.S. House of Representatives, Committee on Military Affairs, *Hearings on a United Air Service*, 66th Cong, 2d sess, 1919, pp 119-125.
44. *Historical Studies: No. 89*, p 22; McClendon, *The Question of Autonomy*, pp 90-91. Also see: Mitchell to The Adjutant General (AG), Aug 27, 1919, Central Decimal File (CDF) 321.9, Record Group (RG) 18, National Archives (NA).
45. *Historical Studies: No. 89*, p 15.
46. *Ibid.*, p 23.
47. Edwin L. Williams, Jr., "Legislative History of the Air Arm," *Military Affairs* XX (Summer 56), 84; *Historical Studies: No. 25*, pp 47-48; *Historical Studies: No. 39*, p 20.
48. *Historical Studies: No. 25*, pp 47-48; Alfred Goldberg, ed, *A History of the United States Air Force, 1907-1957* (Princeton, 1957), pp 29-30. The War Department divided the United States into nine corps areas, with the commander of each having control over the military units located therein.
49. *Historical Studies: No. 89*, p 25; War Department, *Final Report of War Department Special Committee on Army Air Corps* [hereafter cited as the Baker Board Report] (Washington, 1934), p 32; Hurley, *Billy Mitchell*, pp 83-84; Russell F. Weigley, *History of the United States Army* (New York, 1967), pp 399-401.
50. Foulois, *Memoirs*, pp 188-89, 194; Williams, "Legislative History of the Air Arm," pp 84-85; Isaac Don Levine, *Mitchell: Pioneer of Air Power* (New York, 1943), pp 267, 304, 306-12; Craven and Cate, *Army Air Forces in World War II*, I, 24-26; "Information on Aviation and a Department of National Defense," cover letter dated Feb 7, 1934, WPD 888-86, RG 165, NA.
51. William Mitchell, *Winged Defense* (New York, 1925), pp xiii-xviii. Also see: Levine, *Mitchell*, pp 211-12; Hurley, *Billy Mitchell*, pp 42-45; James L. Cate, "Development of Air Doctrine, 1917-41," *Air University Quarterly Review* I (Winter 47), 16-17.
52. Hurley, *Billy Mitchell*, pp 81-82.
53. Training Regulations 440-15, Jan 26, 1926, pp 1-2, AFSHRC 248.211-65A. Also see: Craven and Cate, *Army Air Forces in World War II*, I, 43.
54. See Mitchell, *Winged Defense*, p xvi; Williams, "Legislative History of the Air Arm," pp 84-85; Levine, *Mitchell*, pp 368-370; Craven and Cate, *Army Air Forces in World War II*, I, 20, 43. For more detailed coverage of the events that directly led to Mitchell's court-martial see Levine, *Mitchell*, pp 323-28.
55. *Historical Studies: No. 89*, p 17.
56. Foulois, *Memoirs*, p 197.
57. See Craven and Cate, *Army Air Forces in World War II*, I, 20, 25-26; *Historical Studies: No. 25*, pp 57-58.
58. *Historical Studies: No. 89*, pp 25-26; "War Department Committee Report on the Organization of the Air Service" [hereafter cited as the Lassiter Board Report], approved Apr 24, 1923, pp 1-2, WPD 888-3, RG 165, NA; McClendon, *The Question of Autonomy*, pp 108-110; *Historical Studies: No. 25*, pp 59-60.
59. Lassiter Board Report, pp 1-6, WPD 888-3, RG 165, NA; *Historical Studies: No. 89*, pp 27-28; *Historical Studies: No. 25*, pp 60-61; McClendon, *The Question of Autonomy*, pp 110-11.
60. Hurley, *Billy Mitchell*, p 85; "Chronological Record of Various Studies, Reports, Boards, Committees, etc., concerning the Fixing of the Relative Numbers of Aircraft in Army and Navy Aviation," AFSHRC 145.91-134; McClendon, *The Question of Autonomy*, p 112.
61. U.S. House of Representatives, *Report of the Select Committee of Inquiry into Operations of the United States Air Services* [hereafter cited as the Lampert Committee

Notes, Pages 24-32

Report], H. Rept. 1653, 68th Cong, 1925, p 1.

62. While other Air Service officers testified, Foulois, then a student at Army Command and General Staff School at Fort Leavenworth, did not appear as a witness.

63. Mcclendon, *The Question of Autonomy,* pp 114-15.

64. U.S. House of Representatives, Select Committee of Inquiry into Operations of the United States Air Services (Lampert Committee), *Hearings on Matters Relating to the Operations of the United States Air Services,* 68th Cong, 1925, pp 521-29.

65. *Lampert Committee Report,* pp 8-9.

66. See *Historical Studies: No. 89,* p 28, for indication of the prevailing mood regarding the creation of a separate air arm.

67. Quoted in Levine, *Mitchell,* pp 327, 332.

68. Hurley, *Billy Mitchell,* pp 101-02.

69. *Historical Studies: No. 25,* pp 71-72; *Historical Studies: No. 89,* pp 28-29; Craven and Cate, *Army Air Forces in World War II,* I, 28.

70. Craven and Cate, *Army Air Forces in World War II,* I, 28-29; *Historical Studies: No. 89,* p 29; Edwin H. Rutkowski, *The Politics of Military Aviation Procurement, 1926-1934* (Columbus, 1966), pp 20-21.

71. *Morrow Board Hearings,* pp 505-06, 509.

72. *Ibid.,* pp 476-491. For additional insight into General Patrick's views on autonomy see: 1st Ind (basic unknown), Feb 27, 1926, Patrick to AG, Subject File-Wilcox Bill, 1926-36, Andrews Papers, LC; memos, AG to Chief of Air Service, Sep 26, 1925, and Chief of Air Service to AG, Oct 1, 1925, WPD 888-31, RG 165, NA.

73. Quoted in Levine, *Mitchell,* p 334.

74. *Historical Studies: No. 89,* p 29; *Historical Studies: No. 25,* pp 73-78; *Historical Studies: No. 39,* pp 28-29; Rutkowski, *Politics of Military Aviation Procurement,* p 21.

75. Air Corps Act of 1926, Public, No. 446, 69th Congress (H.R. 10827). Also see Craven and Cate, *Army Air Forces in World War II,* I, 29; *Historical Studies: No. 39,* pp 31-32; Edwin H. Rutkowski, *Politics of Military Aviation Procurement,* pp 21-22. The Air Corps Act of 1926 actually contained conflicting figures with respect to personnel increases. While in one section it called for a total of 1,518 officers and 16,000 enlisted men, in another it provided for increases in the existing allotted strength of the Army air arm by 403 officers and 6,240 enlisted men. The second set of figures authorized the War Department to build the Air Corps up to a total of 1,650 officers and 15,000 men (included 2,500 flying cadets). Due to the wording of the act, the War Department accepted the second set of figures. The 1,800 serviceable aircraft included those to be used for National Guard training.

76. U.S. War Department, "Transcript of the Shorthand Report of Proceedings, Transactions and Testimony, before The Special Committee on Army Air Corps and Air Mail" [hereafter cited as Baker Board Hearings], 1934 (typescript), LC, pp 2140-41, 2171-72. According to Air Corps tables of organization in 1931, three tactical squadrons composed a group, and three groups normally made up a wing. At full strength bomb wings were to contain approximately 150 aircraft, while pursuit and attack wings would have around 280 each. "Organization of the Air Corps" (Army Extension Courses: Special Text 188), 1931, AFSHRC 248.1011-188.

77. U.S. House of Representatives, Committee on Appropriations, *Hearings on War Department Appropriations Bill for 1933,* 72d Cong, 1st sess, 1932, pp 1094-95; Rutkowski, *Politics of Military Aviation Procurement,* pp 22-23. For a comparison of the amounts requested by the Air Corps to carry out its five-year program, those approved by the administration, and what was actually appropriated by Congress, see "Funds Available Under Appropriation 'Air Corps, Army'-by classification-Fiscal Years 1927 to 1935 inclusive," FIN-B-3, Box 19, Foulois Papers; "Estimates of Costs of Five Year Program," by Maj Walter O. Rawls, Oct 31, 1927, DEF-C-lb, Box 17, Foulois Papers; "Relation of Air Corps Expenditures to Total War Department (Military) Expenditures, 1925-1938," AFSHRC 167.65.

78. "Military Flying," *Aviation* XXXIX (May 35), 175; U.S. War Department, *Annual Report of the Secretary of War to the President* (Washington, 1931), p 31.

79. *Annual Report of the Secretary of War,* 1931, p 31.

80. *Ibid.,* pp 171-73; U.S. War Department, "Annual Report of the Chief of the Air Corps, 1935," (mimeographed), LC, p 4.5; *Historical Studies: No. 39,* pp 32-33.

## Notes, Pages 33-42

81. U.S. War Department, "Annual Report of the Chief of the Air Corps, 1932," (mimeographed), LC, p 7; *Annual Report of the Secretary of War,* 1931, pp 171-72; *Historical Studies: No. 39,* p 33; Rutkowski, *Politics of Military Aviation Procurement,* pp 40-42; U.S. War Department, "Annual Report of the Chief of the Air Corps, 1931," (mimeographed), LC, pp 31-32; "Annual Report of the Chief of the Air Corps, 1935," p 4.5. From fiscal years 1927 through 1932 an average of 29 percent of the West Point graduates volunteered and were accepted for pilot training. Of these, an average of 50 percent graduated from pilot training. See *Air Corps Newsletter* XVII (Aug 29, 1933), 192.

82. Rutkowski, *Politics of Military Aviation Procurement,* p 39; "Relationship of Air Corps Expenditures to Total War Department (Military) Expenditures, 1925-1938," AFSHRC 167.65; "Funds Available Under Appropriation 'Air Corps, Army'- by classification-Fiscal Years 1927 to 1935 inclusive," FIN B-3, Box 19, Foulois Papers.

83. Mark Skinner Watson, *Chief of Staff: Prewar Plans and Preparations* (Washington, 1950), p 21; John William Killigrew, "The Impact of the Great Depression on the Army, 1929-1936" (Ph.D. dissertation, University of Indiana, 1960), pp 55-57; John Richard Wilson, "Herbert Hoover and the Armed Forces: A Study of Presidential Attitudes and Policy" (Ph.D. dissertation, Northwestern University, 1971), pp 126-27.

84. Letter, Foulois to Gen Fred T. Austin, Feb 22, 1925, and other correspondence in MIL A-1, Box 41, Foulois Papers; Foulois, *Memoirs,* pp 198, 203.

85. See correspondence between Foulois and Gov John H. Trumbull, June-July, 1927, especially copy of letter, Trumbull to Secretary of War Dwight F. Davis, Jun 30, 1927, MIL A-1, Box 41, Foulois Papers.

86. Foulois, *Memoirs,* pp 207-09.

87. "Biographical Sketch prepared for the Chief, Information Division, AC," by Foulois with cover letter, Foulois to Chief, Information Division, Jan 10, 1931, MIL C-2e, Box 42, Foulois Papers; *USAF Historical Studies: No. 10; Organization of the Army Air Arm, 1935-1945* (Maxwell AFB, Ala., 1956), p 24; Foulois, *Memoirs,* p 211.

88. *Army and Navy Journal* LXVIII (Jan 3, 1931), 413, LXIX (Sep 12, 1931), 27; *New York Times,* Apr 16, 1931, p 5, May 14, 1931, p 6; *Annual Report of the Secretary of War,* 1931, p 33.

89. Copy of Foulois' October 1932 *National Aeronautic Magazine* article, "Keeping America First in the Air," p 7, Foulois File, Box 29, American Institute of Aeronautics and Astronautics Papers, LC.

90. "The 'Air Corps' Mass Migration," *Aviation* XXX (Jul 31), 399; *Curtiss-Wright Review* II (May 31), 12-14; *New York Times,* May 3, 1931, Sec II, p 2, May 13, 1931, p 7; *Air Corps Newsletter* XXVIII (Dec 15, 1935), 6.

91. *New York Times,* May 24, 1931, pp 1, 2, May 27, 1931, p 1, May 28, 1931, p 1, May 16, 1931, p 2, May 19, 1931, p 1, May 23, 1931, p 1, Jun 3, 1931, p 27; *Army and Navy Journal* LXVIII (May 30, 1931), 921, (Jun 6, 1931), 945-46; Foulois, *Memoirs,* p 214. The provisional air division was actually not very strong militarily. Of the aircraft taking part only 449 were combat planes, and of these 238 were observation aircraft. *Annual Report of the Secretary of War,* 1931, pp 29-30.

92. *Annual Report of the Secretary of War,* 1931, p 33; "The Air Corps' Mass Migration," *Aviation,* pp 398-400; *New York Times,* Feb 17, 1933, p 17.

93. See, for example, *New York Times,* Jun 6, 1931, p 5. For Foulois' comments on the importance of the maneuvers to his selection see Foulois, *Memoirs,* p 220.

94. Letter, Foulois to Davison, Jun 9, 1931, MIL A-2, Box 41, Foulois Papers.

95. Letter, AG to Foulois, Jul 13, 1931, MIL A-3, Box 41, Foulois Papers; *Air Corps Newsletter* XV (Jul 21, 1931), 271, XVI (Jan 25, 1932), 5; letter, Henry Arnold to Foulois, Jul 14, 1931, Personal File, Box 4, Arnold Papers, LC.

96. Foulois, *Memoirs,* p 220; *Army and Navy Journal* LXIX (Sep 12, 1931), 27.

97. See Army Regulations 95-5, *Air Corps,* 1930; Army Regulations 170-10, *Corps Areas and Departments, Etc.,* 1930.

98. Memo, Foulois to the Chief of Staff, Dec 24, 1931, PERS G-2, Box 23, Foulois Papers; *Air Corps Newsletter* XVI (Jan 25, 1932), 7.

# Notes

## Chapter II

### Doctrine, Mission, and Employment Concepts, 1931-1933

1. William Star Myers, ed, *The State Papers and Other Public Writings of Herbert Hoover* 2 vols (Garden City, 1934), II, 23. For additional evidence of this strictly defensive bent in national policy see: *Army and Navy Journal* LXXI (Feb 10, 1934), 476; Herbert Hoover, *The Memoirs of Herbert Hoover* 3 vols (New York, 1951-1952). II, 338; Watson, *Chief of Staff*, p 35.
2. See Training Regulations 440-15, Jan 26, 1926, AFSHRC 248.211-65A.
3. Letter, from Lt Gen Ira C. Eaker, Ret, Jan 22, 1975; *Historical Studies: No. 89*, p 52.
4. *USAF Historical Studies: No. 100: History of the Air Corps Tactical School, 1920-1940* (Maxwell AFB, Ala., 1955), pp-vii, 21; *Historical Studies: No. 89*, p 47; "Development of Air Power Doctrine and Concepts Prior to World War II," Air War College Lecture by Maj Gen Follett Bradley, Sep 6, 1951, AFSHRC K239.71651-22.
5. Quoted in *Historical Studies: 89*, pp 40-41.
6. "Doctrine of the Air Force," under cover letter, Commandant, ACTS, to Chief of the Air Corps (C/AC), Apr 30, 1928, CDF 321.9, RG 18, NA.
7. 1st Ind (Basic Unknown), Maj Lawrence A. W. McIntosh, OCAC to Commandant, ACTS, Sep 4, 1928, CDF 321.9, RG 18, NA.
8. *Historical Studies: No. 89*, p 48; letter, from Lt Gen Ira C. Eaker, Ret, Jan 22, 1975; letter, from Gen Orval R. Cook, Mar 10, 1975; Craven and Cate, *Army Air Forces in World War II*, I, 46.
9. "Bombardment Aviation" (ACTS text), 1930, pp 87, 92-93, AFSHRC 248.101-9. Also see: "The Air Force" (ACTS text), Apr 30, pp 69-80, AFSHRC 248.101-l.
10. "The Air Force" (ACTS text), Apr 30, pp 69-80, 110, AFSHRC 248.101-l. Also see: *Historical Studies: No. 100*, p 21.
11. The General Staff maintained that the air component's primary function was to operate as an arm of the mobile army. Army and Navy Joint Board, *Joint Action of the Army and Navy* (Washington, 1927), p 8.
12. "The Air Force" (ACTS text), Apr 30, pp 12, 80, AFSHRC 248.101-l.
13. See Foulois, *Memoirs*, p 225; *Historical Studies: No. 89*, p 40; letter, from Maj Gen Eugene L. Eubank, Apr 4, 1975.
14. "Bombardment Aviation" (ACTS text), Feb 31, p 69, AFSHRC 248.101-9.
15. "The Air Force" (ACTS text), Feb 31, pp 100-101, AFSHRC 248.101-l.
16. "Conference on the Influence of Air Warfare on Future Wars" (Part of the ACTS "Air Force" course), 1932-33, AFSHRC 248.2014A-9.
17. "Conference on Air Force Objectives" (Part of the ACTS "Air Force" course), 1932-33, AFSHRC 248.2014A-4.
18. Quoted in "Conference on Air Force vs. Air Force" (Part of ACTS "Air Force" course), 1932-33, AFSHRC 248.2014A-5.
19. " 'Air Warfare,' by General Giulio Douhet: a translation of the article, 'La Guerre de l'Air' from a French aeronautical magazine by Mrs. Dorothy Benedict," Dec 11, 1933, Box 36, Simonds Papers, LC; *Historical Studies: No. 89*, pp 48-51; *Historical Studies: No. 100*, p 27; letter, C/AC to Copyright Office, Library of Congress, Jul 14, 1933, CDF 032G, RG 18, NA. See Raymond R. Flugel, "United States Air Power Doctrine: A Study of the Influence of William Mitchell and Giulio Douhet at the Air Corps Tactical School, 1929-35" (Ph.D. dissertation, University of Oklahoma, 1965), for a somewhat overstated account of Douhet's influence.
20. *Historical Studies: No. 89*, pp 50-51; Hurley, *Billy Mitchell*, pp 126-130.
21. "Bombardment" (ACTS text), Oct 1, 1933, para 40, AFSHRC 248.101-9.
22. "Air Force Lectures" (ACTS), 1933-34, AF-l, pp 1-4, AFSHRC 248.101-2.
23. *Historical Studies: No. 89*, p 46; Craven and Cate, *Army Air Forces in World War II*, I, 58; "Between the Wars," *Air Force* XL (Aug 57), 122; Caidin, *Air Force*, p 66; "The Status of Military Aviation and

271

## Notes, Pages 50–55

the Trend of Development," Sep 15, 1931, Army War College (AWC) Instructional Records, G-3 Course, 1931-32, RG 165, NA.

24. See *Field Service Regulations, United States Army, 1923* (Washington, 1924), p 77; Training Regulations 440-15, Jan 26, 1926, AFSHRC 248.211-65A.

25. "Report of the Survey of the Military Establishment by the War Department General Staff," Nov 1, 1929, p 45, WPD 3345, RG 165, NA. Also see: AR 95-10, *Air Corps Troops*, Mar 10, 1928, CDF 321.9-B, RG 18, NA.

26. Memo, Assistant Chief of Staff, War Plans Division (Asst C/S, WPD), to the Chief of Staff (C/S), Jan 18, 1932, CDF 032, RG 18, NA; Craven and Cate, *Army Air Forces in World War II*, I, 35; Cate, "Development of Air Doctrine, 1917-1941," pp 13-14. The General Staff's control of publications did not affect those written for internal use by ACTS. Public sentiment, which was quite hostile to thoughts of offensive employment of American military forces, served as an additional constraint on Air Corps overt endorsement of offensive strategic operations.

27. For expressions of the War Department's views on military aviation, see: memo, Asst C/S, WPD, to C/S, Jan 18, 1932, CDF 032, RG 18, NA; "Information on Aviation and a Department of National Defense," under Feb 7, 1934, cover letter, pp 5, 14-16, WPD 888-86, RG 165, NA; "The Truth About the General Staff and the Army Air Corps," by Brig Gen Charles E. Kilbourne (undated article), WPD 888-92, RG 165, NA.

28. Baker Board Hearings, p 1794.

29. "Truth about the General Staff and the Army Air Corps," by Brig Gen Charles E. Kilbourne (undated article), WPD 888-92, RG 165, NA. Also see: "Information on Aviation and a Department of National Defense," under Feb 7, 1934, cover letter, p 5, WPD 888-86, RG 165, NA.

30. "Information on Aviation and a Department of National Defense," under Feb 7, 1934, cover letter, p 5, WPD 888-86, RG 165, NA.

31. See, for example, Army and Navy Joint Board, *Joint Army and Navy Action in Coast Defense* (Washington, 1920), p 50; Army and Navy Joint Board, *Joint Action of the Army and the Navy*, 1927, pp 7, 8, 13-17.

32. "Aircraft in Coast Defense: Controversy Between the Army and the Navy," n.d., pp 1-2, WPD 888, RG 165, NA; *USAF Historical Studies: No. 6: The Development of the Heavy Bomber, 1918-1944* (Maxwell AFB, Ala., 1951), p 131; *Historical Studies: No. 89*, pp 67-68.

33. Quoted in "Aircraft in Coast Defense: Controversy Between the Army and the Navy," n.d., p 1, WPD 888, RG 165, NA.

34. Memo, Patrick to AG, Feb 27, 1926, Subject File: Wilcox Bill, 1926-36, Box 11, Andrews Papers, LC; *Historical Studies: No. 89*, pp 31-35.

35. Quoted in "Aircraft in Coast Defense: Controversy Between the Army and the Navy," n.d., pp 2-3, WPD 888, RG 165, NA. The secondary functions of naval aviation consisted primarily of offshore scouting and patrol. *Joint Action of the Army and the Navy*, 1927, p 14.

36. "Aircraft in Coast Defense: Controversy Between the Army and the Navy," n.d., p 2, WPD 888, RG 165, NA.

37. *Joint Action of the Army and the Navy*, 1927, p 7.

38. Moffett Papers, "P" File, Letter, Moffett to Pratt, Mar 9, 1926, USNA, Nimitz Library.

39. "Historical Digest," Numerical File, 1920-1942, WPD 888-58, RG 165, NA.

40. Testimony of F. Trubee Davison before the Joint Committee on Aerial Coast Defense, May 7, 1929, WPD 888-58, RG 165, NA.

41. Letter, Rear Adm Roger Welles to CNO, May 2, 1929, File A-21 (Confidential), RG 80, NA. Also see Testimony of David S. Ingalls before Joint Committee on Aerial Coast Defense, May 7, 1929, WPD 888-58, RG 165, NA.

42. Wilson, "Herbert Hoover and the Armed Forces," p 166; *Army and Navy Journal* LXVIII (Sep 20, 1930), 53; *Annual Report of the Secretary of War*, 1931, p 38.

43. War Department Press Release, Jan 9, 1931, AFSHRC 168.3952-191. Also see: *Army and Navy Journal* LXVIII (Jan 17, 1931), 457-58.

44. *Army and Navy Journal* LXVIII (Jan 17, 1931), 458.

45. Gerald E. Wheeler, *Admiral William Veazie Pratt, U.S. Navy: A Sailor's Life* (Washington, 1974), pp 356-57, 191. Also see James P. Tate, "The Army and Its Air Arm: A Study of the Evolution of Army

Notes, Pages 56-61

Policy Toward Aviation, 1919-1941" (Ph.D. dissertation, University of Indiana, 1976), pp 114-15.
46. CNO to All Ships and Stations, Nov 28, 1930, Records of the General Board, 449 (1930) Operational Archives, Naval History Division, Washington, D.C. Also see Tate, "The Army and Its Air Arm," pp 114-15.
47. See, for example: Letter, Ingalls to Moffett, Sep 20, 1930, I File, Moffett Papers, USNA; 2d Ind, Senior Member Present to Secretary of Navy, Sep 8, 1931, Records of the General Board, No. 449, Operational Archives, Naval History Division.
48. Letter, Maj Herbert A. Dargue to Commander, Langley Field, Aug 17, 1931, OPS-D, Box 22, Foulois Papers; "Information on Aviation and a Department of National Defense," under Feb 7, 1934, cover letter, p 138, WPD 888-86, RG 165, NA; memo, Asst C/S, G-3, to C/S, Nov 25, 1931, OPS-D, Box 22, Foulois Papers; Foulois, *Memoirs*, pp 215-16.
49. "Information on Aviation and a Department of National Defense," under Feb 7, 1934, cover letter, p 138, WPD 888-86, RG 165, NA; letter, Major Herbert A. Dargue to Commander, Langley Field, Aug 17, 1931, OPS-D, Box 22, Foulois Papers; *New York Times*, Aug 13, 1931, p 24, Aug 14, 1931, p 1, Aug 15, 1931, p 3.
50. *New York Times*, Aug 13, 1931, p 24, Aug 14, 1931, p 1, Aug 15, 1931, p 3; *Army and Navy Journal* LXVIII (Aug 15, 1931), 1195.
51. Quoted in *Army and Navy Journal* LXVIII (Aug 15, 1931), 1195.
52. Letter, Arnold to Spaatz, Aug 26, 1931, Personal File, Box 4, Arnold Papers, LC.
53. Hanson W. Baldwin, "Airplanes vs. Ships," editorial, *New York Times*, Aug 30, 1931, p III-l.
54. *Ibid*.
55. Undated notes in Foulois' hand [ca. Aug-Sep 31], OPS-D, Box 22, Foulois Papers; 4th Ind (basic unknown), Acting C/AC to AG, Nov 18, 1931, OPS-D, Box 22, Foulois Papers.
56. Letter, Andrews to Arnold, Aug 17, 1931, Personal Correspondence-A, 1930-42, Box 1, Andrews Papers, LC; memo, Major John H. Pirie, OCAC to Chief, Materiel Division, Jul 10, 1931, Army Air Forces General File, 1918-35 (AAF), 370.3, RG 18, NA; memo, Foulois to AG, Oct 9, 1931,

AAF 370.3, RG 18, NA; Baker Board Hearings, p 2770.
57. 3d Ind (Foulois to AG, Oct 9, 1931), AG to C/AC, Nov 21, 1931, AAF 370.3, RG 18, NA. Also see: memo, Asst C/S, G3, to C/S, Nov 25, 1931, OPS-D, Box 22, Foulois Papers; Baker Board Hearings, pp 2770-72.
58. *Ibid*.
59. Memo, C/S to Asst C/S, G-3, Nov 12, 1934, AG 352 (10-9-31), RG 407, NA; 4th Ind (Foulois to AG, Oct 9, 1931), Westover to AG, Feb 5, 1932, and 5th Ind (Foulois to AG, Oct 9, 1931), AG to C/AC, Feb 18, 1932, AAF 370.3, RG 18, NA; 2d Ind (basic unknown), Foulois to AG, Dec 14, 1932, AAF 370.3, RG 18, NA; memo, Secretary of General Staff to Major Kilner, n.d., AG 352 (10-9-31) file, RG 407, NA; Progress Reports, 1st Lt Lawrence J. Carr to C/AC, Apr 32-Sep 33, AAF 370.3, RG 18, NA; memo, Lt Col John H. Pirie to C/AC, Feb 6, 1933, AAF 370.3, RG 18, NA; memo, Westover to AG, Jan 10, 1934, AAF 370.3, RG 18, NA.
60. See Training Regulations 440-15, Jan 26, 1926, AFSHRC 248.211-65A.
61. Draft letter, MacArthur to Director of the Bureau of the Budget, with cover letter, Fechet to C/S, Jul 29, 1931 (draft sent as prepared, Aug 12, 1931), CDF 321.9-B, RG 18, NA.
62. Memo, Foulois to AG, Sep 30, 1931, AG 660.2 (9-30-31), RG 407, NA. Also see: memo, Asst C/S, WPD, to C/S, Nov 21, 1931, WPD 1105-55, RG 165, NA.
63. 1st Ind (Foulois to AG, Sep 30, 1931), AG to C/AC, Nov 30, 1931, Box 16, Foulois Papers. Also see: memo, Asst C/S, WPD, to C/S, Nov 21, 1931, WPD 1105-55, RG 165, NA; Baker Board Hearings, pp 2730-31. The Harbor Defense Board consisted of the Chiefs of the Air Corps, Coast Artillery, Engineers, Ordnance, and Chemical Warfare Service, and the Chief Signal Officer. It met infrequently to deal with specific issues. In this case, the War Department directed it to meet to revise certain harbor defense projects which were important to the defense of naval installations. See memo, AG to C/AC, Aug 12, 1931, Box 16, Foulois Papers.
64. U.S. House of Representatives, Committee on Appropriations, *Hearings on the War Department Appropriations Bill for 1933*, 72d Cong, 1st sess, 1932, p 1014.
65. "Principles Covering the Operation

273

of the Air Force in the Defense of the Land and Sea Frontiers," Apr 4, 1932, Box 16, Foulois Papers. Also see: Baker Board Hearings, p 2732.

66. Letter, Maj Gen Harry L. Gilchrist to AG, Jul 7, 1932, with enclosed paper titled "Employment of Army Air Forces in Defense of our Seacoast Frontiers," Box 16, Foulois Papers; memo, Kilbourne to C/S, Nov 28, 1932, WPD 1105-55, RG 165, NA.

67. "Employment of Army Air Forces in Defense of our Seacoast Frontier," under cover letter, Gilchrist to AG, Jul 7, 1932, Box 16, Foulois Papers.

68. Draft memo, Kilbourne to C/S, Sep, 1932, AG 660.2 (7-7-32), RG 407, NA; memo, Kilbourne to C/S, Nov 28, 1932, WPD 1105-55, RG 165, NA.

69. Memo, Foulois to Asst C/S, WPD, Oct 11, 1932, Box 16, Foulois Papers.

70. Ibid.

71. Memo, Kilbourne to C/AC, Oct 27, 1932, WPD 1105-55, RG 165, NA.

72. Memo, Foulois to Asst C/S, WPD, Nov 14, 1932, WPD 1105-55, RG 165, NA.

73. Memo, Foulois to C/S, Dec 13, 1932, Box 16, Foulois Papers; memo, Kilbourne to C/S, Nov 28, 1932, WPD 1105-55, RG 165, NA. Also see: U.S. House of Representatives, Committee on Appropriations, *Hearings on the War Department Appropriations Bill for 1934*, 72d Cong, 2d sess, 1933, pt 1, p 581.

74. Memo, Kilbourne to C/S, Nov 28, 1932, WPD 1105-55, RG 165, NA.

75. Letter, MacArthur to Commanding Generals of Armies, Corps Areas, and Departments, Jan 3, 1933, OPS-A, Box 22, Foulois Papers. Also see: *Historical Studies: No. 89*, p 69; *Historical Studies: No. 25*, pp 89-90.

76. Memo, Westover to AG, "The Air Corps Peacetime Requirements to meet the Defense Needs of the United States," Mar 15, 1933, DEF C-2a, Box 18, Foulois Papers; memo, Foulois to AG, May 23, 1933, DEF C-2a, Box 18, Foulois Papers.

77. Memo, Westover to AG, Mar 15, 1933, DEF C-2a, Box 18, Foulois Papers.

78. Ibid.

79. Baker Board Hearings, p 4146; "Report of the Special Committee of the War Department General Council on the Employment of the Army Air Corps" [hereafter cited as Drum Board Report], p 4,

Oct 17, 1933, WPD 888, RG 165, NA; memo, AG to C/AC, Aug 15, 1933, DEF C-2a, Box 18, Foulois Papers; memo, AG to C/AC, Aug 8, 1933, AG 580 (8-5-33) misc F, RG 407, NA.

80. 1st Lt Kenneth N. Walker, "Bombardment Aviation-Bulwark of National Defense," *U.S. Air Services* XVIII (Aug 33), 15-17; "Statement of Lt Colonel J. E. Chaney before House Military Affairs Committee," and "Statement of Major General B. D. Foulois before House Military Affairs Committee," attachments to memo, Westover to Asst C/S, WPD, Apr 13, 1933, LEGIS 3-G1, Box 27, Foulois Papers; memo, Foulois to Albert Loening, Mar 27, 1933, FIN-C, Box 19, Foulois Papers; *Historical Studies: No. 89*, p 59.

81. Extract of Kilbourne's testimony before Subcommittee No. 3 of the House Military Affairs Committee, n.d. [ca. spring 34], HEARINGS-E, Box 45, Foulois Papers; memo, AG to C/AC, Jun 3, 1933, Box 16, Foulois Papers; Drum Board Report, p 2, WPD 888, RG 165, NA; McClendon, *The Question of Autonomy*, p 153. The three color plans involved dealt with attacks by the following nations: RED, Great Britain; ORANGE, Japan; and GREEN, Mexico. RED-ORANGE was designed to meet attacks from a British-Japanese coalition.

82. "Air Plan for the Defense of the United States," under Jul 13, 1933, cover letter, Westover to AG, WPD 888-75, RG 165, NA. Also see: memos, Chaney to AG, Jun 20, 1933, and Jun 24, 1933, WPD 888-75, RG 165, NA.

83. Ibid.

84. Memo, Foulois to AG, Jul 28, 1933, WD 888-75, RG 165, NA.

85. Memo, Kilbourne to C/S, Jul 25, 1933, WPD 888-75, RG 165, NA.

86. Memo, AG to C/AC, et al, Aug 11, 1933, Box 16, Foulois Papers; Extract of Maj Gen Hugh A. Drum's testimony before Col Walter L. Reed, Jan 31, 1935, IG-G, Box 46, Foulois Papers.

87. "Information on Aviation and a Department of National Defense," cover letter dated February 7, 1934, WPD 888-86, RG 165, NA.

88. "Written Statement of General Foulois in answer to Question 310," n.d. [ca. spring 35] IG-R, Box 47, Foulois Papers; copy of Gen George S. Simond's testimony in investigation of Foulois by the IG, Apr 23, 1935, IG-J, Box 47, Foulois Pa-

Notes, Pages 69-74

pers.
89. Questions and replies of Gen George S. Simonds in IG Investigation of Foulois, under Feb 1, 1935, cover letter, Reed to Simonds, Foulois File, Box 23, Simonds Papers, LC. Also see: Copy of testimony of Generals Simonds, Kilbourne, and Gulick before Subcommittee No. 3, House Military Affairs Committee, n.d. [ca. Jun 34], HEARINGS-E, Box 45, Foulois Papers; U.S. House of Representatives, Committee on Appropriations, Hearings on the War Department Appropriation Bill for 1935, Military Activities, 73d Cong, 2d sess, 1934, p 475.
90. Copy of testimony of Generals Simonds, Kilbourne, and Gulick before Subcommittee No. 3, House Military Affairs Committee, n.d. [ca. Jun 34], HEARINGS-E, Box 45, Foulois Papers.
91. Drum Board Report, WPD 888, RG 165, NA.
92. Ibid. More will be said concerning other facets of the Drum Board Report in subsequent chapters.
93. Drum Board Report, Exhibit III, WPD 888, RG 165, NA.
94. Drum Board Report, WPD 888, RG 165, NA.
95. Memo, C/S to Deputy C/S, Oct 12, 1933, WPD 888, RG 165, NA.
96. Memo, Foulois to C/S, Nov 8, 1932, INS-A, Box 19, Foulois Papers; letter, Lt Col Barton K. Yount to Foulois (and Foulois' penciled notes thereon), Mar 1, 1932, INS-A, Box 19, Foulois Papers.
97. Memo, Foulois to Deputy C/S, Sep 20, 1933 (not sent), DEF C-ld, Box 17, Foulois Papers; memo, Kilbourne to Drum, Jun 12, 1933, MAT DIV B-2b, Box 21, Foulois Papers; memo, Kilbourne to C/S, Oct 12, 1933, WPD 3714, RG 165, NA; Historical Studies: No. 6, p 135; Historical Studies: No. 89, p 69.
98. Letters, MacArthur to Pratt, Jun 22, 1933, and Pratt to MacArthur, Jun 22, 1933, WPD 888, RG 165, NA. Also see: Foulois' penciled marginal notes on the inclosure to "Memorandum for Special Committee of the General Council," submitted by Kilbourne, Sep 15, 1933, Box 16, Foulois Papers.
99. Memo, Lt Robbins to Assistant Chief of Bureau, Sep 15, 1932, Secret File A-21, RG 72, NA; letter, King to Byrd, May 10, 1933, A-D 1933 File, Box 4, King Papers, LC.
100. Minutes of the Meeting of the Aeronautical Board, Nov 8, 1933, A & N-E, Box 38, Foulois Papers.
101. Quoted in Futrell, Ideas, Concepts, Doctrine, p 70.
102. See: Copy of the Navy Report before the Federal Aviation Commission, n.d. [ca. Nov 34], AFSHRC 145.93-97; Army and Navy Journal LXXI (Dec 9, 1933), 294; "Between the Wars," Air Force XL (Aug 57), 122.
103. Minutes of the Meeting of the Aeronautical Board, Nov 8, 1933, A & N-E, Box 38, Foulois Papers; memo, Westover to Foulois, Nov 9, 1933, A & N-E, Box 38, Foulois Papers; memo, Kilbourne to C/S, Nov 28, 1933, MAT DIV B-2b, Box 21, Foulois Papers; letter, Westover to Chief, Materiel Division, May 5, 1932, CDF 452.2E, RG 18, NA,; memo, Executive, OCAC, to C/AC, Oct 21, 1932, CDF 452.2E, RG 18, NA; memo, Foulois to Chief, Materiel Division, Nov 2, 1932, CDF 452.2E, RG 18, NA; memo, Maj John H. Pirie to Westover, Aug 22, 1932, AAF 370.3, RG 18, NA.
104. Memo, Kilbourne to C/S, Nov 28, 1932, Box 16, Foulois Papers; Craven and Cate, Army Air Forces in World War II, I, 63; "The Present Status of Military Aviation and its Trend of Development," prepared by Foulois (delivered as AWC lecture by Westover), Sep 12, 1933, AWC Instructional Records, G-3 Course, 1932-33, RG 165, NA; memo, Foulois to Deputy C/S, Nov 7, 1933, CDF 452.2E, RG-18, NA; memo, Foulois to Asst C/S, WPD, Nov 4, 1933, AFSHRC 145.91-51A; memo, Asst C/S, G-4, to Deputy C/S, Nov 9, 1933, WPD 3690-2, RG 165, NA; memo, Kilbourne to C/S, Nov 2, 1933, WPD 3690-2, RG 165, NA; memo, Kilbourne to Deputy C/S, Nov 8, 1933, WPD 3690-2, RG 165, NA; memo, Kilbourne to C/S, Jul 25, 1933, WPD 888-75, RG 165, NA.
105. Memo, Maj Gen Robert E. Callan to AG, Nov 15, 1933, AG 452.1 (11-3-33), RG 407, NA; memo, AG to C/AC, Jan 12, 1934, AG 452.1 (1-3-34), misc D, RG 407, NA; memo, Callan to C/S, Jan 3, 1934, AG 452.1 (1-3-34), RG 407, NA.
106. Memo, Kilbourne to Deputy C/S, Nov 14, 1933, WPD 1105-55, RG 165, NA.
107. Ibid.
108. Letter, MacArthur to Commanding Generals of Armies, Corps Areas, and Departments, Jan 3, 1933, OPS-A, Box 22, Foulois Papers.

275

## Notes, Page 74

109. Transcript of long distance telephone call between Foulois and Westover, Nov 9, 1933, A & N-E, Box 38, Foulois Papers; memo, Kilbourne to Drum, Dec 5, 1933, WPD 888, RG 165, NA.

110. Editorial, *Washington Sunday Star*, Mar 4, 1934, p D-1.

# Notes

## Chapter III

### Organization: Toward A GHQ Air Force, 1932-1933

1. Letter from General Eaker, Jan 22, 1975; letter from General Cook, Mar 10, 1975; letter from General Hansell, Feb 11, 1975; Mcclendon, *The Question of Autonomy*, pp 138-39; *Historical Studies: No. 25*, pp 84-85.
2. *Army and Navy Journal* LXIX (Feb 32), 576-77; *Historical Studies: No. 25*, pp 86-87. Also see: Dec 31-Feb 32 Correspondence in AG 040 (12-4-30) file, RG 407, NA.
3. U.S. House of Representatives, Committee on Expenditures in the Executive Departments, *Hearings on H.R. 4742 and H.R. 7012: Department of National Defense*, 72d Cong, 1st sess, 1932, pp 104, 110-11.
4. Extract of Foulois' Feb 4, 1932, testimony before the House Committee on Expenditures in Executive Departments, pp 48-49, 56, LEGIS 3-F2, Box 26, Foulois Papers.
5. *Ibid.*, pp 29-30, 46.
6. *Ibid.*, p 56.
7. U.S. House of Representatives, Committee on Expenditures in the Executive Departments, *Hearings on H.R. 4742 and H.R. 7012: Department of National Defense*, 72d Cong, 1st sess, 1932, p 248.
8. *Ibid.*, pp 135-36; Killigrew, "The Impact of the Great Depression on the Army, 1929-36," pp 137-140; memo, Asst C/S, WPD, to C/S, Jan 18, 1932, CDF 032, RG 18, NA; Foulois Interview, Jan 20, 1960, p 54, AFAL; letter, Patrick J. Hurley to Representative John J. Cochran, Jan 5, 1932, LEGIS 3-F, Box 26, Foulois Papers; memo, Acting Asst C/S, WPD, to C/S, Feb 1, 1932, AG 040 (2-1-32), RG 407, NA.
9. *Historical Studies: No. 25.* pp 87-88.
10. *Army and Navy Journal* LXIX (Feb 13, 1932), 553, 576.
11. Letter, John J. McSwain to Foulois, Mar 5, 1932, LEGIS 3-F-2, Box 26, Foulois Papers. Also see: *Army and Navy Journal* LXIX (Feb 20, 1932), 596.
12. U.S. War Department, *Annual Report of the Secretary of War to the President* (Washington, 1932), pp 96-97.
13. See, for example, letter, Secretary of War Dern to Senator Morris Sheppard, Apr 7, 1933, AG 040 (3-15-33), RG 407, NA.
14. Killigrew, "The Impact of the Great Depression on the Army, 1929-36," pp 146-47; *Hearings on the War Department Appropriations Bill for 1934*, 72d Cong, 2d sess, 1933, pt 1, p 586.
15. Levine, *Mitchell*, pp 390-91; correspondence between Mitchell and Roosevelt, Nov 32, especially Roosevelt to Mitchell, Nov 19, 1932, 1932 File, Box 16, Mitchell Papers, LC. A number of letters speaking of, or recommending, Mitchell for the post of Assistant Secretary of War for Air are contained in Box 18, Mitchell Papers, LC.
16. Quoted in Foulois, *Memoirs*, p 186. Also see: McClendon, *The Question of Autonomy*, pp 83-84.
17. Hurley, *Billy Mitchell*, pp 122-23.
18. Quoted in Caidin, *Air Force*, p 66.
19. Editorial, *Army and Navy Journal* LXX (Apr 1, 1933), 616; Killigrew, "The Impact of the Great Depression on the Army, 1929-36," p 148; *New York Times*, Jun 8, 1933, p 3.
20. U.S. War Department, *Annual Report of the Secretary of War to the President* (Washington, 1934), p 4.
21. Quoted in *Army and Navy Journal* LXXI (Mar 17, 1934), 566.
22. *Army and Navy Journal* LXXI (Mar 17, 1934), 566, 584; *New York Times*, Jun 8, 1933, p 3.
23. H.R. 4318, 73d Cong, 1st sess, (1933), LEGIS 3-G, Box 27, Foulois Papers; memo, Kilbourne to C/S, Mar 31, 1933, WPD 635-35, RG 165, NA.
24. "Statement of General Foulois before the House Military Affairs Committee," attachment to memo, Westover to Asst C/S, WPD, Apr 13, 1933, LEGIS 3-Gl, Box 27, Foulois Papers; memo, Kilbourne to C/S, Mar 31, 1933, WPD 635-35, RG 165, NA.
25. Daily memos on the hearings, Kil-

bourne to C/S, Mar 31-Apr 15, 1933, WPD 635-35, RG 165, NA; memo, Drum to Asst C/S, WPD, Apr 10, 1933, LEGIS 3-Gl, Box 27, Foulois Papers.

26. Memos, Kilbourne to C/AC, Apr 11, 1933, Westover to Asst C/S, WPD, Apr 13, 1933, Drum to Westover, Apr 13, 1933, LEGIS 3-Gl, Box 27, Foulois papers. Foulois and Lt Col Chaney were the only two Air Corps witnesses to appear before McSwain's committee.

27. Letter, Foulois to McSwain, May 9, 1933, CDF 032, RG 18, NA. Also see: Foulois Interview, Jan 20, 1960, pp 43-44, AFAL; *Army and Navy Journal* LXX (Apr 15, 1933), 655.

28. Baker Board Hearings, p 3815.

29. Lassiter Board Report, WPD 888-3, RG 165, NA.

30. "Information on Aviation and a Department of National Defense," under Feb 7, 1934, cover letter, WPD 888-86, RG 165, NA.

31. AR 95-10, *Air Corps Troops,* Mar 10, 1928, CDF 321.9-B, RG 18, NA.

32. See: Baker Board Report, pp 43-44; memo, Maj Willis H. Hale, OCAC to C/AC, Sep 28, 1931, DEF C-ld, Box 17, Foulois Papers.

33. Memo, Foulois to Asst C/S, G-3, Oct 23, 1931, AFSHRC 145.93-83; memos, Hale to C/AC, Sep 28, 1931, Maj Walter H. Frank to Chief, Plans Division, OCAC, Sep 22, 1931, Asst C/S, G-3, to C/AC, Sep 11, 1931, DEF C-ld, Box 17, Foulois Papers.

34. U.S. House of Representatives, Committee on Appropriations, *Hearings on the War Department Appropriation Bill for 1933,* 72d Cong, 1st sess, 1932, pp 1049-50.

35. *Ibid.*

36. For an example of the General Staff's attitude, see: memo, Kilbourne to C/S, Sep 20, 1933, WPD 3561-25, RG 165, NA.

37. Memo, Asst C/S, WPD, to C/S, DEF C-la, Box 17, Foulois Papers.

38. *Ibid.*

39. Letter, MacArthur to Commanding Generals of Corps Areas and Departments, Aug 9, 1932, DEF C-lb, Box 17, Foulois Papers; War Department Press Release, Aug 20, 1934, GHQ Air Force, Organization and Operations, 1935 File, Box 9, Andrews papers, LC; *Annual Report of the Secretary of War,* 1934, pp 12-14, 37-38; Killigrew, "The Impact of the Great Depression on the Army, 1929-1936," pp 183-84;

letter, MacArthur to Commanding Generals of the Four Field Armies, Oct 22, 1932, DEF C-lb, Box 17, Foulois Papers.

40. Baker Board Hearings, pp 1788-89.

41. Draft letter, C/S to Corps Area Commanders, etc., Aug , 1932, DEF C-ld, Box 17, Foulois Papers; memo, Westover to Deputy C/S, Sep 19, 1932, DEF C-ld, Box 17, Foulois Papers; letter, Kilbourne to Representative W. Lindsay Wilson, Jun 6, 1934, WPD 888-86, RG 165, NA; memo, Foulois to C/S, Dec 3, 1932, DEF C-ld, Box 17, Foulois Papers; memo, Kilbourne to Foulois, Dec 27, 1932, DEF C-ld, Box 17, Foulois Papers.

42. Memo, Foulois to C/S, Dec 3, 1932, DEF C-ld, Box 17, Foulois Papers.

43. *Ibid.*

44. See Chapter II.

45. Memo, Kilbourne to C/S, Dec 10, 1932, DEF C-ld, Box 17, Foulois Papers. Also see: memo, Kilbourne to Foulois, Dec 27, 1932, DEF C-ld, Box 17, Foulois Papers.

46. Memo, Kilbourne to Foulois, Dec 27, 1932, DEF C-ld, Box 17, Foulois Papers.

47. Memo, Foulois to Kilbourne, Feb 8, 1933, DEF C-ld, Box 17, Foulois Papers. Foulois also maintained that the Chief of the Air Corps should supervise the training of those observation aviation units permanently assigned to divisions, corps, and field armies.

48. Memo, Foulois to Kilbourne, Mar 13, 1933, AFSHRC 167.9-5.

49. *Ibid.*

50. 1st Ind (AG to C/AC, Feb 28, 1933), C/AC to AG, Mar 15, 1933, CDF 321.9-B, RG 18, NA.

51. Memo, Kilbourne to Drum, Mar 31, 1933, WPD 3089, RG 165, NA.

52. Memo, Deputy C/S to Asst C/S, WPD, Feb 22, 1933, CDF 321.9-B, RG 18, NA; Copy of Maj Gen Hugh A. Drum's testimony before Subcommittee No. 3, House Military Affairs Committee, Jun 5, 1934, HEARINGS-F, Box 45, Foulois Papers.

53. See: "Air Corps Officers' Flying Time, F.Y. 1933, by Missions," OPS-C, Box 22, Foulois Papers; Correspondence relating to 1932 inspection trips, 1931-35 File, Box 5, Foulois Papers; TDY orders, Jul 28, 1933, Diary, Apr 3-Jul 31, 1933 file, Box 6, Spaatz Papers, LC.

54. Quoted in copy of testimony of Generals Simonds and Kilbourne before Subcommittee No. 3, House Military Af-

fairs Committee, n.d. [ca. spring 34], p 38, HEARINGS-E, Box 45, Foulois Papers.

55. Letter, MacArthur to Commanding Generals of Armies, Corps Areas, and Departments, Jan 3, 1933, OPS-A, Box-22, Foulois Papers.

56. See: memo, Westover to AG, Mar 15, 1933, DEF C-2a, Box 18, Foulois Papers; draft memo, "Decentralization of Air Corps Activities," n.d., DEF C-la, Box 17, Foulois Papers; Foulois, "Keeping America First in the Air," (article appearing in *The National Aeronautic Magazine*, Oct 32), Box 29, American Institute of Aeronautics and Astronautics Papers, LC; *Army and Navy Journal* LXXI (Feb 10, 1934), 475-76; Drum Board Report, WPD 888, RG 165, NA.

57. Letter, MacArthur to Commanding Generals of Armies, Corps Areas, etc., Feb 6, 1933, AFSHRC 145.93-234.

58. Draft of order, "Directive for Four-Army Organization," under Aug 18, 1933, cover letter, AG to C/AC, DEF C-lb, Box 17, Foulois Papers. Also see: memo, Chaney to C/AC, Aug 17, 1933, DEF C-la, Box 17, Foulois Papers.

59. Memo, AG to C/AC, Aug 12, 1933, AFSHRC 145.93-81; memo, Chaney to C/AC, Aug 17, 1933, DEF C-la, Box 17, Foulois Papers; memo, Collins to AG, Aug 10, 1933, WPD 1474-81, RG 165, NA; Personnel Orders 229, OCAC, Sep 30, 1933, CDF 321.9-A, RG 18, NA.

60. Bryce Wood, *The Making of the Good Neighbor Policy* (New York, 1961), pp 62-63, 71-72.

61. Memo, AG to C/AC, Aug 12, 1933, AFSHRC 145.93-81.

62. 2d Ind [AG 381 (8-15-33) (misc) E], C/AC to AG, Aug 23, 1933, AFSHRC 145.93-81.

63. 1st Ind [AG 381 (8-10-33) (misc) E], C/AC to AG, Aug 23, 1933, WPD 1474-81, RG 165, NA.

64. 2d Ind [AG 381 (8-10-33) (misc) E], AG to C/AC, Sep 1, 1933, AFSHRC 145.93-81.

65. "Information on Aviation and a Department of National Defense," under Feb 7, 1934, cover letter, p 6, WPD 888-86, RG 165, NA; letter, Kilbourne to Representative W. Lindsay Wilson, Jun 6, 1934, WPD 888-86, RG 165, NA; copy of testimony of Generals Simonds and Kilbourne before Subcommittee No. 3, n.d. [ca. spring 34], p 51, HEARINGS-E, Box 45, Foulois Papers; memos, AG to C/AC, Sep 2, 1933, C/A to Asst C/S, WPD, Oct 17, 1933, AFSHRC 145.93-81; copy of Foulois' testimony before the House Military Affairs Committee, Feb 1, 1934, HEARINGS-A, Box 45, Foulois Papers.

66. U.S. War Department, "Annual Report of the Chief of the Air Corps, 1934" (mimeographed), p 9, LC; memo, Lt Col Jacob E. Fickel, OCAC to Asst C/S, WPD, Jan 30, 1934, DEF C-la, Box 17, Foulois Papers; memo, Deputy C/S to Asst C/S, G-3, Dec 22, 1933, OCS 19393-24, RG 165, NA; "Information on Aviation and a Department of National Defense," under Feb 7, 1934, cover letter, p 31, WPD 888-86, RG 165, NA.

67. Drum Board Report, WPD 888, RG 165, NA; Futrell, *Ideas, Concepts, Doctrine*, p 62.

68. Baker Board Hearings, pp 3965-66.

69. "Annual Report of the Chief of the Air Corps, 1935," p 4.5.

70. Lassiter Board Report, p 7, WPD 888-3, RG 165, NA; letter from General Eaker, Jan 22, 1975; copy of testimony of Generals Simonds and Kilbourne before Subcommittee No. 3, House Military Affairs Committee, n.d. [ca. spring 34], pp 2-5, HEARINGS-E, Box 45, Foulois Papers.

71. Quoted in *Army and Navy Journal* LXXI (Feb 3, 1934), 455.

72. See, for example: memos, Spaatz to C/AC, Oct 18, 1933, and Fickel to Westover, Oct 23, 1933, DEF C-ld, Box 17, Foulois Papers.

73. Memo, Fickel to Deputy C/S, Jan 30, 1934, CDF 321.9-A, RG 18, NA; memo, Fickel to Asst C/S, WPD, Jan 30, 1933, DEF C-la, Box 17, Foulois Papers.

74. *Army and Navy Journal* LXXI (Jan 6, 1934), 365; *New York Times*, Jan 7, 1934, p 10.

75. Quoted in *Army and Navy Journal* LXXI (Feb 10, 1934), 475.

76. *Ibid.*

77. Letter, Dern to McSwain, Feb 3, 1934, WPD 888-75, RG 165, NA.

78. Letter, Dern to McSwain, with inclosure, Jan 31, 1934, AG 580 (1-31-34), RG 407, NA.

79. Copy of H.R. 7553, 73d Cong, 2d sess, (1934), WPD 888-86, RG 165, NA.

80. *Ibid.* The personnel increase called for would add 403 officers and over 6,000 enlisted men—the numbers the Air Corps Act of 1926 called for transferring to the Air Corps.

81. Copy of H.R. 7601, 73d Cong, 2d

sess, (1934), CDF 032G, RG 18, NA.

82. *Army and Navy Journal* LXXI (Feb 3, 1934), 445, 455.

83. *Ibid.*

84. For the views of officers in the OCAC, see: "Comments on the Proposal for an Air Force within the War Department similar to the Marine Corps within the Navy Department," prepared by the Plans Division, OCAC, Jan 10, 1934, DEF C-le, Box 18, Foulois Papers; memo, Spaatz to C/AC, Jan 23, 1934, MAT DIV B-2, Box 20, Foulois Papers; memo, Chaney to C/AC, with attached report, Jan 18, 1934, DEF C-le, Box 18, Foulois Papers.

85. Memo, Foulois to C/S, May 20, 1935, LEGIS 7-El, Box 28, Foulois Papers; "Final Statement of General Foulois" (in the IG investigation), n.d. [ca. Jun 35], IG-S, Box 47, Foulois Papers.

86. Copy of Foulois' testimony before the House Military Affairs Committee, Feb 1, 1934, pp 3-7, HEARINGS-A, Box 45, Foulois Papers. More will be said in Chapter IV about the procurement differences which influenced Foulois' testimony.

87. Memo, Asst C/S, WPD, to Asst C/S, G-4, Jan 31, 1934, DEF C-lb, Box 17, Foulois Papers; memo, Asst C/S, G-4, to C/AC, Feb 1, 1934, DEF C-lb, Box 17, Foulois Papers; Baker Board Hearings, p 3962; "Information on Aviation and a Department of National Defense," under Feb 7, 1934, cover letter, WPD 888-86, RG 165, NA.

88. "Information on Aviation and a Department of National Defense," and Feb 7, 1934, cover letter, Asst C/S, WPD, to all other Asst C/Ss, etc, WPD 888-86, RG 165, NA.

89. Letter, Dern to McSwain wth enclosed statement to the House Military Affairs Committee, Feb 21, 1934, Official File 25, Box 2, Franklin D. Rosevelt Library [hereafter cited as FDR].

90. *Ibid.*

91. *Ibid.*

92. Memo for the files from Dern, Feb 19, 1935, AG 580 (7-8-34), RG 407, NA; letter, McSwain to Roosevelt, Mar 14, 1934, 1934 File, Box 19, Mitchell Papers, LC; *Army and Navy Register* XCV (Jun 16, 1934), 462.

# Notes

## Chapter IV

### Funds, Aircraft, and Personnel, 1931-1933

1. Myers, *State Papers of Herbert Hoover*, II, 257-58.
2. Wilson, "Herbert Hoover and the Armed Forces," pp i, 225; Killigrew, "The Impact of the Great Depression on the Army, 1929-1936," p 19.
3. Myers, *State Papers of Herbert Hoover*, II, 41-42.
4. Killigrew, "The Impact of the Great Depression on the Army, 1929-1936," p v; U.S. War Department, *Annual Report of the Secretary of War to the President* (Washington, 1932), pp 1, 5-6.
5. U.S. House of Representatives, Committee on Appropriations, *Hearings on the War Department Appropriations Bill for 1934*, 72d Cong, 2d sess, pt 1, p 5.
6. *Annual Report of the Secretary of War*, 1931, p 40; *Annual Report of the Secretary of War*, 1932, p 58; Watson, *Chief of Staff*, pp 15, 24-25; *Annual Report of the Secretary of War*, 1933, pp 20-21.
7. "Relation of Air Corps Expenditures to Total War Department (Military) Expenditures, 1925-1938," AFSHRC 167.65; "Annual Report of the Chief of the Air Corps, 1935," p 4.5; "Project Airplane Balances," prepared Nov 2, 1938, by Finance Division, OCAC, MAT DIV-B, Box 20, Foulois Papers; *Annual Report of the Secretary of War*, 1933, p 33.
8. "Project Airplane Balances," prepared Nov 2, 1938, by Finance Division, OCAC, MAT DIV-B, Box 20, Foulois Papers; Baker Board Report, p 32; Rutkowski, *Politics of Military Aviation Procurement*, pp 6, 46-47; McClendon, *The Question of Autonomy*, pp 142-43; "Annual Report of the Chief of the Air Corps, 1932," pp 7-8; U.S. House of Representatives, Committee on Appropriations, *Hearings on War Department Appropriations Bill for 1933*, 72d Cong, 1st sess, 1932, pp 1094-95; War Department Statement to the Federal Aviation Commission, Aug 31, 1934, Box 16, Foulois Papers. There was a total reduction of 6,240 enlisted men in the other arms at a rate of 1,248 a year for five years in order to bring the Air Corps up to 15,000 Men. Total losses of other branches were as follows: Infantry-3,108, Cavalry-1,342, Field Artillery-826, Coast Artillery-285, Engineers-243, Quartermaster-150, Ordnance-228, Miscellaneous-63. "Reduction of Other Arms to Permit Increases in the Air Corps Under the Five-Year Program," (undated chart), DEF C-2b, Box 18, Foulois Papers.
9. "Relation of Air Corps Expenditures to Total War Department (Military) Expenditures, 1925-1938," AFSHRC 167.65; Baker Board Hearings, pp 2456, 2551-52, 2564; "Annual Report of the Chief of the Air Corps, 1932," pp 83-84.
10. See note above; U.S. House of Representatives, Committee on Appropriations, *Hearings on the War Department Appropriations Bill for 1933*, 72d Cong, 1932, p 1095; "Extracts from Records Influencing Air Corps 5-Year Program," DEF C-1b, Box 17, Foulois Papers; "Funds Available Under Appropriation 'Air Corps, Army,' by classification, Fiscal Years 1927-1935 Inclusive," FIN B-3, Box 19, Foulois Papers; McClendon, *The Question of Autonomy*, pp 142-43; Rutkowski, *Politics of Military Aviation Procurement*, pp 55-56; U.S. Senate, Committee on Appropriations, *Hearings on the War Department Appropriations Bill for 1935*, 73d Cong, 2d sess, 1934, p 24. The funds referred to were called direct appropriations under the heading "Air Corps, Army." These moneys covered only aircraft procurement, operations and maintenance, and research/development.
11. Memo, MacArthur to Secretary of War, Aug 14, 1931, WPD 888-68, RG 165, NA; *Annual Report of the Secretary of War*, 1933, pp 32-33, 1934, p 45.
12. Memo, MacArthur to Secretary of War, Aug 14, 1931, WPD 888-68, RG 165, NA.
13. *Annual Report of the Secretary of War*, 1933, p 33.
14. See: memo, Kilbourne to Westover, Apr 17, 1933, LEGIS 3-G1, Box 27, Foulois Papers; "Information on Aviation and a Department of National Defense,"

281

under Feb 7, 1934, cover letter, WPD 888-86, RG 165, NA; copy of testimony of Generals Simonds and Kilbourne before Subcommittee No. 3, House Military Affairs Committee, n.d. [ca. spring 34] pp 23-24, HEARINGS-E, Box 45, Foulois Papers.

15. *Army and Navy Journal* LXIX (Nov 7, 1931), 217, 219; *New York Times*, Nov 6, 1931, p 1; Hoover, *Memoirs*, III, 132-33; D. Clayton James, *The Years of MacArthur*, 2 vols (Boston, 1970-1975), I, 359; *Annual Report of the Secretary of War*, 1933, p 16; Wilson, "Herbert Hoover and the Armed Forces," pp 134-35.

16. Memo, Foulois to Davison, Jan 9, 1932, FIN B-3, Box 19, Foulois Papers; *Annual Report of the Secretary of War*, 1932, p 39; "Project Airplane Balances," prepared Nov 2, 1938, by Finance Division, OCAC, MAT DIV-B, Box 20, Foulois Papers; "Funds Available Under Appropriation 'Air Corps, Army' by Classification, Fiscal Years 1927 to 1935, Inclusive," FIN B-3, Box 19, Foulois Papers; *Army and Navy Journal* LXIX (Dec 12, 1931), 337, 340.

17. Killigrew, "The Impact of the Great Depression on the Army, 1929-1936," p 103; Wilson, "Herbert Hoover and the Armed Forces," p 134.

18. Killigrew, "The Impact of the Great Depression on the Army, 1929-1936," pp 127-133, 135; memo, Foulois to Asst C/S, G-3, Oct 23, 1931, AFSHRC 145.93-83; Baker Board Hearings, p 2800; U.S. House of Representatives, Committee on Appropriations, *Hearings on the War Department Appropriations Bill for 1936*, 74th Cong, 1st sess, 1935, pp 36-37; *Hearings on the War Department Appropriations Bill for 1933*, 72d Cong, 1st sess, pp 1051-53; James, *MacArthur*, I, 375.

19. James, *MacArthur*, I, 356-59; *Army and Navy Journal* LXIX (Dec 26, 1931), 385, 396, LXIX (Jan 23, 1932), 481, 483, LXIX (Jan 30, 1932), 503, 507; *New York Times*, Jan 30, 1932, pp 1, 10; Killigrew, "The Impact of the Great Depression on the Army, 1929-1936," pp 110, 120, 129-130.

20. James, *MacArthur*, I, 359-361; *Army and Navy Journal* LXIX (May 14, 1932), 862.

21. *Army and Navy Journal* LXIX (May 21, 1932), 889, 900; *New York Times*, May 20, 1932, p 13; James, *MacArthur*, I, 362.

22. *Army and Navy Journal* LXIX (Jun 4, 1932), 937, (Jun 11, 1932), 961, (Jul 2, 1932), 1025, (Jul 9, 1932), 1052, (Jul 16, 1932), 1067; *New York Times*, Jul 13, 1932, p 1; *Annual Report of the Secretary of War*, 1932, pp 1-2, 60-61; James, *MacArthur*, I, 362; Wilson, "Herbert Hoover and the Armed Forces," p 136; Killigrew, "The Impact of the Depression on the Army, 1929-1936," pp 120-22.

23. *Army and Navy Journal* LXIX (Mar 19, 1932), 673, (Apr 16, 1932), 769, 791, (Apr 23, 1932), 793, (Jun 4, 1932), 937, (Jun 11, 1932), 961, (Jul 2, 1932), 1025-26, (Jul 16, 1932), 1067; Economy Act, Public, No. 212, 72d Cong, 1st sess, 1932; radiogram, AG to All Corps Area Commmanders, Jul 16, 1932, CDF 032G, RG 18, NA; Wilson, "Herbert Hoover and the Armed Forces," p 136.

24. *Army and Navy Journal* LXVIII (Jan 24, 1931), 491, 496; *Annual Report of the Secretary of War*, 1932, p 5.

25. *Army and Navy Journal* LXVIII (Jan 24, 1931), 500; *Annual Report of the Secretary of War*, 1931, pp 40-41; *New York Times*, Dec 2, 1931, p 17; *Annual Report of the Secretary of War*, 1932, pp 5-6; *Annual Report of the Secretary of War*, 1933, pp 35-42; Economy Act, Public, No. 212, 72d Cong, 1st sess, 1932.

26. For comments on life in the Air Corps, see: *New York Times*, Nov 1, 1931, p IX-7; Norman E. Borden, Jr., *Air Mail Emergency—1934* (Freeport, Maine, 1968), pp 25-27; letter, from General Eubank, Apr 4, 1975.

27. "Statement and Recommendations of General Foulois to the Baker Board," Jul 10, 1934, S & R-D, Box 28, Foulois Papers. Also see: *New York Times*, Nov 1, 1931, p IX-7.

28. *Army and Navy Journal* LXX (Oct 29, 1932), 170; letter, Fickel to Spaatz, Apr 5, 1932, Diary, Jan 4-Jun 27, 1932, Box 5, Spaatz Papers, LC; letter, Arnold to Spaatz, Jan 6, 1934, Personal File, Box 5, Arnold Papers, LC; letter, Westover to Brett, Mar 13, 1933, 1931-35 Correspondence File, Box 5, Foulois Papers.

29. "Annual Report of the Chief of the Air Corps, 1932," p 31; U.S. War Department, "Annual Report of the Chief of the Air Corps, 1933," (mimeographed), LC, pp 14, 21, 25; "Annual Report of the Chief of the Air Corps, 1935," pp 4.5, 14.5; *Annual Report of the Secretary of War*, 1932, pp 16-17, 42, 45-46. For information on the reduction of authorized flying time as an economy measure see: *Army and Navy*

Notes, Pages 110–115

*Journal* LXIX (Nov 21, 1931), 265; "Annual Report of the Chief of the Air Corps, 1932," pp 48-50.
30. *Historical Studies: No. 39*, p 94; McClendon, *The Question of Autonomy*, pp 143-44.
31. *Historical Studies: No. 39*, p 95; William B. Huie, *The Fight for Air Power* (New York, 1942), p 57; U.S. War Department, *Annual Report of the Secretary of War to the President* (Washington, 1935), p 10.
32. "Annual Report of the Chief of the Air Corps, 1932," pp 18-19, 37; *Army and Navy Journal* LXIX (Jan 20, 1932), 468, LXX (Apr 8, 1933), 629; U.S. House of Representatives, Committee on Appropriations, *Hearings on the Military Appropriations Bill for 1934*, 72d Cong., 2d sess, 1933, pt 1, p 569; Borden, *Air Mail Emergency—1934*, p 27.
33. "Annual Report of the Chief of the Air Corps, 1935," p 4.5; "Project Airplane Balances," prepared Nov 2, 1938, by Finance Division, OCAC, MAT DIV-B, Box 20, Foulois Papers; *Annual Report of the Secretary of War*, 1932, pp 42-43; Rutkowski, *Politics of Military Aviation Procurement*, pp 48-49. The Assistant Secretary of War for Air, in his annual report, claimed that the Air Corps had 1,254 officers and 1,671 serviceable aircraft in June 1932. Air Corps records present the figures as 1,305 officers and 1,646 aircraft. Of the 1,646 (or 1,671) planes, 152 were used for National Guard training.
34. Correspondence in "Organization and Reorganization of the Air Corps" file, Dec 31-Feb 32, CDF 321.9-B, RG 18, NA; Baker Board Hearings, p 3793; *Army and Navy Journal* LXIX (Apr 16, 1932), 780, LXX (Mar 4, 1933), 532; *Annual Report of the Secretary of War*, 1932, p 41; *Air Corps Newsletter* XVII (Feb 24, 1933), insert in front of p 27; *New York Times*, Mar 2, 1933, p 13; "Annual Report of the Chief of the Air Corps, 1934," p 20; "Annual Report of the Chief of the Air Corps, 1935," p 4.5; memo, AG to C/AC, Feb 23, 1933, CDF 321.9-B, RG 18, NA.
35. *Army and Navy Journal* LXVIII (May 23, 1931), 915, (Jul 4, 1931), 1041, 1060-61; *Annual Report of the Secretary of War*, 1932, p 41; *New York Times*, Mar 2, 1933, p 13; "Annual Report of the Chief of the Air Corps, 1934," p 20.
36. "Annual Report of the Chief of the Air Corps, 1932," pp 48-59; *Army and Navy Journal* LXIX (Nov 21, 1931), 265; *Air Corps Newsletter* XVI (Jan 25, 1932), 9, (Feb 18, 1932), 39; *Annual Report of the Secretary of War*, 1932, p 45; U.S. House of Representatives, Committee on Appropriations, *Hearings on the War Department Appropriations Bill for 1933*, 72d Cong, 1st sess, 1932, p 998; "Annual Report of the Chief of the Air Corps, 1933," p 30; Baker Board Hearings, p 3524.
37. Letters, Arnold to Spaatz, Jul 27, 1933, Aug 4, 1933, Andrews to Westover, Sep 21, 1933, Diary: Apr 3-Jul 31, 1933, Box 6, Spaatz Papers, LC.
38. *Annual Report of the Secretary of War*, 1932, pp 43-44; "Annual Report of the Chief of the Air Corps, 1932," pp 16-17.
39. *Annual Report of the Secretary of War*, 1933, pp 15-16; U.S. House of Representatives, Committee on Appropriations, *Hearings on the War Department Appropriations Bill for 1935*, 73d Cong, 2d sess, 1934, p 12; Killigrew, "The Impact of the Great Depression on the Army," pp 198-202, 216-17.
40. "Funds Available under Appropriation 'Air Corps, Army' by Classification, Fiscal Years 1927 to 1935, Inclusive," FIN B-3, Box 19, Foulois Papers; "Extract from Records Influencing Air Corps Five-Year Program," DEF C-lb, Box 17, Foulois Papers; memo, Westover to War Department Budget Officer, Nov 12, 1932, FIN B-3, Box 19, Foulois Papers.
41. "Keeping America First in the Air," (article by Foulois appearing in the October 1932 *National Aeronautic Magazine*), Box 29, American Institute of Aeronautics and Astronautics Papers, LC; "Statement of Major General Foulois," Dec 3, 1932, pp 1-2, 7-9, FIN B-3, Box 19, Foulois Papers; U.S. House of Representatives, Committee on Appropriations, *Hearings on the War Department Appropriations Bill for 1934*, 72d Cong, 2d sess, 1933, pp 627-28; Public, No. 441, (H.R. 14199), 72d Cong, 2d sess (1933).
42. *Army and Navy Journal* LXX (Apr 8, 1933), 629, (Apr 22, 1933), 669-670; *New York Times*, Apr 18, 1933, p 6, Apr 18, 1933, p 1.
43. Quoted in *Army and Navy Journal* LXX (Apr 29, 1933), 689.
44. Killigrew, "The Impact of the Great Depression on the Army, 1929-1936," pp 225-29.
45. *Army and Navy Journal* LXX (Jun 3, 1933), 789-790, (Jun 17, 1933), 831,

283

(May 20, 1933), 758; *New York Times,* May 30, 1933, p 1; letter, Douglas to Dern, Jun 9, 1933, FIN B-3, Box 19, Foulois Papers; *Annual Report of the Secretary of War,* 1933, pp 15-17; U.S. House of Representatives, Committee on Appropriations, *Hearings on the War Department Appropriations Bill for 1935,* 73d Cong, 2d sess, 1934, p 12; Killigrew, "The Impact of the Great Depression on the Army, 1929-1936," pp 229, 231.

46. "Funds available Under Appropriation 'Air Corps, Army,' by Classification, Fiscal Years 1927 to 1935, Inclusive," FIN B-3, Box 19, Foulois Papers; "Statement and Recommendations of General Foulois to the Baker Board," Jul 10, 1934, S & R-A, Box 28, Foulois Papers; memos, Foulois to C/S, Jun 15, 1933, C/S to C/AC, Jun 16, 1933, FIN B-3, Box 19, Foulois Papers.

47. *Army and Navy Journal* LXX (Apr 1, 1933), 610, (Apr 22, 1933), 669, (May 20, 1933), 764, (Jun 17, 1933), 831, (Jul 15, 1933), 909, (Aug 19, 1933), 1019, LXXI (Sep 2, 1933), 1; Foulois, *Memoirs,* pp 232-33; *New York Times,* May 7, 1933, p 9; *Historical Studies: No. 39,* pp 77-78.

48. *Army and Navy Journal* LXX *(Mar 11, 1933),* 549, (Mar 18, 1933), 569-570, (Apr 1, 1933) 609; *Annual Report of the Secretary of War,* 1933, pp 35-42.

49. Memo, Foulois to Deputy C/S, Mar 11, 1933, DEF C-lb, Box 17, Foulois Papers; memo, Westover to AG, Mar 15, 1933, DEF C-2a, Box 18, Foulois Papers.

50. See Chapter III.

51. H.R. 4318, 73d Cong, 1st sess (1933), LEGIS 3-G, Box 27, Foulois Papers; H.R. 4363, 73d Cong, 1st sess (1933), LEGIS 6-B, Box 27, Foulois Papers; "Statement of General Foulois," and "Statement of Lt. Colonel J.E. Chaney," attachments to memo, Westover to Asst C/S, WPD, Apr 13, 1933, LEGIS 3-Gl,, Box 27, Foulois Papers; *Army and Navy Journal* LXX (Apr 1, 1933), 618, 627; *New York Times,* Mar 30, 1933, p 18, Apr 1, 1933, p 8.

52. Memo, Kilbourne to C/S, Apr 8, 1933, WPD 635-35, RG 165, NA; memo, Kilbourne to Westover, Apr 17, 1933, LEGIS 3-Gl, Box 27, Foulois Papers.

53. Memo, Kilbourne to C/S, Apr 14, 1933, CDF 032G, RG 18, NA; memo, Westover to C/S, Apr 17, 1933, CDF 032G, RG 18, NA.

54. Memo, Deputy C/S to Asst C/S, G-3, WPD, May 18, 1933, WPD 3690-1 & 2 file, RG 165, NA; Foulois' handwritten notes on IG investigation, n.d. [ca. spring 35], IG-J, Box 47, Foulois Papers; memo, Foulois to Asst C/S, WPD, May 22, 1933, CDF 452.1-13, RG 18, NA; memo, Chaney to C/AC, Jun 7, 1933, CDF 032G, RG 18, NA.

55. Memo, MacDill to C/AC, Jun 7, 1933, CDF 452.1-13, RG 18, NA; Foulois' handwritten notes on IG investigation, n.d. [ca. spring 35], IG-J, Box 47, Foulois Papers; memo, Kilbourne to Deputy C/S, May 29, 1933, WPD 3690-1 & 2 file, RG 165, NA; memo, Kilbourne to Drum May 24, 1933, MAT DIV B-2b, Box 21, Foulois Papers.

56. Memo, Drum to Asst C/S, G-3, G-4, WPD, May 27, 1933, WPD 3690-1 & 2 file, RG 165, NA; memo, MacDill to C/AC, Jun 7, 1933, CDF 452.1-13, RG 18, NA; memo, Kilbourne to Deputy C/S, May 31, 1933, WPD 3690-2, RG 165.

57. Memo, MacDill to C/AC, Jun 7, 1933, CDF 452.1-13, RG 18, NA; Baker Board Hearings, pp 3945-47; copy of testimony of Generals Simonds and Kilbourne before Subcommittee No. 3, n.d. [ca. spring 34], pp 26-29, HEARINGS-E, Box 45, Foulois papers; letter, Kilbourne to Richards, Feb 6, 1934, WPD 888-86, RG 165, NA; "Written Statement of General Foulois in answer to Questions 337, 338, 339, 340, 341," n.d. [ca. Apr 35], IG-R, Box 47, Foulois Papers.

58. Memo, Foulois to Asst C/S, WPD, Jun 8, 1933, MAT DIV B-2b, Box 21, Foulois Papers; Foulois' handwritten notes on IG investigation, n.d. [ca. spring 35], IG-J, Box 47, Foulois Papers; memo, Kilbourne to Drum, Jun 10, 1933, MAT DIV B-2b, Box 21, Foulois Papers; Baker Board Hearings, p 4145; copy of testimony of Generals Simonds and Kilbourne before Subcommittee No. 3, n.d. [ca. spring 34], pp 28-29, HEARINGS-E, Box 45, Foulois Papers.

59. Memo, Westover to Kilbourne, Jun 23, 1933, WPD 3690-1 & 2 file, RG 165, NA; memo, Westover to AG, Jul 13, 1933, DEF C-2b, Box 18, Foulois Papers; Baker Board Hearings, pp 2973-74; Army War College Instructional Records, "Conduct of War" course, 1933-34, Vol V, RG 165, NA.

60. Baker Board Hearings, pp 2548-49, 3946-47, 4145; letter, Secretary of War to Federal Emergency Administrator of Public

Works, Sep 5, 1933, MAT DIV B-2b, Box 21, Foulois Papers; Rutkowski, *Politics of Military Aviation Procurement*, pp 65-66; telegram, Reuben H. Fleet to Roosevelt, Jul 22, 1933, letter, Fleet to Roosevelt, Official File 249, Box 1, FDR; letter, McSwain to Roosevelt, May 1, 1933, Official File 25, Box 66, FDR; *New York Times*, Nov 26, 1933, p 27, Dec 3, 1933, p viii-9; Harold L. Ickes, *The Secret Diary of Harold L. Ickes: The First Thousand Days, 1933-36* (New York, 1953), p iii; U.S. House of Representatives, Committee on Appropriations, *Hearings on the War Department Appropriations Bill for 1935*, 73d Cong, 2d sess, 1934, pp 14-15; memo, Westover to Foulois, Nov 9, 1933, A & N-E, Box 38, Foulois Papers; memo, Westover to AG, Dec 7, 1933, CDF 112.4, RG 18, NA.

61. Drum Board Report, WPD 888, RG 165, NA.

62. Ibid. Also see: McClendon, *The Question of Autonomy*, p 155; Futrell, *Ideas, Concepts, Doctrine*, I, 62.

63. Drum Board Report, WPD 888, RG 165, NA.

64. "Annual Report of the Chief of the Air Corps, 1933," p 58; U.S. House of Representatives, Committee on Appropriations, *Hearings on the War Department Appropriations Bill for 1933*, 72d Cong, 1st sess, 1932, pp 1042-46; 1st Ind [AG 452.1 (5-13-33) (misc) D], Chaney to AG, Jun 6, 1933, RG 407, NA.

65. Drum Board Report, WPD 888, RG 165, NA; "Annual Report of the Chief of the Air Corps, 1935," p 4.5; Appendix B to "The Proper Composition of the Air Force," by Captain George C. Kenney, Apr 29, 1933, AFSHRC 248.211-62K; 1st Ind [AG 580 (10-27-33) (misc) D], C/AC to AG, Jan 30, 1934, WPD 888-75 to -85 file, RG 165, NA; memo, Kilbourne to Deputy C/S, Feb 4, 1935, WPD 888-75, RG 165, NA; Futrell, *Ideas, Concepts, Doctrines*, pp 62-63.

66. Memo, Chaney to C/AC, Jan 9, 1934, DEF C-lb, Box 17, Foulois Papers; memo, Asst C/S, G-4, to Asst C/S, G-3, WPD, Nov 27, 1933, MAT DIV B-2b, Box 17, Foulois Papers. The exact number of officers belonging to the Air Corps is difficult to determine. *The Annual Report of the Secretary of War*, for 1933 (p 146) sets the total at 1,320 as of June 30, 1933, but the "Annual Report of the Chief of the Air Corps, 1933" (pp 5-6) says there were 1,282 on that date. A chart in the "Annual Report of the Chief of the Air Corps, 1935," shows 1,334 officers including those detailed to the Air Corps, as of July 1, 1933. Colonel Chaney claims in his January 9, 1934, memo to Foulois that there were but 1,268 Air Corps officers on December 31, 1933.

67. Letter, Kilbourne to Richards, Feb 6, 1934, WPD 888-86, RG 165, NA; newsclipping, *Washington Evening Star*, Jan 29, 1934, MAT DIV B-2, Box 20, Foulois Papers; *Army and Navy Journal* LXXI (Feb 10, 1934), 475-77; copy of General Drum's testimony before Subcommittee No. 3, House Military Affairs Committee, n.d. [ca. spring 34], HEARINGS-F, Box 45, Foulois Papers.

68. Memo, Kilbourne to Drum, Feb 3, 1933, WPD 888-86, RG 165, NA; letter, Kilbourne to Richards, Feb 6, 1934, WPD 888-86, RG 165, NA.

69. H.R. 7553, 73d Cong, 2d sess (1934), WPD 888-86, RG 165, NA; *Army and Navy Journal* LXXI (Feb 10, 1934), 477.

70. H.R. 7553, 73d Cong, 2d sess (1934), WPD 888-86, RG 165, NA.

71. "Information on Aviation and a Department of National Defense," under Feb 7, 1934, cover letter, pp 36, 38, WPD 888-86, RG 165, NA; Foulois' undated handwritten notes on IG investigation, IG-I, Box 46, Foulois Papers; U.S. House of Representatives, Committee on Military Affairs, *Investigation of Profiteering in Military Aircraft, under H. Res. 275*, H. Rept. 2060, 73d Cong, 2d sess, 1934, pp 5-6. See Chapter VII for full coverage of Foulois' reaction to H.R. 7553.

72. *U.S. Air Services* XIX (Feb 34), 38; *Army and Navy Journal* LXXI (Feb 10, 1934), 465; memo, Kilbourne to Asst C/S, G-4, Jan 31, 1934, DEF C-lb, Box 17, Foulois Papers; memo, Asst C/S, G-4, to C/AC, Feb 1, 1934, DEF C-lb, Box 17, Foulois Papers; memo, Foulois to Asst C/S, G-4, Feb 2, 1934, AFSHRC 145.93-81.

73. "Chronological Record of various Studies, Reports, Boards, Committees, etc., fixing of relative numbers of aircraft in Army and Navy Aviation," n.d., AFSHRC 145.91-134.

# Notes

## Chapter V

### The Air Mail Fiasco

1. Baker Board Hearings, p 1144; Foulois, *Memoirs*, p 237.
2. Paul Tillett, *The Army Flies the Mails* (Tuscaloosa, 1955), pp 11, 19-24; Arthur M. Schlesinger, Jr., *The Coming of the New Deal* (Boston, 1958), pp 446-451; Henry L. Smith, *Airways: The History of Commercial Aviation in the United States* (New York, 1942), pp 246-250; Samuel I. Rosenman, ed, *The Public Papers and Addresses of Franklin D. Roosevelt* (New York, 1938), III, 93-94; *New York Times*, Feb 9, 1934, p 1.
3. James A. Farley, *Jim Farley's Story: The Roosevelt Years* (New York, 1948), p 46; *New York Times*, Feb 9, 1934, p 1; Ickes, *Secret Diary*, p 147; letter, Foulois to Paul Tillett, Jul 11, 1954, Box 14, Foulois Papers; Tillett, *The Army Flies the Mails*, pp 28, 58. Also see: Schlesinger, *The Coming of the New Deal*, p 451; Rutkowski, *Politics of Military Aviation Procurement*, p 89.
4. Baker Board Hearings, pp 1144-46, 1170-71; U.S. Senate, Committee on Appropriations, *Hearings on the War Department Appropriations Bill for 1935*, 73d Cong, 2d sess, 1934, pp 42-43; "Statement of Brig Gen J. E. Chaney," (hand-dated February 1934), Diary, Jan 2-Jul 31, 1934, Spaatz Papers, LC; Foulois, *Memoirs*, p 237. Also see: Tillett, *The Army Flies the Mails*, pp 28-29.
5. U.S. Senate, Committee on Appropriations, *Hearings on the War Department Appropriations Bill for 1935*, p 43.
6. Quoted in Foulois, *Memoirs*, p 238.
7. Baker Board Hearings, p 1146; U.S. Senate, Committee on Appropriations, *Hearings on the War Department Appropriations Bill for 1935*, p 43.
8. Executive Order 6591, Feb 9, 1934, Box 14, Foulois Papers.
9. Letter, Dern to Roosevelt, Mar 11, 1934, Official File 19, FDR; *New York Times*, Mar 13, 1934, p 1; U.S. Senate, Committee on Appropriations, *Hearings on the War Department Appropriations Bill for 1935*, pp 44-45; Foulois, *Memoirs*, p 239. Also see James, *MacArthur*, I, 438-39; *Army and Navy Journal* LXXI (Mar 17, 1934), 565-66; Foulois' comments on Tillett, *The Army Flies the Mails*, Mar 25, 1954, p 36, Box 15, Foulois Papers.
10. Baker Board Hearings, pp 1146-47; U.S. Senate, Committee on Appropriations, *Hearings on the War Department Appropriations Bill for 1935*, pp 44-45.
11. *Washington Post*, Feb 10, 1934, p 10.
12. *Washington Evening Star*, Feb 10, 1934, p 1. Also see pp 2-3.
13. Baker Board Hearings, pp 1152-53, 1170-71; Foulois' comments on Tillett, *The Army Flies the Mails*, Mar 25, 1954, pp 4-5, 36, Box 15, Foulois Papers; U.S. House of Representatives, Committee on Appropriations, *Hearings on the War Department Appropriations Bill for 1935*, p 532; U.S. House of Representatives, Committee on Post Office and Post Roads, *Hearings on H.R. 3, H.R. 8578, and other Air Mail Bills*, 73d Cong, 2d sess, 1934, p 104; *Washington Post*, Mar 13, 1934, pp 1-2; *Army and Navy Journal* LXXI (Mar 17, 1934), 566; *New York Times*, Mar 16, 1934, p 14; Tillett, *The Army Flies the Mails*, pp 5, 28-29.
14. U.S. Senate, Committee on Appropriations, *Hearings on the War Department Appropriations Bill for 1935*, p 44; Foulois' comments on Tillett, *The Army Flies the Mails*, Mar 25, 1954, p 5, Box 15, Foulois Papers; Henry H. Arnold, *Global Mission* (New York, 1949), p 143. Also see: letter from Lt Gen Ira C. Eaker, Jan 22, 1975.
15. Personnel Orders 35, Feb 10, 1934, CDF 311.125, RG 18, NA; memo, Foulois to C/S, Feb 10, 1934, Box 14, Foulois Papers; radiogram, AG to Commanding General, First Corps Area, Feb 10, 1934, Box 14, Foulois Papers; Baker Board Hearings, pp 26-27, 226-230; U.S. House of Representatives, Committee on Post Office and Post Roads, *Hearings on H.R. 3, H.R. 8578, and other Air Mail Bills*, pp 97-98; Tillett, *The Army Flies the Mail*, p 41. For excellent brief coverage of the air mail operation see: Eldon W. Downs, "The

Army and the Air Mail," *Air Power Historian* IX (Jan 62), 35-51.

16. Baker Board Hearings, pp 234, 239-242; "Final Report of Army Air Corps Mail Operations," Oct 6, 1934, pp 5-7, Exhibit G, p 2, Box 15, Foulois Papers; *Army and Navy Journal* LXXI (Feb 17, 1934), 485; U.S. House of Representatives, Committee on Post Office and Post Roads, *Hearings on H.R. 3, H.R. 8578, and other Air Mail Bills*, p 97.

17. 1st Ind to Executive Order 6591, AG to C/AC, Feb 10, 1934, Box 15, Foulois Papers; memo, Foulois to C/S, Feb 26, 1934, Box 15, Foulois Papers; letter, Foulois to Farley, Feb 12, 1934, CDF 311.125, RG 18, NA; letter, Foulois to Secretary to the President, Feb 13, 1934, Box 15, Foulois Papers; "Final Report of Army Air Corps Mail Operations," Oct 6, 1934, pp 26-27, Box 15, Foulois Papers; Baker Board Hearings, pp 1115-17, 1122-23.

18. Memo, Foulois to C/S, Feb 26, 1934, Box 14, Foulois Papers; Baker Board Hearings, pp 395-96, 1117-1121; "Final Report of Army Air Corps Mail Operations," Oct 6, 1934, pp 27-28, Box 15, Foulois Papers; memo, Foulois to Secretary of War, Feb 23, 1934, Box 15, Foulois Papers.

19. Statement and Recommendations by General Foulois to Baker Board—titled "Army Air Corps Air Mail Operations," Jul 10, 1934, S & R-E file, Box 28, Foulois Papers; Baker Board Hearings, p 237; Borden, *Air Mail Emergency*, p 29.

20. Letter, Foulois to Branch, Feb 13, 1934, CDF 311.125, RG 18, NA.

21. Ibid.

22. Baker Board Hearings, p 238; "Final Report of the Army Air Corps Mail Operations," Oct 6, 1934, Box 15, Foulois Papers; *U.S. Air Services* XIX (Sep 34), 32.

23. Foulois, *Memoirs*, p 241; Tillett, *The Army Flies the Mails*, p 41; memo, Foulois to Secretary of War, Feb 23, 1934, Box 15, Foulois Papers; Baker Board Hearings, pp 231-32, 257; U.S. Senate, Committee on Appropriations, *Hearings on the War Department Appropriations Bill for 1935*, p 38; U.S. House of Representatives, Committee on Post Office and Post Roads, *Hearings on H.R. 3, H.R. 8578, and other Air Mail Bills*, pp 98, 106; *New York Times*, Feb 13, 1934, p 1, Feb 18, 1934, p 28; letter, Foulois to Rep William N. Rogers, Mar 9, 1934, Box 14, Foulois Papers.

24. Foulois, "Keeping America First in the Air," *National Aeronautic Magazine*, Oct 32, Foulois File, American Institute of Aeronautics and Astronautics Papers, LC; telegram, Foulois to Commander, Middletown Air Depot, Feb 13, 1934, Air Corps Air Mail Operations File, Box 5, RG 18, NA; editorial, *Aviation* XXXIII (Apr 34), 115; *New York Times*, Feb 24, 1934, p 6.

25. Memo, Col James H. Van Horn, Signal Corps, to Deputy C/S, Mar 24, 1934, Box 16, Foulois Papers; memo, Major Volandt, OCAC to C/AC, Feb 21, 1934, Box 14, Foulois Papers; Baker Board Hearings, pp 255-59, 265, 282-85, 570; U.S. Senate, Committee on Appropriations, *Hearings on the War Department Appropriations Bill for 1935*, p 38. The Air Corps' radios were adequate for daylight combat air operations. The thirty-mile range was all that was required to control formations, and the unchannelized feature allowed the use of a multitude of frequencies, thus compounding the enemy's monitoring problem.

26. Air Corps Circular 50-1, Apr 1, 1933, CDF 300.5, RG 18, NA; "Annual Report of the Chief of the Air Corps, 1934," p 25; Baker Board Hearings, pp 310, 320-21; *New York Times*, Sep 9, 1933, p 1. For additional information on the Air Corps' instrument development and training activities between 1931 and 1933, see: *New York Times*, Jul 3, 1932, p VIII-8, Jan 1, 1933, p II-6; "Blind Flying and the Airlines," *Aviation* XXXI (Aug 32), 350; *Air Corps Newsletter* XVI (Jan 25, 1932), 8, (May 28, 1932), 207-08, XVII (May 29, 1933), 116 (Sep 30, 1933), 210-11; U.S. House of Representatives, Committee on Appropriations, *Hearings on the War Department Appropriations Bill for 1933*, 72d Cong, 1st sess, 1932, p 1080.

27. Letter, Andrews to Foulois, Feb 15, 1934, Personal Correspondence-F, 1930-43 File, Andrews Papers, LC.

28. U.S. House of Representatives Committee on Post Office and Post Roads, *Hearings on H.R. 3, H.R. 8578, and other Air Mail Bills*, p 98.

29. Baker Board Hearings, pp 326-27, 3802, 3804-05.

30. *New York Times* Feb 14, 1934, p 5.

31. Report, Capt William C. Goldsborough to Commander, Eastern Zone, May 23, 1934, AAF, Air Corps Air Mail Operations File 200, RG 18, NA; *U.S. Air Services* XIX (Sep 34), 32; Arnold, *Global Mission*, p 143; *Army and Navy Journal*

LXXI (Feb 17, 1934), 503; Tillett, *The Army Flies the Mails*, p 50; article by Reginald Cleveland, *New York Times*, Mar 18, 1934, p VIII-6; Caidin, *Air Force*, p 63.

32. *Army and Navy Journal* LXXI (Feb 17, 1934), 503; article by Reginald Cleveland, *New York Times*, Mar 18, 1934, p VIII-6; editorial in *Aviation* XXXIII (Apr 34), 114-15; *New York Times*, Feb 24, 1934, p 6.

33. Quoted in *New York Times*, Feb 24, 1934, p 6.

34. *Washington Post*, Feb 12, 1934, p 1; Tillett, *The Army Flies the Mails*, pp 34-35.

35. Quoted in *Kansas City Star*, Feb 12, 1934, p 1.

36. Quoted in *New York Times*, Feb 13, 1934, p 16.

37. Quoted in Foulois, *Memoirs*, p 242. Also see: letter, Arnold to Gen Malin Craig, Feb 14, 1934, Personal File, Arnold Papers, LC; Tillett, *The Army Flies the Mails*, p 41.

38. *Congressional Record* LXXVIII, 3619. Also see: letter, Foulois to Rep William N. Rogers, Mar 9, 1934, Box 14, Foulois Papers.

39. Foulois, *Memoirs*, pp 242-43; *New York Times*, Feb 17, 1934, p 6, Feb 18, 1934, p 28; *Congressional Record* LXXVIII, 4501.

40. *Congressional Record* LXXVIII, 3619. Also see: letter, Foulois to Rep William N. Rogers, Mar 9, 1934, Box 14, Foulois Papers.

41. "Ernest Jones File," House of Representatives, Subcommittee No. 3, 1934 File, Box 15, Foulois Papers; Borden, *Air Mail Emergency*, pp 41, 97-98; memo, C/AC to AG, Feb 26, 1934, CDF 311.125, RG 18, NA.

42. Foulois, *Memoirs*, p 243; U.S. Senate, Committee on Appropriations, *Hearings on the War Department Appropriations Bill for 1935*, pp 38-40.

43. Report of Air Mail Operations, Capt William C. Goldsborough to Commander, Eastern Zone, May 23, 1934, AAF, Air Corps Air Mail Operations File 200, RG 18, NA.

44. Borden, *Air Mail Emergency*, p 52; U.S. Senate, Committee on Appropriations, *Hearings on the War Department Appropriations Bill for 1935*, pp 38-40; "Report of Personal Experiences-AACMO," Lt Paul M. Jacobs, May 9, 1934, AAF, Air Corps Air Mail Operations File 201.3,

RG 18, NA; Huie, *The Fight for Air Power*, p 42.

45. *Washington Evening Star*, Feb 19, 1934, p 1; Smith, *Airways*, pp 251-53; Tillett, *The Army Flies the Mails*, pp 42-43; *New York Times*, Feb 20, 1934, p 1.

46. *New York Times*, Feb 20, 1934, p 1; Baker Board Hearings, pp 1140-42; Borden, *Air Mail Emergency*, p 62.

47. *New York Times*, Feb 20, 1934, p 1; Downs, "The Army and the Air Mail," pp 41-42; Foulois, *Memoirs*, pp 243-44.

48. Letter, Early to Farley, Feb 15, 1934, Official File 25, FDR; Smith, *Airways*, p 254; *Washington Evening Star*, Feb 20, 1934, p 1.

49. *Washington Evening Star*, Feb 22, 1934, pp 1, 3; Feb 23, 1934, pp A-1, A-6; *Washington Post*, Feb 23, 1934, p 1, Feb 24, 1934, p 1; *New York Times*, Feb 23, 1934, p 11, Feb 24, 1934, p 1; Foulois, *Memoirs*, pp 244-45.

50. *Congressional Record* LXXVIII, 3619. Also see: "Regulations Governing the Operations of the Army Air Corps' Mail Operations," Feb 26, 1934, Box 14, Foulois Papers; Foulois, *Memoirs*, pp 245-46, 249.

51. *Washington Post*, Feb 25, 1934, p 1; Foulois, *Memoirs*, pp 245-46; *Washington Evening Star*, Jul 26, 1934, p B-6; Foulois' comments on *The Army Flies the Mails*, Mar 25, 1954, p 14, Box 15, Foulois Papers; *Congressional Record LXXVIII*, 3166, 3133-36; *New York Times*, Feb 25, 1934, p 3.

52. *Washington Post*, Feb 24, 1934, pp 1, 3, Feb 25, 1934, p 4; Rosenman, *Public Papers of FDR*, III, 94; Schlesinger, *Coming of the New Deal*, p 453; Tillett, *The Army Flies the Mails*, p 48.

53. Radio Address by Maj Gen Benjamin D. Foulois, Feb 27, 1934, Box 15, Foulois Papers.

54. For indications of the attitudes and feelings of those who participated in the air mail operation see: AAF, Air Corps Air Mail Operations Files 200 and C201.3, RG 18, NA. Also see: *Washington Post*, Feb 25, 1934, p 2; *New York Times*, Feb 25, 1934, p 3, Feb 26, 1934, p 5; Foulois, *Memoirs*, p 25; *Army and Navy Journal* LXXI (Mar 10, 1934), 551.

55. Quoted in *New York Times*, Feb 25, 1934, p 2.

56. *U.S. Air Services* XIX (Sep 34), 32.

57. *New York Times*, Mar 23, 1934, pp 1, 8; "Final Report of the Army Air Corps Mail Operation," Oct 6, 1934, Exhi-

Notes, Pages 140-144

bit G, Box 15, Foulois Papers; *Army and Navy Journal* LXXI (Mar 10, 1934), 551, (Mar 24, 1934), 604; Foulois, *Memoirs*, pp 249-252; draft memo, written by Foulois, Mar 18, 1934, Box 14, Foulois Papers; *U.S. Air Services* XIX (Sep 34), 32.

58. Chart titled "Air Mail Performance," n.d., Box 15, Foulois Papers; Downs, "The Army and the Air Mail," p 45; *Washington Post*, Mar 2, 1934, p 3.

59. Memos, C/AC to AG, Mar 8-9, 1934, CDF 311.125, RG 18, NA; Downs, "The Army and the Air Mail," p 45; *New York Times*, Feb 13, 1934, p 16, Feb 14, 1934, p 14, Feb 16, 1934, p ll; *Army and Navy Journal* LXXI (Feb 17, 1934), 503; memo, Lt Col Jacob E. Fickel, OCAC, to Chief, Press Relations Section, G2, Feb 23, 1934, Official File 25, FDR; letter, Foulois to Rep Brent Spence, Feb 15, 1934, CDF 311.125, RG 18, NA; Foulois' comments on *The Army Flies the Mails*, Mar 25, 1954, pp 6, 42, Box 15, Foulois Papers; "Final Report of the Army Air Corps Mail Operations," Oct 6, 1934, Exhibit F & G, Box 15, Foulois Papers; memo for Foulois (unsigned), May 2, 1934, Box 15, Foulois Papers; Baker Board Hearings, pp 340-43; radiogram, Hickam to Foulois, Mar 15, 1934, Box 15, Foulois Papers.

60. *Congressional Record* LXXVIII, 3614-16, 3618, 3621, 3825-26; *New York Times*, Mar 1, 1934, p 14; Downs, "The Army and the Air Mail," p 45.

61. *Washington Post*, Mar 10, 1934, p 1.

62. Ibid.; *Washington Evening Star* Mar 9, 1934, pp A-l, A-2; *New York Times*, Mar 10, 1934, p 2, Mar 11, 1934, pp 1, 3; Foulois, *Memoirs*, p 253.

63. *Congressional Record* LXXVIII, 4139, 4171; *Washington Evening Star*, Mar 9, 1934, p A-l, Mar 10, 1934, pp A-l, A-2, Mar 11, 1934, pp A-l, A-5; Downs, "The Army and the Air Mail," p 46; editorial in *New York Times*, Mar 12, 1934, p 16; Borden, *Air Mail Emergency*, p 110.

64. Quoted in Foulois, *Memoirs*, p 254.

65. Ibid., pp 253-56; Downs, "The Army and the Air Mail," p 46.

66. Press release containing Roosevelt's letter to Dern, Mar 10, 1934, Box 15, Foulois Papers.

67. Ibid.; Rosenman, *Public Papers of FDR*, III, 138-140.

68. Rosenman, *Public Papers of FDR*, III, 94; *Washington Sunday Star*, Mar 11, 1934, pp A-l, A-5; press release containing Roosevelt's letter to Dern, Mar 10, 1934, Box 15, Foulois Papers.

69. Quoted in *Congressional Record* LXXVIII, 4500.

70. U.S. Senate, Committee on Appropriations, *Hearings on the War Department Appropriation Bills for 1935*, p 2; Foulois' comments on *The Army Flies the Mails*, Mar 25, 1954, Box 15, Foulois papers.

71. Radiogram, Foulois to Central Zone Commander, Mar 10, 1934, Box 15, Foulois Papers; memo, Foulois to C/S, Mar 12, 1934, Box 15, Foulois Papers; *New York Times*, Mar 11, 1934, p 1, Mar 12, 1934, p l; *Washington Post*, Mar 12, 1934, pp 1, 5.

72. Memo, Foulois to C/S, Mar 12, 1934, Box 15, Foulois Papers.

73. Dern's indorsement to Foulois' memo to C/S, Mar 12, 1934, AG 580 Air Mail (2-9-34) file, RG 407, NA.

74. Tillett, *The Army Flies the Mails*, p 55; radiogram, Foulois to Commanding Officer, Central Zone, Mar 12, 1934, Box 15, Foulois Papers; *New York Times*, Mar 15, 1934, p 19, Mar 16, 1934, p 15, Mar 18, 934, p 24; "Report of Air Mail Operations," Capt William C. Goldsborough to Commander, Eastern Zone, May 23, 1934, AAF, Air Corps Air Mail Operations, File 200, RG 18, NA.

75. Foulois' comments on *The Army Flies the Mails*, p 39, Mar 25, 1954, Box 15, Foulois Papers; Foulois, *Memoirs*, pp 254-56; *Washington Post*, Mar 12, 1934, pp 1, 5, Mar 15, 1934, p 2; *New York Times*, Mar 17, 1934, p 7; Tillett, *The Army Flies the Mails*, pp 50-51.

76. Press release, Statement of Gen. Benjamin D. Foulois, Mar 15, 1934, CDF 311.125, RG 18, NA.

77. Radiogram, Foulois to Acting C/AC, Mar 17, 1934, Box 15, Foulois Papers.

78. Radiogram, Acting C/AC to Foulois, Mar 17, 1934, Box 15, Foulois Papers.

79. Letter, Roosevelt to Dern, Mar 18, 1934, AG 580 Air Mail (2-9-34) Sec 1 file, RG 407, NA. Also see: *Washington Post*, Mar 18, 1934, p 1.

80. Letter, Dern to Roosevelt, Mar 18, 1934, AG 580 Air Mail (2-9-34) Sec 1 file, RG 407, NA; Tillett, *The Army Flies the Mails*, pp 56-57. Six days prior to the resumption of air mail flights, Secretary of

289

Notes, Pages 147–149

War Dern ordered an investigation of the Air Corps' performance in the mail operation. See Chapter VIII.

81. "Final Report of the Army Air Corps Mail Operations," Oct 6, 1934, pp 21-22, Box 15, Foulois papers; chart, "Air Mail Performance," n.d., Box 15, Foulois Papers; memo, Maj Asa N. Duncan to Foulois, Mar 31, 1934, Box 15, Foulois Papers; *New York Times,* Mar 19, 1934, p 1; *Washington Post,* Mar 31, 1934, p 1; Downs, "The Army and the Air Mail," p 49.

82. Tillett, *The Army Flies the Mails,* pp 60-61; *Washington Post,* Mar 28, 1934, p 1; "Final Report of the Army Air Corps Mail Operation," Oct 6, 1934, pp 17-22, Box 15, Foulois Papers.

83. *Army and Navy Journal* LXXI (May 12, 1934), 743; Foulois, *Memoirs,* p 259; Downs, "The Army and the Air Mail," p 50; *New York Times,* May 8, 1934, p 1.

84. Memo, AG to C/AC, May 18, 1934, CDF 311.125, RG 18, NA; *New York Times,* Jan 27, 1934, p 22; *Army and Navy Journal* LXXII (Jan 19, 1935), 419; editorial in *U.S. Air Services* XX (Apr 35), 10; Tillett, *The Army Flies the Mails,* p 57.

85. Secretary of War Dern appointed the Baker Board in March 1934. The Air Mail Act of June 1934 created the Federal Aviation Commission, and it began hearings in the fall of the year. Both groups are treated in detail in Chapter VIII.

86. Foulois' comments on *The Army Flies the Mails,* Mar 15, 1954, p 7, Box 15, Foulois Papers.

87. "Funds Available under Appropriation 'Air Corps, Army,' by classification, Fiscal Years 1927 to 1935, Inclusive," FIN B-3, Box 19, Foulois Papers; "Relation of Air Corps Expenditures to Total War Department (Military) Expenditures, 1925-1938," AFSHRC 167.65.

88. "Annual Report of the Chief of the Air Corps, 1934," pp 25-27; Arnold, *Global Mission,* p 144; "Air Corps Training, Heavier than Air," Apr 12, 1933, Box 24, Foulois Papers; "Air Corps Training, Heavier than Air," Apr 16, 1935, Box 24, Foulois Papers; memo, Col James H. Van Horn to Deputy C/S, Mar 24, 1934, Exhibit B, Box 16, Foulois Papers.

89. *Annual Report of the Secretary of War,* 1934, p 54.

90. Quoted in *Army and Navy Journal* LXXI (May 12, 1934), 743.

# Notes

## Chapter VI

### Procurement Troubles, 1933-1935

1. See: U.S. House of Representatives, Committee on Military Affairs, *Investigation under House Resolution 275*, Report No. 1506, 73d Cong, 2d sess, 1934 [hereafter cited as *House Report No. 1506]*.
2. Baker Board Hearings, pp 1968, 2219-2220; letter, Foulois to Col Herbert A. White, Jun 5, 1934, Subcommittee No. 3, 1934 File, Box 45, Foulois Papers.
3. Baker Board Hearings, pp 2247-2253.
4. Air Corps Act of 1926, Public No. 446 (H.R. 10827), 69th Cong.
5. Statement and Recommendations of Foulois to Baker Board, Jul 10, 1934, S & R-H, Box 28, Foulois Papers; Review of Procurement Practices, n.d., MAT DIV B-2a(3), Box 21, Foulois Papers; U.S. House of Representatives, Committee on Appropriations, *Hearings on the War Department Appropriations Bill for 1935*, pp 484-85; memo, Maj Gen Edward A. Kreger to Asst Secretary of War, Aug 3, 1939, Box 23, Simonds Papers, LC; Rutkowski, *Politics of Military Aviation Procurement*, pp 78, 163-64. For an example of how the Air Corps used Section 10(k) and AR 5-240, see: memo, Capt Rudolph W. Propst to C/AC, Apr 25, 1933, CDF 452.1-12, RG 18, NA.
6. Memo, Maj Leslie MacDill to C/AC, May 3, 1932, CDF 452.1-13, RG 18, NA.
7. Statement and Recommendations of Foulois to Baker Board, Jul 10, 1934, S & R-H, Box 28, Foulois Papers.
8. U.S. House of Representatives, Committee on Appropriations, *Hearings on the War Department Appropriations Bill for 1935*, pp 482-84; Baker Board Hearings, pp 2307-2311, 2317-2323; Extract of Testimony of General Henry C. Pratt before the House Military Affairs Committee, Feb 9, 1934, pp 3-6 (hand-numbered), HEARINGS-C, Box 45, Foulois Papers.
9. U.S. House of Representatives, Committee on Appropriations, *Hearings on the War Department Appropriations Bill for 1935*, pp 484, 532-35; *New York Times*, Feb 10, 1934, p 3.
10. U.S. House of Representatives, Committee on Appropriations, *Hearings on the War Department Appropriations Bill for 1935*, pp 478-79, 485,; memo, Lt Col Hugh C. Smith to Assistant Secretary of War, May 17, 1929, LEG-B, Foulois Papers; Foulois, *Memoirs*, p 226; Rutkowski, *The Politics of Military Aviation Procurement*, pp 168-69.
11. Memo, Westover to AG, Dec 7, 1933, CDF 112.4, RG 18, NA; memo, Woodring to Secretary of War, Apr 11, 1934, MAT DIV B-2B, Box 21, Foulois Papers; memos (3), Westover to Assistant Secretary of War, Dec 18, 1933, MAT DIV B-2b, Box 21, Foulois Papers; memo, Kilbourne to C/S, Mar 14, 1934, WPD 888-86, RG 165, NA.
12. Rutkowski, *Politics of Military Aviation Procurement*, pp 71, 81-82, 95, 140-42; letter, James V. Martin to Dern, Nov 6, 1933, CDF 452.1-13, RG 18, NA; memo, written by Gen Henry C. Pratt, addressee unknown, hand-dated Jun 26, 1933, MAT DIV B-2, Box 20, Foulois Papers; memo, Kilbourne to C/S, Mar 14, 1934, WPD 888-86, RG 165, NA; letter, Westover to Pratt, Dec 7, 1933, MAT DIV B-2b, Box 21, Foulois Papers; memo, Woodring to Secretary of War, Apr 11, 1934, MAT DIV B-2b, Box 21, Foulois Papers; "Statement of Costs and Profits on Contracts with the Principal Airplane and Engine Manufacturers," n.d., LEG-C, Box 19, Foulois Papers.
13. Memo, Woodring to Secretary of War, Apr 11, 1934, MAT DIV B-2b, Box 21, Foulois Papers. MacArthur and Drum attended the two-hour conference at Woodring's request but took no part in the discussion.
14. Ibid.
15. Ibid.; Rutkowski, *Politics of Military Procurement*, pp 72-73; *House Report No. 1506*, pp 39-40.
16. U.S. House of Representatives, Committee on Appropriations, *Hearings on the War Department Appropriations Bill for*

291

*1935*, p 521; memo, Foulois to AG, Apr 3, 1934, MAT DIV B-l, Box 20, Foulois Papers.

17. Letter, Woodring to William R. Robertson, Oct 19, 1934, CDF 452.1-13, RG 18, NA.

18. Letter, Harold L. Ickes to Dern, Jan 16, 1934, CDF 112.4, RG 18, NA; memo, Asst C/S, G-4, to C/AC, Dec 26, 1933, MAT DIV B-2b, Box 21, Foulois Papers; U.S. House of Representatives, Committee on Appropriations, *Hearings on the War Department Appropriations Bill for 1935*, p 521; "Notes on Report No. 1506," n.d., MAT DIV B-2b, Box 21, Foulois Papers.

19. Rutkowski, *Politics of Military Aviation Procurement*, pp 67-69, 86-87; *New York Times*, Feb 7, 1934, p 14, Feb 8, 1934, p 10, Feb 9, 1934, p 2; *Washington Post*, Feb 14, 1934, p 3.

20. *New York Times*, Feb 9, 1934, p 2; memo, Kilbourne to C/S, Feb 8, 1934, AG 580 (2-8-34), RG 407, NA; letter, Representative Ross A. Collins to Roosevelt, Nov 10, 1933, CDF 452.1-13, RG 18, NA.

21. *New York Times*, Feb 10, 1934, p 3; "Statement of Costs and Profits on Contracts," n.d., LEG-C, Box 19, Foulois Papers; Extract of testimony of Gen Henry C. Pratt before the House Military Affairs Committee, Feb 9, 1934, HEARINGS-C, Box 45, Foulois Papers; *House Report No. 1506*, pp 20-25; Rutkowski, *Politics of Military Aviation Procurement*, pp 75-79; memo, Kilbourne to C/S, Feb 10, 1934, AG 580 (2-10-34), RG 407, NA; *Army and Navy Journal* LXXI (Feb 17, 1934), 488.

22. Letter, Pratt to Foulois, Feb 20, 1934, MAT DIV B-2a (3), Box 21, Foulois Papers.

23. *House Report No. 1506*, pp 8-20; *New York Times*, Feb 10, 1934, p 3; *Washington Post*, Feb 10, 1934, p 10; Rutkowski, *Politics of Military Aviation Procurement*, pp 70-75.

24. Quoted in *Army and Navy Journal* LXXI (Feb 10, 1934), 475.

25. *Ibid.*

26. U.S. House of Representatives, Committee on Appropriations, *Hearings on the War Department Appropriations Bill for 1935*, pp 482-85; Rutkowski, *Politics of Military Aviation Procurement*, p 82.

27. U.S. House of Representatives, Committee on Appropriations, *Hearings on the War Department Appropriations Bill for 1935*, pp 490-91.

28. Testimony of Foulois before Subcommittee No. 3, Mar 7, 1934, pp 320, 322, HEARINGS-B, Box 45, Foulois Papers; *Washington Evening Star*, Feb 14, 1934, p 1.

29. *New York Times*, Feb 10, 1934, p 3.

30. Quoted in memo, Kilbourne to C/S, Feb 13, 1934, WPD 888-86, RG 165, NA.

31. Memo, Pratt to Foulois, Jun 26, 1933, MAT DIV B-2, Box 20, Foulois Papers. Martin frequently wrote to Secretary of War Dern complaining of poor treatment he received from the Air Corps and charging illegal procurement practices. See, for example: letters, James V. Martin to Dern, Nov 6, 1933, CDF 452.1-13, RG 18, NA, Feb 22, 1934, AG 452.1 (2-22-34), RG 407, NA, Apr 18, 1934, AG 580 (3-12-34), Sec 2 File, RG 407, NA.

32. *New York Times*, Feb 21, 1934, p 10.

33. *Congressional Record* LXXVIII, 3613. Also see: Rutkowski, *Politics of Military Aviation Procurement*, p 86.

34. *Washington Post*, Feb 20, 1934, p 1, Feb 22, 1934, p 1; memo, AG to C/AC, Feb 24, 1934, AG 580 (2-21-34), Misc D, RG 407, NA; memo, AG to C/AC, Feb 24, 1934, AG 580 (2-22-34), RG 407, NA; *Washington Evening Star*, Feb 24, 1934, p A-2.

35. *New York Times*, Feb 26, 1934, p 5, Mar 3, 1934, p 1, Mar 7, 1934, p 28; *Congressional Record* LXXVIII, 3613, 3622.

36. *House Report No. 1506*, pp 26-32; *Washington Post*, Mar 6, 1934, p 1, Mar 7, 1934, p 6.

37. See note above; Rutkowski, *Politics of Military Aviation Procurement*, pp 94-99; *New York Times*, Mar 7, 1934, p 28, Mar 8, 1934, p 7.

38. *House Report No. 1506*, p 32; *New York Times*, Mar 8, 1934, p 7.

39. Rutkowski, *Politics of Military Aviation Procurement*, p 100; *Washington Post*, Mar 8, 1934, pp 1, 2; *New York Times*, Mar 8, 1934, p 7; Testimony of Foulois before Subcommittee No. 3, Mar 7, 1934, pp 319-325, HEARINGS-B, Box 45, Foulois Papers.

40. Testimony of Foulois before Subcommittee No. 3, Mar 7, 1934, pp 339-343, HEARINGS-B, Box 45, Foulois Papers.

41. *Ibid.*

42. Testimony of aircraft manufacturers, Apr 5 and 18, 1934, Transcript of the Testimony, Apr 5, 1934-Apr 15, 1936, Records of the Military Affairs Committee, House of Representatives, relating to an investigation of the War Department, 1934-36 (Preliminary Inventory No. 80), [hereafter cited as Transcript of Testimony, Subcommittee No. 3], RG 233, NA; *Aviation* XXIII (Mar 34), 93-94; Rutkowski, *Politics of Military Aviation Procurement*, pp 105, 140-49. For additional information on the views of larger aircraft firms, see: Baker Board Hearings, pp 1315-16, 1325-26, 1399, 1602-07, 1611, 3049-50; *Army and Navy Journal* LXXII (Nov 24, 1934), 266; *Aviation* XXXIV (Jan 35), 21.

43. *Army and Navy Journal* LXXI (Apr 14, 1934), 645.

44. *Ibid.*

45. Memo, Maj Gen Arthur W. Brown to Assistant Secretary of War, Mar 5, 1934, MAT DIV B-2a(l), Box 20, Foulois Papers; memo, Lt Col Earl North to C/AC, Mar 10, 1934, MAT DIV B-2a(l), Box 20, Foulois Papers; 1st Ind (Basic Unknown), Foulois to Woodring, Apr 14, 1934, CDF 452.1-13, RG 18, NA.

46. Notes from Mar 15, 1934, and Mar 17, 1934, conferences at the Office of the Assistant Secretary of War, MAT DIV B-2(l), Box 20, Foulois Papers; 1st Ind (Basic Unknown), Foulois to Woodring, Apr 14, 1934, CDF 452.1-13, RG 18, NA.

47. *Washington Evening Star*, Apr 3, 1934, p A-1; *New York Times*, Apr 4, 1934, p 11, Apr 20, 1934, p 5; *Army and Navy Journal* LXXI (Apr 7, 1934), 625, (Apr 21, 1934), 666; *Aviation* XXXIII (May 34), 156.

48. *House Report No. 1506*, pp 46-51.

49. *Ibid.*, p 4.

50. *Army and Navy Journal* LXXI (Jul 28, 1934), 972.

51. *Ibid.*, Apr 14, 1934, 646, May 12, 1934, 731; letter, Lt Park Holland to Chief, Materiel Division, May 14, 1934, LEG-B, Box 19, Foulois Papers; *Congressional Record* LXXVIII, 4018.

52. U.S. House of Representatives, Committee on Naval Affairs, *Hearings on Sundry Legislation (1933-34), No. 6: Information as to the Method of Awarding Contracts for Ships and Aircraft for the United States Navy*, 73d Cong, 1st and 2d sess, 1934, pp 279-280, 341, 959, 1000-1003, 1041-44; letter, Pratt to Foulois, Feb 13, 1934, CDF 452.1-13, RG 18, NA.

53. "Extract from the Committee's Final Report," House Committee on Naval Affairs, 73d Cong, 2d sess, Mar 34. Also see: *New York Times*, Mar 19, 1934, p 3.

54. The actions of the two congressional bodies also had far different effects on the careers of the heads of Army and Navy aviation. Admiral King went on to eventually become Chief of Naval Operations. Foulois, branded a lawbreaker and subjected to persistent hounding from Subcommittee No. 3 for the next year and a half, quietly retired in December 1935.

55. Memo, Maj Gen Arthur W. Brown to Assistant Secretary of War, Nov 14, 1934, LEG-B, Box 19, Foulois Papers; letter, Secretary of Navy to Bureau Chiefs, Jul 28, 1934, MAT DIV B-2, Box 20, Foulois Papers; *Army and Navy Journal* LXXII (Jan 26, 1935), 442; notes on Navy Department testimony before the Federal Aviation Commission, Nov 13-15, 1934, DEF A-4, Box 16, Foulois Papers.

56. Memo, Lt Col James K. Crain to C/AC, Apr 20, 1934, CDF 452.1-13, RG 18, NA; *Army and Navy Journal* LXXI (May 5, 1934), 723, (May 12, 1934), 734; letter, Woodring to Rep John J. Cochran, Oct 10, 1934, CDF 452.1-13, RG 18, NA; *Annual Report of the Secretary of War, 1935*, pp 8-10.

57. *Army and Navy Journal* LXXI (May 5, 1934), 723, (May 12, 1934), 734, (May 26, 1934), 774, LXXII (Dec 15, 1934), 322; letter, Comptroller General to Secretary of War, Oct 17, 1934, MAT DIV B-2, Box 20, Foulois Papers; *New York Times*, Jun 30, 1934, p 4.

58. See: U.S. House of Representatives, Committee on Military Affairs, *Investigation of Profiteering in Military Aircraft, under H. Res. 275*, Report No. 2060, 73d Cong, 2d sess, 1934, [hereafter cited as *House Report No. 2060*]. The subcommittee's case against Foulois is treated in Chapter VII.

59. Letter, McCarl to Dern, May 22, 1934, MAT DIV B-2a, Box 20, Foulois Papers; letter, Capt Rudolph W. Propst to C/AC, Apr 25, 1933, CDF 452.1-13, RG 18, NA; Woodring's June 14, 1934, testimony, Transcript of Testimony, Subcommittee No. 3, RG 233, NA; letter, Woodring to Comptroller General, Jul 18, 1934, MAT DIV B-2a, Box 29, Foulois Papers.

60. Memo, Maj Gen Arthur W. Brown to Assistant Secretary of War, Nov 14, 1934, LEG-B, Box 19, Foulois Papers; letter, Attorney General to Secretary of War,

Jan 12, 1935, LEG-B, Box 19, Foulois Papers.

61. Letter, Comptroller General to Secretary of War, Oct 17, 1934, MAT DIV B-2, Box 20, Foulois Papers; letters, Comptroller General to Secretary of War, Dec 12, 1934, Secretary of War to Comptroller General, Jan 10, 1935, Comptroller General to Secretary of War, Feb 19, 1935, CDF 452.1-13, RG 18, NA.

62. *Baker Board Report,* p 21.

63. Federal Aviation Commission, *Report of the Federal Aviation Commission* (Washington, 1935), pp 181-83.

64. Letter, Roosevelt to Dern, Aug 31, 1934, CB-D, Box 28, Foulois Papers.

65. *Annual Report of the Secretary of War,* 1935, pp 38-39, 1936, pp 4, 24-25; *Air Corps Newsletter* XVIII (Jul 15, 1935), 2-3; letter, Rogins to Andrews, Dec 28, 1935, Personal Correspondence "R" 1934-36, Box 6, Andrews Papers, LC; Baker Board Hearings, p 1985; U.S. House of Representatives, Committee on Appropriations, *Hearings on the War Department Appropriations Bill for 1936,* 74th Cong, 1st sess, 1935, pt 1, p 561.

# Notes

## Chapter VII

### The Chief in Trouble, 1934-1935

1. *Washington Post*, Mar 2, 1934, p 3.
2. "Committee Print, Statement of Major General B. D. Foulois Before the Committee on Military Affairs, 73rd Congress, Second Session," Feb 1, 1934 [hereafter cited as Committee Print, Foulois' Feb 1, 1934, testimony], pp 1-2, HEARINGS-A, Box 45, Foulois Papers.
3. In a May 29, 1933, memo to The Adjutant General, Drum directed the channels through which the PWA project would be handled. MAT DIV B-2b, Box 21, Foulois Papers.
4. Foulois' handwritten notes on the IG investigation, n.d., IG-I, Box 46, Foulois Papers. Drum denied that the two men worked on a bill. He called it only a suggestion for the Military Affairs Committee. Copy of Drum's testimony before Subcommittee No. 3, Jun 5, 1934, p 78, HEARINGS-F, Box 45, Foulois Papers.
5. "A Bill," Jan 30, 1934, AFSHRC 145.91-51A.
6. Penciled notes at bottom of *Ibid.*; Foulois' handwritten notes on the IG investigation, n.d., IG-I, Box 46, Foulois Papers; *House Report No. 2060*, pp 5-6.
7. *House Report No. 2060*, pp 4-6. Foulois' original testimony is also found in: Committee Print, Foulois' Feb 1, 1934, Testimony, pp 4-5.
8. *New York Times*, Feb 2, 1934, p 19. The War Department bill (H.R. 7553) called for increasing air strength by an unspecified amount and contained the vague sentence: "That of the increase authorized herein not to exceed two thousand serviceable airplanes, including equipment and accessories, shall be maintained at any time during the next five years." H.R. 7553, 73d Cong, 2d sess, WPD 888-86, RG 165, NA.
9. Committee Print, Foulois' Feb 1, 1934, Testimony, pp 5-12.
10. *Ibid.* For comments on Foulois' ability as a public speaker, see: letter from Lt Gen Ira C. Eaker, Jan 22, 1975; letter from Gen Orval R. Cook, Mar 10, 1975.
11. Committee Print, Foulois' Feb 1, 1934, Testimony, pp 28-29.
12. "Written Statement of General Foulois in answer to Q. 310 and Q. 312," n.d. [ca. spring 35], IG-R, Box 47, Foulois Papers.
13. Testimony of General Foulois before Subcommittee No. 3, Mar 7, 1934, p 340, HEARINGS-B, Box 45, Foulois Papers.
14. Testimony of Thomas A. Morgan and Burdette S. Wright, Apr 5, 1934, Transcript of Testimony, Subcommittee No. 3, RG 233, NA.
15. Quoted in *Army and Navy Journal* LXXI (May 12, 1934), 731. Also see: *New York Times*, May 11, 1934, p 2.
16. *House Report No. 2060*, pp 4-7; *Army and Navy Journal* LXXI (May 19, 1934), 745; copy of testimony of General Drum before Subcommittee No. 3, Jun 5, 1934, pp 101-2, HEARINGS-F, Box 45, Foulois Papers.
17. Copy of testimony of Generals Simonds and Kilbourne before Subcommittee No. 4, n.d. [ca. May 34], pp 2-16, 33, 49, HEARINGS-E, Box 45, Foulois Papers; copy of General Drum's testimony before Subcommittee No. 3, Jun 5, 1934, pp 99-102, HEARINGS-E, Box 45, Foulois Papers; extracts of General Drum's testimony before Colonel Reed, Jan 31, 1935, IG-G, Box 46, Foulois Papers; IG questions for General Simonds and his answers, Feb 1, 1935, Major General Foulois File, Box 23, Simonds Papers, LC; extract of General Kilbourne's testimony in the IG investigation, Feb 5, 8, 1935, IG-H, Box 46, Foulois Papers.
18. Copy of testimony of General Simonds and Kilbourne before Subcommittee No. 3 (General Gulick's comments are also included herein), n.d., [ca. May 34], pp 2-16, 22-24, 31, 38-39, 49, HEARINGS-E, Box 45, Foulois Papers.
19. Copy of General Drum's testimony before Subcommittee No. 3, Jun 5, 1934, pp 81, 84-86, 89, 99-100, HEARINGS-F, Box 45, Foulois Papers.
20. "Statement of Representative Paul J. Kvale, Member of the Committee

## Notes, Pages 179-185

on Military Affairs, Re: Alleged Official Misconduct by Major General Benjamin D. Foulois," Dec 18, 1934, IG-D, Box 46, Foulois Papers. Also see: Rep Frank James' remarks, Jun 14, 1934, Transcript of Testimony, Subcommittee No. 3, RG 233, NA.

21. *Congressional Record* LXXVIII, 3615-18. Also see: *Washington Post*, Mar 3, 1934, p 2.

22. *Congressional Record*, LXXVIII, 3615, 12485; *House Report No. 2060*, p 12.

23. Seven out of the fourteen pages making up the Rogers Subcommittee's Jun 15, 1934 report are devoted to alleged inconsistencies in Foulois' testimony which were used to prove he knowingly lied to congressional committees.

24. Allegations made against General Foulois by Representative Paul J. Kvale, Member of the Committee on Military Affairs, in his statement of December 18, 1934, IG-C, Box 46, Foulois Papers.

25. Quoted in *New York Times*, Jun 16, 1935, p 1.

26. *House Report No. 2060*, pp 3-4.

27. *Ibid.*, pp 2-4, 12-13; Rutkowski, *Politics of Military Aviation Procurement*, pp 107-08; Woodring's Jun 14, 1934, testimony, Transcript of Testimony, Subcommittee No. 3, RG 233, NA.

28. *House Report No. 2060*, pp 4-7.

29. Response of General Simonds to questions regarding the IG investigation of General Foulois, n.d., Major General Foulois File, Box 23, Simonds Papers, LC.

30. *House Report No. 2060*, pp 7-11.

31. *Ibid.*, pp 11-12.

32. Baker Board Hearings, pp 4270-71; testimony of Brig Gen Charles H. Danforth, Apr 26-27, 1934, Transcript of Testimony, Subcommittee No. 3, RG 233, NA; Air Corps Training, Heavier-than-Air, Apr 12, 1933, Box 24, Foulois Papers.

33. Response of General Simonds to questions regarding the IG investigation of General Foulois, n.d., Major General Foulois File, Box 23, Simonds Papers, LC.

34. *House Report No. 2060*, pp 11-12.

35. *Ibid.*, pp 2, 13-14. Subcommittee No. 3 was composed of William N. Rogers, Democrat-New Hampshire, Joseph Lister Hill, Democrat-Alabama, Numa F. Modet, Democrat-Louisiana, Dow W. Harter, Democrat-Ohio, W. Frank James, Republican-Michigan, Edward W. Goss, Republican-Connecticut, Charles A. Plumley, Republican-Vermont, and Paul J. Kvale, Farmer-Labor-Minnesota.

36. Quoted in *New York Times*, Jun 18, 1934, p 1. Also see: *Army and Navy Journal* LXXI (Jun 23, 1934), 868.

37. Memo, Westover to Foulois, Apr 9, 1934, RECORDS-A, Box 46, Foulois Papers; Baker Board Hearings, pp 4774-76.

38. *Congressional Record* LXXVIII, 1248.

39. See: Committee Print, Foulois' Feb 1, 1934, Testimony, pp 1-2, HEARINGS-A, Box 45, Foulois Papers; testimony of General Foulois before Subcommittee No. 3, Mar 7, 1934, HEARINGS-B, Box 45, Foulois Papers.

40. *Congressional Record* LXXVIII, 12485.

41. "Statement Regarding Accusations made against the Chief of the Army Air Corps . . .," n.d., 1931-35 Correspondence File, Box 5, Foulois Papers; *Army and Navy Journal* LXXI, Jun 30, 1934, 898.

42. Letter, Rep William N. Rogers to Foulois, Jul 3, 1934, RECORDS-A, Box 46, Foulois Papers.

43. Editorial, *Washington Evening Star*, Aug 31, 1934, p A-8. For other press comments, see editorials in: *Washington Post*, Jun 19, 1934, p 8, *New York Times*, Jun 24, 1934, p VIII-12; *Aviation* XXXIII (Jul 33), 219; *Aero Digest* XXV (Sep 34), 3; *Army and Navy Journal* LXXI (Jun 23, 1934), 876, (Jul 14, 1934), 936.

44. See note above.

45. Editorial, *U.S. Air Services* XIX (Jul 34), 10.

46. Correspondence in 1927-30 and 1931-35 Correspondence Files, especially, letters, Foulois to Rep Albert C. Willford, Feb 23, 1934, Foulois to Glenn L. Martin, Aug 28, 1934, in 1931-35 Correspondence File, Box 5, Foulois Papers; letter, Andrews to Reuben H. Fleet, Sep 28, 1935, Personal Correspondence "F", 1930-43, Andrews Papers, LC; letter, Arnold to Guy W. Vaughan, Jan 5, 1932, Personal File, Box 4, Arnold Papers, LC; editorial, *Army and Navy Journal* LXXI (Jun 23, 1934), 876.

47. Quoted in *Army and Navy Journal* LXXI (Jul 7, 1934), 909.

48. Letter, Rogers to Roosevelt, Jun 18, 1934, P. REL-B, Box 46, Foulois Papers; *Army and Navy Register* VC (Jun 23, 1934), 486; *Washington Evening Star*, Jun 19, 1934, p A-2; Foulois, *Memoirs*, p 268.

49. "Statement Regarding Accusations made against the Chief of the Army Air

Corps . . .," n.d. [ca. mid-July 34], P. REL-E, Box 46, Foulois Papers; letter, Foulois to Frank Coffyn, Jun 25, 1934, Subcommittee No. 3 File, Box 45, Foulois Papers.

50. Statement and Recommendations of General Foulois to the Baker Board, Jul 10, 1934, S & R-G/H, Box 28, Foulois Papers.

51. 2d Ind [AG 201-Foulois, Benjamin D., Major General (6-18-34) Off], C/AC to AG, Aug 10, 1934, P. REL-B, Box 46, Foulois Papers.

52. *Congressional Record* LXXIX, 9392.

53. *Ibid.*

54. *Ibid.*

55. *Ibid.*

56. *Army and Navy Journal* LXXI (Sep 29, 1934), 98; *New York Times*, Sep 25, 1934, p 8.

57. MacArthur's Dec 7, 1934, testimony, Transcript of Testimony, Subcommittee No. 3, RG 233, NA. For evidence of press reaction to Dern's August 21 statement see: *Washington Evening Star*, Aug 31, 1934, p A-8; *Army and Navy Journal* LXXII (Sep 8, 1934), 26; copies of editorials, Subcommittee No. 3 File, Box 45, Foulois Papers.

58. MacArthur's Dec 7, 1934, testimony, Transcript of Testimony, Subcommittee No. 3, RG 233, NA.

59. *Ibid.*; Rutkowski, *Politics of Military Procurement*, pp 126-29; *Army and Navy Journal* LXXII (Dec 15, 1934), 319; memos, Secretary of War to IG, Dec 13, 1934, OCS 20852-2 through -5, RG 165, NA. The subcommittee mentioned to MacArthur the names of two Air Corps officers who testified against Foulois, Brig Gen Charles H. Danforth and Capt Claire L. Chennault. Danforth was not pleased with Foulois and the senior officers working in OCAC and the Materiel Division. Chennault's testimony is missing. [Transcript of Testimony, Subcommittee No. 3, RG 233, NA.] Criticism by only two men seems hardly enough evidence to argue that Air Corps officers were dissatisfied with Foulois. Other officers have written that the air chief had the full support of the air arm enlisted and commissioned personnel during his time of trouble. See: letter from Lt Gen Ira C. Eaker, Jan 22, 1975; letter from Gen Orval R. Cook, Mar 10, 1975.

60. Memos, Foulois to Strayer, Dec 27, 1934, Strayer to Foulois, Jan 2, 1935, IG-B, Box 46, Foulois Papers; conference notes, Jan 25, 1935 (in code by writing all of the words backwards), IG-E, Box 46, Foulois Papers; Foulois' notes of January activities, n.d., IG-E, Box 46, Foulois Papers; "Unusual Occurrences," Foulois' handwritten notes n.d., IG-Fl, Box 46, Foulois Papers.

61. Extracts of Drum's testimony before Reed, Jan 31, 1935, IG-G, Box 46, Foulois Papers.

62. Extracts from Kilbourne's testimony before Reed, Feb 5, 8, 1935, IG-H, Box 46, Foulois Papers.

63. Copy of General Simonds testimony in the IG investigation, Apr 23, 1935, IG-M, Box 47, Foulois Papers. Also see: Response of General Simonds to questions regarding the IG investigation of General Foulois, n.d., Major General Foulois File, Box 23, Simonds Papers, LC.

64. Final Statement of General Foulois, n.d. [ca. Jun 35], IG-S, Box 47, Foulois Papers. Also see: "Testimony to Colonel Reed between April 26 and May 1, 1935," IG-Q, Box 47, Foulois Papers; "Supplementary Statement of General Foulois," n.d. [ca. May 35], IG-R, Box 47, Foulois Papers.

65. See correspondence in IG-S, Box 47, Foulois Papers.

66. *New York Times*, Apr 16, 1935, p 17, Apr 17, 1935, p 3, Apr 24, 1935, p 2; *Army and Navy Journal* LXXII (Apr 27, 1935), 720, (May 4, 1935), 741.

67. *Congressional Record* LXIX, 9392.

68. *Ibid.*

69. *Ibid.*

70. Memo, Dern to AG, n.d., Major General Foulois File, Box 23, Simonds Papers, LC.

71. *Congressional Record* LXXIX, 9381-82; Rutkowski, *Politics of Military Aviation Procurement*, pp 130-31.

72. Quoted in *Washington Evening Star*, Jun 19, 1935, p A-5.

73. *New York Times*, Aug 9, 1935, p 19; Special Orders 188, Aug 12, 1935, Major General Foulois File, Box 23, Simonds Papers, LC; Foulois, *Memoirs*, p 273.

# Notes

## Chapter VIII

### Organization, 1934-1935: The GHQ Air Force

1. The General Staff was so concerned that it created a 252-page booklet amassing a case aganst autonomy, "Information on Aviation and a Department of National Defense," under Feb 7, 1934, cover letter, WPD 888-86, RG 165, NA.
2. Quoted in editorial, *Washington Sunday Star*, Mar 4, 1934, p D-1. Also see: letter, McSwain to Roosevelt, Mar 14, 1934, Official File 249, FDR; *New York Times*, Mar 14, 1934, pp 1, 3. *U.S. Air Services* kept up the attack on General Staff control in its April issue. *U.S. Air Services* XIX (Apr 34), 10.
3. Letter, Dern to Roosevelt, Mar 11, 1934, AG 580 Air Mail (2-9-34) Sec 1 file, RG 407, NA; news release, "Secretary of War Orders Study of Air Mail Operations," Mar 13, 1934, CG-A, Box 28, Foulois Papers; telegrams, Lindbergh to Dern, Mar 14, 15, 1934, AG 580 (3-14-34), RG 407, NA; telegram, Wright to Dern, Mar 13, 1934, AG 580 (3-13-34), RG 407, NA; *Army and Navy Journal* LXXI (Mar 17, 1934), 566; *U.S. Air Services* XIX (Apr 34), 34. The other four members of group, besides Chamberlin, Baker, and the five officers who composed the Drum Board, included James H. "Jimmy" Doolittle, Dr. Karl T. Compton, President of MIT, Edgar S. Gorrell, President of Stutz Motor Car Co., and Dr. George W. Lewis, Research Director for the National Advisory Committee for Aeronautics.
4. *Baker Board Report*, p 1.
5. News release, "Remarks of Honorable George H. Dern, Secretary of War, Upon Convening the Special Committee for Study of the Army Air Corps," Apr 17, 1934, CB-B, Box 28, Foulois Papers.
6. *Baker Board Report*, pp 2-5; news release, "Aviation Board Resumes Sessions," May 8, 1934, CDF 333.5, RG 18, NA. For information on the scope and depth of the investigation see: Baker Board Hearings.
7. "B-Historical Background," n.d., Box 34, Simonds Papers, LC; McClendon, *The Question of Autonomy*, pp 81-83;

Baker Board Hearings, pp 22-23, 38; letter, Simonds to Moseley, Jul 2, 1934, Box 5, Moseley Papers, LC.
8. Baker Board Hearings, pp 20-22, 3962-65. Also see the testimony of numerous senior ground officers contained in the transcript of the hearings.
9. *Baker Board Hearings*, pp 2747, 2830-2858, 2889, 2913-14, 2960-64, 3322, 3249-3260.
10. *Ibid*.
11. *Ibid*., pp 449, 3180-3223, 3415-3422, 3434, 3438; "Final Statement of General Foulois," n.d., IG-S, Box 47, Foulois Papers; telegram, Patrick to Andrews, Apr 24, 1934, Subject File: Wilcox Bill, 1926-36, Box 11, Andrews Papers, LC.
12. Telegram, Patrick to Andrews, Apr 24, 1934, Subject File: Wilcox Bill, 1926-36, Box 11, Andrews Papers, LC.
13. Baker Board Hearings, pp 3741-44.
14. *Ibid*., pp 3444-45. Also see: pp 3161-3246; *Army and Navy Journal*, LXXI (Jun 2, 1934), 818.
15. *Baker Board Report*, p 28.
16. See Baker Board Hearings; "Statement and Recommendations by Major General B. D. Foulois," submitted to Baker Board, Jul 10, 1934, S & R, Box 28, Foulois Papers.
17. "Statement and Recommendations by Major General B. D. Foulois," submitted to the Baker Board, Jul 10, 1934, S & R-D, Box 28, Foulois Papers.
18. *Baker Board Report*, pp 12-15, 18-19, 62-63, 66.
19. *Ibid*., pp 28-30, 66-67.
20. *Ibid*., pp 46-47, 67-72. Recommendations relating to manpower, aircraft, and training will be dealt with in detail in Chapter X.
21. *Ibid*., pp 60-61.
22. *Ibid*., p 75.
23. For indications of the War Department's receptiveness see: *Annual Report of the Secretary of War*, 1934, pp 46-50.
24. Letter, Dern to Roosevelt, n.d. [ca. late Jul 34], Official File 25, FDR; letter, Roosevelt to Dern, Aug 31, 1934, CB-D,

298

Box 28, Foulois Papers; *New York Times,* Sep 22, 1934, p 16; *Army and Navy Journal* LXXII (Sep 29, 1934), 97, 116.
25. Memo, Westover to Chief, Plans Division, OCAC, Jul 23, 1934, CDF 333.5, RG 18, NA.
26. *Report of the Federal Aviation Commission,* pp 1-2; *Army and Navy Journal* LXXI (Jul 28, 1934), 972; McClendon, *The Question of Autonomy,* pp 165-66. Besides Howell, the commission included Jerome C. Hunsaker, a former naval officer and aeronautical engineer; Edward P. Warner, former Assistant Secretary of the Navy for Air and the editor of an aviation magazine; Franklin K. Lane, Jr., former Secretary of the Interior; and Albert J. Berres, a labor leader.
27. Memo, Drum to AG, Jul 31, 1934, WPD 888-92, RG-165, NA; memo, AG to C/AC, Aug 11, 1934, AFSHRC 145.93-97; memo, Kilbourne to all other General Staff Agencies, Jul 31, 1934, WPD 888-92, RG 165, NA; memo, Kilbourne to C/S, Aug 8, 1934, WPD 888-92, RG 165, NA; letter, Moseley to Simonds, Jul 5, 1934, Moseley Papers, Box 5, LC. Also see other correspondence in "FAC File," WPD 888-92, RG 165, NA.
28. "War Department Statement under the Several Titles and Sub-Hearings submitted in Letter of August 3, 1934, from the Federal Aviation Commission," with Aug 31, 1934, cover letter, Dern to Howell, Box 16, Foulois Papers.
29. Memo, Kilbourne to Chiefs of General Staff Divisions, etc, Sep 11, 1934, Box 16, Foulois Papers; memo, Kilbourne to Westover, etc, Oct 23, 1934, WPD 888-92, RG 165, NA.
30. Memo, Kilbourne to Westover, etc, Oct 23, 1934, WPD 888-92, RG 165, NA.
31. Memo, Kilbourne to Westover, etc, Oct 17, 1934, Box 16, Foulois Papers; letter, Kilbourne to Cone, Sep 11, 1934, WPD 888-92, RG 165, NA.
32. Letter, Monohan to Lt Col Walter R. Weaver, Jul 28, 1934, 1934 File, Mitchell Papers, LC.
33. Handwritten note, Foulois to Westover, Oct 25, 1934, Box 16, Foulois Papers; paper prepared at Foulois' request on the organization of the air arm and the importance of bombardment, n.d. [ca. late Oct 34], DEF B-2, Box 17, Foulois Papers.
34. Memo, Kilbourne to Foulois, Oct 27, 1934, Box 16, Foulois Papers; memo, Kilbourne to Westover, Oct 27,

1934, CDF 334.8, RG 18, NA; "Statement of Foulois before the Federal Aviation Commission," n.d. [ca. Nov 34], Foulois File, Box 29, American Institute of Aeronautics and Astronautics Papers, LC.
35. Westover's Federal Aviation Commission testimony, n.d. [ca. Nov 34], CDF 334.8, RG 18, NA.
36. McClendon, *The Question of Autonomy,* pp 170-71; *Historical Studies: No. 89,* p 52; *Historical Studies: No. 25,* p 98; Claire L. Chennault, *Way of a Fighter: Memoirs of Claire Lee Chennault* (New York, 1949), p 18.
37. "Testimony Presented by Major Donald Wilson, Captain Robert Olds, Captain Harold Lee George, Captain Robert M. Webster, First Lieutenant K. N. Walker before the Federal Aviation Commission," AFSHRC 248.121-3.
38. *Report of the Federal Aviation Commission,* pp 19, 119-120, 123.
39. Ibid.
40. *New York Times,* Apr 17, 1935, p 3.
41. Memo, AG to C/AC, Jul 21, 1934, CDF 321.9-A, RG 18, NA; correspondence under tab "Creation of GHQ Air Force," BBI-A, Box 29, Foulois Papers; memo, AG to C/AC, Aug 15, 1934, BBI-A, Box 29, Foulois Papers; memo, Chaney to Asst C/AC, Aug 19, 1933, CDF 321.9-B, RG 18, NA; Baker Board Hearings, pp 2740-41; Bulletin 3, Jun 11, 1935, GHQAF Bulletins, 1935-37, Box 9, Andrews Papers, LC.
42. Memo, Foulois to Lt Col George W. Cocheu, G-3, Aug 28, 1934, DEF C-la, Box 17, Foulois Papers; memo, Asst C/S, G-3, to C/S, Aug 31, 1934, CDF 321.9-A, RG 18, NA; memo, Foulois to Deputy C/S, Nov 5, 1934, DEF C-la, Box 17, Foulois Papers; memo, Deputy C/S to Asst C/S, G-3, Sep 20, 1934, CDF 321.9-A, RG 18, NA; letter, AG to Commanding Generals of All Corps Areas, etc, Feb 19, 1935, DEF C-la, Box 17, Foulois Papers.
43. For examples of press reports see: *New York Times,* Jul 28, 1934, p 1, Oct 3, 1934, p 1; *U.S. Air Services* XIX (Nov 34), 7.
44. Memo, Foulois to Asst C/S, G-3, Jan 2, 1935, PERS-C, Box 22, Foulois Papers; letter, Andrews to Foulois, Jun 21, 1934, Box 16, Foulois Papers; Baker Board Hearings, p 423.
45. Letter, AG to Commanding Generals of All Corps areas, etc, Dec 31, 1934, BBI-A, Box 29, Foulois Papers; memo, AG

to Andrews, Jan 10, 1935, Official Papers: GHQAF Directives, 1930-37, Box 9, Andrews Papers, LC; *U.S. Air Services* XX (Apr 35), p 16; letter, AG to Commanding Generals of all Corps Areas, etc, Feb 19, 1934, DEF C-la, Box 17, Foulois Papers. For comments on the way other Air Corps officers viewed Andrews see: letter from Lt Gen Ira C. Eaker, Jan 22, 1975; letter from Maj Gen Haywood S. Hansell, Jr., Feb 11, 1975.

46. *Air Corps Newsletter* XVIII (Feb 1, 1935), 31.

47. Quoted in *Army and Navy Journal* LXXII (Dec 29, 1934), 357.

48. Quoted in *U.S. Air Services* XIX (Nov 34), 36.

49. *Annual Report of the Secretary of War,* 1935, pp 61-62.

50. Cy Young, "United We Stand. . . . Divided We Stand for Anything," *Aero Digest* XXVII (Nov 35), 16-17, 68, 70; editorial in *U.S. Air Services* XX (Jun 35), ll; letter from Lt Gen Ira C. Eaker, Jan 22, 1975; "Between the Wars," *Air Force* XL (Aug 57), 124; Craven and Cate, *The Army Air Forces in World War II,* I, 67n; U.S. House of Representatives, Committee on Military Affairs, *Hearings on H.R. 7041, 6810, 4348, 4336, 4351, 4911: To Promote National Defense by Increasing the Efficiency of the Air Corps,* 74th Cong, 1st sess, 1936, pp 1-5, 59-61, 101-3, 183-85. Foulois was not called to testify on the bill.

51. The long-range bomber and the promotion system are taken up in Chapters IX and X respectively.

52. Memo, C/S to Acting C/AC, Nov 6, 1935, Box 16, Foulois Papers; memo, C/S to Andrews, Nov 6, 1935, Official Papers: War Department General Staff, 1935-42, Box 11, Andrews Papers, LC.

53. Memo, C/S to Andrews, Nov 6, 1935, Official Papers: War Department General Staff, 1935-42, Box 11, Andrews Papers, LC.

54. Memo, Westover to C/S, with attachment, Nov 14, 1935, AG 580 (ll-14-35), RG 407, NA.

55. *Ibid.* Also see: "Between the Wars," *Air Force* XL (Aug 57), 124.

56. See: Letter from Lt Gen Ira C. Eaker, Jan 22, 1975; "Between the Wars," *Air Force* XL (Aug 57), 124.

57. Bulletin 5, Nov 2, 1935, GHQAF Bulletins, 1935-37, Box 9, Andrews Papers, LC.

58. Letter, Simonds to Andrews, Aug 10, 1935, Correspondence—GHQ Air Force, Box 23, Simonds Papers, LC; *Historical Studies: No. 10,* pp 1-2; McClendon, *The Question of Autonomy,* p 176.

59. "Preliminary Report of Service Test of GHQ Air Force," Oct 11, 1935, AG 320.2 (9-13-34) file, RG 407, NA. Also see: *Army and Navy Journal* LXXIII (Nov 9, 1935), 185, 188 (Nov 23, 1935), 225, 241, 243.

60. Report of 1935 service test of GHQ Air Force, Andrews to AG, Feb 1, 1936, RG 407, NA.

61. Letter, Andrews to AG, Jun 12, 1935, AG 320.2 (6-12-35), RG 407, NA; letter, AG to Commanding Generals of All Corps Areas, etc, Aug 22, 1935, AG 320.2 (6-12-35) Misc (Ret)-MC, RG 407, NA; "Report of Board Appointed to Survey Personnel Situation of the Air Corps, by letter AGO September 13, 1935," Jan 7, 1936, AG 320.2 (9-13-34) (l) Sec l-c File, RG 407, NA; letter, Andrews to C/S, Mar 26, 1936, AG 320.2 (3-26-36), RG 407, NA; letter, Andrews to C/S, Apr 25, 1936, Personal Correspondence-Malin Craig, Box 2, Andrews Papers, LC.

62. Memo, Westover to C/S, Apr 25, 1936, AG 320.2 (4-25-36), RG 407, NA; McClendon, *The Question of Autonomy,* pp 179-180; letter, AG to Commanding Generals of All Corps Areas, etc, May 8, 1936, AG 320.2 (5-5-36), Misc (Ret)-MC, RG 407, NA; "The GHQ Air Force," Air War College lecture by Maj Gen Frank M. Andrews, Oct 15, 1936, U.S. Army, Center of Military History, Washington, D.C.

63. McClendon, *The Question of Autonomy,* pp 185-87; Craven and Cate, *The Army Air Forces in World War II,* I, 32.

# Notes

## Chapter IX

### Doctrine, Mission, and Employment Concepts, 1934-1935

1. Information on Aviation and a Department of National Defense," under cover letter, Feb 7, 1934, pp 2-3, 16, 21, WPD 888-86, RG 165, NA.
2. Draft memo, enclosed with memo, Kilbourne to AG, Other Asst Chiefs of Staff and Acting Commander, GHQ Air Force, Jun 13, 1934, AFSHRC 145.93-81.
3. Memo, Westover to Asst C/S, WPD, Jun 26, 1934, CDF 321.9-A, RG 18, NA.
4. Memo, C/S to Asst Chiefs of Staff, Commander, GHQ Air Force, etc, Aug 17, 1934, WPD 3664-28, RG 165, NA.
5. Ibid.; memos, Westover to Kilbourne, Jun 26, 1934, Lt Col John P. Smith to Kilbourne, Jul 24, 1934, WPD 3664-28 file, RG 165, NA; Chennault, *Memoirs*, pp 18-19; memo, Kilbourne to Gorrell, Jan 15, 1935, WPD 888-92, RG 165, NA.
6. Baker Board Hearings, pp 3249-3260, 3275-76, 3282, 3284, 3322, 3563-64.
7. Baker Board Report, p 62.
8. "The Air Force" (ACTS text), 1934-35, AFSHRC 248.101-l.
9. Ibid.
10. War Department Statement to the Federal Aviation Commission, Aug 31, 1934, Box 16, Foulois Papers.
11. Brig Gen Frank M. Andrews, "The Air Defense Organization Which the War Department is Building," *U.S. Air Services* XX (Jul 35), 10-11; memo, McNarney to Reardon, Sep 4, 1935, WPD 3798-17, RG 165, NA; "The GHQ Air Force," Air War College lecture by Maj Gen Frank M. Andrews, Oct 15, 1936, U.S. Army, Center of Military History, Washington, D.C.; Baker Board Hearings, p 3322.
12. *Air Corps Newsletter* XVIII (Jan 15, 1935), 14; Foulois, *Memoirs*, p 270; *U.S. Air Services* XIX (Sep 34), 13-15; Arnold, *Global Mission*, pp 145-46.
13. Andrews, "The Air Defense Organization Which the War Department is Building," pp 10-12; *Air Corps Newsletter* XVIII (May 15, 1935), 1-2.
14. *Annual Report of the Secretary of War*, 1934, p 49. Also see: *New York Times*, Sep 23, 1935, p 3.
15. *Annual Report of the Secretary of War*, 1935, p 62.
16. Baker Board Hearings, pp 3993-94.
17. CNO to All Ships and Stations, May 22, 1934, Records of General Board, No. 449 file, Operational Archives, Naval Historical Division.
18. Memo, King to General Board, Mar 31, 1934, Confidential File A1-3(l), RG 72, NA.
19. Memo, King to General Board, Mar 27, 1934, Confidential File A1-3 (l), RG 72, NA.
20. Memo, Chairman General Board to Secretary of Navy, Sep 5, 1934, Confidential File A1-3 (ll), RG 72, NA; memo, CNO to All Bureau Chiefs, Nov 9, 1934, Secretary of Navy Confidential File W, RG 80, NA.
21. U.S. House of Representatives, Committee on Appropriations, *Hearings on the War Department Appropriations Bill for 1935*, pp 54-58; memo, Foulois to Deputy C/S, Feb 2, 1934, MAT DIV B-2, Box 20, Foulois Papers; memo, Westover to C/S, May 1, 1934, CDF 452.2E, RG 18, NA; memo, Spaatz to Foulois, Jul 3, 1934, CDF 334.8, RG 18, NA; memo, Westover to Deputy C/S, Jun 15, 1934, AG 580 (5-16-34), RG 407.
22. *Army and Navy Journal* LXXI (Feb 10, 1934), 476; U.S. House of Representatives, Committee on Appropriations, *Hearings on the War Department Appropriations Bill for 1935*, pp 548-49; editorial in *Washington Sunday Star*, Mar 4, 1934, p D-1; Baker Board Hearings, pp 4133-35; "Memorandum on Conference Held in the Office of the CNO, August 14, 1934," WPD 3774 folder, RG 165, NA; memo, Kilbourne to C/S, Oct 5, 1934, MAT DIV B-2, Box 20, Foulois Papers.
23. "Memorandum on Conference Held in the Office of the CNO, August 14, 1934," WPD 3774 folder, RG 165, NA; memo, Kilbourne to C/S, Oct 5, 1934, MAT DIV B-2, Box 20, Foulois Papers.
24. Memo, AG to Joint Army and

Navy Board, Sep 12, 1934, AG 580 (9-11-34) (Misc) WPD, RG 407, NA; letter, C/S to Commanding Generals of Armies, Corps Areas, Departments, and GHQ Air Force, Oct 17, 1934, AFSHRC 248.12603.

25. Letter, C/S to Commanding Generals . . ., Oct 17, 1934, AFSHRC 248.12603.

26. *Ibid.*

27. See: "Comments . . . on . . . 'Doctrines of the Army Air Corps' . . .," prepared by Lt Col Walter R. Weaver, Jan 18, 1935, AFSHRC 168.6008-13; "A Study of Proposed Air Corps Doctrine . . .," Jan 31, 1935, AFSHRC 145.91-148.

28. Navy Report before the Federal Aviation Commission, n.d. [ca. Nov 34], AFSHRC 145.93-97. Also see: memo, Kilbourne to Drum, Dec 6, 1934, WPD 888-92, RG 165, NA; letter, King to Howell, Dec 13, 1934, File H-R, 1933-1936, Box 4, King Papers, LC.

29. See: penciled notes on Navy Report before the Federal Aviation Commission, n.d. [ca. Nov 34], AFSHRC 145.93-97; War Department-State Department to the Federal Aviation Commission, Aug 31, 1934, Box 16, Foulois Papers; Baker Board Hearings, pp 4134-35.

30. Memo, Andrews to C/S, Nov 25, 1935, Personal File-Chief of Staff, Andrews Papers, LC.

31. Letter, King to Howell, Dec 13, 1934, File H-R, 1933-1936, Box 4, King Papers, LC.

32. Letter, Andrews to Dargue, May 8, 1936, Subject File: Wilcox Bill, 1926-36, Andrews Papers, LC.

33. "Joint Action of the Army and the Navy, (9-11-35)," Chap 4, pp 1-2, AG 062-1, RG 407, NA.

34. *Ibid.*, Chap 5, pp 11, 37-39.

35. In November 1935, the new Chief of the War Plans Division, Brig Gen S. D. Embick, examined the division of defense responsibilities contained in the "Joint Action of the Army and the Navy" as it applied to the island of Oahu. He found that the Navy, because it was charged wth the function of patrolling the coastal zone, would receive the first information of the approach of an enemy force.

"If it is apparent that the objective of hostile forces is shipping within the coastal zone, the primary responsibility rests with the Navy, and it is the duty of the Army to support the Navy by employing its aviation either jointly with naval aviation present or in lieu of naval aviation if none is present. . . . If, on the other hand, it is apparent that enemy forces from overseas intend to attack an objective on shore, then the primary responsibility for repulsing them rests with the Army, and it is the duty of the Navy to support the Army." [Memo, Asst C/S, WPD, to Deputy C/S, Nov 18, 1935, WPD 3885, RG 165, NA.]

36. Memo, Kilbourne to Deputy C/S, Oct 18, 1933, WPD 888-75, RG 165, NA; memo, Drum for C/S, Dec 20, 1933, AG 580 (12-20-33), RG 407, NA.

37. Memo, Kilbourne to C/S, Feb 9, 1935, CDF 321.9, RG 18, NA; memo, Kilbourne to all Asst Cs/S, C/AC, Commanding General, GHQ Air Force, etc, Dec 21, 1934, CDF 321.9, RG 18, NA.

38. Memo, Kilbourne to All Asst Cs/S, C/AC, Commanding General, GHQ Air Force, etc, Dec 21, 1934, CDF 321.9, RG 18, NA.

39. *Ibid.*; memo, Kilbourne to C/S, Feb 9, 1935, CDF 321.9, RG 18, NA.

40. "Doctrines of the Army Air Corps," enclosed in memo, Kilbourne to All Asst Cs/S, C/AC, Commanding General GHQ Air Force, etc, Dec 21, 1934, CDF 321.9, RG 18, NA.

41. *Ibid.*
42. *Ibid.*
43. *Ibid.*
44. *Ibid.*
45. *Ibid.*

46. Memo, C/AC to Deputy C/S, Feb 27, 1935, CDF 321.9, RG 18, NA; "Comments . . . on . . .'Doctrines of the Army Air Corps' . . .," prepared by Lt Col Walter R. Weaver, Jan 18, 1935, AFSHRC 168.6008-31.

47. "A Study of Proposed Air Corps Doctrine . . .," Jan 31, 1935, AFSHRC 145.91-148.

48. *Ibid.*

49. Memo, C/AC to Deputy C/S, Feb 27, 1935, CDF 321.9, RG 18, NA; memo, Asst C/S, G-3, to Asst C/S, WPD, Mar 20, 1935, WPD 3774 file, RG 165, NA; 1st Ind [AG 062.12 (2-9-35) Pub], Andrews to AG, Mar 11, 1935, RG 407, NA; memo, Asst C/S, WPD, to All Asst Cs/S,

C/AC, Commanding General GHQ Air Force, Apr 4, 1935, and 1st Ind, C/AC to Asst C/S, WPD, Apr 9, 1935, CDF 321.9, RG 18, NA; Apr 4, 1935-Sep 3, 1935, correspondence in WPD 3774-4, RG 165, NA.

50. TR 440-15, *Employment of the Air Forces of the Army,* 1935.

51. "Pre-World War II Military Air Doctrine," Air War College lecture by Maj Gen Follett Bradley, Jan 26, 1951, AFSHRC K239.716251-21. Also see Craven and Cate, *The Army Air Forces in World War II*, I, 48-49; *Historical Studies: No. 89*, p 74.

52. Foulois, *Memoirs*, p 229; memos, C/AC to C/S, Dec 5, 1933, Westover to AG, Dec 19, 1933, MAT DIV B-2, Box 20, Foulois Papers; Foulois Interview, Jan 20, 1960, Foulois Files, AFAL; *Historical Studies; No. 6*, pp 14-15; *Historical Studies: No. 89*, pp 46-47.

53. Memos, C/AC to C/S, Dec 5, 1933, Westover to AG, Dec 19, 1933, MAT DIV B-2, Box 20, Foulois Papers; C/AC to AG, Apr 27, 1934, AG 452.1 (4-27-34), RG 407, NA; Foulois, *Memoirs*, pp 229-230; memo, Deputy C/S to C/S, May 12, 1934, and 1st Ind, AG to C/AC, May 16, 1934, AG 452.1 (4-27-34) (Misc) D, RG 407, NA.

54. Memo, Asst C/S, WPD, to Asst C/S, G-4, Dec 29, 1933, MAT DIV B-2b, Box 21, Foulois Papers.

55. See: memo, AG to C/AC, Jan 12, 1934, WPD 3690-1 file, RG 165, NA; *Historical Studies: No. 6*, p 13.

56. Memo, C/AC to Asst Secretary of War, May 9, 1934, AAF General File, 1918-35, 452.1, RG 18, NA; memo, Deputy C/S to C/S, May 12, 1934, and 1st Ind, AG to C/AC, May 16, 1934, AG 452.1 (4-27-34) (Misc) D, RG 407, NA; memo, C/AC to Asst Secretary of War, Jun 22, 1934, AAF General File, 1919-35, 452.1, RG 18, NA; memo, C/AC to AG, Jun 23, 1934, AG 452.1 (6-23-34), RG 407, NA; memo, Deputy C/S to C/S, Jun 25, 1934, AG 452.1 (6-25-34), RG 407, NA; Foulois, *Memoirs*, p 230.

57. See: Craven and Cate, *The Army Air Forces in World War II*, I, 66.

58. *Ibid.*, p 69; memo, C/AC to C/S, Feb 5, 1935, AG 452.1 (2-5-35), RG 407, NA; memo, Acting Asst C/S, G-4, to C/S, Oct 18, 1935, AG 452.1 (10-1-35), RG 407, NA.

59. Foulois, *Memoirs*, p 231.

60. *Ibid.*; *Historical Studies: No. 6*, pp 16-17; *Historical Studies: No. 89*, p 47; memo, Acting Asst C/S, G-4, to C/S, Oct 18, 1935, AG 452.1 (10-1-35), RG 407, NA; memo, C/AC to AG, Oct 1, 1935, MAT DIV B-2, Box 20, Foulois Papers; *New York Times*, Sep 1, 1935, p 10; Arnold, *Global Mission*, pp 156-57. For a sample of the wide press coverage given the XB-17, see: *New York Times*, Jul 5, 1935, p 1, Aug 21, 1935, p 1; *U.S. Air Services* XX (Aug 35), 19; *Aviation*, XXXIV (Sep 35), 50.

61. Inclosure 1 to memo, Acting Asst C/S, G-4, to C/S, Oct 9, 1935, AG 452.1 (10-1-35), RG 407, NA.

62. C/AC to AG, Jul 12, 1935, CDF 452.2E, RG 18, NA; 1st Ind [AG 452.1 (6-17-35) (Misc) E] Westover to AG, Jul 12, 1935, RG 407, NA.

63. *New York Times*, Oct 31, 1935, p 3; *Army and Navy Journal* LXXIII (Nov 16, 1935), 208; *Aviation* XXXIV (Dec 35), 44; memo, Westover to Press Relations Section, General Staff, Dec 21, 1935, CDF 452.1F, RG 18, NA. Gust locks hold the control surfaces in one position and thus prevent them from being damaged by high winds while on the ground. The locking system for the XB-17 was controlled by a lever located in the cockpit. Gust locks for other aircraft were externally controlled.

64. Memo, Andrews to C/AC, Oct 30, 1935, CDF 452.1E, RG 18, NA; letter, Andrews to Robins, Nov 2, 1935, Personal Correspondence-"R", 1934-36, Box 6, Andrews Papers, LC.

65. Memo, Westover to AG, Nov 8, 1935, AG 452.1 (11-8-35), RG 407, NA. Also see: letter, Robins to Andrews, Nov 18, 1935, Personal Correspondence-"R", 1934-36, Box 6, Andrews Papers, LC.

66. Letter, Lt Col John D. Reardan to James Murray, Dec 28, 1935, CDF 452.1F, RG 18, NA.

67. "Between the Wars," *Air Force* XL (Aug 57), 126-27; Craven and Cate, *The Army Air Forces in World War II*, I, 68-70; *Historical Studies: No. 100*, p 34.

68. "Air Force," (ACTS text), approved Apr 11, 1936, AFSHRC 248.101-l; "Statement of General Foulois before the Federal Aviation Commission," n.d.[ca. Nov 34], Foulois File, Box 29, American Institute of Aeronautics and Astronautics Papers, LC; 3d Ind (Basic Unknown), Air Corps Board to C/AC, Jul 15, 1935, MAT DIV B, Box 20, Foulois Papers; letter, Andrews to AG, May 27, 1935, MAT DIV B,

## Notes, Page 234

Box 20, Foulois Papers; 4th Ind [AG 452.1 (5-27-35)], Andrews to AG, n.d. [ca. Aug 35], 7th Ind [AG 452.1 (5-27-35)], C/AC to AG, Sep 28, 1935, RG 407, NA; Foulois, *Memoirs*, pp 228-29; *Historical Studies; No. 89*, pp 55-56; "Bombardment" (ACTS text), Nov 35, AFSHRC 248.101-9.

# Notes

## Chapter X

### Funds, Aircraft, Personnel, and Bases, 1934-1935

1. "Project Airplane Balances," prepared by Finance Division, OCAC, Nov 2, 1938, MAT DIV-B, Box 20, Foulois Papers; memo, Lt Col Jacob H. Rudolph to Foulois, Feb 12, 1934, OPS B-l, Box 22, Foulois Papers; letter, Spaatz to Maj George H. Brett, Diary, August 2-December 27, 1934, Box 6, Spaatz Papers, LC.

2. Baker Board Hearings, p 2550; "Extracts from Records Influencing Air Corps Five-Year Program," n.d., DEF C-lb, Box 17, Foulois Papers.

3. *Ibid.*; U.S. Senate, Committee on Appropriations, *Hearings on the War Department Appropriations Bill for 1935*, pp 2, 26; U.S. House, Committee on Appropriations, *Hearings on the War Department Appropriations Bill for 1935*, pp 551-52; "Annual Report of the Chief of the Air Corps, 1935," pp 48-49.

4. Memos, AG to Chiefs of War Department Arms and Services, Mar 24, 1934, AG to C/AC, Apr 7, 1934, DEF C-lc, Box 17, Foulois Papers; *Washington Post*, Feb 10, 1934, p 10; *Annual Report of the Secretary of War*, 1934, p 42; *New York Times*, May 5, 1934, p 7.

5. Baker Board Report, pp 31, 48, 72; *Annual Report of the Secretary of War*, 1934, pp 4-5; letter, Dern to Roosevelt, n.d. [ca. Aug 34], Official File 25, Box 66, FDR.

6. *New York Times*, Aug 3, 1934, p 17; *Aero Digest*, XXV (Sep 34), 49; memo, Asst C/S, G-3, to C/S, Aug 29, 1934, BBI-A, Box 29, Foulois Papers; memo, Kilbourne to C/S, Oct 5, 1934, MAT DIV B-2, Box 20, Foulois Papers; Killigrew, "The Impact of the Great Depression on the Army," pp 399-402; memo, Asst C/S, G-l, to AG, Dec 29, 1934, AG 580 (12-29-34), and 1st Ind, Judge Advocate General to AG, Jan 11, 1935, RG 407, NA; memo, Acting Asst C/S, WPD, to AG, Feb 15, 1935, WPD 3798-2, RG 165, NA.

7. *Army and Navy Journal* LXXII (Feb 9, 1935), 488; U.S. House of Representatives, Committee on Appropriations, *Hearings on the War Department Appropriations Bill for 1935*, p 9; *New York Times*, Jan 1, 1935, p ll; *Aviation* XXXIV (Feb 35), 64.

8. Public, No. 29 (H.R. 5913), 74th Cong, contained in U.S. War Department, *General Orders, Bulletins, and Circulars* (Washington, 1935), pp 14-15; *New York Times*, Aug 27, 1935, p ll; Killigrew, "The Impact of the Great Depression on the Army," pp 378-84; U.S. House of Representatives, Committee on Appropriations, *Hearings on the War Department Appropriations Bill for 1935*, p 9; memos, Acting Asst C/S, G-3, to C/S, May 20, 1935, Jun 3, 1935, AG 452.1 (5-9-35), RG 407, NA.

9. Andrews, "The Air Defense Organization Which the War Department is Building," p ll; memo, Foulois to AG, May 2, 1935, MAT DIV Box-2c, Box 21, Foulois Papers; memo, Westover to AG, May 8, 1935, CDF 321.9A, RG 18, NA.

10. Foulois, *Memoirs*, p 276; *Army and Navy Journal* LXXII (Feb 9, 1935), 477; *New York Times*, Feb 9, 1935, p 7; Killigrew, "The Impact of the Great Depression on the Army," p 572; letter, Andrews to Robins, May 8, 1935, Personal Correspondence-"R," 1934-36, Box 6, Andrews Papers, LC.

11. *Army and Navy Journal* LXXII (Jul 20, 1935), 1004; letter, Woodring to McSwain, Jul 18, 1935, Official File 25, FDR; *New York Times*, Jul 24, 1935, p 6, Jul 25, 1935, p 20; letter, Rogers to Roosevelt, Jul 23, 1935, Official File 25, FDR; memo, Andrews to C/S, Oct 28, 1935, Personal Correspondence-Malin Craig, Box 2, Andrews Papers, LC.

12. James, *The Years of MacArthur*, I, 458-461; *Annual Report of the Secretary of War*, 1935, pp 65-66.

13. *Annual Report of the Secretary of War*, 1935, pp 7-8.

14. Williams, "Legislative History of the Air Arm," pp 90-93; letter, Dern to Roosevelt, Jan 13, 1936, CDF 452.1-314, RG 18, NA; Futrell, *Ideas, Concepts, and*

## Notes, Pages 241-247

*Doctrine*, p 79.

15. *Annual Report of the Secretary of War,* 1934, p 2, 1935, p 115; "Annual Report of the Chief of the Air Corps, 1935," p 4; *Aero Digest* XXVI (Feb 35), 38.

16. Letter, Foulois to Sen Morris Sheppard, Mar 23, 1934, Box 15, Foulois Papers.

17. *Annual Report of the Secretary of War,* 1935, pp 2, 4-5, 44; U.S. House of Representatives, Committee on Appropriations, *Hearings on the War Department Appropriations Bill for 1936,* pp 36-37; Killigrew, "The Impact of the Great Depression on the Army," pp 378-384, 387-88; memo, Westover to AG, Jul 3, 1935, AG 580 (7-3-35), RG 407, NA; *Army and Navy Register* XCVIII (Jul 6, 1935), 5.

18. Letter, Foulois to Sheppard, Mar 23, 1934, Box 15, Foulois Papers; U.S. House of Representatives, Committee on Appropriations, *Hearings on the War Department Appropriations Bill for 1935,* pp 449-50; "Annual Report of the Chief of the Air Corps 1934," pp 11, 27; "The Air Corps," Army War College Lecture by Westover, Oct 2, 1936, U.S. Army, Center for Military History.

19. *Baker Board Report,* p 69; War Department Statement to the Federal Aviation Commission, Aug 31, 1934, Box 16, Foulois Papers; U.S. War Department, *Annual Report of the Secretary of War to the President* (Washington, 1936), p 33; "The Air Corps," Army War College Lecture by Westover, Oct 2, 1936, U.S. Army, Center for Military History; Williams, "Legislative History of the Air Arm," p 90.

20. "Statement of Major General B. D. Foulois before the Federal Aviation Commission," n.d., Foulois File, Box 29, American Institute of Aeronautics and Astronautics Papers, LC; letter, Arnold to C/AC, Sep 13, 1935, AFSHRC 145.93-81; Baker Board Hearings, pp 2175-79; letter, Andrews to Major George E. Lovell, Jr., Nov 30, 1931, Personal Correspondence-"L," 1929-40, Box 5, Andrews Papers, LC.

21. Letter, Arnold to Andrews, Jul 1, 1935, Personal Correspondence-"A," 1935-37, Box 1, Andrews Papers, LC; Baker Board Hearings, pp 2143, 2158, 2173-74; letter, Andrews to Major George E. Lovell, Jr., Nov 30, 1931, Personal Correspondence-"L," 1929-40, Box 5, Andrews Papers, LC.

22. Memo, Andrews to C/S, Feb 5, 1935, AG 320.2, RG 407, NA; memo, Andrews to C/S, Oct 28, 1935, Personal Correspondence-Malin Craig, Box 2, Andrews Papers, LC; "The GHQ Air Force," Army War College lecture by Andrews, Oct 15, 1936, U.S. Army, Center for Military History.

23. *Army and Navy Journal* LXXIII (Sep 7, 1935), 10; *Annual Report of the Secretary of War,* 1936, p 3.

24. *Army and Navy Journal* LXXI (Mar 31, 1934), 605, LXXII (Jan 12, 1935), 397; *Annual Report of the Secretary of War,* 1935, p 6.

25. *Historical Studies: No. 39,* pp 91, 108-111; memo, C/AC to C/S, May 20, 1935, LEGIS 7-El, Box 28, Foulois Papers; "Information on Aviation and a Department of National Defense," under Feb 7, 1934, cover letter, WPD 888-86, RG 165, NA; letter, MacArthur to President of the General Council, Jul 3, 1934, CDF 210.2, RG 18, NA; memo, Air Corps Board of Officers to Foulois, Jul 19, 1934, CDF 210.2, RG 18, NA.

26. *Baker Board Report,* pp 33, 35-36, 68-69; *Report of the Federal Aviation Commission,* pp 138-39; Statement and Recommendations by Foulois to the Baker Board, Jul 10, 1934, S & R-D, Box 28, Foulois Papers.

27. Air Corps Act, Public, No. 446, 69th Cong (H.R. 10827); Baker Board Hearings, pp 2716, 2826-27, 2910-12; *Baker Board Report,* p 35; memo, Maj Arnold N. Krogstad to Foulois, Feb 6, 1934, CDF 210.2, RG 18, NA; *Historical Studies: No. 39,* pp 100-101.

28. Memo, Asst C/S, G-3, to C/S, Dec 21, 1934; memo, C/AC to Asst C/S, G-3, Jan 2, 1935; memo, C/AC to C/S, Jan 18, 1935; War Department press release, "Temporary Promotions and Standards for Flying Proficiency for Air Corps Officers," Jan 19, 1935, all in PERS-C, Box 22, Foulois Papers; memo, Asst C/S, G-3, to C/S, Jan 8, 1935; memo, C/AC to Asst C/S, G-3, Jan 8, 1935, both in AFSHRC 145.91-86; "Annual Report of the Chief of the Air Corps, 1935," p 5; memo, C/AC to Asst C/S, G-l, Aug 12, 1935, PERS-C, Box 22, Foulois Papers; War Department Circular 7, Jan 25, 1935, BBI-B, Box 29, Foulois Papers.

29. Memo, Asst C/S, G-l, to C/S, Jan 21, 1935, CDF 210.2, RG 18, NA; *Historical Studies: No. 39,* pp 111-12.

30. Copy of H.R. 4351, 74th Cong, 1st

sess, LEGIS 7-E, Box 28, Foulois Papers; *Army and Navy Journal* LXXII (May 11, 1935), 765, (May 18, 1935), 785, 787; memo, Col Arthur G. Fisher, OCAC to C/AC, Feb 5, 1935, CDF 210.2, RG 18, NA; memo, C/AC to C/S, May 20, 1935, LEGIS 7-El, Box 28, Foulois Papers; *Historical Studies: No. 39*, pp 111-13.

31. *Army and Navy Journal* LXXII (Jun 8, 1935), 860, (Jun 15, 1935), 879, (Jun 22, 1935), 917, 921, (Aug 3, 1935), 1045; *Annual Report of the Secretary of War*, 1935, pp 5, 45.

32. Chart, "Effect of Passage of S. 1404 as of August 23, 1935," Nov 7, 1935, G-1/13305 (51-75) file, RG 165, NA.

33. Copy of H.R. 9131, 94th Cong, 1st sess, CDF 032, RG 18, NA; *Army and Navy Journal* LXXII (Aug 17, 1935), 1098; memo, Westover to Asst C/S, G-1, Nov 7, 1935, CDF 032, RG 18, NA.

34. U.S. House of Representatives, Committee on Military Affairs, *Hearings on H.R. 7041, 6810, 4348, 4336, 4351, 4911: To Promote Defense by Increasing the Efficiency of the Air Corps*, pp 61, 185; memo, Capt Alfred W. Marriner to Chief, Personnel Divison, OCAC, Mar 7, 1935, CDF 300.5 D, RG 118, NA; memo, Capt Lester T. Miller to Acting Executive, OCAC, Aug 9, 1935, CDF 210.2, RG 18, NA; article by Lauren O. Lyman in *New York Times*, Jul 21, 1935, p X-8; memo, C/AC to Asst C/S, G-1, Aug 12, 1935, PERS-C, Box 22, Foulois Papers.

35. Memo, C/AC to Asst C/S, G-1, Aug 12, 1935, PERS-C, Box 22, Foulois Papers; memos, Asst C/S, G-1, to C/S, Aug 5, 1935, Col Philip B. Peyton to General Moses, Nov 6, 1935, both in G-1/13305 (51-75) file, RG 165, NA; *Historical Studies: No. 39*, pp 114-17.

36. *Baker Board Report*, p 67; Drum Board Report, pp 19-20, WPD 888, RG 165, NA; memo, AG to C/AC, Sep 28, 1934, AG 320.2 (9-13-34) (Misc) C, RG 407, NA; Conference on Coast Defense (part of "Air Force" course at ACTS), 1932-33, AHSHRC 248.2014 A-6; memo, AG to C/AC, Oct 17, 1933, and 1st Ind, C/AC to AG, Nov 3, 1933, AG 580 (10-27-33) Misc E, DEF C-2c, Box 18, Foulois Papers; memos, Maj Walter H. Frank to C/AC, May 4, 12, 1934, DEF C-2c, Box 18, Foulois Papers; memo, C/AC to Asst C/S, WPD, Jan 21, 1935, DEF C-2d, Box 18, Foulois Papers; memo, Asst C/S, WPD, to C/AC, Dec 21, 1934, WPD 3809 file, RG 165, NA.

37. Memo, Asst C/S, WPD to C/AC, Dec 21, 1934, WPD 3809 file, RG 165, NA; memo, Westover to Asst C/S, WPD, Dec 7, 1934, WPD 3809 file, RG 165, NA; 1st Ind (AG to C/AC, Dec 26, 1934) Maj Roy M. Jones, OCAC to AG, Jan 7, 1935, WPD 3809 file, RG 165, NA; memo, AG to C/AC, Jan 10, 1935, DEF C-2b, Box 18, Foulois Papers.

38. Letter, J. Mark Wilcox to Porter Whaley, Nov 13, 1934, AFSHRC 145.93-290; *New York Times*, Nov 18, 1934, p 25; article by Hans Christian Adamson in *Washington Herald*, Dec 9, 1934, p 2; memo, Kilbourne to AG, Dec 20, 1934, WPD 3798, RG 165, NA.

39. Memo, AG to C/AC, Dec 21, 1934, AFSHRC 145.93-290; memo, Kilbourne to AG, Dec 20, 1934, WPD 3798, RG 165, NA; *Air Corps Newsletter* XVIII (Feb 15, 1935), 45-46.

40. *Congressional Record* LXXIX, 1331-33, 2342. At the time H.R. 4130 was introduced, the Air Corps had tactical combat units stationed at installations in New York, Washington, D.C., Virginia, Louisiana, Texas, Michigan, and California (3). The air arm possessed no bases in New England, the Pacific Northwest, or Alaska.

41. Memo, Kilbourne to C/S, Jan 9, 1935, WPD 3809, RG 165, NA; memo, AG to C/AC, Jan 30, 1935, DEF C-2d, Box 18, Foulois Papers; "A Bill" (War Department Substitute for H.R. 4130), Feb 4, 1935, DEF C-2d, Box 18, Foulois Papers.

42. 3d Ind [AG 580 1-28-35) (Misc) DC of S] C/AC to AG, Feb 7, 1935, RG 407, NA.

43. Copy of Kilbourne's Feb 11, 1935, statement on H.R. 4130 to House Military Affairs Committee, WPD 3798, RG 165, NA; *Army and Navy Journal* LXXII (Apr 27, 1935), 734; Copy of Public, No. 263, 74th Cong, contained in *General Orders, Bulletins, and Circulars*, 1935, Bulletin 7.

44. *New York Times*, Apr 28, 1935, p 28, Apr 29, 1935, p 2, Apr 30, 1935, p 10, May 1, 1935, p 1, May 2, 1935, p 4, May 5, 1935, p IV-7; Rosenman, *Public Papers of FDR*, IV, 141-42; *Aviation* XXXIV (Jun 35), 58, 60.

45. Report of Airdrome Board, under Aug 26, 1935, cover letter, Lt Col John D. Reardan to AG, WPD 3798-17, RG 165, NA; letter, AG to Reardan, Aug 14, 1935, AG 580 (8-13-35) E, RG 407, NA; Report of Special Committee on Air Base Facilities,

under Public, No. 263-74th Congress (H.R. 7022), Dec 28, 1935, WPD 3798-17, RG 165, NA; *Annual Report of the Secretary of War,* 1935, p 10; letter, Acting Director of Bureau of Budget to Roosevelt, Jun 13, 1935, Official File 25, FDR; "The GHQ Air Force," Army War College Lecture by Andrews, Oct 15, 1936, U.S. Army, Center for Military History..

46. U.S. House of Representatives, Committee on Appropriations, *Hearings on the War Department Appropriations Bill for 1936,* pp 50-60; memo, AG to C/AC, Aug 27, 1934, CDF 321.1, RG 18, NA; *Historical Studies: No. 100,* pp 17-18. For examples of the increased flying training requirements, see: "Air Corps Training, Heavier-than-Air," Apr 12, 1933, and Apr 16, 1935, Box 24, Foulois Papers; Air Corps Circular 50-1, Mar 22, 1935, Entry 193, Office of Chief of Air Corps, Air Corps Circulars, 1924-41, RG 18, NA; Circular 6, Jan 24, 1935, *General Orders, Bulletins, and Circulars,* 1935. For a review of some of the air maneuvers see: *New York Times,* Jan 5, 1935, p 19, Jan 27, 1935, p II-15; memo, Andrews to C/S, Dec 21, 1935, Personal Correspondence-Malin Craig, Box 2, Andrews Papers, LC.

47. Benjamin D. Foulois, "America's Position in the Air," *National Aeronautic Magazine* XIII (Oct 35), 12-13; Foulois, *Memoirs,* p 276.

48. Foulois Interview, Jan 20, 1960, pp 18-19, Foulois Files, AFAL; *Army and Navy Journal* LXXIII (Jan 4, 1936), 346-47.

49. Memo, Foulois to Westover, Nov 12, 1935, 1931-35 Correspondence File, Box 5, Foulois Papers; Foulois, *Memoirs,* p 280. For example of the laudatory treatment of Foulois in the trade journals see: *Aviation* XXXIV (Sep 35), 52; *Army and Navy Register* XCVIII (Aug 10, 1935), 125.

50. Foulois, *Memoirs,* p 275.

# Glossary

| | |
|---|---|
| A-12 | Single-engine, all-metal, low-wing attack plane. Two crew, the gunner seated behind the pilot. Fitted with four fixed .30-caliber Browning machineguns in landing gear farings. Rear gunner had a single flexible .30-caliber Browning machinegun. Bombload, 400 pounds. Maximum speed, 175 miles-per-hour at sea level. Cruising speed, 150 miles-per-hour. Endurance, 3 to 4 hours at cruising speed. Service ceiling, 15,150 feet. |
| AAF | Army Air Forces |
| ACTS | Air Corps Tactical School |
| adm | admiral |
| AEF | American Expeditionary Force |
| AFAL | United States Air Force Academy Library, Colorado Springs, Colorado |
| AFB | Air Force base |
| AG | The Adjutant General, United States Army |
| AFSHRC | Albert F. Simpson Historical Research Center, Maxwell Air Force Base, Alabama |
| asst | assistant |
| AWC | Army War College |
| B-6A | Biplane light bomber, powered by two 575-horsepower air-cooled radial engines. Crew of five (2 pilots, bombardier, front and rear gunners). Armed with three .30-caliber Browning machineguns and 2,500 pounds of bombs. Maximum speed, 121 miles-per-hour. Cruising speed, 103 miles-per-hour. Service ceiling, 14,100 feet. Range, 363 miles. |
| B-7 | Gull-wing monoplane with two 600-horsepower engines on struts beneath the wing. Main wheels retracted backwards. Crew of four had open cockpits. Armament comprised 1,200 pounds of bombs and two .30-caliber machineguns. Maximum speed, 182 miles-per-hour at sea level. Combat range, 411 miles. Service ceiling, 20,400 feet. |
| B-9 | Two engine, all-metal, low-wing monoplane bomber with retractable landing gear. Four crewmembers (pilot, navigator/bombardier, 2 gunners). Fitted with one .30-caliber machinegun each in front and rear cockpits. Could carry 2,000 pounds of bombs at a top speed of 186 miles-per-hour. Service ceiling, 20,000 feet. Combat range, 600 miles. |
| B-10 | Besides design features of the B-9, this bomber had an enclosed cockpit, front and rear turrets, and newly designed engine cowling. Crew of four (pilot, radio operator, 2 gunners). Armament consisted of one .30-caliber Browning machinegun each in the nose and rear turrets and in the floor behind the bomb bay. Bombload, 2,260 pounds. Top speed was around 210 miles-per-hour, with a service ceiling of over 21,000 feet and a combat range of 600 miles. (The B-10B version's service ceiling was 24,200 feet and its range was 1,240 miles.) |
| B-12 | Revised version of the B-10. A number of these bombers were modified for coast defense duties, equipped with large floats so they could operate off water. |

309

# FOULOIS AND THE U.S. ARMY CORPS

| | |
|---|---|
| B-17 Flying Fortress | Four-engine, midwing bomber, developed by Boeing. Used widely during World War II in Europe and the Mediterranean area. Nine crewmembers. The combat version of the B-17 gave up the graceful lines of the YB-17. The slim rudder yielded to a broad dorsal fin enclosing twin .50-caliber machineguns in the tail. Top and belly turrets with jutting guns bulged from the fuselage. Gunners stood at open side hatches to train their .50s on enemy planes. |
| brig gen | brigadier general |
| ca. | about, approximately |
| C/AC | Chief of the Air Corps |
| capt | captain |
| CCC | Civilian Conservation Corps |
| CDF | Central Decimal File |
| CG | commanding general |
| chap | chapter |
| CNO | Chief of Naval Operations |
| co | company |
| col | colonel |
| Cong | Congress |
| C/S | chief of staff |
| DC-2 | Twin-engine, commercial monoplane with retractable landing gear. Maximum speed, 213 miles-per-hour. Cruising speed at 14,000 feet, 205 miles-per-hour. Service ceiling, 23,700 feet. Cargo and mail compartment held 1,000 pounds with an additional cargo and baggage compartment aft of the cabin. Two crew, 14 passengers. |
| DC of S | deputy chief of staff |
| def | defense |
| div | division |
| *et al (et alii)* | and others |
| FDR | Franklin D. Roosevelt Library, Hyde Park, New York |
| fin | finance |
| 1st lt | first lieutenant |
| G-4 | Assistant Chief of Staff, G-4 (Logistics) |
| gen | general |
| GHQ | General Headquarters |
| GHQAF | General Headquarters Air Force |
| gov | governor |
| H.R. (with number) | House Bill |
| H. Rept. (with number) | House Report |
| H. Res. (with number) | House Resolution |
| IG | The Inspector General |
| ind | indorsement |

# GLOSSARY

| | |
|---|---|
| LC | Library of Congress, Washington, D.C. |
| lt | lieutenant |
| lt col | lieutenant colonel |
| lt gen | lieutenant general |
| ltr | letter |
| maj | major |
| maj gen | major general |
| mat | material, materiel |
| M-day | Day on which mobilization begins or is postulated to begin. |
| memo | memorandum |
| misc | miscellaneous |
| MIT | Massachusetts Institute of Technology |
| n | note, footnote (plural nn) |
| NA | National Archives (National Archives and Records Service), Washington, D.C. |
| n.d. | no date |
| OCAC | Office of the Chief of the Air Corps |
| ops | operations |
| P-26A | One-crew, single-engine fighter and the first all-metal production model aircraft accepted by the military. Had a maximum speed of 234 miles-per-hour at 7,500 feet, a cruising speed of 199 miles-per-hour, a service ceiling of 27,400 feet, and a range of 360 miles. Armed with 2 fixed forward-firing .30-caliber machineguns and 112-pound bombs (carried externally). |
| para | paragraph |
| pers | personnel |
| pt | part |
| PWA | Public Works Administration |
| rear adm | rear admiral |
| ref | reference, refer |
| rep | representative |
| RG | Record Group |
| sec | section |
| 2d lt | second lieutenant |
| sess | session |
| temp | temporary |
| TR | training regulations |
| USNA | United States Naval Academy, Annapolis, Maryland |
| vice adm | vice admiral |
| WPD | War Plans Division |
| XB-15 | Plans were laid at Wright Field in 1933 for a bomber with a 5,000-mile range. Winning the design competition, Boeing began building the XB-15 prototype in 1935. The bomber did not fly until 1937 and later tests proved it too large for the engines available at the time. Boeing's labor, however, enabled the company to produce the prototype for the B-17 in 1935. |

# FOULOIS AND THE U.S. ARMY CORPS

XB-17　　　　　　　　Boeing started work on the prototype for this four-engine, midwing bomber in 1934 and first flew it in 1935. The plane's flying characteristics were outstanding for the time. It could carry 2,500 pounds of bombs 2,260 miles and could attack closer targets with up to 9,000 pounds of ordnance. Accepted by the military in January 1937 as the YB-17 Flying Fortress, the aircraft had a top speed of 256 miles-per-hour at 14,000 feet. Service ceiling was 30,600 feet. Loaded with 10,496 pounds of bombs, its maximum range was 1,377 miles.

XB-18　　　　　　　　Single-wing, twin-engine, medium bomber. Six crew. Maximum speed, 217 miles-per-hour at 10,000 feet. Service ceiling, 24,200 feet. Combat range, 1,200 miles. Armament: three .30-caliber machineguns in nose, ventral, and dorsal positions. Maximum bombload, 6,500 pounds.

# Bibliographic Note

Primary source material on the Air Corps during the early 1930s is abundant but requires digging to sort out what is pertinent. The Foulois Papers in the Manuscript Division, Library of Congress, offer a wealth of information about both the Army Air Corps and General Foulois. Other collections in the Manuscript Division, as noted below, are of less value for the 1931-35 period, although the Andrews Papers are quite good on the organization of the General Headquarters Air Force. Personal papers in the Albert F. Simpson Historical Research Center at Maxwell Air Force Base, Alabama, are well cataloged, but offer little of value for the period covered by this study. However, the center does contain a number of documents on the Air Corps and the Air Corps Tactical School, as well as extremely important interviews of Foulois. The Roosevelt Papers in the Franklin D. Roosevelt Library, Hyde Park, New York, have little of substance on the Air Corps between 1931 and 1935. The Operational Archives, Naval Historical Division, Washington, D.C., provides useful material on the Navy's views, particularly on the coast defense issue, in its Records of the General Board. The collections at the Air Force Academy Library are of marginal value for this period.

The National Archives contains a tremendous amount of Air Corps-related material, but it frequently requires paging through numerous documents to locate one or two that are applicable to 1931-35 military aviation history. This is especially true when dealing with The Adjutant General's Records (Record Group 407). The War Plans Division Numerical File (Record Group 165) contains a great deal of material on the Air Corps, and it is well indexed for easy use. WPD numbers 888 and 3798 are particularly valuable. The Army Air Forces Central Decimal File (Record Group 18) is loaded with significant documents but is not as well indexed. It uses The Adjutant General's numbering system and, while this is somewhat helpful, it still requires the researcher to check a multitude of entry numbers and to page through numerous inapplicable documents to locate pertinent ones. The most fruitful index numbers in this file are 032, 311.125, 321.9, 333.5, and 452.1. The most helpful entries within The Adjutant General's Files (Record Group 407) include 320.2, 352, 452.1, and 580. Record Group 255, Records of the Joint Board, is particularly disappointing, for it holds few documents relating to the 1931-35 years. Record Group 72, Bureau of Aeronautics Correspondence, is invaluable for the Navy's outlook on aviation matters. General Records of the Navy Department, Office of the Secretary (Record Group 80) is less useful from the aviation standpoint. Record Group 233 includes some of the transcripts of the 1934 secret hearings

# FOULOIS AND THE U.S. ARMY AIR CORPS

of Subcommittee Number 3 of the House Military Affairs Committee as well as subcommittee correspondence. However, the researcher needs to secure clearance from the Clerk of the House to view these documents—a task in itself.

## I. MANUSCRIPT COLLECTIONS

Annapolis, Maryland. United States Naval Academy, Nimitz Library.
  William Adger Moffett Papers.
Colorado Springs, Colorado. United States Air Force Academy Library.
  Benjamin D. Foulois Collection.
Hyde Park, New York. Franklin D. Roosevelt Library.
  Roosevelt Papers, Official Files 25 and 249.
Maxwell Air Force Base, Alabama. Albert F. Simpson Historical Research Center.
  Major General Benjamin D. Foulois Collection.
  Brigadier General Harold A. McGinnis Collection.
  Brigadier General H. Conger Pratt Collection.
  Major General Oscar Westover Papers.
  Lieutenant General Ennis C. Whitehead Collection.
Washington, D.C. Library of Congress, Manuscript Division.
  American Institute of Aeronautics and Astronautics Papers.
  Frank M. Andrews Papers.
  Henry H. Arnold Papers.
  Benjamin D. Foulois Papers.
  Ernest Joseph King Papers.
  William "Billy" Mitchell Papers.
  George Van Horn Moseley Papers.
  George S. Simonds Papers.
  Carl Spaatz Papers.

## II. PUBLIC RECORDS AND DOCUMENTS, UNPUBLISHED

Maxwell Air Force Base, Alabama. Albert F. Simpson Historical Research Center. Cataloged records of the Air Corps and Air Corps Tactical School as well as various interviews of General Foulois.
Washington, D.C. Center of Military History. United States Army.
  Army War College Lectures, 1935–36.
Washington, D.C. Library of Congress.
  "Annual Report of the Chief of the Air Corps" (annually, 1931–35). (Mimeographed).
  "Transcript of the Shorthand Report of Proceedings, Transactions and Testimony, before the Special Committee on the Army Air Corps and Air Mail." 1934. (Typescript).
Washington, D.C. National Archives.
  Record Group 18.
    Army Air Forces Central Decimal Files, 1917–1938.
    Army Air Forces General File, 1918–1935.
    Army Air Forces Air Mail Operations, 1934, File.
    Air Corps Circulars, 1924–1941.
    Air Corps Letters, 1926–1942.
    Headquarters Air Force Combat Command, 1935–1942.
      Secret Correspondence.

# BIBLIOGRAPHIC NOTE

Record Group 72.
 Bureau of Aeronautics, Confidential Correspondence, 1922-1944.
 Bureau of Aeronautics, General Correspondence, Secret, 1939-1942.
Record Group 80.
 General Records of the Navy Department, Office of the Secretary.
Record Group 107.
 Assistant Secretary of War for Air File.
Record Group 165.
 Army War College Instructional Records.
 War Plans Division Numerical File.
Record Group 225.
 Records of the Joint Board, 1903-1947.
Record Group 233.
 Records of the Military Affairs Committee, House of Representatives, relating to an investigation of the War Department, 1934-1936. (Preliminary Inventory No. 80).
Record Group 407.
 Adjutant General Central Files, 1926-1939.
Washington, D.C. Operational Archives. Naval History Division.
 Records of the General Board of the Navy.

## III. PUBLIC RECORDS AND DOCUMENTS, PUBLISHED

*Boards and Commissions*

Federal Aviation Commission. *Report of the Federal Aviation Commission.* Washington: Government Printing Office, 1935.
Joint Board of the Army and the Navy. *Joint Army and Navy Action in Coast Defense.* Washington: Government Printing Office, 1920.
Joint Board of the Army and the Navy. *Joint Action of the Army and the Navy.* Washington: Government Printing Office, 1927.
President's Aircraft Board. *Hearings before the President's Aircraft Board.* Washington: Government Printing Office, 1925.
*Report of the President's Aircraft Board.* Washington: Government Printing Office, 1925.

*U.S. Congress*

*Congressional Record,* Vols 75, 78, 79.
*House Committee on Appropriations*
 Hearings on War Department Appropriations Bill for 1933. 72d Cong, 1st sess, 1932.
 Hearings on War Department Appropriations Bill for 1934. 72d Cong, 2d sess, 1933.
 Hearings on War Department Appropriations Bill for 1935. 73d Cong, 2d sess, 1934.
 Hearings on War Department Appropriations Bill for 1936. 74th Cong, 1st sess, 1935.
*House Committee on Military Affairs*
 Hearings on H.R. 7041, 6810, 4348, 4336, 4351, 4911: To Promote National Defense by Increasing the Efficiency of the Air Corps. 74th Cong, 1st sess, 1936.
 Hearings on a United Air Service. 66th Cong, 2d sess, 1919.
*Other*
 House. Committee on Expenditures in the Executive Departments. *Hearings on H.R. 4742 and H.R. 7012: Department of National Defense.* 72d Cong, 1st sess, 1932.

315

# FOULOIS AND THE U.S. ARMY AIR CORPS

House. Committee on Naval Affairs. *Hearings on Sundry Legislation Affecting the Naval Establishments, 1933-34.* No. 6, 18. 73d Cong, 1st and 2d sess, 1934.
House. Committee on Post Offices and Post Roads. *Hearings on H.R.3, H.R. 8578, and other Air Mail Bills.* 73d Cong, 2d sess, 1934.
House. Select Committee of Inquiry into Operations of the United States Air Services. *Hearings on Matters Relating to the Operations of the United States Air Services.* 68th Cong, 1925.
House. *Investigation of Profiteering in Military Aircraft, under H. Res. 275.* H. Rept. No. 2060. 73d Cong, 2d sess, 1934.
House. *Investigation under House Resolution 275.* H. Rept. No. 1506. 73d Cong, 2d sess, 1934.
House. *Report of the Select Committee of Inquiry into Operations of the United States Air Services.* H. Rept. No. 1653. 68th Cong, 1925.

*Senate*

Committee on Appropriations. *Hearings on War Department Appropriations Bill for 1935.* 73d Cong, 2d sess, 1934.
Committee on Military Affairs. *Hearings on Reorganization of the Army.* 66th Cong, 2d sess, 1919.
Committee on Post Offices and Post Roads. *Hearings on S. 3012, A Bill to Revise the Air Mail Laws.* 73d Cong, 2d sess, 1934.
*Army Air Corps Stations and Frontier Defense Bases.* S. Rept. No. 888. 74th Cong, 1st sess, 1935.

*U.S. Departments*

Navy. *Annual Report of the Secretary of the Navy* (1933-1941). Washington: Government Printing Office, 1933-1941.
War. *Annual Report of the Secretary of War to the President* (1931-1936). Washington: Government Printing Office, 1931-1936.
_____. *Army Regulations 95-10.* Washington: Government Printing Office, 1928.
_____. *Field Service Regulations, United States Army, 1923.* Washington: Government Printing Office, 1924.
_____. *Final Report of War Department Special Committee on Army Air Corps.* Washington: Government Printing Office, 1934.
_____. *General Orders, Bulletins, and Circulars* (1932-1935). Washington: Government Printing Office, 1933-1936.

# IV. OFFICIAL STUDIES

*Army Air Forces Historical Studies: No. 25: Organization of Military Aeronautics, 1907-1935.* Washington: Historical Division, Assistant Chief of Air Staff, Intelligence, 1944.
*Army Air Forces Historical Studies: No. 39: Legislation Relating to the Air Corps Personnel and Training Program, 1907-1939.* Washington: AAF Historical Office, 1945.
*Army Air Forces Historical Studies: No. 50: Materiel Research and Development in the Army Air Arm, 1914-1945.* Washington: AAF Historical Office, 1946.
Craven, Wesley F., and Cate, James L., eds. *The Army Air Forces in World War II.* Vol I: *Plans and Early Operations, January 1939 to August 1942.* Chicago: University of Chicago Press, 1948.
Futrell, Robert Frank. *Ideas, Concepts, Doctrine: A History of Basic Thinking in the United States Air Force, 1907-1964.* Maxwell Air Force Base, Ala.: Air University, 1971.

# BIBLIOGRAPHIC NOTE

McClendon, R. Earl. *The Question of Autonomy for the U.S. Air Arm, 1907-1945.* Maxwell Air Force Base, Ala.: Documentary Research Division, Air University, 1950.

*USAF Historical Studies: No. 6: The Development of the Heavy Bomber.* Maxwell Air Force Base, Ala.: USAF Historical Division, Air University, 1951.

*USAF Historical Studies: No. 10: Organization of the Army Air Arm, 1935-1945.* Maxwell Air Force Base, Ala.: USAF Historical Division, Research Studies Institute, Air University, 1956.

*USAF Historical Studies: No. 89: Development of Air Doctrine in the Army Air Arm, 1917-1941.* Maxwell Air Force Base, Ala.: USAF Historical Division, Research Studies Institute, 1955.

*USAF Historical Studies: No. 100: History of the Air Corps Tactical School, 1920-1940.* Maxwell Air Force Base, Ala.: USAF Historical Division, Research Studies Institute, Air University, 1955.

Watson, Mark Skinner. *Chief of Staff: Prewar Plans and Preparations.* Washington: Government Printing Office, 1950.

## V. PUBLISHED MEMOIRS AND PAPERS

Arnold, Henry H. *Global Mission.* New York: Harper & Bros, 1949.

Chennault, Claire L. *Way of a Fighter: The Memoirs of Claire Lee Chennault.* New York: G. P. Putnam's Sons, 1949.

Farley, James A. *Jim Farley's Story: The Roosevelt Years.* New York: McGraw-Hill Book Co, 1948.

Foulois, Benjamin D., and Glines, Carroll V. *From the Wright Brothers to the Astronauts: The Memoirs of Major General Benjamin D. Foulois.* New York: McGraw-Hill Book Co, 1968.

Hoover, Herbert. *The Memoirs of Herbert Hoover.* 3 vols. New York: The Macmillan Co, 1951-1952.

Ickes, Harold L. *The Secret Diary of Harold L. Ickes: The First Thousand Days, 1933-1936.* New York: Simon & Schuster, 1953.

Myers, William S., ed. *The State Papers and Other Public Writings of Herbert Hoover.* 2 vols. Garden City: Doubleday, Doran & Co, 1934.

Patrick, Mason. *The United States in the Air.* Garden City: Doubleday, Doran & Co, 1928.

Rosenman, Samuel I., ed. *The Public Papers and Addresses of Franklin D. Roosevelt.* Vols II-IV. New York: Random House, 1938.

## VI. BOOKS

Borden, Norman E., Jr. *Air Mail Emergency—1934.* Freeport, Maine: Bond Wheelwright Co, 1968.

Caidin, Martin. *Air Force: A Pictorial History of American Airpower.* New York: Rinehart & Co, 1957.

Glines, Carroll V. *The Saga of the Air Mail.* Princeton: D. Van Nostrand Co, 1968.

Goldberg, Alfred, ed. *A History of the United States Air Force, 1907-1957.* Princeton: D. Van Nostrand Co, 1957.

Huie, William B. *The Fight for Air Power.* New York: L. B. Fischer, 1942.

Hurley, Alfred F. *Billy Mitchell: Crusader for Air Power.* New York: Franklin Watts, 1964.

James, D. Clayton. *The Years of MacArthur.* 2 vols. Boston: Houghton, Mifflin Co, 1970-1975.

King, Ernest J., and Whitehill, Walter M. *Fleet Admiral King: A Naval Record.* London: Eyre & Spottiswood, 1953.

# FOULOIS AND THE U.S. ARMY AIR CORPS

Levine, Isaac D. *Mitchell: Pioneer of Air Power.* New York: Duell, Sloan & Pearce, 1943.
Millis, Walter. *Arms and Men: A Study of American Military History.* New York: G. P. Putnam's Sons, 1956.
Mitchell, William. *Winged Defense.* New York: G. P. Putnam's Sons, 1925.
Nelson, Otto L., Jr. *National Security and the General Staff.* Washington: Infantry Journal Press, 1946.
Rutkowski, Edwin H. *The Politics of Military Aviation Procurement, 1926-1934: A Study in the Political Assertion of Consensual Values.* Columbus: Ohio State University Press, 1966.
Schlesinger, Arthur M., Jr. *The Coming of the New Deal.* Boston: Houghton, Mifflin Co, 1958.
Smith, Henry L. *Airways: The History of Commercial Aviation in the United States.* New York: Alfred A. Knopf, 1942.
Spencer, Francis A. *Air Mail Payment and the Government.* Washington: Brookings Institution, 1941.
Tillett, Paul. *The Army Flies the Mails.* Tuscaloosa: University of Alabama Press, 1955.
Weigley, Russell F. *History of the United States Army.* New York: Macmillan Co, 1967.
Wheeler, Gerald C. *Admiral William Veazie Pratt, U.S. Navy: A Sailor's Life.* Washington: Naval History Division, 1974.
Wood, Bruce. *The Making of the Good Neighbor Policy.* New York: Columbia University Press, 1961.

## VII. NEWSPAPERS AND PERIODICALS

*Aero Digest*, 1933-1935, Vols XXII-XXVII.
*Air Corps Newsletter*, 1931-1933, 1935, Vols XV-XVIII.
*Army and Navy Journal*, 1931-1936, Vols LXVIII-LXXIII.
*Army and Navy Register*, 1934-1935, Vols VIIIC-VC.
*Aviation*, 1931-1935, Vols XXX-XXXIV.
*New York Times*, May 1931-December 1935.
*U.S. Air Services*, 1931-1935, Vols XVI-XX.
*Washington Evening Star*, February-August 1934.
*Washington Post*, May 1931-December 1935.

## VIII. ARTICLES

"Between the Wars." *Air Force* XL (August 1957), 113-129.
Bonney, Walter T. "Chiefs of the Army Air Force." *Airpower Historian* VII (July 1960), 129-142.
Cate, James L. "Development of Air Doctrine, 1917-1941." *Air University Quarterly Review* I (Winter 1947), 11-22.
Crabbe, William M., Jr. "The Army Airmail Pilots' Reports." *Airpower Historian* IX (April 1962), 87-94, 128.
Downs, Eldon W. "Army and the Air Mail—1934." *Airpower Historian* IX (January 1962), 35-51.
Eaker, Ira C. " 'The Little Big One' or 'The Last of the First.' " *Aerospace Historian* XVII (Winter 1970), 140-43.
Finney, Robert T. "Early Air Corps Training and Tactics." *Military Affairs* XX (Fall 1956), 154-161.

# BIBLIOGRAPHIC NOTE

Foulois, Benjamin D. "America's Position in the Air." *National Aeronautic Magazine* XIII (October 1935), 12-13, 34.

──── . "Early Flying Experiences: Why Write a Book?—Part I." *Air Power Historian* II (April 1955), 17-35.

──── . "Early Flying Experiences: Why Write a Book?—Part II." *Air Power Historian* II (July 1955), 45-65.

──── . "Early Flying Experiences: Why Write a Book?—Part III." *Air Power Historian* III (April 1956), 114-133.

──── . "Past Failures—What to Do About Them." *U.S. Air Services* II (November 1919), 18-21.

Glines, Carroll V. "When the Air Corps Carried the Mail." *Air Force and Space Digest* LI (July 1968), 82-87.

Pegasus (pseud.). "The Forty-Year Split: The First Twenty Years, 1920-1940." *Army* XV (July 1965), 46-51.

Wilkins, Fred J. "One-Man Air Force." *Army Digest* XXV (March 1970), 38-41.

Williams, Edwin L., Jr. "Legislative History of the Air Arm." *Military Affairs* XX (Summer 1956), 81-93.

## IX. UNPUBLISHED MATERIALS

Cook, Gen Orval R., Ret. Letter to author, March 10, 1975.

Eaker, Lt Gen Ira C., Ret. Letter to author, January 22, 1975.

Eubank, Maj Gen Eugene L., Ret. Letter to author, April 4, 1975.

Flugel, Raymond R. "United States Air Power Doctrine: A Study of the Influence of William Mitchell and Giulio Douhet at the Air Corps Tactical School, 1921-1935." Ph.D. dissertation, University of Oklahoma, 1965.

Hansell, Maj Gen Haywood S., Jr., Ret. Letter to author, February 11, 1975.

Killigrew, John W. "The Impact of the Great Depression on the Army, 1929-1936." Ph.D. dissertation, University of Indiana, 1960.

Tate, James P. "The Army and Its Air Corps: A Study of the Evolution of the Army Policy Towards Aviation, 1919-1941." Ph.D. dissertation, University of Indiana, 1976.

Wilson, John R. M. "Herbert Hoover and the Armed Forces: A Study of Presidential Attitudes and Policy." Ph.D. dissertation, Northwestern University, 1971.

# Index

Accidents: 6, 109
Aero Squadron, 1st: 6-8
Aeronautics, Department of, proposed: 12, 15, 24
Air base squadrons: 210
Air bases
    construction programs: 31, 102, 111, 121, 249, 252, 262
    for GHQ Air Force: 249, 251-252
    station complement organization: 204. *See also* base squadrons strikes against: 66
Air Corps (*see also* Air Service; Aviation Section, Signal Corps; Foulois, Benjamin F.; Westover, Oscar)
    accidents in: 109
    activated: 25, 31
    air doctrine formulation: 31, 34-35, 40, 43-46, 61-75
    in airmail service. *See* Airmail service
    aircraft procurement and allotment. *See under* Aircraft
    autonomy movement: 11-17, 21-22, 24-29, 31, 76-81, 83-84, 90, 92-98, 171, 173, 176, 178, 189, 193-199, 202-203, 207, 209-210, 256-258, 263
    bombing demonstrations by: 18, 56-58
    budget control by: 80, 82-83, 97-98, 178, 181, 210, 259
    casualties in: 109
    Chief authorized: 31
    and Civilian Conservation Corps: 112
    and coast defense mission: 24, 46, 51-52, 54, 56-66, 132, 224, 256, 262-263
    and Coast Guard aviation control: 221
    command and control in: 31, 40, 42, 61-64, 86, 97, 263
    Congressional criticism of: 138, 141-144
    duty routine: 109
    efficiency, inquiry into: 194-195
    enlisted authorization and strength: 31-32, 102-103, 111, 122, 241-242
    and escort missions: 234
    expansion program: 31, 97, 102, 111
    flying cadets strength and shortages: 31, 33
    funding programs: 31, 33, 102-105, 107, 113-116, 120-124, 145, 148, 150, 152, 197, 236-237, 239, 254, 256, 258-259
    General Staff, representation on: 25, 31, 198, 252-253
    GHQ Air Force, views on: 97, 203
    interdiction missions: 70
    maneuvers by: 34-40, 112
    manpower expansion: 102
    Navy, cooperation with: 64-65
    officers' authorizations and strength: 31-33, 102, 107, 111, 116, 122, 241, 244, 248
    physical training program: 109
    pilots, strength and shortage: 32-33
    pay and allowances: 109, 244
    promotion policies and practices: 97, 109-110, 244, 246-248
    reconnaissance missions: 65, 67, 69-70, 72-74
    reserve officers use: 102-103, 242-243

# FOULOIS AND THE U.S. ARMY AIR CORPS

roles and missions agreements: 52-54, 86
safety measures: 135-136, 138-139, 145-146
safety records: 40
and strategic air operations: 256, 263
and tactical unit organization: 65, 85-86, 88, 111
Air Corps Act (1926): 97, 102, 104, 107, 111-112, 150-151, 154-155, 157, 160-169, 179, 195, 198-199, 236-237, 241-242, 245-246, 258
Air Corps Board: 253
Air Corps Tactical School
    and air arm autonomy: 203
    air doctrine formulation: 44-51, 216, 228
    on coast defense mission: 228
    on strategic air operations: 234
    on tactical air operations: 228
Air Corps Training Center: 35, 112, 128, 132, 182
Air Division, 1st: 87
Air doctrine formulation
    Air Corps views on: 31, 34-35, 40, 43-46, 51, 61-75
    Air Corps Tactical School views on: 44-51, 216, 228
    Andrews views on: 229
    Baker Board proposals: 198, 203
    Bradley views on: 229
    Drum Board proposals: 69, 93, 203, 225-226, 260
    Fechet views on: 45
    Foulois views on: 3, 6, 16-17, 45-46, 48, 61-63, 65, 77, 84, 86, 120-121, 189, 228-229, 256
    Hughes views on: 229
    Kenney views on: 47-48
    Kilbourne views on: 226, 228-229
    MacArthur views on: 225-226
    Patrick views on: 22-23
    War Department views on: 84-85, 95, 212-213, 225-229, 257-263
Air-drop missions: 112
Air-ground communications, first: 3
Air Mail Act (1934): 169, 200
Air Service (*see also* Air Corps; Aviation Section, Signal Corps)
Air Service
    autonomy movement: 11-12
    aviation cadets strength: 18, 23
    becomes Air Corps: 25, 31
    Chief authorized: 17-18
    coast defense mission: 24
    combat arm status: 17
    command and control in: 12, 15, 17-18
    enlisted strength: 15, 17-18, 23
    officer strength: 12, 15, 17-18, 23
    tactical unit organization: 17-18
    World War I experience: 11
Air Service Field Officers School: 44
Air superiority, maintaining: 11, 46-47, 69
Aircraft
    allotments. (*See* procurement and allotment, *below*)

# INDEX

altitude capabilities, advances in: 50
beacon guidance for: 131
bombers. *See* Aircraft types
bombload capacities: 11, 43, 50, 72, 231-232
characteristics sought in: 131
combat range capabilities: 11, 50, 72, 231-232
command and control of: 17-18, 52, 61-62
design development programs: 50, 229-232, 256, 260, 263
dirigible, first acquired: 2
fire direction and control by: 11, 61
instrumentation: 127, 130-132, 136-139, 146-147, 149
land-based, controversy over: 52-56, 70, 72
landing lights for: 131
maintenance and repair: 6, 136, 140, 146-147, 204, 210
mapping, use in: 3, 216-219
night flying equipment: 127, 131
number requested and allotted: 23, 31-32, 67-68, 70, 97, 102-105, 111, 117-122, 172, 236
number serviceable: 8, 18, 31-32, 102-103, 111, 117, 119, 120, 122-123
observation, use in: 3
performance, advances in: 50
photography, use in: 3
procurement and allotment: 2-8, 24-25, 32-33, 67-70, 95-96, 102, 104, 106, 114, 117, 119-124, 141, 150-181, 185-186, 190-191, 233-241, 254, 257, 260, 262-263
radio equipment in: 3, 64, 130-131, 136, 146, 149, 173, 178
in reconnaissance missions: 3, 11
seatbelt introduced: 3
shortages in: 31-32
speed requirements and performances: 50, 155, 231
types. *See* Aircraft types
weather service for: 131
wheels introduced: 3
Aircraft types
   A-3: 38
   A-12: 135
   amphibians: 72-73, 232
   B-2: 37-38, 143
   B-6: 137, 141
   B-7: 135
   B-9: 49-50
   B-10: 49-50, 148, 216-219
   B-17: 229-230, 234, 263-264
   B-18A: 235
   DC-2: 136
   experimental: 151-153, 155, 231-233
   JN-2: 7
   O-19: 142
   P-12: 143
   P-26: 167-168
   SE-5: 30
   types requested and allotted: 118, 121-122
   Wright B: 4

XB-12: 231
XB-15: 231, 232
XB-17: 231-233
XB-18: 231, 233
XB-19: 231-233
Airfields. *See* Air bases
Airline Pilots Association: 141
Airmail service: 120, 124, 231. *See also* Aircraft; Pilots
  administration facilities: 136
  aircraft, number assigned: 130
  aircraft, suitability for: 133
  airfields for: 130
  altitude limitations in: 135
  Andrews role in: 132
  Arnold role in: 128, 136, 146
  Baker Board views on: 199
  Branch role in: 125-127, 129-130, 149, 182
  casualties in: 135, 137-138, 141-144, 146-148, 193
  command and control in: 128
  Congressional action on: 125, 128-129, 140, 147-148, 156, 160-161
  costs of operations: 148
  Dern role in: 124, 126, 128, 144-147, 194
  Drum role in: 126-129
  enlisted strength in: 128, 130
  equipment required and assigned: 131
  Farley role in: 125, 129-130, 149
  Foulois role in: 125-136, 139-147, 149, 171, 176, 178-180, 182, 190-191, 253, 257, 265
  funding for: 129-130
  ground crews in: 140
  headquarters centers: 128
  Hickam role in: 128, 136, 141, 146
  Ickes role in: 126
  Jones role in: 128, 136, 146
  MacArthur role in: 126-127, 144-145
  mileage logged: 130, 145, 147
  officers, number assigned: 128
  pilots, number assigned: 130, 132-133
  planning for: 130-131
  political issues in: 125-126, 138-139
  reserve officers in: 128, 132-133, 140
  Rogers role in: 171, 176, 178-180, 182
  Roosevelt role in: 124-128, 132, 134, 138-139, 141-148, 257
  safety measures in: 135-136, 138-139, 145-146
  sorties completed: 148
  supply system in: 136
  War Department role in: 127, 129, 140
  weather encountered: 132, 135, 137-144, 147, 149
  Westover role in: 128, 130, 147
Alaska defenses: 65, 69, 216-219, 250-251
Allen, James: 3
Altitude capabilities, advances in: 50
Ammunition shortages: 112

# INDEX

Amphibian aircraft units: 122
Anchorage, Alaska: 217
Anderson, Orvil A.: 28
Andrews, Frank M.: 264
   on air base construction: 252
   and air doctrine formulation: 229
   on aircraft procurement: 233, 239-240
   and airmail service: 132
   and Civilian Conservation Corps: 112
   on coast defense mission: 217, 224
   on command and control: 209-210
   commands GHQ Air Force: 206-208, 246
   and Navy land-based aircraft: 224
   on officer authorizations and strength: 243-244
Antisubmarine missions: 222
Army. *See* United States Army; War Department
Army-Navy Joint Board: 23, 52-53, 63-64, 71, 77, 222-223, 225, 227, 229
*Army and Navy Journal*: 54-55, 97, 114, 163, 184
Arnold, Henry H.: 39
   on air arm autonomy: 16, 207
   in airmail service: 128, 136, 146
   appointed Assistant Chief of Air Corps: 254
   and bombing demonstrations: 58
   and Civilian Conservation Corps: 112
   as Foulois successor: 254
   on pilots capabilities: 135
   and promotion proposals: 248-249
   on strategic air operations: 215
   Washington-to-Alaska flight: 216-219
Around-the-world flight (1924): 28
Artificial horizon: 131-132
Artillery branch. *See* Ground forces
Assistant Chief of Air Corps. *See* Westover, Oscar
Assistant Chief of Staff, G-1: 249
Assistant Chief of Staff, G-3. *See* Hughes, John H.
Assistant Chief of Staff, G-4. *See* Callan, Robert E.
Assistant Secretary of War. *See* Woodring, Harry H.
Assistant Secretary of War for Air (*see also* Davison, F. Trubee)
   authorized: 25, 31
   controversy over office: 81-82, 173, 198
Associated Press: 127
Atlantic region defenses: 69
Attack units organization: 65, 111, 122
Attorney General. *See* Cummings, Homer S.; Mitchell, James
Aviation cadets. *See* Flying cadets
Aviation Section, Signal Corps: 6


Baker, Newton D.: 12, 14, 194-195. *See also* Baker Board; War Department Baker Board
   (1934)
   on air arm autonomy: 194-198
   on air base construction: 249

# FOULOIS AND THE U.S. ARMY AIR CORPS

    Air Corps efficiency inquiry: 194-195
    on air doctrine formulation: 198, 203
    and air representation on General Staff: 198, 252-253
    on aircraft allotment: 198
    on aircraft procurement: 169, 237, 241
    on airmail service: 199
    appointed: 100, 148, 193
    and Assistant Secretary of War for Air: 198
    on coast defense mission: 220, 222
    on command and control: 198-199
    Dern reaction to report: 199
    Federal Aviation Commission reaction to report: 201, 204
    and Foulois competence inquiry: 183, 185-186, 190
    Foulois reaction to report: 199-200
    on GHQ Air Force: 198-199, 205-206, 259
    promotion proposals: 199, 245, 248-249
    on reserve officers training: 242
    on strategic air operations: 214-216
    on training programs: 198-199
    War Department reaction to report: 199, 201-202, 260
Baldwin, Hanson W.: 58
Barksdale Field, La.: 111
Bases. *See* Air bases
Beacon guidance: 131
Bingham, Hiram: 39
Black, Hugo L.: 125, 156
Blind flying. *See* Instrument flying; Night flying
Boeing, William E.: 156
Boeing Airplane Corporation: 153, 163, 167, 231-232
Bogen, William L.: 82
Bolling Field: 14, 59, 94, 206, 217, 219
Bombardment Brigade, 1st: 90, 93-94
Bombardment Groups
    2d: 112
    19th: 59
Bombardment training: 112
Bombardment units organization: 65, 111, 122
Bombing demonstrations: 18, 58-58
Bombing missions. *See* Strategic air operations
Bombload capacities: 11, 43, 50, 72, 231-232
Bombsight design development: 234
Boston, Mass.: 137
Bradley, Follett: 196, 207, 229
Branch, Harllee: 125-127, 129-130, 149, 182
Brown, Albert E.: 195
Brown, Arthur W.
    aircraft procurement rulings: 151-153, 161-165, 167-169, 181
    promotion rulings: 246
Brown, Walter F.: 125, 138
Browning, William S.: 210
Bureau of the Budget. *See* Douglas, Lewis W.
Burwell, Harvey (Henry B. S.): 197

# INDEX

Byrd Field, Va.: 136
Byrns, Joseph W.: 76, 106

California air maneuvers: 112
Callan, Robert E.: 73, 124, 172
Canada: 69, 252
Canal Zone
    air bases in: 250
    air unit assignments: 31, 65, 111
    naval land-based aviation in: 53
Carberry, Joseph E.: 7
Carrier-borne aircraft: 66
Casas Grandes, Mexico: 7
Casualties: 2, 109, 135, 137-138, 141-144, 148, 193
Chamberlin, Clarence D.: 193-194
Chaney, James E.: 66, 117
Cheney Award: 82
Chesapeake Bay defenses: 65
Cheyenne, Wyo.: 136, 141, 147
Chicago, Ill.: 128, 136, 146
Chief of Air Corps. *See* Fechet, James E.; Foulois, Benjamin F.; Westover, Oscar
Chief of Air Corps
    authorized: 31
    lieutenant general grade for: 97, 163
    office organization: 41, 261
Chief of Air Service: 17. *See also* Patrick, Mason M.
Chief of Coast Artillery: 60. *See also* Gulick, John W.
Chief of Finance: 129
Chief of Staff, U.S. Army. *See* Craig, Malin; MacArthur, Douglas
Civilian Conservation Corps: 110, 112, 115
Cleveland, Ohio: 141
Close air support. *See* Tactical air support
Coast defense mission
    Air Corps views on: 24, 46, 51-52, 54, 56-66, 132, 224, 256, 262-263
    Air Corps Tactical School views on: 228
    Air Service in: 24
    Andrews views on: 217, 224
    Baker Board proposals: 220, 222
    Baldwin views on: 58
    Chaney views on: 66
    Davison views on: 54
    Dern views on: 99
    Drum views on: 73
    Drum Board proposals: 68-70, 222
    Fechet views on: 60
    Federal Aviation Commission views on: 223
    Foulois views on: 56, 58-65, 68-70, 74, 83, 92, 116, 221, 257, 259
    GHQ Air Force role in: 216-217, 222, 228-229
    Gulick views on: 68, 95
    Hoover views on: 54
    Hurley views on: 54
    Kilbourne views on: 63-65, 68, 70, 74

# FOULOIS AND THE U.S. ARMY AIR CORPS

    King views on: 72, 224
    MacArthur views on: 54-55, 59-60, 64-66, 71, 74, 92, 221-223, 259-260
    Mitchell views on: 52
    Moffett views on: 53-54, 56, 72
    Navy views on: 51-52, 61, 63, 65, 70-72, 220-225, 262
    Patrick views on: 52
    Pratt views on: 54-55, 71, 259
    Simonds views on: 72, 220
  Standley views on: 72, 220
    training programs: 59-60, 132
    War Department views on: 51-54, 59-63, 74, 92, 212, 220-225, 227, 259-260
  Collins, Ross A.
    on air arm autonomy: 84
    on Air Corps funding: 114
    on aircraft procurement: 158, 160-161
    and Army manpower cuts: 106-107
  Columbia Broadcasting System: 139
  Columbus, Ohio: 136
  Combat range capabilities: 11, 50, 72, 231-232
  Command and control
    Air Corps views on: 31, 40, 42, 61-64, 86, 97, 263
    in Air Service: 12, 15, 17-18
    of aircraft: 17-18, 52, 61-62
    Andrews views on: 209-210
    in Army: 87
    aviation, issues in: 11
    Baker Board proposals: 198-199
    Craig views on: 210
    Drum views on: 90, 95, 206
    Fickel views on: 95-96
    Foulois views on: 15, 42, 63, 77-78, 85, 88-90, 93, 95, 97-98, 128, 206, 209-210, 213-214, 259
    by GHQ Air Force: 64, 87-90, 204-207, 209-211, 225
    Inspector General views on: 210
    Kilbourne views on: 89-90, 95, 213
    MacArthur views on: 94, 214
    Patrick views on: 23-24
    Pershing views on: 9, 11-12
    of schools: 87-88, 90
    Simonds views on: 209
    War Department views on: 17-18, 23, 31, 52, 85-87, 90-93, 206, 210-211, 226, 259
    Westover views on: 210, 213-214
    Wilson views on: 11
  Commerce, Department of: 126, 128, 130-131, 133
  Communications systems, first: 3
  Composite units organization: 65
  Comptroller General. *See* McCarl, John R.
  Congress (*see also members by name*)
    on air arm autonomy: 15-17, 21, 24-25, 76-80, 90
    on air base construction: 250-252
    Air Corps criticized by: 138, 141-144
    and Air Corps funding: 31, 150, 237, 239, 254

# INDEX

and aircraft procurement: 120, 141, 150, 156-169, 171-172, 174-176, 185, 238-241, 254, 262
and airmail service: 128-129, 140, 147-148, 160-161
and Army expansion: 32, 262
committees and subcommittees. *See under name of chairman*
and defense appropriations: 101-103, 105-108, 113, 262
and Defense Department organization: 76-78, 83, 90
and flight pay: 115
Foulois relations with: 9
and mandatory furlough program: 115
manpower authorizations: 242, 244
and Navy Air expansion: 122-123
and Navy aircraft procurement: 166
pay legislation by: 115, 244
promotion legislation by: 247-249, 262
and reserve officers training: 242, 262
Consolidated Aircraft Corporation: 153, 159, 161
Continental United States, air units assignments: 31, 111
Contract awards. *See* Aircraft, procurement and allotment
Cook Inlet, Alaska: 217
Coolidge, Calvin: 21, 25, 31-32
Craig, Malin
  on aircraft procurement: 234
  appointed Chief of Staff: 208
  on command and control: 210
  and GHQ Air Force: 208
  and Navy land-based aircraft: 224
  on strategic air operations: 234
  on tactical air support: 260
Crain, James K.: 154-155
Cross-country flights: 3, 136-137, 148
Crowell, Benedict: 12
Crowley, Karl A.: 125
Cuban political crisis: 92-94
Cummings, Homer S.: 125, 169
Curry, John F.: 214-215
Curtiss Co.: 174
Curtiss-Wright Corporation: 154, 161, 163, 174

Dargue, Herbert A.: 7, 57
Davison, F. Trubee: 32, 39, 60
  on aircraft procurement and allotment: 114, 150, 152
  on coast defense mission: 54
  and Foulois appointment: 40
  on promotion policies: 245
  resignation: 81
  and training programs: 112-113
  and Westover appointment: 42
Dayton, Ohio: 232
Daytona Beach, Fla.: 141
Defense, Department of, proposed: 24, 29-31, 76-81, 83-84, 90, 96-98, 116
Denver, Colo.: 143
Depots. *See* Supply system

Deputy Chief of Staff. *See* Drum, Hugh A.; Moseley, George Van Horn; Simonds, George S.
Dern, George H.
   on air arm autonomy: 96, 99, 193-195
   on air base construction: 251
   on aircraft procurement: 119-120, 151-152, 167-169, 238-241
   airmail service, role in: 124, 126, 128, 144-147, 194
   and Assistant Secretary of War for Air: 81-82
   on Baker Board proposals: 199
   on coast defense mission: 99
   and defense budget: 115
   on Federal Aviation Commission report: 201
   and Foulois competence inquiry: 185-187, 190-192
   Foulois reprimand by: 191
   and promotion policies: 248
   on Washington-to-Alaska flight: 219
Deshler, Ohio: 137
Design development programs: 50, 229-232, 256, 263
Detroit air races (1922): 22
Dietz, Harold L.: 137
Directional gyroscope: 131-132
Dirigible, first acquisition: 2
Dodd, Roy D.: 82
Doolittle, James H.: 195, 199
Douglas, Lewis W.
   and Air Corps funding: 96, 103-105, 113, 181, 191, 236-239
   and airmail service funding: 129
   and coast defense mission funding: 60
   and officer strength reduction: 118
   and War Department funding: 114-116
Douglas Aircraft Company: 163, 231
Douhet, Giulio: 47-48, 84
Drum, Hugh A.: 91
   on air arm autonomy: 195
   on air base construction: 249
   and aircraft procurement: 118-119, 123-124, 172, 237-239
   airmail service, role in: 126-129
   and coast defense mission: 73
   on command and control: 90, 95, 206
   on Defense Department proposal: 83-84
   and Federal Aviation Commission report: 201
   on Foulois competence: 176-178, 181, 189-190
   on GHQ Air Force: 94-95, 206
   on officer authorizations: 243
   on reconnaissance mission: 222
   on tactical units organization: 85
Drum Board (1933)
   on air arm autonomy: 193, 195
   on air base construction: 249-250
   on air doctrine formulation: 69, 93, 203, 225-226, 260
   on aircraft allotments: 68, 121-122
   appointed: 121

## INDEX

on coast defense mission: 68-70, 222
Foulois on procedures: 172-174, 181
on GHQ Air Force: 94-96
MacArthur reaction to: 70, 121
on tactical air operations: 69-70
on tactical units organization: 122

Eastman, James Y.: 135
Escort missions: 234
Eubanks, Eugene: 28

Fairbanks, Alaska: 217-218
Fairfield Air Depot, Ohio: 37
Farley, James A.: 125, 129-130, 149
Fechet, James E.: 60
   on air base construction: 250
   on air doctrine formulation: 45
   appointed Assistant Chief of Air Corps: 34
   and bombing demonstrations: 57
   on coast defense mission: 60
   retirement: 40
Federal Aviation Commission
   aeronautics administration study: 199-204
   on air arm autonomy: 203-204
   on air base construction: 250
   on aircraft procurement: 169
   on Baker Board proposals: 201, 204
   on coast defense mission: 223
   Dern reaction to: 201
   Drum reaction to: 201
   on GHQ Air Force: 204
   Kilbourne reaction to: 201-202
   MacArthur reaction to: 201-202
   Moseley reaction to: 201
   Navy reaction to: 201
   on promotion policies: 245
   on strategic air operations: 216
   War Department reaction to: 201-204, 258
Federal Employment Stabilization Board: 119
Federal Reserve Bank: 126
Fess, Simeon D.: 144
Fickel, Jacob E.: 95-96
Fire direction and control by aircraft: 11, 61
First air-to-ground communications: 3
First casualty: 2
First tactical unit: 6-8
Fish, Hamilton, Jr.: 141
Fleet, Reuben H.: 159
Flight pay. *See* Officers; Pay and allowances; Pilots
Flight records
   around-the-world: 28
   cross-country: 3, 136-137, 148
   by Foulois: 3

# FOULOIS AND THE U.S. ARMY AIR CORPS

    Juneau-to-Seattle: 217
    Seattle-to-Dayton: 231-232
    Washington-to-Alaska: 216-219
Flight training. *See* Training programs
Flying cadets
    strength and shortages: 18, 23, 31, 33
    training programs: 122
Florida defenses: 65, 69
Fort Defiance, Ariz.: 113
Fort Myer, Va.: 2
Fort Sam Houston, Texas: 5
Foulois, Benjamin F.: 60, 82
    accomplishments reviewed: 256-257, 263-264
    on air arm autonomy: 11-16, 25-29, 76-79, 83-84, 92, 98, 171, 173, 176, 178, 189, 197, 202, 210, 256-257
    as air attaché: 18
    on air base construction: 249-251
    on Air Corps Board assignments: 253
    on Air Corps budget control: 80, 98, 178, 181, 210, 259
    and Air Corps funding: 102-105, 107, 114-116, 150, 152, 197, 254, 256, 259
    on air doctrine formulation: 3, 6, 16-17, 45-46, 48, 61-63, 65, 77, 84, 86, 120-121, 189, 228-229, 256
    on aircraft allotments: 172-173, 202
    and aircraft design development: 231-232, 256
    aircraft evaluation and modifications by: 2-3
    and aircraft procurement: 67-68, 95-96, 106, 114, 117-124, 150-175, 178-181, 185-186, 190-191, 233, 236-237, 239-241, 257
    airmail service, role in: 125-136, 139-147, 149, 171, 176, 178-180, 182, 190-191, 253, 257, 265
    on amphibian aircraft: 72-73, 232
    appointed Assistant Chief of Air Corps: 34
    appointed Chief of Air Corps: 40
    on Arnold as successor: 254
    on Assistant Secretary of War for Air: 83, 173
    aviation expansion plans: 8-9
    Aviation Section assignment: 8
    on Baker Board proposals: 199-200
    on bombing demonstration: 57-58
    on casualty rates: 146-147
    on coast defense mission: 56, 58-65, 68-70, 74, 83, 92, 116, 221, 257, 259
    on command and control: 15, 42, 63, 77-78, 85, 88-90, 93, 95, 97-98, 128, 206, 209-210, 213-214, 259
    commands maneuvers: 34-40
    on commercial pilots: 140-141
    communications systems development: 3
    competence, inquiry on: 171-192, 254, 257, 263
    Congress, relations with: 9
    on Cuban crisis: 93
    on Defense Department proposal: 76-79, 83-84, 98
    and detail system: 15
    on Drum Board procedures: 172-174, 181
    early flying experience: 2

# INDEX

early service and commissioning: 1-2
as first pilot: 3-4
first crash: 3
first solo flight: 3
on flight pay: 115
flight records by: 3
flight training: 2-3
flying activity: 91
General Staff, relations with: 8-9, 171-178, 181, 189-192, 254, 257-258, 263
on GHQ Air Force: 89-90, 92-95, 171-172, 197-198, 200, 206-208, 256-257, 259
on instrument flying: 132-133
instrument flying by: 131
Kilbourne, relations with: 62, 91
lobbying by: 34, 40, 98, 260
Mackay Trophy award: 39-40
maintenance and repair by: 6
and maneuvers program: 253
material, stress on: 106
and material procurement: 173, 178
in Mexican Punitive Expedition: 3, 6-8
as Mitchel Field commander: 30, 34
Mitchell, relations with: 9-11, 21
on naval air superiority: 70
on officer authorizations and strength: 117, 241, 243
Pershing, relations with: 9
personal traits: 10-11, 184, 263-265
on physical training programs: 109
pilots capabilities, defense of: 132, 139, 145, 148, 171, 180, 182
promotion: 110
on promotion proposals: 98, 110, 173, 244-249
on radio procurement: 173, 178
on reconnaissance mission: 63, 221
relief recommended: 183, 185-187, 254
reprimanded: 191
on reserve officers pay: 173
on reserve officers training: 242-243
on roles and missions: 77, 86
retirement: 192, 254-255
Roosevelt criticism of: 139, 144-145, 185
safety measures, stress on: 135-136, 138-139, 145-146
on school attendance: 243
Signal Corps assignment: 2
on strategic air operations: 258
on tactical units organization: 63-69, 88-90, 92-93, 95, 111, 122, 217-219
training programs: 6, 59, 89, 113-114, 136, 149, 180, 182, 253, 263
and Washington-to-Alaska flight: 217, 219
work habits: 91, 263-265
World War I experience: 9-11
Four-army plan: 64, 66, 86-87, 92-93
Frank, Walter H.: 195-196
Fremont, Ohio: 138
Furlough program: 108, 115

# FOULOIS AND THE U.S. ARMY AIR CORPS

General Board, U.S. Navy: 24, 70
General Headquarters, Air Force *(see also* Andrews, Frank M.)
    activation: 93-94, 100, 256
    air bases for: 249, 251-252
    Air Corps views on: 97, 203
    aircraft allotments: 69, 172, 239-240
    and antisubmarine mission: 222
    Baker Board proposals: 198-199, 205-206, 259
    and coast defense mission: 216-217, 222, 228-229
    command and control: 64, 87-90, 204-207, 209-211, 225
    Craig views on: 208
    Drum proposals for: 94-95, 206
    Drum Board proposals for: 94-96
    Federal Aviation Commission views on: 204
    Foulois views on: 89-90, 92-95, 171-172, 197-198, 200, 206-208, 256-257, 259
    inception: 85-86
    Kilbourne views on: 89, 195
    Langley Field as headquarters: 206
    MacArthur views on: 92, 94-96, 123, 207, 214, 222, 226-227, 260
    maneuvers by: 253
    McSwain views on: 123, 156
    Moseley views on: 87
    Navy views on: 223, 225
    officers authorization and strength: 243-244
    organization: 204-205
    promotions in: 246
    and reconnaissance missions: 222-223
    in strategic air operations: 202-203, 213, 216-217, 262
    in tactical air operations: 62-63, 67, 69, 207, 212-213, 216, 224, 229
    War Department views on: 86, 88, 92-96, 98-100, 171-172, 195, 203-207, 210, 212, 220, 225, 259
    Westover views on: 94, 208, 210
General Staff, War Department. See Kilbourne, Charles E.; MacArthur, Douglas; War Department
George, Harold L.: 203
Giles, Barney M.: 264
Gilmore, William E.: 34
Goss, Edward W.: 162-163, 174
Great Lakes defenses: 35, 67
GREEN war plan: 67, 120
Grenier, Jean D.: 135
Ground crews training: 6
Ground forces
    air components control: 17, 22-23, 85
    air support of. See Strategic air operations; Tactical air operations
    reorganizations: 17-18, 64, 66
    troop shortages: 33
Groups organization: 111
Gulick, John W.: 60, 177
    on coast defense mission: 68, 95
    on Drum Board procedure: 176, 181
    on Foulois competence: 176, 189
Gunnery training: 112

# INDEX

Harbor Defense Board: 60-61, 63, 67, 249, 259
Harding, Warren G.: 21
Hawaii
    air bases in: 250
    air unit assignments: 31, 65, 111
    naval land-based aviation in: 53
Hickam, Horace M.: 30
    on air arm autonomy: 29
    airmail service, role in: 128, 136, 141, 146
Hill, Joseph Lister
    on airmail casualties: 179
    and Foulois competence inquiry: 178, 180, 188
Hoover, Herbert
    on air arm autonomy: 76, 78
    and Air Corps maneuvers: 35
    and Army expansion: 33
    and Assistant Secretary of War for Air: 81
    on coast defense mission: 54
    and Defense Department proposal: 76, 78, 81
    defense policies and funding: 43, 101, 103-104, 108, 111-112, 262
    and Foulois appointment: 40
    mandatory furlough plan: 108
Hopi, resupply of: 112
House of Representatives. *See* Congress
Housing construction programs: 102, 118, 121
Howell, Clark: 200, 204. *See also* Federal Aviation Commission
Hughes, John H.: 229, 245-246
Humphreys, Frederic E.: 3
Hurley, Patrick J.: 54, 104-105, 134

Ickes, Harold L.: 126, 155
Indians, air resupply of: 112
Infantry branch. *See* Ground forces
Inspector General
    on command and control: 210
    Foulois competence inquiry: 188-192, 228, 257
Instrument flying: 145
    Foulois stress on: 131-133
    training programs: 131-133, 135-136, 147-149, 198, 253, 263
Interdiction missions: 70
Instrumentation in aircraft: 127, 130-132, 136-139, 146-147, 149

James, William F.: 157, 176
Japan, potential war with: 67, 69, 120
Jerome, Idaho: 135
Joint Board. *See* Army-Navy Joint Board
Jones, Byron Q.:
    airmail service, role in: 128, 136, 146
    on pilots capabilities: 135
Judge Advocate General. *See* Brown, Arthur W.
Juneau-to Seattle flight: 217

# FOULOIS AND THE U.S. ARMY AIR CORPS

Kenney, George C.: 47-48
Kentucky air maneuvers: 112
Kilbourne, Charles E.: 177
    on air arm autonomy: 83, 195, 202
    on air base construction: 250-252
    on Air Corps funding: 117, 258
    on air doctrine formulation: 226, 228-229
    and aircraft procurement: 67-68, 118-120, 123, 176
    on amphibian aircraft: 72-73
    on coast defense mission: 63-65, 68, 70, 74
    on command and control: 89-90, 95, 213
    on Defense Department proposal: 83
    on Drum Board procedure: 181
    on Federal Aviation Commission proposals: 201-202
    Foulois, relations with: 62, 91
    on Foulois competence: 176-178, 189
    on GHQ Air Force: 89, 195
    and naval air superiority: 70
    on officer authorizations and strength: 117-118
    on reconnaissance missions: 73-74, 213, 222
    on schools control: 90
    on strategic air operations: 202-203, 213, 260
    on tactical air operations: 51, 62-63, 213, 260
    on tactical units organization: 88-89
King, Ernest J.: 71
    on aircraft procurement: 166
    on coast defense mission: 72, 224
    on land-based patrol aircraft: 220-221, 224
    on manufacturers profits: 156
Kvale, Paul J.: 157, 179-180, 185

Lahm, Frank P.: 3
Lampert Committee (1924): 24-25, 29, 31
Landing lights: 131
Langley Field, Va.: 44, 90, 93
    air unit assignments: 90, 93-94, 111
    and bombing demonstrations: 18, 56-58
    as GHQ Air Force headquarters: 206
    navigation school: 132, 136
Las Vegas, Nevada: 142
Lassiter Board (1923): 23-24, 84, 94-95, 259
*Lexington* USS: 71
Lindbergh, Charles A.: 134, 193-194
Lines of communication, strikes against: 11, 66
Lobbying activities: 156, 159-160
Lowry, Durward O.: 137

MacArthur, Douglas: 80
    on air arm autonomy: 78-80, 207
    on air base construction: 251
    Air Corps, confidence in: 127
    on Air Corps capabilities: 127

# INDEX

    on Air Corps funding: 104, 115, 123-124, 237, 239, 258
    and Air Corps maneuvers: 35
    on air doctrine formulation: 225-226
    on aircraft allotments: 172
    on aircraft procurement: 68, 102, 104, 122-123, 157-158, 180, 238-239, 260
    airmail service, role in: 126-127, 144-145
    on Assistant Secretary of War for Air: 81-82
    on budget allotments: 101-102, 105-106, 112-115
    on coast defense mission: 54-55, 59-60, 64-66, 71, 74, 92, 221-223, 259-260
    on Coast Guard aviation control: 221
    on command and control: 94, 214
    and Defense Department proposal: 78
    and Drum Board report: 70, 121
    and Federal Aviation Commission report: 201-202
    and Foulois competence inquiry: 187-188
    on four-army plan: 87
    on GHQ Air Force: 92, 94-96, 123, 207, 214, 222, 226-227, 260
    and mandatory furlough plan: 114-115
    on manpower reductions: 106-107
    manpower, stress on: 240
    on officers authorizations and strength: 117, 242
    on pay and promotion: 108, 244, 247
    on reconnaissance missions: 64, 72, 223, 260
    on roles and missions: 214, 220, 222
    Roosevelt criticism of: 144
    on strategic air operations: 217-220, 226-227, 260
    on tactical air operations: 61, 96, 120, 214, 220, 226-227, 260
    on tactical units organization: 66, 96
    training, stress on: 106
    and Westover appointment: 42
MacArthur-Pratt agreement: 54-56, 60, 63, 70-72, 74, 221-222, 259
MacDill, Leslie: 118-119
Maintenance and repair: 6, 136, 140, 146-147, 204, 210
Mackay Trophy award: 39-40
Maneuvers by Air Corps: 34-40, 112, 253
Manufacturers. *See* Aircraft, procurement and allotment
Mapping, aircraft role in: 3, 216-219
March Field, Calif.: 111, 143
Martin, Charles H.: 77-78
Martin, James V.: 159
Martin (Glenn L.) Company: 153, 159, 167, 231
Martin Aircraft Company of New Jersey: 159
Maxwell Field, Ala.: 44, 196. *See also* Air Corps Tactical School
McCarl, John R.: 165-167
McSwain, John J.: 78
    air arm autonomy legislation: 78-79, 96-100, 122, 124, 156, 163, 171, 173, 176, 193, 195, 201, 207, 231, 262
    on aircraft procurement: 120, 141, 156-160, 169, 172, 175, 239-240
    Defense Department legislation: 83-84, 96-97, 116
    on Foulois competence: 189, 191
    on GHQ Air Force: 123, 156
    on officer authorizations and strength: 107, 116-118

promotion legislation: 244, 247-248
pilots capabilities, defense of: 138, 141
Mechanics. *See* Ground crews
Menoher, Charles T.: 12, 14, 17
Mexican Punitive Expedition: 3, 6-8
Mexico, potential war with: 67, 86
Miami, Fla.: 252
Mitchel Field, N.Y.: 132, 146
Mitchell, James: 32
Mitchell, William: 22, 28
    and air arm autonomy: 16-19, 21-22, 24-29, 81
    on aircraft procurement: 156
    and bombing demonstration: 18
    on coast defense mission: 52
    court-martial and resignation: 21, 25, 31
    criticism of authorities: 25, 29
    and Defense Department proposal: 29
    Foulois, relations with: 8-11, 21
    personal traits: 10-11
    on strategic air operations: 19-21
    on tactical air operations: 18-19, 29, 43, 48
Moffett, William A.: 53
    on coast defense mission: 53-54, 56, 72
    on Defense Department proposal: 78
Morgan, Thomas A.: 163, 174
Morrow Board (1925): 25-29, 195
Moseley, George Van Horn: 51, 87, 201
*Mount Shasta,* SS: 56-58

National Aeronautics Association: 39-40
National Air Frontier Defense Association: 250
National Guard
    aircraft allotments: 32
    in maneuvers: 35
    tactical units organization: 87, 122
National Industrial Recovery Act: 72-73, 118, 120
Navajo, resupply of: 112
Navigation training: 59, 132, 136, 149, 253
Navy, Department of the. (*See also* King, Ernest J.; Pratt, William V.; Standley, William H.)
    air arm expansion: 72, 103
    and air arm autonomy: 12, 21, 24
    Air Corps cooperation with: 64-65
    aircraft procurement and allotments: 70, 122-124, 155, 166, 172
    carrier-borne aircraft: 66
    on coast defense mission: 51-52, 61, 63, 65, 70-72, 220-225, 262
    Congress on air expansion: 122-123
    on Defense Department proposal: 78
    on Federal Aviation Commission proposals: 201
    on GHQ Air Force: 223, 225
    parochial outlook: 51
    land-based aviation, controversy over: 52-56, 70, 72

# INDEX

on promotion legislation: 247-249, 262
on reconnaissance missions: 222, 227
roles and missions agreements: 52-55, 72, 224. *See also* MacArthur-Pratt agreement
Roosevelt interest in: 81
on strategic air operations: 234
on tactical air operations: 23-24
New England: 65, 69, 137
New York City: 128, 137
*New York Times:* 57, 135, 173
Newark, N.J.: 136-137, 148
Night flying
    equipment for: 127, 131
    training programs: 131-133, 149, 180, 182, 198, 253, 263
Norden bombsight: 234
Northrop Corporation: 153, 167

Observation missions, aircraft role in: 3
Observation units organization: 65, 111, 122
Ocean City, N.J.: 38
Office of Chief of Air Corps. *See* Chief of Air Corps; Fechet, James E.; Foulois, Benjamin F.; Westover, Oscar
Officers *(see also* Reserve officers; Pilots)
    Air Corps authorizations and strength: 31-33, 102, 107, 111, 117, 122, 241, 243-244, 248
    Air Service strength: 12, 15, 17-18, 23
    Army authorizations and strength: 18, 97, 102, 108, 114, 117-118, 241-242, 244, 247-248
    GHQ Air Force authorization: 243-244
    pay and allowances: 109, 244
Omnibus Economy Bill (1932): 108, 110
ORANGE war plan: 67, 86
Organized Reserve, officers of. *See* Reserve officers
*Ostfriesland:* 18, 20
Overman Act (1918): 11

Panama. *See* Canal Zone
Patrick, Mason M.: 22, 28, 53
    on air arm autonomy: 22, 24-29, 84
    on air doctrine formulation: 22-23
    appointed Chief of Air Service: 18
    appointed Chief of Air Service, AEF: 9
    on coast defense mission: 52
    on command and control: 23-24
Patrol units. *See* Reconnaissance units
Pay and allowances
    of Air Corps officers: 109, 244
    Congressional action on: 115, 224
    increases and reductions: 108, 110, 114, 116, 244
    MacArthur views on: 108, 244, 247
    of pilots: 115, 129, 140, 182
Pearl Harbor, attack on: 225, 263
Pershing, John J.: 8-12
Philatelists, demands by: 137

Philippines
    air bases in: 250
    air unit assignments: 31, 65, 111
Photography, aircraft role in: 3
Physical training program: 109
Pilots (*see also* Flying cadets; Officers; Reserve officers)
    capabilities defended: 132, 135, 138-139, 141, 145, 148, 171, 180, 182
    casualties among: 2, 109, 135, 137-138, 141-144, 148, 193
    commercial, in airmail service: 133, 140-141
    dedication and morale of: 137, 139-140
    duty routine: 109
    hours logged annually: 133
    inexperience criticized: 132-135, 138-139, 145, 148, 171, 180, 182
    living conditions: 140, 182
    pay and allowances: 115, 129, 140, 182
    strength and shortages: 32-33
    training programs: 2-3, 6, 33, 110-112, 122, 128, 132-133, 148, 263
Port Columbus Airport, Ohio: 136
Post Office Department: 125-126, 128-130, 145. *See also* Airmail service
Pratt, Henry C.: 39, 60, 154, 156-158, 164
Pratt, William V.: 55
    on aviation as fleet element: 55-56
    on coast defense mission: 54-55, 71, 259
Promotion
    Air Corps policies and practices: 97, 109-110, 244, 246-248
    Army policies and practices: 108-110, 244-249
    Arnold proposals: 248-249
    Baker Board proposals: 199, 245, 248-249
    Brown rulings on: 246
    Davison views on: 245
    Dern views on: 248
    Federal Aviation Commission proposals: 245
    Foulois proposals: 98, 110, 173, 244-249
    in GHQ Air Force: 246
    Hughes proposals: 245-246
    MacArthur views on: 108, 244, 247
    McSwain legislation: 244, 247-248
    Navy views on legislation: 247-249, 262
Public Works Administration grants: 118-120, 150, 153-157, 160-163, 166-169, 172-175, 179, 181, 223, 227, 239-240, 262
Public works program: 118, 120
Pursuit Groups
    1st: 206
    17th: 133
Pursuit units organization: 65, 111
Pursuit Wing (Provisional), 1st: 38

Radio equipment: 3, 64, 130-131, 136, 146, 149, 173, 178
Rainey, Henry T.: 141, 190
Reconnaissance missions (*see also* Coast defense mission)
    aircraft role in; 3, 11
    Air Corps role in: 65, 67, 69-70, 72-74

# INDEX

controversy over: 223, 227
Drum views on: 222
Foulois views on: 63, 221
GHQ Air Force role in: 222-223
Kilbourne views on: 73-74, 213, 222
MacArthur views on: 64, 72, 223, 260
Navy role in: 222, 227
Reconnaissance units organization: 65, 122
RED war plan: 67, 86, 120
RED-ORANGE war plan: 67, 69, 120
Reed, Walter L.: 189-191
Reserve components. *See* National Guard; Organized Reserve; Reserve officers
Reserve officers
    Air Corps use: 102-103, 242-243
    Baker Board proposals for: 242
    casualty rate: 109. *See also* Casualties
    number on active duty: 122
    pay and allowances: 173
    training programs: 107, 112, 116, 128, 242-243, 262
Retirement policies: 248
Richmond, Va.: 136
Richmond Air Transport and Sales Company: 136
Rickenbacker, Edward V.
    flight demonstrations by: 136-137, 148
    on pilots inexperience: 134-135, 138
Rockwell Field, Calif.: 59, 132, 136
Rocky Mountains region: 137
Rogers, Edith N.: 141-144
Rogers, Thomas J.: 82
Rogers, Will: 134
Rogers, William N.:
    air arm autonomy legislation: 163, 193
    aircraft procurement legislation: 160-169, 171, 174-176, 179, 185, 239-240
    on airmail service: 171, 176, 178-180, 182
    Foulois competence inquiry: 171-192, 254, 257, 263
Roles and missions *(see also* MacArthur-Pratt agreement)
    Air Corps agreements on: 52-54, 86
    Foulois views on: 77, 86
    MacArthur views on: 214, 220, 222
    Navy agreements on: 52-55, 72, 224
    War Department agreements on: 52-55, 85-86, 224
Roosevelt, Elliott: 145
Roosevelt, Franklin D.: 82
    on air arm autonomy: 81, 97, 193
    on air base construction: 252
    on Air Corps funding: 120-121, 145, 148, 236-237, 254, 258
    on aircraft procurement: 169, 238-241, 254
    airmail service, role in: 124-128, 132, 134, 138-139, 141-148, 257
    on Assistant Secretary of War for Air: 81
    and Baker Board proposals: 199
    and Civilian Conservation Corps: 112
    and Cuban political crisis: 93

# FOULOIS AND THE U.S. ARMY AIR CORPS

and defense budget: 114, 117, 262
on flight pay: 115-116
Foulois criticized by: 139, 144-145
on Foulois relief: 185
MacArthur criticized by: 144
mandatory furlough plan: 114-116
and manpower authorizations: 118, 242
Navy, interest in: 81
and pay reductions: 114, 116, 244
public works program: 118, 120
on safety measures: 144-147

Safety measures: 135-136, 138-139, 145-147
Safety records: 40
St. Mihiel offensive: 11
Salt Lake City, Utah: 128
San Diego defenses: 65, 69
San Francisco defenses: 65, 69, 148
Sawyer, Donald H.: 119
Schools (see also Training programs)
    command and control of: 87-88, 90
    established: 31, 44
    navigation: 59
    officers detailed to: 243
Seatbelt introduced: 3
Seattle defenses: 65, 69, 217
Seattle-to-Dayton flight: 231
Selfridge, Thomas E.: 2
Selfridge Field, Mich.: 22, 111
Senate. See Congress
Service squadrons organization: 204, 210
*Shenandoah,* USS: 25-27
Sheppard, Morris: 241
Sheridan, Hiram W.: 28
Signal Corps: 6, 11
Simonds, George S.: 177
    on air arm autonomy: 195
    on coast defense mission: 68-69, 95
    on command and control: 209
    on Drum Board procedure: 176, 181
    on Foulois competence: 176, 181-182, 189-190
Smith, Howard S.: 39
Smith, Sumpter: 28
Sneed, Albert L.: 39
Spaatz, Carl A.: 39
Speed requirements and performances: 50, 155, 231. See also Flight records
Sperry bombsight: 234
Squadrons. See Tactical units organization; also by type
Standley, William H.: 72, 220, 224
Staten Island, N.Y.: 37
Strategic air operations
    Air Corps Tactical School views on: 234

# INDEX

Air Corps views on: 256, 263
Arnold views on: 215
Baker Board proposals: 214-216
Craig views on: 234
Curry views on: 214-215
doctrine formulation: 43-51, 61-75, 212
Federal Aviation Commission views on: 216
Foulois views on: 258
GHQ Air Force role in: 202-203, 213, 216-217, 262
Kilbourne views on: 202-203, 213, 260
MacArthur views on: 217-220, 226-227, 260
Mitchell views on: 19-21
Navy role in: 234
War Department views on: 75, 215, 223, 226-227, 262-263
Westover views on: 202-203, 213
World War I experience: 11
Strayer, Thorne: 188-189
Supply System: 31, 40

Tactical air operations
    Air Corps Tactical School views on: 228
    doctrine formulation: 43-46, 51, 61, 70, 86
    Craig views on: 260
    Drum Board proposals: 69-70
    GHQ Air Force role in: 62-63, 67, 69, 207, 212-213, 216, 224, 229
    Kilbourne views on: 51, 62-63, 213, 260
    MacArthur views on: 61, 96, 120, 214, 220, 226-227, 260
    Mitchell views on: 18-19, 29, 43, 48
    Moseley views on: 51
    Navy role in: 23-24
    War Department views on: 16-17, 19-21, 23, 43, 46, 50-51, 62-63, 66-75, 86, 212-216, 227, 258
    Westover views on: 46-47
    World War I experience: 11
Tactical units organization: 204
    Air Corps plans for: 65, 85-86, 88, 111
    in Air Service: 17-18
    amphibian units: 122
    attack units: 65, 111, 122
    bombardment units: 65, 111, 122
    composite units: 65
    Drum views on: 85
    Drum Board proposals: 122
    first: 6-8
    Foulois views on: 6-8, 63-69, 88-90, 92-93, 95, 111, 122
    in ground forces: 17, 22-23, 85
    groups: 111
    Kilbourne views on: 88-89
    MacArthur views on: 66, 96
    National Guard: 87, 122
    observation units: 65, 111, 122
    pursuit units: 65, 111

reconnaissance units: 65, 122
service units: 204, 210
training programs: 112
War Department views on: 66, 85-86, 93, 204, 224
wings: 111
Woodring views on: 66
TAN war plan: 92-94
Tinker, Clarence L.: 133
Training programs: 40. *See also* Schools
    Baker Board proposals: 198-199
    Blind flying. *See* Instrument flying, *below*
    bombing: 112
    coast defense: 59-60, 132
    Davison views on: 112-113
    flying cadets: 122
    Foulois stress on: 6, 59, 89, 113-114, 136, 149, 180, 182, 253, 263
    ground crews: 6
    gunnery: 112
    instrument flying: 131-133, 135-136, 147-149, 198, 253, 263
    MacArthur stress on: 106
    Military Academy graduates: 252-253
    navigation: 59, 132, 136, 149, 253
    night flying: 131-133, 149, 180, 182, 198, 253, 263
    pilots: 2-3, 6, 33, 110-112, 122, 128, 132-133, 148, 263
    reserve officers: 107, 112, 116, 128, 242-243, 262
    unit training: 112
    War Department stress on: 106, 253
    weather flying: 132-133, 136
    by Wright brothers: 3
Trumbull, John H.: 34

Unification of armed services. *See* Defense, Department of, proposed
United Aircraft and Transport: 156
United Kingdom, potential war with: 67, 69, 86 120
United States, continental. *See* Continental United States
United States Army *(See also* War Department)
    combat effectiveness: 101-102
    command and control in: 87
    enlisted authorizations and strength: 18, 97, 102, 241-242
    first tactical air unit: 6-8
    furloughs, mandatory: 108
    manpower authorizations: 242, 244
    materiel deficiencies: 102
    officer authorizations and strength: 18, 97, 102, 108, 114, 117-118, 241-242, 244, 247-248
    pay increases and reductions: 108, 110, 116, 244
    promotion policies and practices: 108-110, 244-249
    reorganizations: 17-18, 64, 66, 86-87, 92, 102
    retirement policies: 248
    roles and missions agreements: 52-55
United States Coast Guard: 221
United States Navy. *See* Navy, Department of the

www.ingramcontent.com/pod-product-compliance
Lightning Source LLC
Chambersburg PA
CBHW020635230426
43665CB00008B/186